Notes from a Different Drummer

Notes from a Different Drummer

A Guide to Juvenile Fiction Portraying the Handicapped

by Barbara H. Baskin
and Karen H. Harris

R. R. Bowker Company
New York & London • 1977

Published by R. R. Bowker Company
1180 Avenue of the Americas, New York, N.Y. 10036
Copyright © 1977 by Barbara H. Baskin and Karen H. Harris
Printed and bound in the United States of America

Library of Congress Cataloging in Publication Data

Baskin, Barbara Holland, 1929–
    Notes from a different drummer.

    Includes indexes.
    1.   Children's literature—Bibliography.
2.   Mentally handicapped in literature—Juvenile
literature—Bibliography.   3.   Physically handicapped
in literature—Juvenile literature—Bibliography.
I.   Harris, Karen H., 1934–   joint author.
II.   Title.
Z1037.9.B37   [PN1009.Z6]   028.52   77-15067
ISBN 0-8352-0978-4

Contents

Illustrations

Preface

Our purpose in writing this book is to create a comprehensive guide to juvenile fiction written between 1940 and 1975 that depicts handicapped characters. Unfortunately, there is no clear demarcation that precisely separates books in this category from all others; rather, blurred distinctions exist that demand decisions that may seem arbitrary. Although some books are clearly children's works and others are clearly adult, the burgeoning adolescent market and new perceptions about teenage interests have extended traditional ideas beyond what was formerly the upper limit of the juvenile spectrum. Editorial judgments that result in some novels being marketed as adult and similar ones as juvenile seem capricious. Our decision of whether or not to include such works hinged primarily on whether or not the crux of the story reflected predominately adolescent concerns.

Fiction, we believe, is the literary genre that permits the widest latitude for the full expression of contemporary perceptions and values. Separating this from all other literary forms poses certain problems: Biographies, while a distinct entity, blend into fictionalized biographies and then into biographical fiction, the latter category being one we wish to include as part of this collection. Nonfiction creates another puzzle: Ostensibly, this is an excludable genre, but we discovered many essentially didactic works that were embedded in an identifiable story form. Those endeavors that had a viable, if often uninspired, plot, we dubbed quasi-fiction and incorporated into the collection. The contribution of folklore to social perceptions and attitudes is only briefly explored, as a comprehensive report and analysis of myths and legends involving disability would require a separate, extensive volume. Therefore, reluctantly, such works are excluded from this compendium.

Books originally written for adults or stories transposed from other formats are not included.

Books written abroad but distributed domestically have become part of this study since they both parallel and help shape domestic attitudes. Out of print books are likewise considered important since so many are still found in children's collections and it is realistic to assume that they may continue to reside there for many more years. Their examination is especially useful in illuminating some perceptions no longer popularly expressed but that may still have currency among segments of the population.

The terms "handicap," "disability," "exceptionality," "dysfunction," "impairment," and "special needs" and their variations are all used interchangeably throughout the book to provide some variety for the reader. "Handicapped" was selected for the subtitle because of its greater familiarity among nonspecialists in this field. Technically, a *disability* is a reality, for example, the loss of vision. The restrictions and opportunities imposed by society determine whether or not the disability becomes a *handicap*. That is, "handicap" actually should be understood to be situational and attitude bound. The term "emotional dysfunction" is used instead of "mental illness" to bypass the connotation of sickness and to suggest a lack of permanence.

In Chapters 1, 2, and 3 we have tried to place our analysis of individual juvenile titles in its historic, cultural, and literary context. In Chapter 4, the titles are viewed from a macrocosmic perspective, identifying patterns and trends that emerge when the field is viewed in its entirety. It is Chapter 5, entitled "An Annotated Guide to Juvenile Fiction Portraying the Handicapped, 1940–1975," that forms the bulk of this book.

Juvenile titles selected for inclusion in Chapter 5 contain child or adult characters who have special needs by reason of intellectual, visual, auditory, speech, orthopedic, or cosmetic impairments; neurological or specific learning disabilities; emotional dysfunction; or such special health problems as diabetes, asthma, and cardiac disorders. Books containing handicapped animals have been rejected unless they also feature human characters with disabling problems. Also excluded is fiction dealing with such rare or exotic diseases as leprosy. Books having temporarily injured characters, especially where rehabilitative problems are not a significant part of the story, or those containing characters who suffer terminal ailments are omitted. Again, there are gray areas that allow for different interpretations as to whether or not an individual book should have been included.

Every book that described or alluded to a disabled character was not selected for inclusion in Chapter 5 since some were of such minor significance that comment would have been strained. In other instances, important insights were available even when the disabled character was peripheral to the novel's main thrust, and the volume was added to the corpus of books selected for evaluation. Such vignettes often seemed to portray disabled persons in more important ways than did other presentations totally devoted to problems of exceptionality.

The extent of disablement a character manifested in order to have it considered an impairment was another issue. Stories describing mild forms of an identified disability have been included when either rehabilitation and adaptation or exploration of attitudes was a major focus. A number were excluded despite the author's or reviewers' use of disability labels when the appellation and the described behavior were incongruent. Conversely, stories with characters not labeled but who display behaviors consistent with standard clinical definitions were added to the collection.

Stories whose characters suffer economic hardships or are delinquent or socially maladjusted are left out of this work. The sheer numbers of books being published about characters manifesting conduct disorders would unreasonably expand the size of this volume.

Locating books to be analyzed presented some difficulties. Such standard references as *The Children's Catalog*, *Subject Guide to Children's Books in Print*, and the card catalog of the main children's collection at the New York Public Library yielded few titles and considerable overlap among the identified works. Textbooks and source books on children's literature were somewhat more helpful. The prime sources were specialized bibliographies, such as those prepared for bibliotherapeutic purposes or compiled by professional or advocate groups interested in specific impairments. Many of these listings included inconsequential problems. For example, it was somewhat startling to see such subcategories as "freckles" and "shortness" listed as physical handicaps; such attributes are considered outside the scope of this work.

A retrospective and ongoing search of professional reviews of juvenile titles unearthed additional works, although, since most reviewers lacked our particular perspective presented here, they often neglected to mention the presence of a character with an impairment. Publishers' catalogs were scoured and publishing houses contacted. Here, too, our correspondents occasionally failed to identify their own products. We presumed that a common reason was failure to note, or see as salient, this component of the story. Whenever we located a book by a new author, we checked his or her other publications and not infrequently it was found that writers cognizant of the problems of disability (or aware of the dramatic potential of such topics) tended to include one or more impaired characters in other writings.

Interested and resourceful school and public librarians, as well as our own students, turned up additional appropriate books. Finally, we were reduced to simply reading shelves for likely candidates and in this we surveyed the collections of dozens of libraries.

Inevitably, some books were overlooked: Certain out of print titles were not available through network or other interlibrary loan facilities; others, undoubtedly, were missed, and for these omissions we apologize. Our search did turn up books of every major genre and interest area, including contemporary and historical fiction, fantasy, science fiction, romance, sports, animal, and mystery stories. Those works purporting to be realistic are not necessarily the most forthright, accurate, or honest about disability. Such sought-after qualities exist independent of genre and are present in every prose category.

Annotations of the identified books are designed to respond to presumed user needs. Although some labeling is inevitable, we have assiduously tried to minimize the practice. Too often labels have assumed pejorative connotations, have called up a host of incorrect assumptions, and have provided a barrier rather than a shortcut to understanding. Labeling practices also suggest that people be perceived primarily on the basis of impairment, thus emphasizing loss or malfunctioning rather than strengths and achievements. In an effort to minimize conceptualization of characters in those terms, individual annotations are not grouped by disability, and descriptions emphasize behavior rather than etiology. Specific impairments, nonetheless, are often of particular interest to the reader and of importance in this analysis. All of the books annotated are grouped by pertinent disabling condition in the Subject Index. Also, in Chapter 5, one or more of nine broad descriptive terms are used with each annotation to indicate classifications of impairment: Auditory Impairment, Cosmetic Impairment, Emotional Dysfunction, General Health Problems, Intellectual Impairment, Neurological Impairment, Orthopedic Impairment, Speech Impairment, and Visual Impairment. Where specified, the particular disorder is identified within the annotation itself.

It seemed important to us to include a plot summary in each annotation, since it is this aspect of the book that most interests the potential child reader. Our synopses often tend to concentrate disproportionately on those aspects that reveal attitudes or convey information about impairments, since they are our prime concern. This caveat should be kept in mind when reading the annotations.

The second component of each annotation is the *Analysis*, which evaluates how impairments are treated as well as the literary qualities of the title in question. Evaluation of the treatment of the disabled character focuses on accuracy and honesty of the depiction; plausibility of reported psychological, rehabilitative, and social responses to the impairment; the role of the affected character in the story; and the tone and attitude expressed toward handicaps. We are especially critical of patronizing, pitying, or romanticized depictions. We have commented extensively on mixed messages—those works that seem to be calling for compassion but that, on another level, emphasize the differences, real and hypothesized, between the disabled and the rest of society—in effect establishing persons with special needs as a discrete category of humanity.

However admirable the intent of an individual work, it ultimately succeeds or fails on the basis of literary merit. Literary criticism is inevitably a highly personal art, so we have tried to indicate specific examples of what we feel are laudable or censurable elements.

Illustrations, particularly in books for the very young child, carry a significant portion of the book's impact, directly or subtly communicating attitudes or information about impairments. However, it is not unusual for illustrators to omit all representations of difference, even in instances of characters with obvious, visible anomalies. Such omissions are themselves expressions of attitude. Pictorial representations therefore, have also been evaluated.

Many individuals helped to bring this work to fruition. The task of locating our books was made considerably easier by the efforts of Ruth Heatley of the Emma S. Clark Memorial Library of Setauket; by Sandra Feinberg of the Middle Country Library; and by the staff of the children's section of the Smithtown Library—all in New York. Elizabeth Ashin and Evelyn Chandler assisted us tremendously and we are grateful for their interest and help. We are appreciative of the good counsel of Evert Volkerz and of the assistance with our research and analysis by Francine Lucidon and Amy Baskin. Special mention must be made of the support and encouragement given by Betty Carter who, among a host of librarians, read these stories to her children and generously reported their reactions. Credit should also be given to the multitude of parents and teachers who have, over the years, provided us with new titles as well as extensive feedback from youthful readers. Perhaps most important are the innumerable authors and storytellers we were exposed to who readily communicated to us not only their excitement about good fiction but also their belief that the content of a story had meaning that could illuminate our lives.

Introduction

Chance, trauma, genetics, environmental stress, and a host of other factors combine to shape our lives. The resultant variations among people are an immutable fact of existence. When normative values are superimposed on these differences, when occult etiologies are presumed, or when sentimentality or exclusionary behavior are prescribed responses to these differences, then such variation is perceived as deviance.

Like everyone else, people with impairments are still just people—individuals who are good and bad, wise and foolish, congenial and aloof. Their core human needs are the same, and their differences are in degree, not in kind. Undeniably, their pursuit of goals is affected by the fact and severity or complexity of their disabilities, but this is only part of the picture. Helen Keller asserted that the heaviest burdens of disability arise from personal interaction and not from the impairment itself. While little control can be exerted over the reality of the disability, changes in the quality of the social context can have an immediate, as well as long term, beneficent impact.

Society is contaminated with negative perceptions regarding disability. The philosophy on which this book is based holds that impairment should neither be exaggerated nor ignored, neither dramatized nor minimized, neither romanticized nor the cause of devaluation. Among antidotes to rejection are increased contact with disabled individuals and honest objective depictions, particularly for the young. Books that children read provide continuous stimuli through their formative years, and latent and overt messages in stories of exceptional individuals accumulate to form subsequent perceptions. Literary presentations that avoid distortion and that accurately reflect the reality of impairment help readers separate the disability from the false superstructure imposed by society.

The promise of full participation for the disabled remains to be met. Translating rhetoric into reality requires the abandonment of inaccurate and rejecting perceptions and their replacement by enlightened, accepting ones. Literature can help in this quest by presenting models for the restructuring of a more hospitable, supportive society. When diversity is not equated with deviance, Thoreau's words will be finally realized, and, without criticism or condemnation, we shall all be free to march to the beat of our different drummers.

> *If a man does not keep pace with his companions, perhaps it is because he hears a different drummer. Let him step to the music which he hears, however measured or far away.*
>
> Thoreau, *Walden*, Conclusion

1

Society and the Handicapped

Janus-like, literature looks back, summing up the cultural precepts of the past while simultaneously projecting and structuring future social reality. Thus it is both a product and an agent of change, preserving old ideas but modifying concepts as they are reinterpreted and reformulated. To understand children's literature about the handicapped—the focus of this work—it is necessary to examine the social context from which it emerged. The culture is suffused with unexamined attitudes and beliefs that have endured through generations and find expression in language, literature, and symbols. Radical changes in society affect perceptions and responses toward people who are atypical and such alterations are, not unexpectedly, detectable in the literature.

As fiction distills the essence of social thought into a comprehensible and enjoyable format, the sentient reader, by examining the content of traditional and contemporary literature, can discern the persistence of certain beliefs about the exceptional person. By looking at attitudes in early examples of fiction and comparing these with modern fiction, one can note continuities as well as some significant quantitative and qualitative changes. Since literature contributes to value formation through information generation and transmission of culturally determined models and emotional responses, it is instructive to examine the information, models, and values manifested in fiction for young readers. It is during the period of childhood when understandings have not yet crystallized that the individual is most amenable to influence and fictional models may have great impact. Because values in fiction about disability are inextricably bound to social realities, these first must be examined in some detail before looking at the fictional representations.

1

Traditional Social Responses to Disability

Historically, those attitudes that derived from the perception of handicaps varied among different societies, cultures, and social classes, and were further differentiated by time, place, age, sex, and religious dimensions, as well as by the actual handicap itself. Some early attitudes have survived in our culture in a variety of forms—customs, superstitions, metaphors, clichés—that are now the common currency of daily life, refusing to be interred. The disabled have been a sensitive barometer of the social climate throughout the ages. Infantile treatment of adults, lionization, protectionism, witch burning, exploitation, institutionalization (more often for the "protection" of society than for assistance to the individual), medical experimentation, and charity have all been manifested at one time or another in policies and practices of governments. To some degree, modifications of these practices still exist and continue to be part of the social response.

However, the common function among societal responses to handicaps has been to separate those individuals sustaining such conditions from the privileges and communality of the rest of society. Although a handicap is only a single aspect of the myriad descriptions possible of a person, it has tended to overtake and cloak other characteristics, suppressing their importance in the eyes of others. Its existence dominates the person being perceived; its power is superordinate.

Society has always reacted strongly, although not consistently, to disabling conditions, imbuing them with mystery and magic and endowing people who possessed such properties with extranormal abilities or attributes that were caricatures of those of the average person. These distortions arose from ignorance, awe, or confusion. The necessity to interpret these differences and reduce the anxiety created by their existence generated stories, myths, superstitions, idiomatic expressions, and other such literary responses. The resultant stereotypes functioned to "explain" the condition, authenticate the "normalcy" of those who did not evidence such difference, proscribe, prescribe or sanction social roles for the disabled, and indicate acceptable patterns of response among the nondisabled.

Patterns varied from veneration to outright rejection and were frequently passed on from generation to generation, often extending from small clusters of individuals to entire societies and becoming part of the cultural baggage that still burdens us today. Even though information about the origin and implications of physical and emotional conditions is available in the common culture as a result of widespread media coverage, still the ghosts from the past continue to haunt us.

For example, Monbeck, who has worked with the American Foundation for the Blind and has edited major publications for blind persons and professionals working in the area, identified three commonly held irrational beliefs about blindness that seem anachronistic in the twentieth century, in that they are not based on lack of information or incomplete data about loss of sight, but reflect superstitious feelings and ideas. First, he cites the practice of "blaming the victim," that is, "the notion that blindness is a punishment for some past sin, a sign of some moral failing."[1] Father Carroll, long interested in this topic, states that "this belief is reinforced whenever blindness is called an 'affliction,' . . . The word, by its nature and by its derivation, suggests punishment."[2] Monbeck also asserts that the general public considers venereal disease a prime cause of blindness, a convenient item of misinformation that assuages guilt in the sighted for not furthering associations with a blind person. Finally, and most critically, popular thinking holds that "for some unknown reason he (or she) has been singled out and marked with the 'sign' of blindness" with the implication "that the person is not only abnormal, but that he is physically, psychologically, morally and emotionally inferior."[3] To support his contention, Monbeck cites cases where blind persons were pressured not to marry sighted individuals or were prevented from becoming blood donors, regardless of the origin of their condition.[4] The belief that immorality and disability are coupled is common, and is not restricted to the blind. Reisman reports that at the turn of the century, children with learning difficulties were described as having "moral defects."[5]

Childlike Treatment

Attitudes toward exceptional people are frequently patronizing and condescending; the handicapped often complain, justifiably, that they are treated as children. The most demoralizing example of such practice can be observed among professionals who work with youths or adults but refer to them as "children." Grannis, in a superb article on book selection practices of librarians, convincingly argues that protectionist attitudes characterize policies in selecting reading material for mature blind patrons. Too often librarians overload collections with inspirational, safe, or insipid braille and disc materials in lieu of contemporary "adult" novels, practical nonfiction, particularly in certain occupational areas, and titles that are more intellectually demanding.[6] This practice not only reflects a demeaning attitude about the special needs reader but has additional serious vocational implications and reduces possibilities of social interaction when other persons are discussing controversial events or a current best-seller.

Sheltering blind readers is not a new practice. In 1930 Langworthy reported that in an analysis of 442 titles at the Perkins Library (a major

library for blind readers), distortions were prevalent in literary portrayals of blind persons.[7] Even in a collection where depictions could
expect to be challenged by a knowledgeable readership, representations
of blind persons were overwhelmingly inaccurate, with abilities and
virtues either exaggerated or grossly undervalued.

Romanticization

The plight of someone suffering frequently moves people to pity or
into action to ameliorate the problem. While certain types of exceptionality are treated with aversion, others are romanticized. Throughout time, individuals have always idealized heroes and heroines who
survived their own odyssey or trial. Helen Keller's impressive achievements captured everyone's imagination and respect—not, of course,
with the fervor reserved for a Lindbergh or an Armstrong. Our admiration for intellectual or esthetic achievements has tended to be more restrained compared with physical accomplishments. Yet, who is to say
which achievement is the more meritorious?

The idiomatic expressions "He paid his dues" or "Why *me*?" (the
implication being that I am not so wicked as to deserve such heavy
punishment) reflect the widespread belief that the world is, at base,
fair. People often believe that there must be some compensation for a
handicap, and when there is not, ascribe compensatory characteristics
to the person sustaining the problem. Typical is the assumption that
loss of sight is compensated for by extraordinarily acute hearing or notable musical ability. The laudable achievements of some disabled individuals may have been oversold and have emerged to represent ideal
prototypes. Such gifted individuals as Beethoven, Edison, or the math-
ematical and engineering genius, Steinmetz, are described as people
who "rose above" their auditory or orthopedic problem and it is implied that other handicapped people should emulate such models, an
implausible goal for all but the most minute section of any population.
There is often a vast discrepancy between the grubby reality of a handicap and the idealized version.

Spread

Wright analyzes another seemingly contrary but related phenomenon—the concept of spread.[8] People often presume that if one is blind,
one's hearing is also impaired or if one has a serious physical disability,

then one is also retarded. In addition, despite any one of a hundred descriptive terms an observer might select, when the person described has a disability, he or she is most likely referred to in terms of that disability, for instance, "I saw that crippled woman this morning." Even professionals who work with the disabled use the disability label as a communication shortcut, as in such remarks as, "I worked with that CP (person with cerebral palsy) today." Unfortunately, the result is that the individual is conceptualized as the sum of the disabling characteristics rather than as Ms. Y or Mr. Z.

Differential Patterns of Avoidance

Different incapacities can result in identical consequences. The social cost of deafness, blindness, or emotional dysfunction may be loneliness, underemployment, or loss of civil rights. Yet, on a number of dimensions, the nonhandicapped have developed differential attitudes toward various categories of handicaps. Shears and Jensema adapted a social distance scale to measure these various attitudes. Respondents indicated a willingness to be more accepting as long as contact was minimal, that is, the greater the social distance, the greater the tolerance. However, when the hypothesized relationship was characterized as closer or more socially demanding, rejecting attitudes emerged. Whenever respondents perceived that communication might be a problem (such as with individuals having faulty speech or hearing), they also chose to avoid a close relationship.

Selected items from their study are that 79 percent of the respondents would be willing to have an amputee as a friend and 95 percent would be willing to live in the same neighborhood; 65 percent would consider a person who stuttered as a pal but only 83 percent would want to live in the same neighborhood; 38 percent would have a friend with cerebral palsy, but only 65 percent expressed willingness to have this kind of person as a neighbor. Some did not wish to *live in the same country* with such people. By and large, the study revealed that acceptance of exceptional people decreased as level of intimacy increased.[9]

It might be logical to assume that there is a direct correlation between the severity of the disability and the degree of social ostracism. This is not always true. Oddly enough, for example, teachers who work with children with visual impairments report that social acceptance of the totally blind is often better than that evidenced toward the child with moderately impaired vision. Behaviors associated with blindness are commonly known and areas of deviance are predictable and thus not upsetting. However, the partially seeing child's behavior is often unclear, puzzling, vacillating, or inconsistent. The seeing peer is confused and cannot react automatically and naturally when encountering a child who can identify colors but sometimes uses braille and sometimes large print or who can participate in some games and not in others. Children have neither the knowledge nor social experience to respond appropriately to such apparent inconsistencies. An unfortunate, but commonly reported reaction is to avoid any confrontation altogether.

One simplistic way to respond to unusual behavior is to ignore subtle differences and apply the label of incompetence or insanity to all deviance. Involuntary movement, blindisms, drooling, and voice irregularities may be so perceived. Exceptional people often have disability-related gaps in their experiential base. The deaf person may be totally divorced from the popular music scene and the person with severely reduced mobility may not know about elements of his or her immediate environment. On the basis of some behaviors that are the direct outcomes of reduced knowledge or experience, the exceptional person is tagged as ignorant.

Disabled adults sometimes report avoidance by others presumably because of threatening social consequences. Despite an obvious illogical basis, the nondisabled fear contagion. The intact individual is reminded of her or his own social vulnerability and fragility. They suspect they may also be avoided along with the person they befriend.

People often sidestep personal interaction with those who are handicapped, substituting the more distant involvement of giving money. These contributions support the feeling that responsibility belongs to family, researchers, physicians, therapists, technicians—in fact, anyone but themselves. This rationalization excuses them from becoming involved. With the general public's affection for instant panaceas, it is difficult to come to terms with the possibility that some problems do not have an immediate or palatable solution. Conventional wisdom assumes that social, economic, or personal difficulties can be resolved if only the proper (and distant) intervention agent would effect the appropriate prescription. Inviting a child into a play group, supporting a local hostel, or providing employment has more widespread positive consequences for the disabled than the charitable donation of hundreds of dollars.

Sometimes people can be encouraged, cajoled, or pressured into making isolated grand gestures, but they lose interest in the mundane problems of day-to-day follow-up care. To some extent, the gesture benefits the giver more than the receiver. The cloak of benevolence surrounds the worker for the telethon and much publicity attends the presentation of wheelchairs or the ribbon-cutting ceremony for a new facility. But the real needs of the exceptional person are reflected more in long-term, ongoing provision of professional services and social intercourse than in observable materials. The brace supports the leg, but the therapist in daily training sessions provides the skill and techniques that make walking possible. The socially supportive environment provides the walker with some place to go and someone with whom to share experiences. Those factors that can be accommodated through surgical, prosthetic, or therapeutic means are the most readily attended to. More often, however, the movement or growth of a child is impeded by social barriers that tend to be more handicapping than the original disability. This is true because social conditions are less amenable to remediation or control; they are often accepted as inevitabilities and are reaffirmed constantly and perpetuated in social exchange through our language forms.

Use of Disability in Humor and Figurative Language

One tactic for dealing with fears is to defuse their potency with humor, thus reducing them to manageable dimensions. Years ago, the ubiquitousness of the moron jokes was testimony to this. The "humor" of the characterizations of the deaf on the television show *Saturday Night* or on such buttons as "Support Mental Health or I'll Kill You" represents recent attempts to cope with common unspoken fears. The clumsy, stumbling, stuttering character is a stock comedy role. Speech hesitations are an automatic clue to an audience that the character, almost exclusively male, is a confused, weak, or inadequate person. Sometimes the situation and the dialogue are simply not funny; the intended hilarity derives from difficulties in speech and coordination. The use of this device is particularly offensive when the characterization approximates some of the physical symptoms of cerebral palsy.

There appear to be unusual variations in viewers' concepts about humor related to disability. Deafness is sometimes considered amusing, blindness is rarely funny (Mr. Magoo being one obvious exception), but irregularities in speech are commonly exploited for "merriment."

Figurative language also reveals unconscious values and beliefs about others. Skinner, in analyzing the function of terms, recognized that metaphors are mechanisms for extending the essential privacy of the experiential process.[10] Such expressions as "stone deaf," "deaf as a post," "blind as a bat," and "blind drunk" are used as linguistic radicals to describe the most extreme situations. These phrases are universally negative: "a lame duck" (someone who still retains a position after losing the power), "crept up on their blind side" (their weakest, most vulnerable quarter), "went down a blind alley" (took a hopeless, dead-end route). In virtually every language context, the simile or metaphor used to describe an unpleasant or disagreeable situation is identical to or derivative of the words naming the disability itself. Fernandez, an anthropologist, asserts that metaphor is a strategy, sometimes used to

> make it appear that the incumbent occupies a desirable or undesirable place in the continuum of whatever domain has been chosen. As Aristotle says, "To adorn, borrow metaphor from thing superior, to disparage, borrow from things inferior."[11]

Moreover, he claims that metaphor has a critical social function that relates to "the occupancy of various continua which in sum constitute a cultural quality space. Persuasive metaphors situate us and others with whom we interact in that space."[12]

Words relating to disability sometimes seem to have emotionally charged meaning, as if the very words carry magical power. Monbeck, in *The Meaning of Blindness: Attitudes toward Blindness and Blind People*, mentions the reluctance of individuals even to use the word "blind" in discussion of or conversation with sightless individuals.[13] Supporting this, Harold Krents, a blind lawyer and best-selling author, sardonically reports the following personal experience:

> When I go to the airport and ask the ticket agent for assistance to the plane, he or she will invariably pick up the phone, call a ground hostess and whisper . . . "We've got a 76 here." I have concluded that the word "blind" is not used for one of two reasons: Either they fear that if the dread word is spoken, the ticket agent's retina will immediately detach, or they are reluctant to inform me of my condition of which I may not have been previously aware.[14]

Counselors report that parents, students, and teachers respond selectively to different words. For example, they find the expression "learning disabled" preferable to "slow learner" and "emotional illness" more acceptable than "insanity." Such preferred terms emphasize that the involved person is not responsible for the condition. Even children are highly attuned to the impact of words, effectively and typically employing an epithet like "retard" to tease and anger others.

Maintenance of Social Distance

We place a high premium on youth and attractiveness; therefore it is not surprising that we are less tolerant toward older handicapped persons who carry the double burden of age and disability. Young children often become poster subjects, are displayed on telethons, and are the recipients of the charitable efforts of many individuals. As adults, these same people are denied access to public buildings, jobs, housing, and basic civil rights. The child, because of the projection of vulnerability, invites a protective response. Older handicapped persons often must deal with aversion, which has replaced the pity and concern shown them as children. Differential treatment of children and adults with handicaps is quite obvious; this is a similar response expressed toward other minority groups.

Nevertheless, one is not surprised to discover that sociometric studies frequently (but not always) reveal that exceptional children are rejected and ostracized by their peers, and in high-density, potentially explosive situations, such as lunchrooms or playgrounds, they are subjected to social abuse. The older person is also highly vulnerable to social stress, but this is very often manifested by neglect rather than by direct hostility or abuse. Certainly, recent exposés of institutions for the retarded and nursing homes reveal the incredible amount of tolerance for negligence society holds toward helpless, often multiply handicapped, individuals.

There is a general belief that people with impairments have neither the capability nor the interest in living independent adult lives. Despite their overall superior record as conscientious and efficient employees, the handicapped share similar rebuffs with other outgroups: discriminatory hiring practices and low wages, for example. The latter problem is especially onerous for those physically disabled workers who have extra travel costs because they are unable to use public transportation. Although preferential hiring by the government is an accepted practice, especially of disabled veterans, these posts tend to be at low occupational levels and are frequently in certain defined occupations sometimes "reserved" for them, such as concessionaires in government buildings in the United States or lottery vendors in foreign countries.

Additionally, disabled individuals are often excluded from participation in a variety of social situations deliberately or inadvertently. Many handicapped adults will testify to being refused opportunities to register in vocational training programs, rejected as airline passengers, excluded from residences, and a host of similar experiences that painfully reflect their rejected status. Krents reports, for example, that despite his high class rank and cum laude degree from Harvard Law School, he was turned down by more than 40 law firms because of his blindness.[15] In other instances, the needs of the handicapped person have never even been considered; to borrow Ellison's apt epithet, they are invisible. Because of architectural barriers, houses of worship, museums, libraries, and innumerable other social settings are frequently closed to those with mobility handicaps. It is quite clear that the needs of the disabled, despite their prevalence in society, are not considered in the planning of those agencies whose central purpose presumably is to serve the public.

Economically as well as socially, shortsighted views that result in cutbacks in prevocational training, massive underfunding of rehabilitative programs, inadequately trained personnel engaged in preparing transition from institution to community living, and difficulty in funding appropriate local housing for adults who are capable of living partially independently all act to restrict the ability of the adult with special needs to function as an independent, economically able citizen. Such programs are considered low priority items, particularly in times of fiscal distress.

Past practices had reaffirmed the common belief that the disabled require lifelong custodial care. They were housed in institutions where the director, invariably a medical doctor, quite naturally gave preeminence to medical concerns rather than to rehabilitative measures designed to return the residents to community settings. These forbidding structures were frequently in scenic but remote rural locations, effectively removing handicapped individuals from the geographic and psychological proximity of their families, their communities, and, in effect, society.

The widespread acceptance of the practice of isolating disabled people from the proximity and hence the protection of those most apt to be concerned for their welfare has provided an historic irony. Totalitarian regimes have exploited the indifference of the citizenry to the abuse of the emotionally disturbed and have used incarceration in so-called mental institutions as a technique to silence dissenters. While the implications of such behavior are primarily political, it also clearly demonstrates the vulnerability and low status of persons labeled mentally ill. In these circumstances the label provides a cover for conscienceless persecution.

Social distance can also be created in the opposite direction. The accomplishments of a handicapped person, implying superhuman effort and achievement, may be valued far beyond their true worth. The public reads a newspaper feature story of a blind woman who graduates magna cum laude or of a man who learns to paint or type with a headstick. Certainly these are important and noteworthy accomplishments, but they are hardly newsworthy. Many disabled individuals are competent in areas where they have learned to bypass their impairments and are involved in adapted activities on a daily basis. The tone of awe and incredulity in these reports is what many disabled readers find distasteful.

Disabled people, like other minorities, inevitably have been affected by the attitudes of the dominant culture in shaping their own self-image. Consequently, some have evaluated themselves as less deserving, less worthy than others. Ghettoization, neglect, and the pandemic presence of architectural barriers reinforce this belief. Daily experience provides ample evidence that the disabled are not considered part of the mainstream of the common citizenry and that their needs are not factored into social planning.

The handicapped share similarities with other social outgroups in the United States. Despite tremendous heterogeneity, class characteristics are ascribed and often solidify into stereotypes. The deaf are assumed to have a suspicious nature, the blind are expected to be passive and serene, and the retarded or disturbed are expected to have uncontrollable sexual drives or, alternatively, to be totally sexually inactive. Retarded and emotionally dysfunctional persons are often perceived as a threat; note the panic in localities where a halfway house for rehabilitated adults or a school for disturbed or retarded youngsters may be built or extended. Although the ostensible motive for the local cover stories is purported to be based on economic factors (it is alleged such a facility will lower property values), the intensity of the community's frantic reactions would tend to belie these claims.

The Challenge of Increased Mainstreaming

Such traditional behaviors as isolating and stigmatizing the disabled are comfortable social responses because they reduce the need for coming to terms with the problem of how to respond to persons with impaired functioning. However, as more and more individuals with special needs are deinstitutionalized, mainstreamed, and included in myriad social situations and contexts, increasing numbers of the nonhandicapped will be exposed to behaviors that are currently unfamiliar to them. The advent of mainstreaming, with the prospect of reduced stigmatization and marginality, offers a tremendous opportunity for a richer, more sociable, fuller life for those who are disabled, as well as for those who are not.

It is important to remember, however, that disabled children originally were removed from regular school programs because conditions there were inhospitable, unsuitable, or unresponsive to their special needs. Unless these destructive components are eliminated completely and a supportive climate established, the return may be even more traumatic than their present isolation. Inadequate diagnosis or remediation, unprepared and undertrained teachers, and sometimes hostile administrators[16] can sabotage intended advantages of mainstreaming. The issue here is not just movement, but beneficial change.

Parents have often refused to permit their children to play with "special" children; principals have often segregated special classes in basements or distant wings of buildings or in temporary shelters and have organized school lunch, bus, or activity periods at different times from those of the regular school population. To exacerbate the situation, teachers of these children report that they too are frequently isolated and excluded from the activities of the rest of the school faculty.

Recent Trends toward Activism

In the past, the disabled had very few spokespersons who were at the same time eloquent, persuasive, and politically influential. Although there have been a few strong advocates or advocacy-linked agencies calling for equity and justice, in many instances requests were soft-pedaled or muted and subsequently downgraded to pleading appeals for improvements. Among the disabled, there was little unity or militancy. Because of exclusion from access to power, they were often leaderless, inexperienced, and unfamiliar with basic techniques for manipulating events for their own interests or attracting media recognition and support. Moreover, agencies that purported to represent the disabled had few handicapped individuals or their selected representatives on governing boards and their goals were sometimes at variance with either the immediate goals or long-range objectives of their constituency.

There is evidence that significant changes are taking place that will move the handicapped person from peripheral or second-class status to fuller participation in American life. A need for self-determination has moved groups of the disabled to join militant advocates in pressing for abolition of exclusionary practices and provision of supportive legislation and administrative interpretations. They have mounted legal challenges against discriminatory actions that have resulted in favorable judicial decisions. They have become knowledgeable and skilled in using the structure of government to bring about long overdue reform. The snaillike pace of social response to the problems of the disabled is evidenced in the fact that the federal government has passed the Education of All Handicapped Children Act, with 1978 as the implementation date. Although education for all children has long been mandatory, provisions guaranteeing disabled children access to this basic service have been painfully slow in coming.

Organizations are increasingly influenced by the personal involvement of the disabled themselves in terms of policymaking and have expanded their focus from fund raising and direct service to extensive public relations as well as political action. Despite inexperience and exclusion from channels of influence in the past, the disabled have begun to learn how to organize and recruit others and to raise the general consciousness by tapping the potential of the media. The efforts of parent groups and professional organizations have resulted in modest improvement in the functioning of institutions. Political, sports, and entertainment personalities have publicly and assertively identified themselves closely with issues related to problems of the handicapped. Business and industry have realized the prospective size of the handicapped consumer market and are providing more adapted materials and specialized services. In addition to direct service, these efforts have alerted the populace to the rights and needs of the disabled, but, more critically, they also have functioned to notify decision makers in various sectors of society of their social responsibility.

Problems of Self-Concept and Group Membership

Although the disabled share a low social status with Blacks, Native Americans, and women, in some distinctive ways their social status and self-regard are significantly different. Perhaps the factor that most differentiates disabled children from youngsters in other minority groups is the nearly complete absence of close adult models either to consult with or to emulate. The psychological benefits of group identification and cohesion are largely absent except in those rare cases where another family member shares the same problem. For young children with a disability, this presents perplexing dilemmas. How are identities to evolve? How does their immediate world relate to these differences? How shall they perceive and value themselves?

For adults, identification and membership in groups composed solely of the similarly handicapped arouse ambivalent feelings. Such organizations provide a support community of people who have experienced equivalent problems and developed ameliorative coping behaviors. Psychological, familial, social, and vocational difficulties can be shared with those who can truly empathize, provide moral support, and suggest pragmatic solutions. On the other hand, by affiliation with such organizations, individuals accept the disability label and, in a sense, cut themselves off from the "normal" world. The psychological pressure to be indistinguishable from others can be so great that one may be willing to bypass essential needs in exchange for just the illusion of belonging. When the disability is the prime reason for the association, then there is the danger that it may become the salient identity factor, not only in the perception of others but in self-definition as well. An individual, then, is seen not in terms of skills, personality characteristics, interests, or even family, religious, or ethnic ties, that is, in terms of positive affiliations or abilities, but rather in the area of the most obvious deficiency.

Media Portrayal of the Disabled

Visual and print media have been critically underused by the public relations supporters in the cause of the disabled. Yet there is evidence that, paralleling the assertions of other minority groups, films and television create images that potently affect attitudes toward people who differ from the norm. Just as the white hat was an instant identifier of the hero in early western films, so disability is often used symbolically to convey instant messages to the viewer.

Handicapped characters are rarely, if ever, just "there," a part of the background (a passerby seated in a wheelchair but mobile in a street scene, or a shopper with a hearing aid not having a problem with a purchase) unless there is some specific role or function for that character subsequently to play. When a specific role has been planned it oftentimes is that of the villain, the victim, the foil (as in the humorous sidekick role), the "brain" or, rarely, the hero. Just as the comic-strip readers of Dick Tracy instantly recognize the villains by their physical stigmata, so the fans of James Bond know the enemy—physical disability or atypical behavior is usually the signal. Dr. No and Dr. Strangelove, as well as characters in the films *The Third Man* and *Fuzz* and the unknown perpetrator in the long-lived television show *The Fugitive* are all examples of this egregious device. Television heroes have been in evidence, such as Longstreet (a blind insurance investigator) and Ironside (a crippled ex-police official); the ironies of the names are noteworthy. An English version is found in "The Avengers": "Mother," a man, was the head of an intelligence operation run by the two featured characters and was confined to a wheelchair.

Television biographies or vignettes of real handicapped people often present considerable information about personal modes of coping or adjustment. Although romanticization is not uncommon, certain programs have offered invaluable insights. On his educational television program for children, Mister Rogers has consistently included guests who have had to adapt to impairment and complements their visits with informative, relevant discussions.

In films, coverage of this topic is frequently by means of a feature film of an actual person. In biographical films on Franklin Roosevelt, Jill Kinmont, Helen Keller, and so on, great emphasis is placed on the energy and tenacity of these individuals in triumphing over their misfortune; their success, moreover, augments their stature as persons.

Not only have the protests and demonstrations by the disabled and the Special Olympics been covered as television news events but extensive coverage in newspapers and magazines has been growing at a rapid pace. Some television stations regularly present signed and captioned shows for the deaf, and radio programs for the blind have appeared on which commentators read extensive selections from newspapers and magazines. From discussion shows, television and radio fans have learned that stellar personalities, particularly in politics and the entertainment business (Hubert Humphrey, Beverly Sills, and John Kennedy, for example), have family members for whom special educational or medical adaptations have been made. Producer Josh Logan has spoken freely about his psychiatric problems and entertainer Nanette Fabray has been open and casual about her deafness. Governor George Wallace and Senator Thomas Eagleton, on the other hand, prefer to downplay such issues. Both are sensitive to the exigencies of being political candidates with known difficulties and undoubtedly are aware that extensive publicity on this matter would be incompatible with their image and ambition. The senator's concern proved well founded when revelations of his treatment for emotional stress cost him the Democratic vice-presidential nomination.

Media have contributed to an increased awareness of the problems of disability. Yet, by their very nature, media have built-in limitations. Pacing is predetermined and fixed, allowing little time or opportunity for elaboration, explication, or reflection. There is reason to question whether the information and perceptions presented through the major media are adequate, especially in their present state, to effect attitudinal change. To do so it will be necessary to provide vicarious experiences wherein the nonhandicapped can identify with the problems and aspirations of the disabled, see themselves, temporarily at least, in such a role, and empathize over an extended period of time with the frustrations and limitations they confront. A pattern of rejecting behavior can best be challenged through channels providing more sustained and profound involvement than is possible through nonprint media. The instrumentality most apt to provide just such heightened sensitivity is literature.

Notes

1. Michael E. Monbeck, *The Meaning of Blindness: Attitudes toward Blindness and Blind People* (Bloomington, Ind.: Indiana University Press, 1973), p. 11.
2. Thomas J. Carroll, quoted in Monbeck, *The Meaning of Blindness*, p.11.
3. Monbeck, *The Meaning of Blindness*, p. 12.
4. Ibid.
5. John M. Reisman, *The Development of Clinical Psychology* (New York: Appleton-Century-Crofts, 1966), p. 42.
6. Florence Grannis, "Philosophical Implications of Book Selection for the Blind," in *The Special Child in the Library*, ed. by Barbara H. Baskin and Karen Harris (Chicago: American Library Association, 1976), pp. 29–33.
7. Jessica L. Langworthy, "Blindness in Fiction," *Journal of Applied Psychology* 14 (1930): 269–286.
8. Beatrice A. Wright, "An Analysis of Attitudes—Dynamics and Effects," *New Outlook for the Blind* 68 (March 1974): 109.
9. Lyoda M. Shears and Carl J. Jensema, "Social Acceptability of Anomalous Persons," *Exceptional Children* (October 1969): 91–96.
10. B. F. Skinner, "The Operational Analysis of Psychological Terms," in *Cumulative Record* (New York: Appleton-Century-Crofts, 1961), pp. 272–286.
11. James W. Fernandez, "Persuasions and Performances: Of the Beast in Every Body . . . And the Metaphors of Everyman," *Daedalus* (Winter 1972): 45.
12. Ibid.
13. Monbeck, *The Meaning of Blindness*, p. 5.
14. Harold Krents, "Darkness at Noon," *New York Times*, May 26, 1976, p. 39.
15. Ibid.
16. Reflecting on the District of Columbia decision chastising the Board of Education for failure to provide appropriate educational opportunities for exceptional children, an editorial comment in *The School Administrator* declared that administrators will find *"little solace and little comfort* in this contempt citation, solutions might have to come from the diversion of funds from ongoing regular grade programs." Italics added. Editorial, *The School Administrator* 32, 5 (May 1975): 8.

2

Literary Treatment of Disability

Chaos is intolerable. Life must have order and meaning. If events are capricious, we can ascribe no purpose, predictability, or security to our existence. If events confound our expectations, our fragile sense of security is threatened. Phenomena, once explained, can be dealt with, even controlled. The norm, of course, needs no justification; it is the standard by which the authenticity of one's own purpose or place is measured. But deviance demands explication. For if anomalous events are understood or rationalized, similar or related circumstances and events can be likewise interpreted, and the world will seem safe and orderly.

Myths in the Prescientific World

In the prescientific world, people were at the mercy of the environment and needed to be constantly alert to actual as well as imaginary threats. They had to protect themselves and looked for guidance to reduce their fears, avoid fatal pitfalls, and find some sense of certitude and safety in a turbulent, unpredictable world. Diviners and storytellers, assuming this responsibility, imposed order through magical or mystical interpretations.

Among the occurrences that required explanation were obvious variations in body structure, physiology, and behavior. Patterns of interpretation of these differences were manifested in the myths of many cultures. It seemed clear that disability was inextricably linked to social role and status: the handicapped were exposed, abandoned, or put to death, or, at the other extreme, were elevated to the role of demigod, shaman, or tribal leader. The gods mark those who are to be set apart,

17

but is the mark one of favor or contempt? The answer varied among societies and through time, although forms or combinations of forms are discernible through an analysis of mythology and other literary devices.

Despite variations in the myths, most attempted to rationalize the reasons for atypicality. Mythic stories functioned to dictate approved behaviors. Thus, societal response was not to the true impact of the handicap and the real adjustment it imposed, but to the attributed mythic meaning it had been assigned. By examination of some of these pervasive, enduring myths relating to disability, conscious and unconscious perceptions are revealed that have shaped social attitudes in the past and continue to do so today.

The appearance of disabled characters in children's fiction has its roots in mythic, biblical, classical, and contemporary literary forms. In effect, these manifestations in fiction for children echo recurrent themes. In this matrix, it is useful to consider children's stories not as isolated, ahistoric phenomena, but as the continuing social expression of persisting beliefs.

Although handicapped characters are remembered for attributes other than their disability, the disability is not incidental to the roles they will play. Their "blemish" is a reminder that the person is somehow set apart and will act out a predetermined destiny, extreme in nature and significantly different from those of other people.

Ironically, the same outward sign frequently symbolized opposite meanings: power or impotence, favor or rejection, good or evil. That lameness is a sign of disfavor was a belief of early peoples.[1] Since kings or chiefs were considered divine, their health and virility were causally linked to tribal prosperity. The vitality and number of children, the well-being of herds and crops, and the success of the hunt were all reflections of the perfection of the leader and, hence, the favor of the gods. Any sign of physical weakness, especially as it symbolically suggested impotence, was anathema. Oedipus[2] is the classical personification of that belief. Crippled in infancy, he destroys the Royal House of Thebes. His very name draws attention to his foot, which lamed, further cues the audience that a tragic destiny will unfold. The bodily signs of injury are not accidental, they presage events.

Authors of juvenile books of historic fiction are aware of these prescientific beliefs and reflect them in their work. In the adolescent novel *The Crows of War*, which is set in the first century A.D., this idea is dramatized. During the course of the Roman conquest, Airmid is blinded. Although her heroic actions save many of her people, she cannot marry Beon, the newly named tribal leader:

A chieftain has to be whole. And so, too his wife, that their children are not tainted with blemish! Any who are maimed are barred. Is that not the law? You know it is so![3]

The marked character as an agent of destruction finds expression in a Norse myth. The beautiful and beloved Baldur is killed by his blind brother, Hoder. The malicious Loki tricked him into committing this fratricidal act. In *Viking's Sunset*,[4] this myth is told twice—once in a storytelling exchange by characters within the story proper and later echoed in the climax. Heome, whose hands are mutilated, is deceived by his father's enemies, but is also self-deceived. He is the instrument through which his brother, Wawasha, as brave and handsome as Baldur, dies.

In *The Stronghold*, set in the time of the druids, Coll, the young hero, is lame. His design for a fort to protect the tribe from the marauding Romans is ultimately accepted. Its success ordinarily would have ensured his candidacy as tribal leader, but he is at first rejected, for: ". . . how then could the tribe survive with only a cripple to lead them?"[5]

Conversely, physical imperfection was often a sign of special favor. Moses stuttered. Jacob, lamed in a struggle with an angel, founded a nation. In children's books this presentation is a more frequent occurrence than the use of disability as a sign of a negative fate, and even Coll, the protagonist in *The Stronghold*, is eventually installed as king. O-Tah-Wah, in *Prisoner of the Mound Builders*,[6] is captured when his lame foot prevents his escape. The injury is regarded as a special sign of favor by his captors and is instrumental in his being specifically selected as a sacrifice to accompany the dying chief in his afterlife. Eventually, O-Tah-Wah escapes and, like Jacob, becomes the eponymous creator of a new nation.

Other positions in a society were frequently reserved for the disabled. Surprisingly, the role of medicine man or healer was often held by a disabled person. In Iroquois folklore, for example, Hadui, a crippled man, knew the secrets of medicine and curative herbs. Similarly, Tatlek, an Athabascan Indian, in the children's story *At the Mouth of the Luckiest River*, has an underdeveloped foot. Tatlek earns the enmity of the tribal medicine man, who fears him, seeing him as a future challenge to his power and an unwanted successor. As his grandfather tells Tatlek, "[he fears you since] He knows that some of the greatest medicine men of our people were born with weak bodies."[7] Tatlek fulfills this prophecy and proves that his yegas, or divine spirits, are more powerful than those of his antagonist. Nummer, of *Antelope Singer*,[8] has a withered and nearly useless arm. After years of rejection by his tribe, he becomes the one who divines where the herds of antelope are so that the hunters can provide food for his people. Thus he achieves an esteemed tribal position.

The ancient role of storyteller was a powerful one, and often held by the disabled. In modern times, the role has the connotation of one who amuses with entertaining little tales. Ancient storytellers were those who passed on the accumulated wisdom of a people and who foretold and interpreted life. Ahijah, the blind prophet of the Old Testament, and Tiresias, the blind seer of classical Greek literature, are examples of handicapped persons performing this prophecy function. In *The Son of the Leopard*,[9] the hero's future is foretold by a blind man and interpreted by a lame one. As the title states, the fortune teller is blind in *The Boy and the Blind Storyteller*,[10] the blind harpist is adviser to the king in *Warrior Scarlet*,[11] and the shaman in *Hunters of the Black Swamp*[12] has a back deformity. In a modern setting, Dave, the war-ravaged character in *Camilla*,[13] is the one Frank and Camilla turn to for an understanding of love and life's purpose. His suffering appears to have endowed him with special, more profound insights.

Handicaps are often associated with punishment. There is ample biblical and mythological precedent for this. Among others, Zedekiah blinded and Zacharias rendered mute; Rhoecus blinded by a dryad for negligence toward her messenger; Phineus, a Greek soothsayer who was blinded for abusing his gift of prophecy; and Tobit, blinded for disobeying Hebrew commandments to maintain ritual cleanliness—all reflect this punishment theme. In folklore, Peeping Tom was blinded for gazing at Lady Godiva. This latter instance reflects a popular supposition that blindness is a punishment for seeing what should not be looked upon.

Relationship between Disability and Character

Early literary forms illustrate the belief that the body reflects the quality of the inner person. In fairy tales, the prince and princess are beautiful; the wicked witch or villainous troll is hideous, ugly, and malformed—their external form mirroring their interior evil. Shakespeare presents Richard III as the most "subtle, false and treacherous" of men.[14] His twisted body reveals and provides justification for his villainy. He is self-described as:

Deform'd, unfinish'd, sent before my time
Into this breathing world scarce half made up,

And that so lamely and unfashionable
That dogs bark at me as I halt by them.[15]

Being by nature unsuited to goodness, he declares: "I am determined to be a villain."[16]

In more modern literature, physical appearance is often the objective correlative of the fortunes and virtues of characters. The evil, lame Quilp of *The Old Curiosity Shop*[17] and blind Stagg of *Barnaby Rudge*[18] in the stories of Charles Dickens are but two examples. Sir Leicester Dedlock's physical decline parallels the disintegration of his life and forms one of the most compelling symbols in *Bleak House*.[19] Stevenson's Pew, the wicked blind character from *Treasure Island*,[20] is yet another instance of a disability being the external evidence of internal evil.

Rarely is a physical mark the sign of wickedness in juvenile literature. With such minor exceptions as the malevolent Shrecker in *Ox Goes North*,[21] Uncle Russell in *Flambards*,[22] or Claws Johnson in *The Bright High Flyer*,[23] the perception of disability as wickedness is mainly confined to works of historic fiction. In *Johnny Tremain*,[24] when Johnny is crippled while working on the Sabbath, his injury is seen by his employer's family as God's punishment for breaking His law. Similarly, in *The Witch's Brat*, Lovel is regarded by the villagers as having demonic powers. The villagers see his deformed back and leg as signs of the devil. They turn on him and stone him, yelling: "Drive him out, the misshappen imp!"[25] Eilian, the title character of *The Change Child*,[26] is suspected of being a changeling. The most telling evidence for this is her limp.

The opposite perception, that disability is a sign of goodness, is more often reflected in contemporary children's books, and it, too, has its origins in earlier beliefs. Both Norse and Roman smiths, Weyland and Vulcan, are generally represented as lame. In *A Christmas Carol*,[27] the crippled child, Tiny Tim, is a symbol of innocence and hope. He is even more crippled by the cruel society he lives in than by his physical limitations and can be seen as an ironic counterpart of the wicked Mr. Cripples of *Little Dorrit*.[28]

One of the six children of the Templeton family in *A Crack in the Sidewalk* is seven-year-old Pleas, a name that is open to various interpretations. He is so severely impaired that he can neither talk nor move independently. His father sees him as having "a beautiful soul in a sorry body."[29] His older sister, although sad that he cannot participate more fully in the family, muses: "Maybe Pleas has been given a special compensation from where his happiness flows, and we are foolish to spend a moment pitying him. Maybe he is aware that he is luckier than we are."[30]

A more subtle variation on the idea of special grace can be found in Joey's story in the beautifully constructed *The Hayburners*.[31] Joey, an adult resident of an institution for the retarded, spends one summer working for a farm family. In his lack of knowledge and naivete, he is unaware that the decrepit steer he cares for is a hayburner, a "loser." Because he does not know it is impossible, he transforms the hopeless creature into a prize-winning animal. (See Figure 1.)

FIGURE 1.   From *The Hayburners* by Gene Smith. Illustrated by Ted Lewin. Illustrations copyright © 1974 by Ted Lewin. Reprinted by permission of Delacorte Press.

Disability and Social Commentary

Social perception of disability is ambiguous, motivated by compassionate and hostile forces, understanding and misunderstanding, curiosity and aversion. That the representation of these perceptions in literature should be paradoxical is not surprising. This device enables writers to make ironic statements about the human condition. A mute person may symbolize the essential isolation of humankind and the inability of one person to share fully ideas and feelings with another. The use of such a character can demonstrate that speech is often employed to hide, deceive, and dissemble and, hence, acts as a barrier to real communication. The mad character may be used to comment on an irrational world. The profound sayings of the fool in Elizabethan drama frequently serve to illuminate the folly of society. Lear gone mad is more perceptive than when sane. Gloucester, sighted, never observes the villainy of his son Edmund and does not truly see or comprehend until he is blinded. Lear admonishes him, saying: "A man may see how the world goes with no eyes."[32]

The "seeing" blind man is the most common fictional manifestation of superior functioning linked to loss. It is not until Odin sacrifices an eye that he gains wisdom or clearly "sees." Blind Tiresias is a prophet or seer, and this gift of special vision—insight or prophecy—is common. Oedipus, blind to the meaning of his own behavior, later develops prophetic ability when sightless in *Oedipus at Colonus*.[33]

In Jean Merrill's retelling of the Taoist legend *The Superlative Horse*, the message is conveyed twice. When Han Kan is questioned about the extraordinary horse he has purchased for the duke, he can offer no description. He has noted neither color nor gender, yet he has identified the most magnificent horse in all of China. Undistracted by the external, visible, and, hence, irrelevant aspects of the beast (despite his intact vision!), he has been able to see its essential qualities. And the final words of the book give a special message:

> This horse so impressed the artists who visited the court that for years they could draw no other. However, the quality of this great horse eluded every artist but one—an old man who had lost his eyesight studying the stallion and then, when he was entirely blind, carved in stone what is said to be a vivid likeness of the horse.[34]

It is only by not seeing the superficial world that one is finally able to see the essence. There is considerable objective truth in this observation; humanity's present and persisting unwillingness to "see" the implications of individual behavior, social policy, or global confrontations makes the metaphor of blindness a popular literary device. Juvenile fiction is replete with its usage.

Racial Issues

It is not coincidence that the most commonly occurring disability in books containing black characters is blindness. *The Dark of the Cave*,[35] *Sugar Bee*,[36] *Treasure of Green Knowe*,[37] and *The Cay*[38] have a brotherhood message that pivots on the need to see beyond the externals to an essential common humanity.

The Cay has been the subject of considerable controversy. The recipient of several major book awards for excellence in writing and for the promotion of interracial understanding, nevertheless it has recently been attacked as a paternalistic, racist book. The story is set in the Caribbean in the early days of World War II and revolves around Phillip, an eleven-year-old white child and Timothy, a seventy-year-old West Indian. The ship they are on is torpedoed and Phillip is blinded. After making their way to an island, Timothy teaches Phillip to take care of himself, to move freely around the island, to fish, and to perform other essentials of survival. During a fierce storm, Timothy is killed. Only because of the teachings of Timothy is Phillip able to survive until rescue comes.

The charges of racism against *The Cay*, which led to the withdrawal of the Jane Addams Children's Book Award, focus on the portrayal of Timothy as ugly, self-effacing, sycophantic, ignorant, and self-sacrificing. In regard to the latter, it is charged that the death of Timothy "has the ring of a metaphorical statement to the effect that it is for Blacks to serve and die and whites (white civilization) to *be served* and prevail."[39]

Clearly, other interpretations of this same event can be made. The situation might be seen as pointing out the need for the old order to give way to the future, that Timothy, a victim and symbol of bigotry and repression, must give way to the young boy, who embodies the enlightened future. Phillip, under the tutelage of Timothy, has abandoned the prejudices of his parents and has moved to a new level of understanding.

Taylor's response to the charges of racism includes his rationale for Phillip's blindness:

Much has been said about my purposely "blinding" Phillip. Why could he not learn his lessons while sighted? Insofar as prejudice is concerned, I honestly felt that Phillip was already blind, as was his mother, long before he suffered the injury. I believed that Phillip should dramatically know that much of prejudice is a matter of eye-sight (as with ugliness)—my own opinion. Finally, I wanted him to reach the point where "color" made no difference, leading to the line, "Are you still black, Timothy?"[40]

The last line, as might be expected, was central to the controversy. Taylor meant it to epitomize Phillip's dilemma. His upbringing had forced him to consider West Indians inferior and dangerous, but his experience had confronted him with an intelligent, gentle, and com-passionate man. Yet Phillip's question, when taken alone, suggests that blackness is incompatible with these qualities. The problem in inter-pretation seems to lie within the framework in which the question ap-pears. The context would seem to be the crisis point at which Phillip must abandon the false precepts he grew up with and acknowledge the validity of Timothy's behavior. Thus, although Timothy dies, he lives in the sense that his ideas prevail in the changed sensitivity and con-sciousness of Phillip, who now "sees" what Timothy is.

The young, anonymous black narrator of *Sound of Sunshine, Sound of Rain* is blind. His sister and Abram, a young man who befriends him, give him conflicting interpretations of the world he is unable to see. The boy recounts:

My sister says the park is ugly and dirty.

Abram says there are a few bits of paper, and a couple of cans and some bottles, but he says he can squint up his eyes and all those things lying around shine like flowers. Abram says you see what you want to see.

My sister says the park is just for poor folks, and that no one would ever come here if they had a chance to go anywhere else.

Abram says the park is just for lucky people, like him and me. He says the people who come to this park can see things inside themselves, instead of just what their eyes tell them.[41]

Abram tells him about colors too: "There isn't a best color. . . . Colors are on the outside. They aren't important at all. They're just cov-ers for things, like a blanket."[42] But when his sister takes him home one day, she is humiliated because of their color. Her brother tries to comfort her: "Abram says color don't mean a thing." She asks if Abram is black and he admits he doesn't know. " 'You don't even know if your friend is black or not,' says my sister. 'I wish everyone in the world was blind.' "[43]

On one level the sister is right. Color is of overwhelming importance in that it is the cause of the abuse she suffers. Paradoxically, Abram is also right. On a deeper level, color does not matter. The sister sees the world through pain; Abram through hope.

The author's message is clear as she contrasts reality and wish as determiners of perception. In this book, the youngster's blindness and youth are metaphors for innocence and contrast with the gratuitous cruelty of a society that countenances the abuse of children because of their color.

Another book in which these two elements are bracketed is *Listen for the Fig Tree*.[44] Muffin, black and blind, is not concerned with interracial problems but with an understanding of the implications of her own emerging personal and racial identity. The superficial focus on a dress for the Kwanza festival is subordinated to the search for self and her wider quest for connectedness to the black community. Muffin can be viewed, in the totality of her problems, as representing the social and economic handicaps under which Blacks have functioned. As Muffin copes with the limitations imposed by family problems, visual loss, and ghetto life, she draws from the strengths of the Black experience and her own undimmed, indomitable will to survive. Thus it is only when Muffin reconciles the various components of her conflicting experiences that she sees her own role clearly for the first time.

Romanticization or Diminution of Disability

In many novels, the heroes accomplish feats that their disabilities would seem to make impossible. Billy Gimp, the lame hero is the "runner" and key connection in *The Bladerunner*.[45] Although mute, the hero of *Atu, the Silent One*[46] is chosen to be the storyteller of his tribe, his drawings transmitting his message through generations. Auguste, also mute, in *Burnish Me Bright*,[47] is able to communicate with a supposedly dying child and a mad dog, actions that the speaking populace is unable to accomplish.

Neufeld, in the futuristic novel *Sleep Two, Three, Four!*,[48] uses the nearly blind Indian as a guide for the youngsters who are fleeing tyranny. Raph cannot see that which is close to him (the present), yet his distance vision (the future and past) is acute.

This symbolic use of disability seems quite of a different order from the literal achievement of characters who succeed *despite* their disability. The latter usage signals a denial of the implication of the handicap and is usually bound to a roseate view of the world in general and of disability in particular.

Tom, the central figure of *A Cry in the Wind*,[49] is a bright, perceptive, analytical boy, although he is described as mentally retarded. The presentation of maladaptive behavior is not metaphorical, but rather an obvious and heavy-handed plea for understanding and acceptance of children with retarded mental development. The fatal flaw in this presentation arises from the diminution of credibility as the young hero saves a life, outfaces the school bully, deduces who has vandalized the school taking full responsibility for his apprehension—complete with incriminating evidence. Similarly, eleven-year-old Chris in *Mister O'Brien*,[50] despite a hip deformity that necessitates a built-up shoe with a complex brace of leather straps and metal rods, participates in a walkathon for charity, and is able to walk, though in considerable pain, for ten miles.

The difference between Tom and Chris, on the one hand, and Billy Gimp, on the other, is critical. Although superficially they seem alike, they differ in this vital aspect: Billy Gimp's club foot is real; the agony he suffers as a result of the work he must do to establish a better society symbolizes the effort involved in resisting tyranny. It further signifies that the abandonment of security will be painful, that one must be willing to sacrifice in the area of greatest vulnerability. Billy is not a decathlon athlete; he is a runner who delivers messages and instruments that will enable the people he works with to continue their humane medical work and resist the pressures of a society that would ruthlessly control them. The walk Chris takes would have been demanding for a physically able-bodied child, and for one with Chris' limitation it is manifestly absurd. Chris' walk dramatizes a cliché: We forget our own burdens when we help others.

The message of *The Bladerunner* is that people are inadequate in the very areas in which competence is most needed. The case that one must surmount the barriers imposed by one's own limitations and do what ethics and social survival demand is argued effectively in Billy Gimp's fictional world.

Conversely, an unwarranted diminution of the implication of a disability is present in many other books. The condition is named, often extensively described, but its true impact is so reduced that it seems not much more than a slight inconvenience. The effects of polio on the characters in *Key of Gold*,[51] *The Mystery Gatepost*,[52] and especially *Green Door to the Sea*[53] are of the most trivial order. The medical sequelae have no more impact than dueling scars. They are romanticized and noninterfering badges that provide stories with artificial crises or the characters with excessively heroic stances. This minimization of a disability is a form of denial, discounting the reality of the problem and thus diluting the relevant message.

Search for Self

Another literary device for examination of the human experience is the metaphorical odyssey. Several of the books dealing with handicapped characters involve a search for self or for meaning in life. The disability is often a critical factor in the process. Aremis Slake of *Slake's Limbo*—myopic, abandoned, uncared for, and persecuted—escapes his tormentors by hiding out in the New York subway system. He sells used newspapers and does janitorial work in a below-ground coffee shop, thereby earning enough money for subsistence. Slake finds shelter in the broken wall of a subway tunnel. There he remains until he gains some confidence in his own powers and some control over his own life. He literally and metaphorically emerges from the purgatory of darkness and loneliness. The clearer vision provided by new glasses parallels his brighter vision of the world:

> He turned and started up the stairs and out of the subway. Slake did not know exactly where he was going, but the general direction was up.[54]

The deaf central character of *David in Silence*[55] escapes an angry mob of boys through a long dark tunnel. When at last he emerges, he is lost and unable to get help since his speech is so poor that no one he approaches can understand him. Safe at last, his adventure is regarded with awe and his former tormentors are ready to admit David to their circle of companions.

Margaret, from *A Dance to Still Music*,[56] lost her hearing as a result of an illness. She and her mother move from Maine to Florida, and Margaret, restless in her new home, undertakes a cross-country trip back to where she once was happy. Although she never reaches her geographic destination, her emotional journey is more successful. Supported by an understanding, compassionate adult who deals with Margaret's hearing loss in an accepting, unstressful way, and diverted from her self-absorption by an injured animal, Margaret is able to explore and finally articulate her own personal goals. The unmoving houseboat, her temporary home, transports her on a voyage of self-discovery.

In *Let the Balloon Go*, John's quest is fulfilled at the top of an 80-foot tree. His parents' fears for the safety of their spastic child have bound him tightly with prohibitions. Although safe, he is suffocating, and when he is unexpectedly left alone he laboriously climbs the forbidden tree, thereby proving to himself that "He was strong. He was free. He was a boy like any other boy."[57] Although still limited by the reality of his physical problem, he will no longer tolerate infantile treatment by his parents. John has established the right to take those risks necessary to achieve maturity and freedom.

Suffering as Payment for Grace and Enlightenment

The concept of suffering as necessary for grace or enlightenment suffuses Western thought. The central Christian symbol and the legends of innumerable saints attest to this. In an earlier manifestation, Odin paid for a draught from the well of wisdom with the sacrifice of an eye and later for the secret of the runes by mortification. In *A Single Light*,[58] Anna, a discarded and isolated deaf-mute young woman, is hounded by the villagers when she tries to hide and preserve a statue of the Christ Child. Only recently had its potential economic value to the community been realized, and the impoverished people see it as an instrument of their financial salvation. In their frenzied pursuit of Anna, they turn on a crippled man who they think has hidden her and stone him to death. At the last minute, the local curate rescues Anna and confronts the villagers with the knowledge of the suffering they caused, hoping that their shame will turn them from avarice and hate to feelings of love.

The similarity to Christian legend is hardly accidental. Anna was almost christened Maria at birth, but her imperfection prevented her from being so named; nevertheless, her relationship to the Christ Child is established. Her loving regard for the statue contrasts with the peasants' desire to exploit its monetary possibilities. The village is called Almas (souls in Spanish). The handicapped man must die and Anna suffer as the price for the villagers' redemption. The repeated juxtaposition between worldly and spiritual goals strengthens the analogy.

Into the Forest[59] is another Christian allegory of the search for the Kingdom of God after the "Great Destruction." Three of the major characters are disabled: one blind, one deaf, and one lame. They wander in the woods, losing their way and encountering great peril. The children receive help from (St.) Christopher, who describes the haven they will have to reach. He tells them stories of other travelers and helps them deal with their own failings. At last they are rewarded when "the lands that glisten" are laid out before them. The disabilities of the characters magnify the arduousness of the search, and are a metaphor for the inadequacies and vulnerability of all who undertake the search for salvation.

A Single Light and *Into the Forest* are complex, deliberate parables, and exhibit some literary skill. But the same idea of redemption through suffering and sacrifice, using disability as a central metaphor, is also present in the most mundane and superficial of stories. When the myth is eviscerated, generally all that remains is soap opera. In *A Bright Star Falls*, Rosellen, a handicapped adolescent, endures tremendous suffering without a word of complaint. This paragon prefers death to the possibility of being a burden. Her stoic model inspires all who know her; and when she does die, it is clear that her friends are better people—more humane, more compassionate for having known her, for her "loving warmth permeated the room the minute she entered. Some magic in her made every boy gallant and solicitous . . . and smoothed out edges and drew out the kindness and goodness in everyone."[60]

The shallow, self-centered prom queen heroine of *The Shining Moment*[61] is disfigured by facial scarring acquired in an accident. Unable to face her former friends, Janey retreats to the relative anonymity of a small town where she redirects her energies toward community projects. No longer self-absorbed, she finds out "what life is all about." Her scar fades as enlightenment dawns and she returns to a more open life, wiser and almost as pretty as ever. The pain has had a purpose: Janey has confronted her former value system and discovered a fractionally deeper purpose in life.

The idea that pain somehow ennobles is ingrained in our culture. The hard reality is that it is more apt to lead to frustration, anger, or despair. Such beliefs die hard, though, and their perpetuation in the literature shapes false expectations toward real-life counterparts.

Suffering of the Impaired Benefits Others

Suffering is not always portrayed as leading to the purification of the sufferer. Sometimes a displacement occurs and the impaired person is the agency for the deliverance of others. This is reminiscent of the pagan concept of a scapegoat, where the faults and crimes of the community were loaded on an animal whose sacrifice freed all of their guilt while providing a cathartic release of hostility. Much variation and transposition occur in the presentation of this somber theme in juvenile literature. When a little girl is hurt in *Hey, Dummy*,[62] without the slightest bit of evidence the crowd assumes that Alan, a retarded boy, is responsible. In the climactic scene, Alan is shot. His guilt or innocence is less an issue with the crowd than the provision of a sacrificial victim to whom they can assign guilt. The scapegoat role is most obvious in *Dark Dreams*.[63] The victim of community violence, Joey J., a harmless retarded man, is adjudged its perpetrator. Banished to an institution, he soon dies.

Faith Leading to Cure

As suffering can lead to grace, so faith can lead to cure. Zacharias, struck dumb for doubting God's word, has his speech restored when at last he obeys God's command. Restoration of speech is also the climactic incident in two children's books, *A Certain Small Shepherd*[64] and *Nacar, the White Deer*. In the former, Jamie, mute since infancy, speaks clearly when he presents a gift to the infant born on Christmas day to a homeless couple seeking shelter in a stable. In the second story, Lalo, also mute, is entrusted with the care of a white deer. After an arduous and dangerous journey, he delivers the animal to the king, who proposes that it be the target of a hunt. Lalo cries out to save it. " 'Our Lady opened your throat because your heart is good,' said the King. 'I consider it a miracle.' "[65]

Monasteries are the settings for two other miraculous cures. Strength is restored to Rowan's muscles through the ministrations of Brother Tomaso and the intercession of God in *The Keys and the Candle*.[66] Hugh, a young lad, is left by his father in the care of some monks in *The Hidden Treasure of Glaston*. In the midst of a fire, after he had courageously rescued one of the monks, he finds that his limp has completely vanished. Hugh wonders: "When had it happened? The vision in the flameswept Chapel of St. Joseph flashed before his mind's eye. *That* had been it. Healing had come in the presence of the Holy Grail!"[67]

In three of these four stories, goodness is rewarded with an instantaneous and total recovery. An inference can be readily drawn that perhaps those who still sustain a disability are less deserving since the models presented lose their handicap as a reward for courage, generosity, and other commendable virtues.

The Handicapped as Catalysts in the Maturation of Others

In juvenile literature, the handicapped person frequently is the unwitting agency through which other characters fulfill their destinies. In Molly Cone's *Simon*,[68] in *Summer of the Swans*,[69] and in *A Year to Grow*,[70] retarded youths are the catalysts in the maturation process of the main characters. Although the dimensionality of the characters varies from the well-developed Charlie in *Summer of the Swans* to the less clearly delineated Julia in *Simon* and Jimmy in *A Year to Go*, their function is identical: Out of the seeds of the crises in each of their lives comes the insight and energy for the central characters' passage to adulthood.

An interesting variation on this theme, found in *The Rose Round*,[71] involves the maturation of a fully grown man. Theo is the scorned adult son of a wealthy, bitter, hostile, and rejecting mother, who, through her imperious behavior, keeps Theo in a dependent, self-effacing role. His surreptitious involvement in a school for severely handicapped children allows him to act for the first time in a decisive, responsible manner. Theo's deformed hand, a continual focus of his mother's contempt and loathing, diminishes in importance as a barrier to his full functioning and ceases to serve as an excuse for self-imposed isolation. When the school faces imminent financial collapse, Theo moves the children into his own home despite the strenuous objections of his mother. Gaining inspiration and strength from the resolution of the school's eviction crisis, he is able to shed the chrysalis of subjugation and self-disparagement and emerge at last as a mature, independent adult.

Portrayal of the Social Realities

Convinced of the potency of the pen as a tool of reform, skilled authors have long used fiction to draw attention to a variety of social and political ills. Novels often ignite the imagination of the reading public more effectively than a mountain of public reports. So, too, in juvenile fiction are there realistic books dealing with social issues. Among these are books about the physical, psychological, rehabilitative, and/or social implications of having a specific handicap. Despite a tendency to romanticize some problems, the treatment tends to be honest and such books can be highly informative. Material is developed on multiple levels with characters playing complex and sometimes ambivalent roles; actions have complicated ramifications and problems may only be partially resolved. Although conclusions may be unclear in some of these adolescent novels, most end with a definite, although not always pleasant, resolution.

One example of this kind of book, *The Trembling Years*, is a detailed examination of the effects of polio on a vibrant young woman. The onset of the disease, the hospital stay, the emotional trauma, the questions and fears about her future, the therapy and rehabilitative process, the probable extent of recovery, the familial adjustments, the financial costs, and the factors that will prevent an unfettered resumption of her former lifestyle—all are painstakingly chronicled. There is no attempt to gloss over the psychological or physical pain, nor is there a tempering of the expected social difficulties. In a powerful scene, Kathy asks another patient in the hospital who is badly crippled:

"Max, is the worst over or yet to come?"

He replied tersely out of experience. "To come. I have never walked myself. But I'd say for you the worst will come when you leave the hospital and live among normal people."

"Do you ever really get used to it?"

"Never."

"Where is there help? I don't mean doctors. But for courage or—or whatever? I—I'm scared sometimes." She kept picking at the sheet, trying to keep from wailing, hating to confess even to Max how scared she could be.

Terribly she craved comfort, but today Max had no comfort.[72]

The attentive reader can hardly fail to learn a great deal about polio from its description in the novel. But, in addition to the informational function, there is a strong affective component that makes ready identification with the heroine likely. Poliomyelitis is the single most common disorder found in juvenile books about handicapped characters. The treatment in *The Trembling Years* is one of the most honest and thorough.

Twyla[73] is unique in both content and style. It is the story of a retarded adolescent told mainly through her letters to Wally, a college student about whom she has created a fantasy love life. Her letters show that she does not have the coping skills needed to function adequately in contemporary society and there is neither personal nor community help for her. She is badly used by her peers and is often the butt of their cruel jokes. Her restricted functioning is an impediment to her ability to predict or understand the results of her own or others' behavior. Poverty, a fragmented family, and an inadequate school clearly exacerbate the effects of low intellectuality. In sum, the problems of mental retardation are seen as complex and interdependent and not restricted to poor academic functioning.

The Trembling Years and *Twyla* have implications that extend beyond the lives of two literary heroines to their real-life counterparts. Characters in the book and, by extension, the readers, have a social responsibility toward those who are excluded, ignored, or reviled.

Gift of Gold is concerned almost exclusively with the adjustments necessitated by blindness. It is a junior novel of simple construction and relatively uncomplex characterization, less demanding than the preceding two titles. Cathy, the heroine, is portrayed as an attractive, intelligent young woman who makes reasonable and understandable adaptations to her blindness. Her associates are sensitive or callous, considerate or indifferent, kind or exploitive, helpful or obstructive in their relationships with her, consistent with their overall character. Her blindness causes her some particular difficulties, but it does not prohibit the possibility of a full, reasonably happy, and productive life.

In *Gift of Gold* several common prejudices are effectively explored, including the particularly nefarious fallacy that the blind should seek their own ghettoization. Cathy wants to be a speech therapist, but she is counseled to work instead with blind children:

> "Have you ever thought of directing your own studies toward work with the blind?"
>
> "No," Cathy said, startled into curtness. . . .
>
> She had been braced for practically anything but a train on this old track. What she resented was the implication the question always carried that, because she was blind herself, both necessity and natural inclination should restrict her activities to the world of the blind.[74]

In works such as these, with the extended examination they provide of a single disability, there is ample opportunity to explore the subtle and multitudinous ramifications of the attendant problems. It should not be assumed, however, that a realistic style of book that focuses on a disability is necessarily a guarantee of accuracy, balance, or extensive data. Authors have proven themselves capable of writing highly misinformed books of this type, as well as those with cardboard characters or the imposition of fairy-tale endings for what are initially serious themes.

Character Portrayal

In assessing the value of books on disability, one of the key questions is: Are the characters with exceptionalities treated as people or devices? Any story is suspect that suggests that a handicapped person is inevitably and forever set apart from the mainstream of human experience. When the character is unnaturally or outrageously endowed, blessed, or heroic, the effect is emphasis on the differences between a disabled person and the presumed nondisabled reader. If the book is intended to increase acceptance for people with special needs, the heroic, talented, or otherwise admirable disabled character must be developed as credible, natural, and three-dimensional. Saintliness in characters is not credible. The believable character does invite identification.

The aspects of character, behavior, and situation that the author stresses also require evaluation. When serious problems are minimized, where unconscious limitations or biases are superimposed, or when sin and punishment seem natural and inevitable partners of disability, the ultimate consequence is to reduce and dehumanize. This assertion holds true whether the character is a major, minor, or incidental one.

Underlying Messages

Although some children report that the story line itself remains in their memory long, long after the initial reading, it is more likely that the essence of the story lingers in a distilled, nonlinguistic format of feelings, images, and stirrings. That is, when the details of the story fade, it is necessary to consider what attitudinal traces will remain. If a book's messages are ambivalent or contradictory, those that tend to be the most powerful and responsive to the psychological needs of the reader will endure. If certain thematic elements pervade the book, such as death, evil, and violence, these, by their very nature, carry more emotional weight and more impact than a Panglossian resolution. The story should also be examined to see what it stresses quantitatively, because, despite disclaimers, the author's real interests can often be inferred from the amount of space expended on various aspects of the story. If the story is heavily laden with purposeless violence, later condemnation is insufficient to attenuate the impact of the brutality.

The question must arise: Do children read solely on a literal, story-line level, or are they able to detect the profound and subtle undertones in their reading? Researchers from diverse disciplines have reported that, at remarkably early ages, children do internalize messages relevant to social role and status. It is not necessary that they be specifically articulated; in fact, the best and most potent delivery may be on the sub- or pre-conscious level. Children's books are just one more agency that endorses traditional cultural mores. Juvenile fiction is not unique—it is derivative and reflective of the same perceptions found in classical and popular literature. As such, it contains a range of positive and negative images and of overt and latent messages. When selecting books to be recommended or used, it is essential to consider what perceptions are being shaped or reinforced vis-à-vis the exceptional person.

Notes

A short form of reference is used for works cited fully in Chapter 5.

1. For a fascinating and provocative discussion of the lame character in adult fiction, see Peter L. Hays, *The Limping Hero; Grotesques in Literature* (New York: New York University Press, 1971).
2. Sophocles, *Oedipus, the King* (Minneapolis: University of Minnesota Press, 1972).

3. Steven Rayson, *The Crows of War*, p. 254.
4. Henry Treece, *Viking's Sunset*.
5. Mollie Hunter, *The Stronghold*, p. 190.
6. Lloyd Harnishfeger, *Prisoner of the Mound Builders*.
7. Arnold A. Griese, *At the Mouth of the Luckiest River*, p. 4.
8. Ruth M. Underhill, *Antelope Singer*.
9. Harold Courlander, *The Son of the Leopard*.
10. Paul Anderson, *The Boy and the Blind Storyteller*.
11. Rosemary Sutcliff, *Warrior Scarlet*.
12. Lloyd Harnishfeger, *Hunters of the Black Swamp*.
13. Madeleine L'Engle, *Camilla*.
14. William Shakespeare, "The Tragedy of King Richard, the Third," in *The Histories* (New York: Heritage Press, 1958), p. 780.
15. Ibid., p. 779.
16. Ibid., p. 780.
17. Charles Dickens, *The Old Curiosity Shop* (London: J. M. Dent, 1907).
18. Charles Dickens, *Barnaby Rudge* (New York: Dutton, 1906).
19. Charles Dickens, *Bleak House* (New York: Heritage Press, 1942).
20. Robert Louis Stevenson, *Treasure Island* (New York: Scribners, 1907).
21. John Ney, *Ox Goes North: More Troubles for the Kid at the Top*.
22. K. M. Peyton, *Flambards*.
23. Margaret J. Baker, *The Bright High Flyer*.
24. Esther Forbes, *Johnny Tremain*.
25. Rosemary Sutcliff, *The Witch's Brat*, p. 9.
26. Jane Louise Curry, *The Change Child*.
27. Charles Dickens, *A Christmas Carol* (Philadelphia: Lippincott, 1964).
28. Charles Dickens, *Little Dorrit* (New York: Heritage Press, 1956).
29. Ruth Wolff, *A Crack in the Sidewalk*, p. 32.
30. Ibid., p. 33.
31. Gene Smith, *The Hayburners*.
32. William Shakespeare, "The Tragedy of King Lear," in *The Tragedies* (New York: Heritage Press, 1958), p. 837.
33. Sophocles, *Oedipus at Colonus*, ed. by Gilbert Murry (Oxford University Press, 1948).
34. Jean Merrill, *The Superlative Horse* (Reading, Mass.: Addison-Wesley, 1961), p. 79.
35. Ernie Rydberg, *The Dark of the Cave*.
36. Rita Micklish, *Sugar Bee*.
37. Lucy Maria Boston, *Treasure of Green Knowe*.
38. Theodore Taylor, *The Cay*.
39. Council on Interracial Books for Children, "*The Cay*: A Position Paper," *Top of the News*, April 1975, p. 283.
40. Theodore Taylor, Letter to the Editor, *Top of the News*, April 1975, p. 287.
41. Florence Heide, *Sound of Sunshine, Sound of Rain*, unpaged.
42. Ibid.
43. Ibid.
44. Sharon Bell Mathis, *Listen to the Fig Tree*.
45. Alan E. Nourse, *The Bladerunner*.
46. Frank Jupo, *Atu, the Silent One*.
47. Julia Cunningham, *Burnish Me Bright*.
48. John Neufeld, *Sleep Two, Three, Four!*
49. L. Dean Carper, *A Cry in the Wind*.

50. Prudence Andrew, *Mister O'Brien*.
51. Cora Cheney, *Key of Gold*.
52. Jean Bothwell, *The Mystery Gatepost*.
53. Erick Berry, *Green Door to the Sea*.
54. Felice Holman, *Slake's Limbo*, p. 117.
55. Veronica Robinson, *David in Silence*.
56. Barbara Corcoran, *A Dance to Still Music*.
57. Ivan Southall, *Let the Balloon Go*, p. 109.
58. Maia Wojciechowska, *A Single Light*.
59. Rosamund Essex, *Into the Forest*.
60. Lenora Mattingly Weber, *A Bright Star Falls*, p. 91.
61. Mildred Lawrence, *The Shining Moment*.
62. Kin Platt, *Hey, Dummy*.
63. C. L. Rinaldo, *Dark Dreams*.
64. Rebecca Caudill, *A Certain Small Shepherd*.
65. Elizabeth Borton de Trevino, *Nacar, the White Deer*, p. 145.
66. Maryhale Woolsey, *The Keys and the Candle*.
67. Eleanore M. Jewett, *The Hidden Treasure of Glaston*, p. 282.
68. Molly Cone, *Simon*.
69. Betsy Byars, *Summer of the Swans*.
70. Felice Holman, *A Year to Grow*.
71. Meriol Trevor, *The Rose Round*.
72. Elsie Oakes Barber, *The Trembling Years*, p. 79.
73. Pamela Walker, *Twyla*.
74. Beverly Butler, *Gift of Gold*, p. 21.

3

Assessing and Using
Juvenile Fiction
Portraying the Disabled

Our literary inheritance is strong and enduring, yet is constantly modified and reinterpreted in the cauldron of social change. Radical transformations in society caused by shifts in political, sociological, and social class positions have impact on the content, format, and style of contemporary literature. The posture of outgroups, for example, has profoundly changed. Now the tone of their writings is frequently more abrasive, strident, and demanding rather than obsequious. Their quest is both qualitative and quantitative, seeking greater visibility and more positive characterization. The plea for mere tolerance has been replaced by an insistence on equality of treatment in the literary context. Initial evidence of success for these groups can be seen in the outpouring of books concerning formerly socially marginal populations.

Juvenile literature, paralleling adult literary changes, has been profoundly affected by the new societal realities. Previously taboo content is now commonplace. Those topics once considered too sophisticated, emotionally devastating, complex, or exotic are now deemed appropriate for young readers. Furthermore, style and form have expanded from the traditional third person, expository, chronological mode to a variety of literary formats, including mixed sequence, first person presentations, absurdist, surrealistic, or impressionistic styles, and other forms common in adult writings.

Concurrent with this development is a new recognition of children's literature as a legitimate art form worthy of the attention of serious writers. Earlier, children's classics were often disparaged—even by their own creators—as frivolous entertainments. Although in the distant past, lesser talents were considered good enough to write for children, now there are many first-rate authors who view juvenile literature as the major forum for their creative efforts and some who move easily between writing for juvenile and adult audiences.

As these contemporary authors make more stringent artistic demands upon themselves, so they tend to make greater intellectual demands upon their young audiences. Serious writers perceive of themselves not as mere purveyors of entertainment or didactic messages, as in the past, but frequently as interpreters of the social order as well as shapers of a new consciousness.

Earlier Children's Fiction

Historically, children's stories were neither conceptualized nor evaluated in literary terms. Rather, they were thought of primarily as vehicles for reinforcing moral instruction or for providing academic information in palatable form. The bulk of the books produced for juvenile audiences exhorted, intimidated, cajoled, or threatened. Models of probity were contrasted with dire examples of the tragic consequences of misbehavior. Puritan literature warned of eternal damnation for what seem today to be relatively minor vices. Later generations of writers, commonly and extravagantly reflecting the work ethic, promised social and economic rewards for industriousness and cooperation with others. Still later, consideration, persistence, and diligence were extolled. Although mores of society, as reflected by authors, changed and their emphases altered, didactic intent persisted and even today permeates a large portion of writing for children.

Unfortunately, throughout the history of children's books in America, the desire to teach and to preach has overridden the need to produce good literature. The result has been a torrent of forgettable books that have found their well-deserved place in oblivion. Yet, during their period of popularity, these stories often reflected the conventional wisdom and today provide insights into contemporary attitudes and perceptions.

In those early books for children, of which we still have some record, disabled characters were rarely found. On those occasions when they were portrayed, they usually played restricted, particularized roles. Often they served as models of forbearance and humility or as rightfully punished malefactors. The onset of the disability was especially fertile ground for gleaning object lessons. If the disability were the result of an accident, then carelessness or misbehavior by the victim was the usual cause. In *Adventures of a Pincushion*,[1] for example, a young girl who told a lie was kicked by a horse and crippled for life! The author hastened to assure the reader that cause and effect were at work in this calamity.

Although the humor and absurdity in this typical incident are apparent to modern audiences, the moral lesson in the story reflected contemporary beliefs. The idea that there is a physical marking or punishment as a natural and inevitable outcome for immoral behavior was explicitly stated in Kingsley's aside to the readers in *The Water Babies*: ". . . for you must know and believe that people's souls make their bodies, just as a snail makes its shell."[2]

Occasionally the handicapped were perceived as unfortunate victims rather than culprits to be punished. Young readers were invited to observe the poor crippled child, à la Tiny Tim, who, although having great burdens to bear, was unwaveringly kind, humble, and considerate—unlike certain ungrateful boys and girls who fail to appreciate their own good fortune. Typical of this presentation was an incident from a book called, apparently without sarcastic intent, *Happy Home Stories*. This little volume was published by the American Tract Society, a popular producer of many unenduring similar works.

> When Charlie Reed was a year old, his nurse let him fall on the floor, and his back was so badly hurt that he could never walk without crutches. The poor fellow used to feel very sad, when he grew older, as he saw other boys running and jumping and playing as much as they pleased, while he had to be on his bed nearly all the time, and could only limp around a little with his crutches.
>
> Charlie used to watch at the window every day for a little apple-girl, of whom he always bought an apple, and she felt so sorry for the lame boy that she saved her largest apple for him.
>
> "You are rich and have all the money you want," she said to Charlie once.
>
> "You are richer than I, for you can walk," answered Charlie.[3]

Juliana Horatia Ewing was one of the most celebrated authors of children's novels in the second half of the last century. Two of her stories dealing with disabled characters typify the attitudes of the day. They depict the exceptional person as a paragon of virtue, wonderfully patient, good-natured, and brave under any and all circumstances. The hero of *The Story of a Short Life* was crippled trying to save his dog's life. Although still young when he died as a result of his injuries, he was able to endure his suffering by imagining himself a soldier wounded in battle.[4] In the story "The Blind Man and the Talking Dog" from *Dandelion Clocks and Other Tales*, the resigned and uncomplaining blind man was contrasted with the "selfish and imperious" mayor's son. The former was patient and undemanding, finding happiness in the warm sunshine, the few pennies dropped in his hat, and his dog's loyalty and affection, while riches and the love of his fair wife were insufficient to satisfy the greedy young man.[5]

The Little Lame Prince and His Travelling Cloak[6] is still popular today. A fantasy, it presented the title character as one who, though exiled, isolated, and imprisoned, remained kind, gentle, loving, and forgiving. It was clear that his lameness made these qualities all the more praise-worthy. Heidi[7] included in its cast of characters a blind grandmother, a lame girl, and a slow-learning boy. These characters were better devel-oped, more credible, and less sentimentalized than Ewing's, but the improvement was only relative. Clara, the wealthy crippled girl, was taught to walk by Heidi. Although her first steps were painful, Clara's discomfort diminished by the third step, and buoyed by Heidi's cheer-ful determination and the therapeutic alpine air, she made an almost instantaneous recovery.

Another story from the last century, Otto of the Silver Hand,[8] can still be found in libraries today. The treatment of disability was very dif-ferent in this romantic, swashbuckling retelling of a violent old legend by a highly gifted writer. Otto's amputation was a deliberate and ruth-less act of revenge. The villain selected a mutilation that was directed at Otto's father, symbolically dramatizing his intention to deny the pas-sage of power from father to son. Otto's body was the battleground for the expression of conflict between opposing forces. Pyle could not resist a parting moral, bluntly stating that personal loss was preferable to bru-tal villainy: "Better a hand of silver, than a hand of iron."[9]

Two stories from the early days of the twentieth century, The Christ-mas Tree Forest[10] and Johnny Blossom,[11] used disabled characters to deliver sermons about unselfishness and concern for others. In the former nov-el, Grandfather Christmas left presents every year for children to choose for their friends. One day a stranger suggested that every one should choose gifts for him- or herself instead. Only one boy, Inge, rejected the idea and decided he would rather get presents to give to his sister, "the poor crippled child [who] could not go a step toward the forest."[12] None of the other children was able to find gifts, but the noble Inge found plenty and soon "there are many toys piled up about the little cripple's chair."[13]

Johnny Blossom demonstrated his generosity by paying for an op-eration so that his grandmother's sight could be restored, providing spiritual comfort for a man with an injured back, and inviting a "crippled boy with big solemn eyes" and "Katerina the dwarf" to his party. Fortunately, there were enough disabled characters around to provide adequate expression for Johnny's goodness. These two books illustrate practices commonly used in such tales. The disabled person was known by his or her disability. Often, as in *The Christmas Tree Forest* or "The Blind Man and the Talking Dog," the handicapped character had no name; in other stories, such as *Johnny Blossom*, the disability formed part of the name, as, for example, when one character was always referred to as "Katerina the dwarf."

Emergence of Realism

As the twentieth century progressed, a gradual and continuing improvement in realistic books for children was evident. Characters with handicaps began to emerge as believable people rather than pasteboard props. However, implications of disability were rarely examined in depth and fairy-tale solutions remained dominant. The disabled began to be depicted as having a secure and viable place in the family structure. Many of the stories provided warm and cozy portraits of home life. For example, Francis was a central character in *The Cottage at Bantry Bay*[14] and also in the sequel, *Francie on the Run*.[15] He had a severe limp of unspecified origin that did not in any way impede his adventurousness.

However, in these stories, descriptions of real problems associated with the disability are intermixed with totally unrealistic resolutions to problems. Francie expressed concern about how his leg would be when he was grown and whether it would affect how others would regard him. His mother assured him that "greatness comes from the brains and heart, not from the feet."[16] This seems the kind of natural and supportive response a sensitive and loving mother might give. But, on another occasion, Francie and his brother discovered some of that buried treasure so elusive in reality and so common in children's books. It allowed them to pay for an operation to correct Francie's orthopedic problem and the author to find a convenient and happy ending for her story. In the sequel, Francie left the hospital where he had been for seven(!) months and successfully made his way home across Ireland by himself. Problems were beginning to be honestly stated, but resolutions often continued to be preposterous.

Probably the best-known disabled character from the first half of this century was Laura's sister, Mary, from such Laura Ingalls Wilder novels as *Farmer Boy*[17] and *On the Banks of Plum Creek*.[18] The perennially popular series was, above all, a tale of a loving and mutually supportive family. Mary's life, like that of her sister's and parents,' was filled with the crises of frontier living, in her case exacerbated by the problems of blindness. Mary never gave way to despair, nor lashed out and railed against a cruel and unjust fate, nor became bitter or withdrawn. Such common manifestations of human emotion were not a part of children's literature of the time, no matter what the provocation or subject matter. Most writers of the period apparently took seriously the advice given in a well-known manual entitled *Writing for Children* in which authors were enjoined to "make the characters live the lives of ordinary, *healthy* [emphasis added] human boys and girls."[19]

Although the dominant pattern of juvenile fiction presented a carefully laundered view of life, a new and growing trend, roughly coinciding with the onset of World War II, could be discerned. Perceptions of what children were like were changing. In education, for example, the image of the child as a passive recipient of the teacher's knowledge was changing to that of discoverer or even, on a modest scale, to that of decision maker. It followed naturally that if children were to be given the responsibility of making decisions, then it was essential that they have the requisite information on which to base suitable judgments.

The construct of childhood as a happy, carefree time was seen to have evolved more from nostalgia than derived from an honest, objective observation of young people. Illness, accidents, infirmity, and personal and social disruptions are facts of life. The prevailing attitude that such things were not fit topics for the young left children ill-equipped to cope with crises when they occurred. Some writers began to realize that efforts to protect children from knowledge of a threatening, unhappy, or capricious world, rather than providing security, left them unprepared and therefore vulnerable. As these psychological insights gained popular currency, books began to appear on such formerly forbidden subjects as divorce, death, institutionalization, racial discrimination, and disability. Nevertheless, the treatment of these issues remained romanticized and "happily ever after" continued to be the favored ending. The barriers were being breached, however, and the unnameable could at last be discussed. Gradually more honest and realistic presentations would appear.

Relative Incidence of Disabilities Portrayed

One major change from post-World War II to the present was the increase of disabilities considered appropriate thematic material for young readers. Blindness and orthopedic conditions were the most frequently selected disabilities in early children's literature. In junior fiction, polio was the major cause of orthopedic problems and, as a fictional device, had great dramatic potential. It provided a character test, the resolution of which established the heroic credentials of the character. In essence, instead of a ritual slaying of a dragon, the satisfactory confrontation of the consequences of a feared viral agent would be substituted. Since the residual physical effects of polio could range from minimal crippling to near total paralysis, the writer could control the impact of the illness. By electing minimal disablements, the credibility of virtually unlimited achievement could be sustained.

Poliomyelitis was in fact a major crippler and its ubiquitous expression in the literature at that time reflected contemporary incidence and concern. Blindness, however, which is relatively rare, was represented in fiction far in excess of its actual occurrence. In the 1940s and 1950s other disorders were grossly underrepresented or totally absent. Stories about persons who manifested conditions of developmental disability, emotional dysfunction, deafness, or cardiac or neurological impairment were almost nonexistent.

There is no conclusive evidence to explain why certain functional disorders were popular and others were not. However, several factors are suggestive. Considerable historic precedent exists for the utilization of blind and lame characters in both adult and early children's fiction. Additionally, except for cerebral palsy, there appears to be a relationship between the visibility or obviousness of the condition and the likelihood of its presence in a story in which the author wishes to include disabled characters. Such overt manifestations of disability were readily comprehensible to readers and drew upon presumed sympathetic perceptions. Wheelchairs and guide dogs were conspicuous, clear signals that alerted the reader to a specific response set. (The recent movement away from concentration on highly visible disabilities to less apparent ones, such as deafness, asthma, emotional dysfunction, and so on, has created more demands on authors since it diminishes common obvious cues to youthful readers; writers must make more refined uses of dramatization, interaction, and characterization to elicit empathic reactions.)

Well-known contemporary figures often raised public consciousness about particular handicapping conditions, creating in the process a heightened interest and receptivity toward books on the subject. Public identification with Franklin Delano Roosevelt and awareness of his struggles to rise above his disabling condition provided a model to be replicated and emulated in children's fiction. Years later, the Kennedy family's association with mental retardation lent it "respectability" and soon thereafter fictional books on this topic found their way to the juvenile literary marketplace.

Recent Expansion of Scope. Beginning in the 1960s, there was an explosion of books on difficult subjects, ushering in a new climate wherein more complicated or subtle differences in human behavior or conditions could be explored. Although there are still underrepresented areas—speech problems, epilepsy, specific learning disabilities—this situation is gradually being redressed. Furthermore, fictional treatment of impairments has changed radically. The complexities of many problems, the unlikelihood of easy solutions, and the social conflict and abuse sustained by the involved characters and their families are being probed and scrutinized in detail. Moreover, there has been a shifting of focus to an internal perspective as the intricate, multiple ramifications of the involved character's life unfold.

Impact of Social Statements in Literary Works

The most complex, sophisticated level of literary experience is the esthetic. Educators ultimately want children to understand not only the literal meaning of fiction but also to appreciate how structure, symbolism, idea, and style enhance the beauty and meaning of a work of art. However, using literature for other than esthetic purposes is also a legitimate academic goal. Fiction can be used as a means of pleasurable presentation of information and as a vehicle for understanding oneself and society.

Major authors, such as Dickens, Dostoyevsky, and Camus, were able to create impressive literary works that simultaneously made profound social statements. Yet writers of lesser renown have also shaped beliefs that have triggered social or political response. Despite an unimaginative plot, banal language, and stereotyped characterizations, Harriet Beecher Stowe's *Uncle Tom's Cabin* so dramatized the plight of slaves that President Lincoln reportedly remarked upon meeting her, "So you're the little woman who wrote the book that made this great war"[20]—an excessive claim that nevertheless acknowledged the impact her book had on enlisting public sentiment for emancipation. Thus, books of social protest, through their own momentum, brought into high relief certain egregious wrongs and generated energy for the initiation of social change.

Fiction has the capacity to translate vast societal abuse into individual terms. In this transformation, an author personalizes a problem, reducing it to comprehensible scope and enabling the reader to identify with the individual undergoing stress. Once that identification has been established, generalization to the affected group is facilitated. Through such techniques, novels may deliver both cognitive and affective messages.

But even information alone may generate affective spinoff. Learning the manual alphabet and using finger spelling as a communication tool enable the learner to realize that the motions are simple movements in a comprehensible standard code—motions that have as their base the familiar alphabet—and that all those rapid and apparently confusing movements are not an esoteric, unknowable choreography. In this manner, knowledge demystifies and, in the process, may act to show commonalities and ultimately to foster connectedness and identification. Fiction, however, has a powerful advantage over nonfictional formats in that its inherent drama highlights, illuminates, and directs the changing sensibilities of the reader, potentially on a profound emotional level.

Increasing the quantity of a child's knowledge is a comparatively easy task. Factual data and their interpretation are the central core of the academic experience. Hence, increasing one's store of knowledge is basically a cumulative act. The process of changing attitudes, however, may require the abandonment of comfortable and entrenched beliefs and their replacement by new or opposite formulations. Such long-held beliefs may be psychologically reassuring but, if stereotyped or based on faulty information, may ultimately be socially destructive as well as inimical to individual growth. The ongoing task of dislodging these biased ingrained assumptions, beliefs, and values is a formidable challenge.

Implicit in the recommendation to use fiction to foster attitudinal change is the belief that literature has the power to expand and deepen understanding of the human condition. Juvenile books have been suggested as effective social change agents by Huck, Arbuthnot, and others. It is almost a tenet of faith, as exemplified in the title *Reading Ladders for Human Relations*,[21] that books have the potential for behavioral impact. There is widespread support for the use of books as tools for benign intervention in the campaign to change common social prejudices. Indeed, the conviction that books have a potent, whether good or nefarious, influence is virtually unanimous. Religious and political zealots and special-interest groups have engaged in extensive action to promote, censor, or eliminate books, clearly on the presumption of literature's ability to influence and shape attitudes or action. As Rosenblatt states:

> The experience of literature, far from being for the reader a passive process of absorption is a form of intense personal activity. . . . Through books, the reader may explore his own nature, become aware of the potentialities for thought and feeling within himself, acquire clearer perspective, develop aims and a sense of direction.[22]

Furthermore, history reveals that adults have been especially sensitive to the malleability of children's minds and have designed didactic campaigns to mold behavior for a variety of causes. But the process of modifying attitudes and values is a subtle one. The assumption that a simple direct correlation exists between story message and subsequent reader behavior is naive. Nevertheless, literature supplements other factors in its ongoing incremental role in values clarification. As Frank reports:

> an individual's course through life is not determined by one force but is the product of many. His choices of action, his response to situations, to experiences within the family and outside it grow out of what he was born with plus the many influences that play on him through his environment—and reading is one of these influences.[23]

Concern with Integration of Exceptional Children

Mildly and moderately disabled children are being mainstreamed into nonspecial schools in greater and greater numbers. The extent of their psychological and social integration will be mediated to a large extent by the attitudes of their nondisabled peers. Children with disabilities previously were excluded from regular classrooms because those environments were basically dysfunctional, unwelcoming, and unaccommodating. To return them to a setting containing the same inimical components could result in considerable psychological damage.

Many disabled adults, in describing their childhood, claim that coming to terms with their impairment was a minor issue compared with the more painful problems of isolation, overprotection, segregation, pity, or other similar rejecting or punitive behavior. Because of hospitalization, maladaptive schools, or similar factors restricting experience, significant and obvious academic differences between themselves and their peers often arose. Additionally, they felt physical atypicality had been a terrible burden in the many settings that inordinately valued physical beauty or motor skills. The inhospitable psychological climate that resulted inhibited personal growth and social acceptance and added an often intolerable burden to whatever limitations their impairment caused.

Obviously, considerable care must be taken to avoid the repetition of such mistakes. Those educators actively concerned with social as well as physical integration of exceptional children have concluded that adapted physical plants and curricula are insufficient since they deal only with externals and do not alter the psychological climate. Sociometric studies have indicated that while children with special needs might be able to function academically in such modified circumstances, their acceptance and social adjustment are frequently inadequate, and, without intervention, these children tend to be rejected or excluded from desirable social constellations of their peers. Studies have shown that attempts to reduce rejecting behaviors by proximity alone or information alone also tend to be unsuccessful. However, when contact is sensitively arranged and is buttressed by appropriate cognitive and affective understanding, the probability of acceptance is enhanced. That is, as positive, direct personal encounters are structured and information that normalizes and clarifies is internalized, rejection decreases.

Problems arise from lack of knowledge about what is appropriate behavior in contacts between a disabled and a nondisabled child, since in many instances the latter have had little or no exposure to play or academic activities or even indirect contact with affected peers. In the absence of role models (an inevitable consequence of exclusion), unaffected youngsters are unsure not only of possible actions to take but of the receptivity of their behavior once that choice is made. A further concern involves the response of nonaffected peers. If children fear that the isolation handicapped youngsters endure is contagious, then even though they may feel guilty about not becoming involved, avoidance may seem preferable. In addition, confusion about whether to offer assistance to a slow-moving child in a wheelchair or whether to invite a blind classmate to parties or outings is often unsettling.

Although these concerns may seem trivial, it is just such mundane aspects of social exchange that function to foster relationships. Through the presentations of like situations in fictional settings, young readers can vicariously explore a whole array of alternatives and glean some insight both into the process and value of social exchange with disabled peers.

The behavior of handicapped children is often subject to misinterpretation. Lack of response to social overtures by a disabled individual is often interpreted as ineptness or rejection, when in reality it may be the result of misunderstanding or blocked communication. Nondisabled children often assume that the visible aspect of an impairment is its totality, and base their expectations on their observations. In truth, the most significant components may be invisible, and this lack of understanding can form a barrier to building friendships.

Literary Manipulation Is Counterproductive

Literature can have both preparatory and sustaining functions in the process of providing knowledge and altering attitudes toward the handicapped. One major problem that touches on the role of a library in a free society needs clarification in this regard. The handicapped join many special-interest groups that clamor for favorable representation in books. But calling for literary manipulations is a dangerous game. The analogy to politics is pertinent. Blatant attempts to merchandise political candidates through selling their imagined virtues and ignoring issues have made many citizens angry about the packaging of those held up for public adulation.

Implicit in such personality manipulations are the legitimizing of Madison Avenue techniques in the remaking of human images. While the intent may be either sincere or self-serving, the process itself is corrupting. As an image campaign is conceptualized, values seen as positive are elevated and inflated and those perceived as derogatory are ignored or grossly minimized. These actions thus falsify the human so treated: The individual becomes a product and the act degenerates into propaganda. Inevitably, the humanity of the person is reduced and the astute consumer, angry at the hard sell and the presumption of his or her ready pliability, resents this approach.

Many advocates of outgroups assert that the public must be saturated with models that reflect prodigious accomplishments or quintessential goodness—models that are antidotes to the ubiquitous stereotypes found in many cultural forms. This posture frequently surfaces in children's literature where the focal character is so idealized that resemblance to an actual person vanishes. The result is a packaged item, like a gas-ripened tomato, superficially attractive in its untroubled perfection, but without taste, substance, or relation to its real counterpart.

As a corollary to including exclusively favorable depictions, special-interest groups also insist that unfavorable portrayals be eliminated from holdings or be actively boycotted in future purchases. If this were allowed, then the right to free access to information and interpretation would be endangered. Adhering to such demands would not only place intolerable burdens on libraries but could be self-defeating as well. Clearly, different reviewers reading the same book might come to diametrically opposed conclusions as to whether or not the depiction was favorable. Moreover, permitting this kind of censorship, no matter how noble the intent, opens the way to continuous review by any agency or individual vociferous enough to command a hearing. While the job of countering misinformation and prejudice may be subject to subversion by some of the holdings of the library, restraints to free access are clearly intolerable.

Assessing Fiction to Facilitate Mainstreaming Goals

While it is not the function of libraries to actively promote selected social causes, educators can deliberately and effectively use carefully chosen library holdings to further mainstreaming goals. It is therefore essential that a wide spectrum of books that offer insight into the problems of the disabled be made available and aggressively promoted. When books are used to facilitate the integration process, much care must be taken in their selection. All books about disability or that contain disabled characters *cannot* automatically be presumed useful; some even may be counterproductive. Occasionally, these works have inaccuracies that destroy or seriously diminish their potential effectiveness.

Importance of Accuracy

One of the first obligations of a writer is the presentation of truth. This is a particularly difficult task in this field since mythology, a strong sense of mission, or moral outrage often becloud the author's vision. Nevertheless, unless a sizable portion of literature deals honestly with these problems and issues, this absence denies identity, even existence, and reduces the handicapped reader to a feeling of invisibility. The nonhandicapped reader, if exposed to inaccurate writing, may misperceive the disabled and behave inappropriately when confronted with the real-life equivalent. Readers' literary experiences should not conflict with accurate perceptions of the real world. If they do, children learn to mistrust the literary message as distorting or to devalue their own observations. Accuracy in relation to specifics and to overall situations is a significant criterion in writing about this population.

In assessing this genre, the following questions should be posed: Is the nomenclature accurate? If the author is purposely vague, does this detract from the description or development of the character? Is the description of the handicapping condition consistent with medical or psychological practice? Are the accoutrements and paraphernalia associated with the disability correctly described and utilized? Has the author ignored critical aspects of the disability or distorted them in any way? Are the social, psychological, and emotional ramifications of exceptionality developed in a credible manner? Are the genesis, current conditions, and prognoses harmonious with reasonable expectations? Is the resolution of the story dependent on improbable events or illogical behavior on the part of characters? Is the vocabulary consonant with age, developmental level, or situation of the speaker? In summary, do the parts of the structure, as well as the final impression generated by the story, contribute to an accurate perception by the reader?

In those books that are unsatisfactory because of misinformation, errors seem to be of three major types: those that incorrectly describe symptomatology, treatment, or prognosis; those that misrepresent societal conditions by distortion or omission; and those that describe highly improbable human behavior by either the handicapped or other characters in response to disabling conditions.

Alan's sister in *Hey, Dummy*[24] is referred to as autistic. From descriptions of her behavior, the label is inappropriate. Although inaccurate, this error is trivial in terms of its significance in the story. However, in *He Is Your Brother*,[25] Lawrence, the "autistic" child, is a major character and flaws in his presentation are critical. An assessment more in keeping with his actions would be that of a severely conduct-disturbed child who is able to cloak himself in autisticlike behavior as a means of manipulating his environment. A further incongruity concerns this six-year-old's ability to play spontaneously and without instruction "the slow movement from the Dvorak." Although some autistic children have outstanding musical ability, the episode described is unbelievable.

Errors appearing in other works are often of central import, creating faulty impressions in the minds of unknowledgeable readers. Some learning-disabled children exhibit writing reversals that generally involve confusion of individual words, such as reading "saw" for "was," or individual letters, such as "d" for "b." The kind of reversal exemplified in the title *Whales to See The*[26] is so unlikely as to be unique and gives a distorted impression of this aspect of the behavior of learning-disabled children.

Occasionally, the disparity between the identified disorder and its manifestation in a fictional character is so incongruent as to grossly subvert understanding. Dawn, the severely retarded child in *The Fortune Cake*,[27] is able to write a 99-word message—a feat far beyond the abilities of such children. Anne, Cathy's stepsister, is diagnosed, described, and placed in a school for mentally retarded children in *Cathy at the Crossroads*.[28] In the sequel, *Cathy's Secret Kingdom*,[29] this label is retroactively altered to emotional dysfunction. The change in labels blurs the distinction between two different disorders.

Rehabilitative misrepresentation concerning faulty descriptions of therapeutic intervention is seen in *Whales to See The*.[30] The strong impression that heavy daily drug dosage is standard therapy for all learning-disabled children is given in this novel. Such an impression is erroneous. One of the most controversial techniques for treatment of developmentally disabled children is that in which patterning procedures are employed. *The Deep Search*[31] and *Listen, Lissa!*[32] hint at its remediative success with children exhibiting retarded behavior. To suggest these questionable therapies in juvenile literature seems inappropriate when the results claimed by practitioners are presently questioned by major researchers in the professional community.

Spontaneous cure is a frequently used device for resolution of problems created by disability. The idea that shock or trauma is a remedy for physical or psychological impairments does not seem to diminish in popularity in fictional works despite its lack of prevalence in reality. Edward, in *Key of Gold*, is crippled as the result of polio. His clairvoyant doctor predicts that a shock would "make him forget himself some day and he will begin to walk involuntarily."[33] Needless to say, Edward recovers in just this manner. In *Pablito's New Feet*,[34] the central character's sudden spontaneous ability to walk, despite months of futile therapy, provides an example of both deficient medical knowledge and slipshod plot structure. In *Wisdom to Know*,[35] a woman who has been committed to a mental institution for many years begins an amazingly speedy recovery after hearing a song that she had written being played on the piano. This kind of instant rehabilitation, more commonly reported by writers than psychiatrists or physicians, has more dramatic than medical viability.

Miraculous cures, especially through divine intervention, present unique problems for the young reader. In *A Certain Small Shepherd*,[36] a mute child's gift to a young woman who gives birth to an infant on Christmas Day results in the restoration of speech. In *A Charm for Paco's Mother*,[37] a Mexican boy, who makes a pilgrimage to a shrine to pray for his blind mother, is delayed by the many acts of goodness he performs. He returns home disconsolate, convinced he has failed, only to find that in his absence a traveling American ophthalmologist has generously offered his mother free surgery. The author makes it abundantly clear that the mother has been "given" this reward for her son's Good Samaritan-like behavior. The bracketing of spontaneous remission or cure with payment for selfless behavior must inevitably suggest the converse—that those who remain uncured have not demonstrated their worthiness.

Social responses to disabled persons are often distorted in fiction for young readers. Frequently, institutions or social agencies described in these books are more reflective of wishful thinking than of reality. Lovingly decorated rooms, large, well-trained and totally devoted staffs, generous budgets, and provision of fresh flowers and similar amenities for retarded or emotionally dysfunctional residents of public institutions portray an apotheosized world only dreamed of by professional workers in the field, but endemic in children's books.

Whales to See The[38] features a special educator with a sufficiently ample budget to allow the chartering of a boat to take her class to observe the migration of whales. The teacher in *A Cry in the Wind*[39] apparently has no personal demands on his time whatsoever and is able to devote his leisure as well as his working hours to the welfare of his students. Undoubtedly, there are many dedicated teachers, social workers, and institutional attendants, but the quality and extent of self-lessness displayed in children's books are truly mind-boggling.

Fairy godparents and their corporeal counterparts populate the world of children's stories. Waiting in the wings are numerous kindly benefactors with sacks of money eager to bestow their largess on deserving handicapped children. An unknown neighbor leaves a house to Tom's family in *A Cry in the Wind*;[40] a wealthy rancher agrees to finance Tony's college education in *Birkin*;[41] and a grateful royal stranger pays for Musa's surgery in *Musa the Shoemaker*.[42] Except for a dwindling body of innocents, even preadolescents are skeptical about the orderliness and benevolence of a universe in which the just are so opportunely and fittingly rewarded.

Accuracy in Illustrations. Illustrations are particularly vulnerable to criticism of inaccuracy in that they frequently ignore, minimize, or show a partial or obscured view of the disability. In *Mister O'Brien*, Christopher wears a "big, thick black boot" on his right leg with a brace "supported by two iron rods and buckled around by three leather straps."[43] The cover illustration, however, shows the boy with his impaired foot positioned behind the other and almost none of the elaborately described prosthesis is visible. Mr. O'Brien, an amputee, is positioned sufficiently far forward in the picture that, although shown to be on crutches, the cause is not evident. The heroine of *The Shining Moment*,[44] a former beauty queen, spends virtually the entire book recovering from a disfiguring facial scar. Yet the dustcover shows an unblemished teenager. In *Scarred*, as the title hints, the central character's hellish existence stems from responses to the surgical scar from his cleft lip repair. Yet the jacket illustration presents an anomaly so minute as to be readily overlooked if the title did not point to its significance.[45]

Literary Qualities

Books concerning handicapped characters are subject to the same literary flaws as other works. A few are extraordinarily good, having strong characterizations, well-developed plots, good sense of time and place, and excellent language usage. Most are works of more modest quality and some are spectacularly inept. If all readers were sensitive and reflective about what they read, then only the highest quality novels might be recommended. But many youngsters are unready to meet the demands of these more sophisticated works and are comfortable only with simpler stories. Fortunately, within this category may be found some that have the power to affect and enlighten.

Librarians report that such a journeyman effort as *Follow My Leader*[46] seems to provide an important sensitizing experience. Although the plot is fast-paced, some of the incidents are contrived, the characterization is flat, the dialogue weak, and the tone didactic. This old favorite has none of the subtlety or effective use of language of *Bow Island*[47] or *Dark Dreams*.[48] Yet the value of Garfield's book is undeniable. Students report being able to recall large sections of the story and their responses to it many years later.

The ideal book, of course, would combine excellent writing, wide appeal, and accurate, honest, and sympathetic portrayals of exceptional people. Such books are as rare in this field as in any other and some compromise will have to be made when selecting books about exceptional characters.

Character Development. Of literary flaws, the most grievous is usually that of poor character development. Ginny and her teachers in *Wheels for Ginny's Chariot*,[49] Rosellen of *A Bright Star Falls*,[50] and Almena of *Almena's Dogs*,[51] to name but a few, are so sweet and good as to be offensive. A more subtle problem is that of vague and insubstantial portrayals of severely disabled characters. The suicidal girl in *A Time to Dance*[52] and Dawn in *The Fortune Cake*[53] have no discernible personality. Almost nothing is known about who they are or how they feel about events; they exist primarily in their relationships with other nondisabled characters or as catalytic agents to explain, facilitate, or expedite the denouement. Uncontestably, it takes heightened skills to portray impaired characters so well that the world can be viewed through their eyes, but Twink in *Touching*,[54] Alan in *Hey, Dummy*,[55] and Joey in *Dark Dreams*[56] emerge as knowable human beings.

Perhaps one of the most mystical approaches is that in which the disabled character is likened to a nonhuman creature. For example, in *The Magic Moth*,[57] the life spirit of a dying child is transmuted into a fragile insect, an attempt at conceptualization, however lyrical, that reduces the believability of the deceased girl. By contrast, another author, sensitive to the demeaning quality of such a comparison, uses it as a metaphor for the clumsy, pitying behavior the heroine is subjected to. In the excellent novel, *The Trembling Years*,[58] a clergyman, attempting to be kind, calls attention to Kathy by describing her to the congregation as "a bird with a broken wing." This episode is intended to epitomize the humiliation she endures in a sentimental but insensitive society.

The disabled person often plays a symbolic role in children's books. Certainly this is a legitimate literary usage, but one that, if not handled with great skill, can reduce the human dimensions of the designated character. This technique in the hands of a talented writer is capable both of illuminating a social message and simultaneously dramatizing the implications of impairment. Tall Boy, one of the central characters in *Sing Down the Moon*,[59] is handicapped. The Indian's arm, wounded and rendered impotent in a fight to protect his future wife, symbolizes the destruction of the American Indian. Garfield uses a visually impaired judge to symbolize blind justice in *Smith*.[60] In an ironic use of symbolism, the author of *The Hayburners*[61] movingly develops the concept that being a loser is a matter of circumstance and opportunity. As a symbol, Joey represents the lost chances of other retarded individuals who have been swindled out of their future by a society that has labeled them "hayburners." Far from being a loser, Joey demonstrates those qualities that define a humane person.

Didactic Messages. Didactic books for children find their full flowering in works about handicapped characters. A common fatal literary defect is the excessively obvious superimposition of a cumbersome message on the story. Rosen has succinctly dealt with the difficulty of deliberately fostering the writing of books for the express purpose of raising consciousness or altering attitudes. Her comments, written from the viewpoint of the women's movement, apply equally to all "minority" literature. In discussing role-model books, she avers this "has meant a call to tract writing sweetened with fictional effects. These are the hardest to talk about without seeming to turn against what is so bravely meant. But the truth is, fiction dies under the duress of ideology."[62] Such juvenile message books as *The Light*[63] and *Land of Silence*[64] attest to the truth of her assertions.

Some books are undisguised efforts to promote specific social causes. Blatter, in discussing her novel *Cap and Candle*,[65] asserts that her intention was to write a book that would recruit women to work as nurses in Turkey. She efficiently pursues this aim, providing much professional information in the course of the story. Unfortunately, literary goals are secondary to her missionary objective. Similarly, *The Road to Agra*[66] strings together a series of adventures about a blind girl and her sighted brother's attempts to obtain medical help for her. Although the story paints a graphic picture of poverty in India, its main intent, strongly underscored by the ending, appears to be an explanation and endorsement of the work of the World Health Organization.

Humor. The overwhelming majority of the books reported here are straight, chronological, omniscient narratives. Humor is rarely used, but its appearance in *Spectacles*,[67] *Dinky Hocker Shoots Smack!*,[68] and *Ox Goes North*[69] illustrates the premise that serious treatment need not necessarily preclude wit. One effort at humor seems in extremely poor taste. *The Tattooed Potato and Other Clues*[70] uses rather obvious and not very clever puns in an unsuccessful attempt to vitalize an exploitive story line.

Emotional Tone. The issue of the emotional content or tone of these books is a ticklish one. Frank characterizes literature about the handicapped as "infused with emotions which call for tears and lamentations." She adds that the compassion that books call forth should be "informed rather than sentimental, and strengthening rather than resigned."[71] Yet compassion is not as desirable a reaction as empathy. The latter focuses on acceptability based on knowledge and closeness, while the former concentrates on the suffering aspects of the situation as though they were the primary response stimulus.

Although a segment of the literary effort in children's literature encompasses writing that is suffused with emotionalism, the advent of candor and realism in this area has made many radical changes in the content and methods that writers have utilized. Just as sentimental, unwarrantedly optimistic, and romanticized books are limited in value, so are those that present a picture of unrelieved despair or cruelty. Bettelheim[72] and Karl[73] insist that children must be offered some element of hope, some ray of light in their books. Narratives such as *Fly Away Paul*[74] or *Scarred*[75] are so suffused with brutality and deceit that the reader is repelled and overwhelmed, feeling it is useless to protest or resist such a pitiless and relentless fate. As Frank observes:

> In the recent trend toward presenting realism in books for young people, some have offered, in the name of "reality" sheer ugliness and evil, unrelieved by any resolution. The reassurance that good *does* exist, and *can* overcome evil, is a basic need for all of us, but especially for the young people who cannot yet draw on their own experiences to reinforce their faith in the goodness of life. A book in which the boy or girl protagonist is so emotionally disturbed as to have lost touch with truth, with all the adults so evil or so uncaring as to offer neither hope nor charity, can hardly provide a healthy reading experience for the young.[76]

Books such as *Sleep Two, Three, Four!*,[77] *The Planet of Junior Brown*,[78] and *Slake's Limbo*,[79] which examine serious problems and contain unsettling elements, nevertheless conclude on a note of hope for some presumed future happiness or betterment.

The new realism has spawned another problem that requires particular attention. Violence has assumed pandemic proportions, and in books about the disabled this hostility is most frequently directed against characters with impairments. Books containing such elements cannot be dismissed for that reason alone. *Hey, Dummy*[80] is replete with instances of physical and psychological violence, yet the author causes the reader to react angrily to the pain-imposing aspects of society represented in the story. In this case, the violence is purposeful, instructive, and essential to underscore the broad social implications of the story.

There are some superficial similarities between *Hey, Dummy* and *Whales to See The*.[81] Both contain cruelty to handicapped children and feature an educator who inadvertently sets in motion the action that will lead to the tragic denouement. But there are critical differences in the treatment of characters and the use of violent episodes that result in differing reader responses. Ironically, even though the first-named novel involves a killing and the psychological ruin of the main character, it offers more hope than the latter, which includes an aborted, almost casual suicide and mindless, near-sadistic deception. In *Whales to See The*, neither the teacher nor the learning-disabled children are sufficiently developed to evoke strong reader identification or even concern. The special children are casually and gratuitously humiliated. The victims seem almost peripheral to the authors', hence the reader's, interest, since they display little dimensionality. There is no compelling sense of literary inevitability to the shocking surprise ending, which, while chillingly clever, provides no guidance for reader interpretation. Although the mature reader is aghast at the abuse of these children, condemnation stems from a value system that is external to the story. The authors' pious endorsement of the whales' benevolent social structure is totally vitiated by the amoral conclusion.

The brutality displayed in *A Single Light*[82] involves the persecution of a deaf-mute girl and the stoning to death of a crippled man. There is a sense of inevitability in these deeds that simulate sacrificial behaviors, since it is in the aftermath of their savage actions that enlightenment comes to their perpetrators. This same exploitive use of violence is seen in *Dorp Dead*.[83] Egoff's defense of this aspect of the book shows questionable logic: "Brutality . . . is actually inseparable from the realization of love and personal fulfillment of the young protagonist, Gilly: had he not been the victim of a sadistic adult, he would have become entrapped in a cage of self-alienation."[84] To link brutality and love, presuming the latter can be a consequence of the former, is to deny mountains of evidence that demonstrate that behavior is modeled and mirrored. The victims of child abuse become the next generation of child beaters—a tragic heritage demonstrating incontrovertibly that brutality brutalizes both abuser and victim. The presumption that being alienated is demonstrably worse than being the victim of a homicidal sadist is a shaky one at best. Those who escape from childhood oppression frequently discover that they have not been unmarked and often carry corrupting scars throughout their lifetimes.

It would be unreasonable to condemn books solely on the basis that they contain elements of violence. The purpose and effect of such actions must be assessed. Life is not free of violence. To ignore or deny this fact is deceptive as well as dishonest. The division between what is or what is not an acceptable depiction pivots precisely on whether violence is used in an exploitive, sensual, titillating manner or as a means to illuminate the iniquitous aspects of individual and collective behavior. Authors are attracted to the use of violence because its attention-getting power ensures an audience. Its appearance in books about the disabled is not surprising because of the common perception of the handicapped person as victim. Books that perpetuate this linkage must be closely examined. If the presentation of violence sheds light, either on aspects of the reader's own nature or on corrosive elements in society, then it serves a valid purpose.

Treatment of Special Groups. In recent years, some critics have evaluated books exclusively in terms of what messages they deliver about women, various ethnic groups, or other minorities. Books featuring disabled characters are not free from sexist, racist, or negative portrayals of members of special groups. For example, the title character in *No Tears for Rainey*[85] is discouraged from pursuing her interest in chemistry. She is told cooking is more suitable and, after all, much like chemistry. This offensive message, probably overlooked at the time the book was published, is now seen as intolerable. Yet, despite this and similar sexist incidents, the book clarifies some important aspects of mental disorders, particularly problems related to reincorporating into the family structure a member who has been institutionalized.

Brave Companions[86] concerns a young soldier blinded in the Pacific in World War II. This novel presents substantive information about the practical and psychological problems attendant upon adjustment to blindness. However, its virulent racial slurs toward the Japanese people radically diminish its usefulness.

Few books can satisfy every special-interest group—nor should they be expected to—but some messages are so destructive of humane values that endorsement is impossible. This problem is extremely complex and involves books in which objectionable comments or situations may be trivial as well as others in which offensive components are too qualitatively or quantitatively important to be ignored. Examination must be broad-gauged—with careful appraisal of the treatment of the disabled but awareness of episodes or dialogue that misinforms or diminishes other groups. The majority of children's books written before

1970 are sexist to some degree, but their elimination would consign to oblivion many otherwise valid books. As the only viable alternative to retroactive censorship, it may be necessary to deliberately help children understand attitudes that emerge from and reflect a specific historic context or perception.

Many books combine positive social attitudes toward various out-groups. The pairing of blackness and blindness, as previously noted, often yields statements supportive of both populations. However, in some instances, it is a disabled character who is cast in the role of a villain. An author may exploit latent prejudice against the handicapped in an effort to show, by contrast, the good qualities of another abused social group. The hero of *Sticks and Stones*[87] is almost destroyed by accusations of homosexuality. The spoiler in the book is a lonely slow learner, another outsider. The book's intent, to affirm the right of people to be free from persecution regardless of sexual predilections, ironically casts a member of another maligned population into the role of offender.

Quasi-Fiction

Included in the collection of books dealing with the disabled is a special category herein classified as quasi-fiction. This is an amorphous grouping consisting of books that are neither strictly fiction nor non-fiction but that contain elements of each. Such works are primarily extended instructional messages delivered through the medium of a story. Most often they embody generous amounts of specific cognitive information, but recent titles seem more interested in promoting attitudinal changes than in presenting facts or explanations. *About Handicaps*[88] is really two books in one. The story addressed to primary-age children ostensibly concerns a young child who learns to be friends with a boy who has cerebral palsy. Explanatory notes, which comprise the "other" book (some of which appear in smaller type on the same pages as the child's text), are addressed to adults and interpret the unfolding events. Using the device of a contrived and unsubtle story line, commonly held negative attitudes toward disabilities are expressed and shown to be without validity. It is an impressively effective and moving work despite its consciously didactic intent.

Thus, quasi-fiction as a category should not be presumed to indicate works of inferior quality. This coined term merely represents a grey area in terms of classification and includes under this rubric books ranging from the truly abysmal to those excellent in conceptualization and realization.

Works of quasi-fiction addressed to young readers often encounter two problems whose resolution is generally unsatisfactory. Those stories about disabilities that have little or no visible manifestations are difficult to present meaningfully in picture books. Claims are made of exceptionality for those who give no outward discernible sign of deviation. In effect, the child reader is asked to accept the author's designation on faith without tangible evidence to support the assertion. Another separate but related obstacle is that of finding terminology both accurate and comprehensible. Too frequently such works are weighted down with a technical vocabulary having no real meaning to the neophyte reader.

Characters who have leg braces or hearing aids can readily be identified as people with special problems and needs. But the child in *One Little Girl*[89] is retarded and the boy in *Please Don't Say Hello*[90] is autistic, and their portrayals are complicated by the invisibility of the respective impairments. Assuming a target audience of children in the early school years, as the format would indicate, these authors have the delicate task of presenting nonvisible concepts in the kinds of concrete, specific terms young readers can comprehend. Authors must simplify complex material without distorting it. In terms of its cognitive goals, *Please Don't Say Hello* fails in that the reader has little better comprehension of autism after finishing the book than before. The bizarre conduct seems as unreasonable and arbitrary as ever. Yet, two points are made clear: The seemingly inexplicable behavior of the autistic child is neither deliberately antisocial nor culpable and the proper response to such a child is patience and tolerance.

Books like *Mom! I Need Glasses*[91] and *Katie's Magic Glasses*[92] are direct quasi-fictional homilies stressing the necessity of good vision and simultaneously explaining how glasses can help to achieve that vital goal. These slim books are replete with information about the physiology of the eye and the visual process. They end happily as their newly bespectacled heroines carry on a more functional life. Authors, here too, have a conflict between the level of the intended audience and the complexity of the material they wish to present. For example:

> "Ring the bell and walk in." Susan read the sign on the green door.
> Inside the waiting room sat a young lady in a white uniform.
> "You must be Susan Monti," she said. "And this is your mother." "That's right," said Mrs. Monti.[93]

Since Susan is seven and a half and the above quoted short, choppy sentences are typical of primers, the target audience is certainly beginning readers. Despite this, the author includes words like "pertinent," "shatterproof," "prescription," and "elastic." Furthermore, there are explanations of the function of the eye, refraction, and muscle change—topics well beyond the understanding and, probably, the interest of these children. Such books are generally considered good for children, a quality almost certain to ensure their avoidance. The cheery, virtuous titles and unwaveringly tractable heroines are a dead giveaway to their obvious didactic nature.

While *Mom! I Need Glasses* and *Katie's Magic Glasses* are very close to nonfiction, two others that deal with the same subject are slightly more infused with fictional structure. *The Cowboy Surprise*[94] is a simple, not particularly creative story that suggests that if cowboys and Indians wear glasses, such devices can't be all bad. Farther along the spectrum toward an authentic story is *Spectacles*,[95] which presents a perfectly charming, recalcitrant heroine who is finally persuaded of the glamorous potential of glasses in this amusing and cleverly illustrated tale.

Selecting Books about the Disabled

Fortunately, as mainstreaming accelerates the need for more material about the handicapped, publishers are responding with a wide array of books: fiction, quasi-fiction and nonfiction now explore relatively untouched topics relating to disability and widen the choices available to the older adolescent as well as to the very young child. In selecting a book for a particular situation, more needs to be known about it than just the disability label and the appropriate age level of the prospective readers. A multitude of factors, including theme, tone, style, attitudes, and the presence or absence of such components as purposeless violence, social biases and peripheral messages, would affect its suitability.

Considering the quality, scope, and variety of novels containing handicapped characters, a simple listing of books divided into age and disability categories is therefore insufficient since any single work may exhibit positive, negative, neutral, or mixed utility. The mere presence of a disabled character in a book does not ipso facto signify that that title should be included on a recommended list about the handicapped. Indeed, many bibliographies contain entries that vary astonishingly in quality, apparently included on the assumption that any book about the handicapped is informative. Unless there is a disclaimer or accompanying critical annotation for each novel listed, the user of such a roster might reasonably expect that such inclusion implies endorsement. *The Bright High Flyer*,[96] *Old Con and Patrick*,[97] and *The Trembling Years*[98] all contain characters who have had polio, yet the latter is light-years away from the first two in informational accuracy, sensitivity, and literary quality.

Limitations of Criticism and Reviews

Abbreviated reviews tend to focus exclusively on plot—rarely the most salient element in determining utility. On the contrary, the decision to select a book may hinge on the treatment, values, or attitudes that the author generates, topics that the one-line review either omits or reduces to a precis so emaciated that it might better have been omitted. Reviews, particularly in this sensitive area, must be quantitatively extensive, their scope permitting adequate analysis of both surface and latent qualities.

Criticism of children's literature is a generally toothless affair, eschewing stringent standards for simple commentaries on illustrations, content, or style. As Trease complains, "criticism has adopted the habit . . . of being uniformly laudatory and approving."[99] This fault is serious when particularized knowledge and informed judgments are urgently needed. If critical or analytical comments are not made about works that evoke pity, purvey misinformation, present faulty models, or otherwise endorse basically inadequate material, critics are abdicating their professional responsibility.

Reviews of children's books containing disabled characters are subject to two major failings. Some reviewers may see these books from limited perspectives. Either they concentrate on literary components, overlooking medical, psychological, or social aspects of impairment, or they focus on the information-transmitting potential of the story, unconcerned with traditional literary considerations. On the one hand, well-written, totally erroneous books may be endorsed; on the other, informative, inane potboilers may be promoted.

Despite Heins' dictum that "a children's book deserves to be probed as much as an adult book for general questions of diction, structure, significance of detail and literary integrity,"[100] modest examples of literary accomplishment are often welcomed and proliferate in this subset of children's fiction. An aura of sentimentality distorts perception of books about disability, thus precluding objective evaluation. Even worse, Schuman charges that reviewers, children's editors, and librarians get carried away in chronic spasms of enthusiasm, and consequently are frequently guilty of the "highly recommended" syndrome. She suggests that such individuals "take a cue from the general consumer movement, which is calling for advice and warnings, as well as recommendations."[101] Nesbitt, concurring, sees this in a larger framework:

Creative literature . . . should . . . call forth creative criticism. . . . Criticism may manifest itself in various forms. In the form of the book review, it should serve a utilitarian as well as a stimulating purpose. . . . If criticism is to have the effect . . . of convinced acceptance of children's literature as an integral and significant part of the total body of literature of any country, then it must not only, in Arnold's words, "learn to know and propagate the best," it must also learn to know and discourage the worst. Of equal importance is the discernment of positive versus negative qualities in a book, the pinpointing of the positive and the negative, and the relationship between them. For it is true that a book may have weaknesses but may at the same time accomplish something so positive, so worthwhile, so constructive as to negative [sic] its faults.[102]

Some critics appear to feel that any book about a person with special needs serves an important social goal, and therefore critical analysis is bypassed. Too often these well-meaning efforts, bland and uninteresting as oleo, are described as "a heartwarming story" or one that "serves as an inspiration to those similarly afflicted."

The practice of recommending books about disabled characters to children having similar impairments should be carried out with extreme caution. Children want and need to see themselves and their own special problems reflected in their literature. But when books are recommended on the basis of the similarity between a fictional character and the intended reader, the person suggesting the book is linking it to the reader primarily on the basis of the identified attribute. That is, of the multitude of qualities of an individual, the one singled out for recognition in this instance is the disability. Ralph Ellison vividly described the pain of invisibility,[103] and for too long many disabled children have been invisible, hidden from public view in special institutions and missing from representation in cultural phenomena. This absence has resulted in a lack of role models upon whom the handicapped youngster can pattern his or her behavior and aspirations.

The disabled, unlike the nondisabled, know they are *more* than their guide dog or their wheelchair. Therefore, their role models could be individuals who share, for example, vocational or avocational interests, but who do not necessarily share an identical impairment. While reading books about disabled heroes or heroines is of value, restriction to only these models is confining. Sutherland, in her provocative article "On the Need of the Severely Handicapped to Feel That They Are Human," has eloquently testified to the insights she gained about herself as a result of reading "books which deal with the entire range of human experience," and not just those recommended by her parents and teachers, which endorsed the "feeling that I was mentally different from most other people." She adds: "The young, severely handicapped person desperately searches for a normal person who feels the way he does about life. His search is so intensive that he is most apt to identify himself, though the image is vastly distorted, with whomever he is reading about."[104]

Uses of Fiction That Focus on the Disabled

Children's images of themselves are composed in large measure of the cumulative, reflected perceptions of others. When the disabled child is perceived of as *more* than his inabilities or incapacities, as someone similar in many ways to other students, then companionship, affection, and other social and emotional interactions are distinct possibilities. While special children need role models, a more urgent necessity is greater acceptance by their peers. The climate developed by contact and exposure to new ideas can reduce the inflated and distorted meanings frequently superimposed on the disability. Thus, books that focus on handicapped characters should be used primarily with the nonimpaired as facilitators or interpreters of attitudes and information.

Clearly, literature alone will not transform rejecting children into accepting ones, but it can be a powerful aid in altering those perceptions that impede integration and in structuring understandings that will foster it. As Jerzy Kosinski observed, fiction offers "new insights into the tides and drifts of one's own life. The reader is tempted to venture beyond a text, to contemplate his own life in light of the book's personalized meanings."[105] It is precisely in transferring insights available in literature to parallels in the reader's own life where most assistance and guidance must be provided.

If books are to be used effectively for the integration of exceptional children, then a deliberate, concerted program needs development. The optimal time to begin building positive attitudes is in early childhood before stereotypes have crystallized. Reading aloud, discussion, and role playing should all start in the primary grades. Since young children are willing, sometimes eager, to hear the same story several times, various aspects of a single book can be examined on different occasions. Children need time to digest ideas, to try them out, and to test them over extended periods. Immediate positive response will scarcely be the product of a single story-reading session. Teachers, librarians, and parents must allow time for understanding to flourish, but such enlightenment must be planned and not trusted to appear spontaneously.

Books on the identical disability and for the same age group may serve different purposes. *Howie Helps Himself*,[106] for instance, is a story about how a child with cerebral palsy learns to use his wheelchair independently. The things Howie can and cannot do, his frustrations and pleasures, his means for learning to compensate for his disability, his problems of loneliness and dependence, his instructional and therapeutic paraphernalia and apparatuses, his classroom structure, his difficulties with muscle control and mobility—all are topics discussed in the text. As such, this book is very useful in providing the kind of information that can make the disorder seem less threatening to the nondisabled child. (See Figure 2.)

Another book on the same topic, *About Handicaps*,[107] zeroes in on the response of a fully functioning child to one who has cerebral palsy. This particular perspective has utility in different ways. By examining the attitudes of a nondisabled child and his view of the disability as a danger to himself, this book provides a model for readers to work through their possible fears and aversions. Through *Howie Helps Himself*, they learn that handicapped children are very like themselves in the things that are most important and they begin to understand some of their specific problems. In *About Handicaps* they can learn that their worries are not unique or wicked and that they can confront their fears and through this heuristic experience successfully overcome them.

When children are mature enough to talk about these problems, they may still be too unskilled to read these books or comprehend or internalize the implications unaided. Adults can readily lead discussion toward desired goals, asking children to draw parallels from their own lives and to express their feelings about the characters and events. Each book may fulfill a different function. *Howie Helps Himself* focuses on the adaptations of a disabled child and *About Handicaps* examines the feelings an unimpaired child has about disabled persons. If the adult can identify the approach that is most needed by the listeners, then the appropriate book can be chosen.

It should be noted that an absolute correlation between a disability a child exhibits and that discussed in a particular book need not exist for the book to be effective. In some instances it might be advisable to select a book with a superficially unrelated disability in order to avoid too obvious attention to a particular child. The problem *About Handicaps* deals with is social rejection of handicapped persons. Avoidance and isolation are social problems often experienced by blind, deaf, retarded, and physically handicapped children. The resultant loneliness and unhappiness can be felt by all children. Thus the book can be used to explore the consequences of rejection rather than the specific problems of a cerebral-palsied child.

As they grow older, if children and youth continue to be read to, then consideration should be given to the role played by disabled characters in the stories used. Books that promote empathic responses to the handicapped can readily be included. Older students may need guidance in interpreting what they have read since their perception is often selective and self-serving. Misinterpretations and misunderstandings are commonplace, and the adult reader should take the opportunity to go deeply into the story, responding to questions, clarifying literal misperceptions, and exploring inferential aspects as well.

FIGURE 2.   From *Howie Helps Himself* by Joan Fassler. Illustrated by Joe Lasker. © 1975 by Joe Lasker. Reprinted by permission of Albert Whitman.

Some books dealing with exceptional characters can be read aloud in their entirety. *Twyla*,[108] *A Dance to Still Music*,[109] *Ransom*,[110] and *The Hayburners*,[111] for instance, have enough dramatic tension and excellent writing to sustain interest in adolescent listeners. Occasionally, the educator may want to deal with just one aspect of a story; then single chapters or segments can be read in isolation. The ramifications of a character's behavior, other options that might have been chosen, and the implications of such choices can be discussed or role-played. Comparisons with real-life situations can be drawn and suggestions for specific behavioral changes can be projected.

Every worthwhile book about disability cannot be the object of an academic exercise or the subject of library story hours. Children need to be encouraged to include books on this topic in their recreational reading. Appropriate works can easily be included on recommended reading lists and subject bibliographies. Children who are disconsolate when all the Helen Keller biographies have been checked out may be guided to fiction that features blind or deaf heroines of their own age.

Books that not only present positive attitudes toward the disabled but that also provide good historic information and a sense of life in former times are natural supplements to the study of history. For example, *Johnny Tremain*,[112] an exceptionally well-researched book, is set in America in Revolutionary times. From the story, the reader gets a sense of the character and political importance of some of the founding fathers. The puritanical perception of disability as a punishment for sin is painfully dramatized, an historic fact also worth studying. Beyond this, the daily life of the citizens, the religious beliefs and practices, and some major political events are revealed through the channel of an exciting story.

Wings[113] is a marvelous work of social history. Set in the late 1920s, it evokes the bohemian world then emerging—the romantic, daring glamor of early planes and flyers and the impact of the film industry on the fantasy life and recreational habits of the time. *No Promises in the Wind*[114] recreates not only the economic impact of the Great Depression but also its social cost to the nation. Much that is eliminated from juvenile histories and social studies texts is put forth in this powerful and compelling novel.

The attitudes toward the disabled in each of the above works are honest and realistic. The inclusion of these and similar books in social studies curricula could provide an indirect but valuable reinforcement for attitudes of acceptance for handicapped persons.

Children have a multitude of interests and are often eager to read books on their current passions. There are several excellent romances, sports stories, or books on hobbies containing characters with special needs that can be promoted as recreational reading for this audience. *On the Outside Looking In* [115] is an easy-to-read juvenile romance. The central male character is an amputee. His doubts about his self-worth and his consequent defensive behavior realistically reflect the basic concern faced by people in like situations.

For young readers who are sports enthusiasts, *Run with the Ring* [116] and *Dead End Bluff* [117] are two books that might be suggested. The former concerns a blind track star who is also a ham radio operator; the latter is about a blind swimmer. Both books may surprise youngsters who perceive of blindness as an ineffably debilitating disorder. The accent in each is heavily on the achievement possibilities of blind adolescents and their athletic capabilities. The problems are greatly simplified and their solutions facile but they are nonetheless useful introductions to what might otherwise be a little known aspect of human experience and achievement.

As a supplement to the study of acoustics, it would not be inappropriate for the science instructor to suggest books like *A Dance to Still Music*, [118] which dramatizes the ramifications of hearing loss. Teachers of health courses might well recommend *The Trembling Years* [119] and those teaching geography of, say, Australia, would find that *The Bates Family* [120] could contribute enormously to an awareness of how that environment shapes lives. Classes in value clarification would have much substantive content to deal with by analyzing *Ben and Annie* [121] or *A Sporting Proposition*. [122] Teachers of English, exploring such literary elements as symbolism and imagery, could study *Dark Dreams* [123] or *The Transfigured Hart*. [124]

These suggestions for school use are attractive since they approach the topic of handicaps in subtle ways. Currently, teachers, particularly at the elementary level, are including a curriculum unit that focuses entirely on the handicapped. For these instructors, related fictional works can be an invaluable aid.

In sum, no claim is made that literature should be the only agency or even the premier mechanism to change the social climate. Nevertheless, books have unique attributes that have been largely ignored in the campaign strategy of those who are concerned with making the school and the neighborhood conducive to the social growth of the child with special needs. Because literature affects people at a deep emotional level, it is uniquely suited for this sensitizing purpose.

One of the critical junctures children with serious disabilities have to confront is a transition period in which other children become accustomed to their manifested difference and begin to relate to them as people. Heisler relates the story of a mother of a ten-year-old cerebral-palsied boy who observed her son on the playground one day and was dismayed to observe that he was being taunted by a group of strange boys. She restrained her impulse to rush in protectively. When Ken, her son, joined her a little later, she asked him: "Why did you stay with those boys when they were treating you like that?" Ken replied simply, "I was giving them time to get used to me."[125] It is hoped that wide exposure to sensitizing reading materials will effectively reduce the "orientation" time that exceptional children must often endure.

Notes

A short form of reference citation is given here for those works that are cited fully and annotated in Chapter 5.

1. Mary Jane Kilner, *Adventures of a Pincushion* (Worcester, England: Isaiah Thomas, 1788).
2. Charles Kingsley, *The Water Babies: A Fairy Tale for a Land Baby* (London: Macmillan, 1863), p. 54.
3. American Tract Society, *Happy Home Stories* (New York: American Tract Society, 1885), p.44.
4. Juliana Horatia Ewing, *The Story of a Short Life* (London: Society for Promoting Christian Knowledge, 1885).
5. Juliana Horatia Ewing, "The Blind Man and the Talking Dog," in *Dandelion Clocks and Other Tales* (London: Society for Promoting Christian Knowledge, 1887?).
6. Dinah Maria Mulock Craik, *The Little Lame Prince and His Travelling Cloak* (London: Daldy, Isbister, 1875).
7. Johanna Spyri, *Heidi* (Boston: Ginn, 1899).
8. Howard Pyle, *Otto of the Silver Hand* (New York: Scribners, 1888).
9. Ibid., p. 192.
10. Raymond M. Alden, *The Christmas Tree Forest* (New York: Bobbs-Merrill, 1906).
11. Dikken Zwilgmeyer, *Johnny Blossom* (Boston: Pilgrim Press, 1912).
12. Alden, *The Christmas Tree Forest*, unpaged.
13. Ibid.
14. Hilda Van Stockum, *The Cottage at Bantry Bay* (New York: Viking, 1938).
15. Hilda Van Stockum, *Francie on the Run* (New York: Viking, 1939).
16. Van Stockum, *The Cottage at Bantry Bay*, p. 154.
17. Laura Ingalls Wilder, *Farmer Boy* (New York: Harper & Row, 1933).
18. Laura Ingalls Wilder, *On the Banks of Plum Creek* (New York: Harper & Row, 1937).
19. Arthur Groom, *Writing for Children*, cited in *Tales Out of School*, by Geoffrey Trease, 2nd ed. (London: Heinemann Educational Books, 1964), p. 110.
20. Charles Edward Stowe and Lyman Beecher Stowe, *Harriet Beecher Stowe: The Story of Her Life* (Boston: Houghton Mifflin, 1911), p. 203.
21. Muriel Estelle Crosby, ed., *Reading Ladders for Human Relations*, 4th ed. (Washington, D.C.: American Council on Education, 1963).
22. Louise M. Rosenblatt, *Literature as Exploration* (New York: Appleton Century Crofts, 1938), p. vi.

23. Josette Frank, *Your Child's Reading Today*, rev. ed. (Garden City, N.Y.: Doubleday, 1969), p. 143.
24. Kin Platt, *Hey, Dummy*.
25. Richard Parker, *He Is Your Brother*.
26. Glendon and Kathryn Swarthout, *Whales to See The*.
27. Hope Dahle Jordan, *The Fortune Cake*.
28. Nancy W. Faber, *Cathy at the Crossroads*.
29. Nancy W. Faber, *Cathy's Secret Kingdom*.
30. Glendon and Kathryn Swarthout, *Whales to See The*.
31. Theodora Koob, *The Deep Search*.
32. Earlene W. Luis and Barbara F. Millar, *Listen, Lissa!*.
33. Cora Cheney, *Key of Gold*, p. 92.
34. Dawn Thomas, *Pablito's New Feet*.
35. Regina J. Woody, *Wisdom to Know*.
36. Rebecca Caudill, *A Certain Small Shepherd*.
37. Louise A. Stinetorf, *A Charm for Paco's Mother*.
38. Glendon and Kathryn Swarthout, *Whales to See The*.
39. L. Dean Carper, *A Cry in the Wind*.
40. Ibid.
41. Joan Phipson, *Birkin*.
42. Louise A. Stinetorf, *Musa the Shoemaker*.
43. Prudence Andrew, *Mister O'Brien*, p. 7.
44. Mildred Lawrence, *The Shining Moment*.
45. Bruce Lowery, *Scarred*.
46. James B. Garfield, *Follow My Leader*.
47. Bo Carpelan, *Bow Island*.
48. C. L. Rinaldo, *Dark Dreams*.
49. Earlene W. Luis and Barbara F. Millar, *Wheels for Ginny's Chariot*.
50. Lenora Mattingly Weber, *A Bright Star Falls*.
51. Regina J. Woody, *Almena's Dogs*.
52. Regina J. Woody, *A Time to Dance*.
53. Hope Dahle Jordan, *The Fortune Cake*.
54. John Neufeld, *Touching*.
55. Kin Platt, *Hey, Dummy*.
56. C. L. Rinaldo, *Dark Dreams*.
57. Virginia Lee, *The Magic Moth*.
58. Elsie Oakes Barber, *The Trembling Years*.
59. Scott O'Dell, *Sing Down the Moon*.
60. Leon Garfield, *Smith*.
61. Gene Smith, *The Hayburners*.
62. Norma Rosen, "Who's Afraid of Erica Jong," *New York Times Magazine*, July 28, 1974, p. 50.
63. Jany Saint-Marcoux, *The Light*.
64. Anna Rose Wright, *Land of Silence*.
65. Dorothy Blatter, *Cap and Candle*.
66. Aimée Sommerfelt, *The Road to Agra*.
67. Ellen Raskin, *Spectacles*.
68. M. E. Kerr, *Dinky Hocker Shoots Smack!*
69. John Ney, *Ox Goes North: More Trouble for the Kid at the Top*.
70. Ellen Raskin, *The Tattooed Potato and Other Clues*.
71. Frank, *Your Child's Reading Today*, p. 136.

72. Bruno Bettelheim, *The Uses of Enchantment; The Meaning and Importance of Fairy Tales* (New York: Knopf, 1976).
73. Jean Karl, *From Childhood to Childhood—Children's Books and Their Creators* (New York: John Day, 1963).
74. Peter Davies, *Fly Away Paul*.
75. Bruce Lowery, *Scarred*.
76. Frank, *Your Child's Reading Today*, p. 127.
77. John Neufeld, *Sleep Two, Three, Four!*.
78. Virginia Hamilton, *The Planet of Junior Brown*.
79. Felice Holman, *Slake's Limbo*.
80. Kin Platt, *Hey, Dummy*.
81. Glendon and Kathryn Swarthout, *Whales to See The*.
82. Maia Wojciechowska, *A Single Light*.
83. Julia Cunningham, *Dorp Dead*.
84. Sheila Egoff, "Precepts and Pleasures," in *Only Connect*, ed. by Sheila Egoff, G. T. Stubbs, and L. F. Ashley (Toronto: Oxford University Press, 1969), p. 440.
85. Lila Perl, *No Tears for Rainey*.
86. Ruth Adams Knight, *Brave Companions*.
87. Lynn Hall, *Sticks and Stones*.
88. Sara Bonnett Stein, *About Handicaps*.
89. Joan Fassler, *One Little Girl*.
90. Phyllis Gold, *Please Don't Say Hello*.
91. Angelika Wolff, *Mom! I Need Glasses*.
92. Jane Goodsell, *Katie's Magic Glasses*.
93. Angelika Wolff, *Mom! I Need Glasses*, unpaged.
94. William Wise, *The Cowboy Surprise*.
95. Ellen Raskin, *Spectacles*.
96. Margaret J. Baker, *The Bright High Flyer*.
97. Ruth Sawyer, *Old Con and Patrick*.
98. Elsie Oakes Barber, *The Trembling Years*.
99. Geoffrey Trease, *Tales Out of School*, 2nd ed. (London: Heinemann Educational Books, 1964), p. 166.
100. Paul Heins, "Coming to Terms with Criticism," *Horn Book* 46 (August 1970), p. 370.
101. Patricia Schuman, "Concerned Criticisms or Casual Drop Outs," in *Issues in Children's Book Selection* (New York: Bowker, 1973), p. 196.
102. Elizabeth Nesbitt, "The Critic and Children's Literature," in *A Critical Approach to Children's Literature*, ed. by Sara I. Fenwick (Chicago: University of Chicago Press, 1967), p. 121.
103. Ralph Ellison, *Invisible Man* (New York: Random House, 1952).
104. Prudence Sutherland, "On the Need of the Severely Handicapped to Feel That They Are Human," in *The Special Child and the Library*, ed. by Barbara H. Baskin and Karen H. Harris (Chicago: American Library Association, 1976), p. 151.
105. Jerzy Kosinski, quoted in *The Plug-in Drug; Television, Children and the Family* by Marie Winn (New York: Viking, 1977), p. 64.
106. Joan Fassler, *Howie Helps Himself*.
107. Sara Bonnett Stein, *About Handicaps*.
108. Pamela Walker, *Twyla*.
109. Barbara Corcoran, *A Dance to Still Music*.

110. Lois Duncan, *Ransom*.
111. Gene Smith, *The Hayburners*.
112. Esther Forbes, *Johnny Tremain*.
113. Adrienne Richard, *Wings*.
114. Irene Hunt, *No Promises in the Wind*.
115. Joan Oppenheimer, *On the Outside Looking In*.
116. Kathryn Vinson, *Run with the Ring*.
117. Elizabeth Witheridge, *Dead End Bluff*.
118. Barbara Corcoran, *A Dance to Still Music*.
119. Elsie Oakes Barber, *The Trembling Years*.
120. Reginald Ottley, *The Bates Family*.
121. Joan Tate, *Ben and Annie*.
122. James Aldridge, *A Sporting Proposition*.
123. C. L. Rinaldo, *Dark Dreams*.
124. Jane Yolen, *The Transfigured Hart*.
125. Verda Heisler, *A Handicapped Child in the Family* (New York: Grune and Stratton, 1972), p. 111.

4

Patterns and Trends in Juvenile Fiction, 1940–1975

Individual fictional works can be analyzed to understand one author's particular perspective. To see the representativeness of that effort, how it articulates or compares with other books on the same topic, how it shares or deviates from other popular perceptions, and how it reflects, interprets, or defies contemporary mores, the genre must be assessed as an entity.

In examining the universe represented by over 300 books, it is possible to catalog not only pertinent demographic information but also to comment on social values that are represented in that world. Some data, such as types of disability, age of impaired characters, settings, or rehabilitation or intervention procedures, are readily tabulated. Other observations, such as the congruence of events in the story with reality, require an interpretative rather than a tabular report. Since reducing amorphous, complex material to discrete categories sometimes tends to distort the contents, a census of this fictional population is coupled with description, in narrative form, of behaviors, roles, and interactions taking place in that universe.

Types and Incidence of Disability Portrayed

Paralleling an increase in public awareness and interest in disability, characters who are handicapped have appeared with increasing frequency in children's fiction over the 36-year span examined in this book. Each five-year period from 1940 to 1960 reveals a slight rise in the number of novels containing a central or secondary disabled character. The decade of the 1960s introduced a rapid growth and the years 1966–

1975 generated roughly twice as many books as had the prior 26 years combined.

Two phenomena that occurred during this period—one literary and the other social—may have strongly influenced this increased output. The 1960s produced a deluge of "problem" stories for young readers in which formerly taboo ideas and issues were confronted. These included family fragmentation, social dislocations, and personal trauma. Within that expanded context, impairment became a more viable subject, readily interacting with those other topics. Simultaneously, disability advocacy groups grew increasingly skillful in raising the consciousness of the public about the needs and scope of their constituency. This momentum persisted into the 1970s and later publications exhibited more variation in kinds of disablement, as well as greater complexity and ambiguity in treatment.

Orthopedic problems, representing one-third of the collection, are the most commonly presented disabilities. These disorders, of which polio is the single most frequently identified cause, range in seriousness from modest problems, like a slight limp, to near total paralysis. Although orthopedically disabled characters form the single largest segment in this universe, it is also the most rapidly decreasing one. Diminished incidence of polio as a medical problem is at least in part responsible for its virtual disappearance from juvenile literature. In the wake of this decrement, other disabilities are receiving more attention and consequently supplanting presentation of that illness. Hence, when mobility restriction is selected as a story factor, other etiologies tend to be substituted.

The practice of specifically establishing the source of orthopedic impairments became more common in the 1970s. Before that period, one out of every five orthopedic impairments was not explained in terms of cause. Since then, only a half dozen physically disabled characters have appeared on the scene without a medical diagnosis.

One area that has received increased attention since 1970 is orthopedically related birth defects: There are as many such stories written from 1970 to 1975 as in the preceding 30 years. This shift in literary emphasis followed changes within advocacy organizations as they refocused their mission goals, and public consciousness about congenital birth anomalies rose.

Battle-caused orthopedic handicaps are found almost exclusively in characters injured in World War II or prior conflicts. Viet Nam veterans are conspicuously absent from juvenile fiction. Although numerous male amputees appear, only two females are mentioned with this problem, both of whom play identical roles. These nameless females, found in Beyond the Bridge[1] and The Shield of Achilles,[2] are used to symbolize the horrors of war. Both writers evidently view this depiction as especially powerful, and its use reinforces the pacifist orientation of those novels.

The next most frequently found disorders in these stories are those associated with visual impairment. Individuals with vision loss represent almost one-fifth of all disabled characters, a fraction grossly in excess of its actual incidence in the population. When only this subset is examined, blind characters exceed those with reduced visual acuity by a ratio of three to one. Excluding quasi-fiction (devoted mainly to the virtues of wearing glasses), the ratio of blind to visually deficient characters jumps to six to one, close to the reverse of reality. The dramatic potential of blindness (compared to mild vision loss) is great and this may account for its disproportionate representation in fiction. The reiteration of mythic messages and the obvious possibilities inherent in the linkage between blindness and social issues continue to appeal to writers. But recent years have yielded evidence of increased attention to characters with less severe visual problems.

The next largest group is composed of individuals who exhibit emotional disorders. This segment, representing about 13 percent of the fictional disabled population, has increased sharply in recent years—well over half of these characters appear after 1970. These are individuals who have been hospitalized, have undergone prolonged psychiatric treatment for severe disorders, are self-destructive, engage in irrational asocial acts, or have been specifically clinically labeled. In the absence of medically attributed criteria, delimitation was difficult and some deductive judgments were required. As an example, *A Blues I Can Whistle*[3] was excluded. That novel explores anti–Vietnam protest and contains a character who plans to immolate himself. While some may consider this prima facie evidence of instability, this has been interpreted here as a political response. On the other hand, several books contain characters whose aphasia derives from psychological trauma and they are considered temporarily emotionally dysfunctional rather than speech-impaired.

However, origins of emotional instability are infrequently stated. When attributed, they are usually seen as situational, often precipitated by a single event, such as the death of a baby or an abrupt, unwelcome change in lifestyle. Here, females exceed males by a ratio of five to four and dysfunction is increasingly seen as a problem of adult women. Surprisingly, emotionally impaired young girls are relatively rare in these fictional accounts.

Books about retarded characters constitute about 10 percent of this genre. Novels about retardation peaked between 1966 and 1970, a period that produced half of all the output on this subject for juvenile readers. The overall ratio of males to females was two to one, again a

disproportionate figure compared to actual data. More retarded characters exhibit severe rather than mild involvement, again reversing actual
incidence.

The other disabilities, in decreasing order of occurrence, are auditory impairment, speech impairment, general health, and neurological
problems. This latter category includes cerebral palsy, stroke, and specific learning disabilities, a subset that has been the object of particular
interest recently. Cosmetic problems, representing 4 percent of the total, form the smallest group.

The change in status of the impaired character often provides the
central crisis in many novels. However, in three-fifths of the stories,
health or adjustment of such characters remains unchanged. Many of
these people either play cameo roles or are adults for whom intervention options no longer exist. After 1973, the complete "cure" almost
disappears and there is a marked movement toward realistic, partial
resolutions. Miracle cures and spontaneous remission of symptoms as a
denouement have all but vanished. Such contrivances as car accidents
that immediately restore total vision have apparently lost their literary
popularity. Instead, a wide spectrum of therapeutic interventions has
been introduced that is more harmonious with conventional practices:
physical therapy, vocational training, prosthetics, and similar components of rehabilitative activity.

Schooling is the next most frequently employed remediative agent.
Medical and psychiatric authorities are also widely consulted, but with
mixed results. Early books posited that willpower or determination was
the critical variable in ameliorating a particular condition, but this echo
of the Puritan Ethic has declined radically in recent years. Almost 15
percent of the impaired characters either decline in health or die by
book's end, a development particularly evident in the last three years of
this survey.

Characteristics of the Disabled Portrayed

In actuality, there are far more disabled males than females in the
population. Overall, in the juvenile fiction surveyed, impaired males
represent almost two-thirds of the disabled characters, a proportion
which does reflect but in fact underrepresents disabled males in the
population at large. In books about adolescents, however, disabled females appear almost as often as disabled males. Disability occurs in the
books surveyed in almost equal proportions among children, adolescents, and adults.

The overwhelming majority of disabled characters are Caucasian. Although there are less than a dozen important black characters, they often serve dual functions in the novels: carrying social messages as well as playing out their dramatic role. For example, in *On the Move*,[4] a black character dramatizes the consequences of racial discrimination, and the lame boy in *Roosevelt Grady*[5] personalizes the plight of migrant workers. When nonhandicapped Blacks appear, they frequently act as catalysts, precipitating experiences that generate insights for the impaired person. The other minority group most commonly portrayed is the American Indian, whose culture and traditions are key elements in the story. Although some novels are patronizing, most attempt to present a balanced picture of Indian societies. Unfortunately, these stories are set almost exclusively in the past. Only a handful of Oriental characters can be found in this collection, each of whom is in a story containing a social or political message.

Jews are the only other specifically identified minority group that serves a symbolic purpose. Though rarely portrayed as disabled (*Our Eddie*,[6] *The Trembling Years*,[7] and *Other Sandals*[8] are the major exceptions), they appear in social message books where their function is to exemplify the role of outgroup members, allowing parallels to be drawn between themselves and the handicapped. *The Great Brain*,[9] *Secret of the Emerald Star*,[10] and *Joyride*[11] are typical of this usage.

When the disabled are portrayed as employed, they are often shown in jobs requiring minimal human contact. One-third of the workers are in menial or blue-collar occupations, though a few are in industry and the skilled trades. Reflecting popular romanticized misperceptions, 13 percent of those working are shown as artists of some sort, for example, musicians, potters, or mimes. The prophet or seer role, derived mainly from historic fiction, continues to surface, but represents only 8 percent of the described occupations. A fifth of those employed are shown in professional (physician, judge, accountant) or power-related positions. The latter category is characterized by such singular roles as a sultan or the founder of a nation.

Characters often select careers related to their own impairment. In *The Green Gate*,[12] the visually impaired student teacher works with blind children. The young woman who stutters in *The Immediate Gift*[13] trains as a speech therapist. The deaf girl in *Water Rat*[14] is hired as a swimming instructor in an institution with deaf and blind students.

Stress, associated with aspects of the job, as in *No Tears for Rainey*,[15] or in forced retirement from a job, in both *The Phaedra Complex*[16] and *The Drowning Boy*,[17] is depicted as precipitating the dysfunctional behavior of the workers. Occupations may also have symbolic functions. In *The

Dream Time,[18] the protagonist's artistic ability represents the creative forces of humanity. The war-wounded Greek amputee in *The Shield of Achilles*[19] sells postcards that ironically celebrate the beauty of his country, soon to be ravaged again by warfare.

Family Situations Portrayed

In addition to identifying and describing the disabled, authors also inevitably comment about the social context. The primary milieu for the disabled is the family, and over two-thirds of the books show them in this setting. The actions by various family members or surrogates run the gamut from loving support to deliberately destructive behavior.

Typical of the majority of books that show the family as benevolent are *Little Town on the Prairie*[20] and its sequel, *These Happy Golden Years*.[21] These novels are characterized by warm relationships, concerned parents, and responsible siblings who willingly provide for the needs of the impaired family member. Other instances of support range from simply providing a stable, nurturant home life, as in *Su-Mei's Golden Year*,[22] to moving across country in order to obtain proper therapy, in *Key of Gold*.[23] The epitome of unswerving loyalty is found in *A Crack in the Sidewalk*,[24] in which the family accepts the profoundly retarded child exactly as he is and gives fully and unconditionally of their love.

Some books show clearly that even a totally committed family may be unable to protect its handicapped member. Twink's mother in *Touching*[25] scours the country for the best medical and educational intervention for her cerebral-palsied daughter. Nevertheless, a catastrophic decision is made and the more complex situation is presented of a well-meaning parent inadvertently contributing to the worsening of her child's condition.

Overprotection is seen as a major barrier to the growth and development of a handicapped child in *Let the Balloon Go*[26] and *The Watchers*.[27] Parents are trapped by their inability to find a reasonable balance between guarding their child's safety and permitting the kinds of contact with the world that, while potentially dangerous, allow for psychological as well as physical maturation.

Sometimes the impaired character becomes just one more contributing agent in an already conflict-ridden family. Distraught over his mother's threat to institutionalize his retarded brother, Paul, in *Escape the River*,[28] runs away with him. In *Deenie*,[29] disability is the cause of conflict as the mother proposes a lenient interpretation of the doctor's orders and the father demands strict compliance.

Denial of the true status of the child is a behavior attributed predominantly to fathers who see disability as an insupportable blow to their egos. In both *Take Wing*[30] and *Nancy and Her Johnny-O*,[31] fathers delay seeking remediation for their retarded sons because of an unwillingness to acknowledge that any intervention is necessary. Absorption in their own lives renders some families oblivious to the developing problems of impaired members. Mrs. Hocker, in *Dinky Hocker Shoots Smack!*,[32] is so preoccupied with social causes that she ignores her niece's maladaptive behavior.

Other families actively intensify the difficulties that impairments create. *The Top Step*[33] introduces a parent who demands that his son be more "manly" as the price of his father's love, a pressure that propels the severely asthmatic child into circumstances causing physical as well as psychological pain. The perpetually unfulfilled promises of the mother to her son in *The Unmaking of Rabbit*[34] increase the emotional disequilibrium of the stuttering boy.

The absence of one or both parents is common in books containing disabled characters. Undue weight should not be accorded this since it is a ubiquitous contrivance in juvenile fiction. Actual abandonment, however, takes many forms—from Rennie's father's suddenly increased business demands in *The Lionhearted*[35] to the father's severance of all ties in *Me Too*.[36] The ultimate in nonsupportive families is found in *The Boy Who Could Make Himself Disappear*[37] and *Flambards*.[38] In the former, the parents literally cause their son's emotional disorder and, in the latter, the youth is driven to self-mutilation to escape his father's abuse.

When it is the parent who is disabled, the children's responses are rarely rejecting. In the absence of other adult family members, the burdens of responsibility are generally willingly, but ineptly, shouldered. As exemplified in *The Bears' House*,[39] the children desperately try to carry on despite their pathetically limited resources. In that novel, as in such others as *Celebrate the Morning*,[40] outsiders must finally be called upon to salvage the deteriorating situation.

The effect of disability on marriage or romance was not generally treated seriously prior to the 1960s. With only one exception, impairment was seen as a fact in the relationship, not a factor in structuring it. Handicaps were not viewed as a barrier to successful male-female relationships except if the prospective alliance involved a retarded character. There are no instances of intellectually impaired marriage partners, and the sole romance is one-sided and characterized by complete rejection of the retarded person. During the decade of the 1960s, stories emerged that featured disability as a complicating factor in the relationship. Emotional dysfunction was the single most common impairment explored in the marriage or romance context during that period, and it still continues to interest contemporary writers. Although responses to dysfunction varied, it was not considered an impediment to developing or maintaining relationships; marital breakups were not presented as possible options in the 1960s. The response by marriage partners after 1970 became vastly more complex. Abandonment, divorce, and exploitation all appear for the first time.

In sum, the past five years have shown the most dramatic increase in portrayals of families whose behavior is detrimental to the interests of the handicapped member. The phenomenon of the idealized family as the fictional norm has been replaced by one beset with a multitude of problems, many of which undercut the functioning of the disabled person.

Depiction of Professionals

Handicapped individuals, more than other segment of the citizenry, are dependent on social agencies and services. Authors see professionals and institutions as varying widely in the quantity and quality of support they offer. Doctors are shown in the most consistently positive light, depicted as generously donating their skills to remove cataracts (*A Charm for Paco's Mother*[41]) or to excise a brain tumor (*The Immediate Gift*[42]). These projections, while panegyrized, are essentially stereotypical, presenting cardboard characters whose intervention is manipulated for the resolution of the story line.

Professionals serve a very particularized function. Not only do they speak as characters in a story but they also provide a channel through which the author can lecture readers directly on technical aspects of the disability. As the orthopedist explains scoliosis to Deenie, he also interprets this spinal problem to the readership. Educators, psychologists, therapists, and other allied professionals all impart information in this manner.

Medical Personnel and Social Agencies

A positive and fully developed portrayal is found in *Deenie*,[43] in which the orthopedist diagnoses, interprets, prescribes, and supervises the rehabilitative procedure in a concerned and professional manner. A mixed depiction is developed through the actions and negligence of the physician in *The Trembling Years*.[44] Although adequate medical treatment is provided, the young woman recovering from polio is left to cope alone with her attendant anxieties without interpretation or prognosis. The most dramatic divergence from the generally admiring perception of doctors occurs in *Touching*.[45] The surgeon uses the heroine casually and cavalierly in experimental surgery and feels neither remorse nor responsibility when Twink becomes blind as a direct result of his treatment.

Except for the exemplary nurse in *The House in the Waves*,[46] few strong characterizations of this profession appear. Social workers, encountered almost exclusively in contemporary novels, are pictured almost universally as inept. They are shown as unable to recognize the symptoms of a seriously disturbed woman, failing to assign safe and proper custody of a vulnerable child and too deficient even to process forms properly. Although a congenial person, the social worker in *Celebrate the Morning*,[47] neither competent nor especially resourceful, completes this dreary literary profile of a disparaged occupation.

Teachers and Schools

Teachers are the single most commonly represented professional group. They are seen predominantly as they interact with children rather than as they perform academically. There is no single unified image projected of educators, only an array of characterizations ranging from cruel and abusive to sensitive and dedicated.

The teachers in *From Anna*[48] and *Sue Ellen*[49] create an unpressured therapeutic learning environment that fosters growth and self-acceptance in their charges. These portrayals feature exceptionally talented women who manipulate classroom and situation variables in constructive, exciting ways, markedly reducing the impact of the children's impairments. The coach in *Long Shot for Paul*[50] and the teacher in *Nobody Likes Trina*[51] exemplify the accommodations made to foster the social integration, as well as the functioning, of special-needs students.

These educators are counterbalanced by numerous teachers who, through their ineptness or cowardice, either create a climate devastating to the interests of the impaired child or actively harass or demean their students. The teachers in *Kristy's Courage*,[52] *Shutterbug*,[53] and *He's My Brother*[54] tolerate the teasing, terrorizing, and ostracising of exceptional students and, by their noninvolvement and passivity, ensure the continuation of this treatment. School scenes often demand courage from teachers. The one center stage in *Hey, Dummy*[55] and his colleagues in *Lisa, Bright and Dark*[56] are notably deficient in this attribute. In their anxiety to protect themselves, they endanger the lives of their charges.

Other books dramatize scenes of cruelty: The lisping speech of the emotionally distraught youth in *The Boy Who Could Make Himself Disappear*[57] is mocked by his instructor, and the poor handwriting of the child with arm muscles damaged by polio is held up for public ridicule in *Screwball*.[58] Many episodes portray teachers who use questionable strategies in instructing their exceptional pupils. In a misguided attempt at protection, Harold's teacher in *Wings*[59] foolishly exempts him from demands made on the other children. Her actions exaggerate his limitations and succeed in insulating him temporarily from social contacts.

Educators in the residential schools for the blind in *Light a Single Candle*[60] and *Run with the Ring*[61] illustrate diametrically different approaches to the developmental needs of their students. The faculty in the first novel encourage dependence, passivity, and low aspirations. Conversely, the staff in the latter book require student participation, encourage independence, and motivate the children to seek more demanding goals.

The only schools free from critical comment are schools that train blind people to use dogs for mobility. Day schools, displaying the same array of qualities as do teachers, range from highly idealized settings to destructive, oppressive ones. Residential institutions frequently are presented in extremes. Idealized centers are typically found in naive, lightweight novels set in the present day. These are characterized by unflaggingly dedicated staffs, resortlike grounds, and abrupt, dramatic instances of recovery among the residents.

When books have multilevel messages, institutions are often synonymous with death and the assignment of characters there seems more a sentence than a prescription. In historic fiction, asylums were seen as functioning more for the convenience of the family than for the welfare of their inmates. There are some balanced presentations, but in these, information tends to be essentially inferential rather than explicit. That is, much of the action takes place offstage, and the effect on the character generates the impression that the milieu has been supportive. In contrast with large institutions, small agencies dealing with day care, vocational training, or recreation are seen as much more involved in personalized service, and it is lack of adequate financing rather than incompetence or malevolent intent that limits their efficacy.

Depiction of Other Aspects of the Community

Although religious themes are extant in many books, except for historic novels, ecclesiastical institutions are surprisingly rare. Some religious figures are portrayed in a positive light, but this is in no way a universal depiction. Moreover, there is a surprising absence of representation of the contemporary church as a haven, a source of comfort, support, or hope.

The community at large is generally represented as oblivious, indifferent, or unresponsive to the special needs of the disabled. Savitz, a writer who has written extensively on this topic, particularly stresses how architectural barriers and underfinancing of supportive agencies increase the difficulties of handicapped persons. Absence of readily accessible or early intervention developmental centers is also widely deplored.

The implications of poverty and its deleterious effect on disability are common themes. Correlation between the fictional world of poverty and the real world is high. The poor are not only portrayed as less able to pay for remediative services; they are also less able to identify, locate, or utilize these opportunities, and, lacking the savvy to manipulate events or establishments, usually end up as victims.

Other Characteristics of the Stories

Although stories take place in every continent, on shipboard, as well as in unidentifiable or imaginary lands, two-thirds of these novels are set in the United States and almost an additional quarter in Europe. There appears to be no pattern of deliberately selecting exotic frameworks, which could have had the effect of diminishing identification. Many of the novels are written by foreign nationals who use their own countries as locales, and these books were translated or reprinted for American audiences. In domestic fiction, the shift from rural to urban settings parallels that generally found in other juvenile literature.

While most of these novels are contemporary, time frames range from the prehistoric to the unspecified future. Twice as many handicapped males as females appear in historic fiction and orthopedic impairments surface with astonishing frequency, being twice as prevalent as the combined total of all other disorders. In stories set in very early times, disability is either associated with mystical or divine powers or is the consequence of violence. Monasteries are a popular locale for stories taking place during the Middle Ages. These are shown as benevolent institutions that provide protection, instruction, and moral support with a religious figure or group acting as a parental surrogate. Futuristic novels gloomily forecast that abuse and deprivation for the handicapped will worsen. Repressive societies are postulated in which the disabled are projected as readily victimized.

Beliefs and Attitudes Represented toward the Handicapped

In addition to exploring the tangible environment, authors have described those intangible components that comprise the fictional world of the disabled. These consist of beliefs and attitudes expressed and inferred and social roles projected as appropriate for the handicapped.

Naming and labeling are common unfortunate societal practices reflected in these stories. Nicknames that are pejorative or denigrating and reduce the character to the disability are pervasive. "Gimpy" in *Crazylegs Merrill*,[62] "Squinter" in *The Contrary Orphans*,[63] "Dummy" in *Hey, Dummy*,[64] and "Rabbit" in *The Unmaking of Rabbit*[65] are typical. In some instances, these appellations are both contrived and unlikely, as, for example, the term "Weak Willies" in *Shutterbug*[66] or "Crippled Crutchers" in *Almena's Dogs*.[67]

The perception that name connotes status is best exemplified in *Red Eagle*.[68] The despised name of "Lame Foot" is gratefully replaced by an esteemed one after the young Indian has earned it through his heroic actions. When impairment was seen as the salient attribute, the boy's name reflected this. However, when he proved his fearlessness, a non-derogatory name (without reference to the disability) was awarded.

More subtle is the use of partial names. "Mike" in *Screwball*[69] and "Orry" in *He Is Your Brother*[70] are used when the boys are low achievers. Their names change to Michael and Lawrence, respectively, only after they improve in their functioning and consequently in their status. The significance of a name is further demonstrated in *Mountain Magic for Rosy*[71] in which the superstitious mother fears that naming her sickly baby may precipitate its death.

It is commonplace in these stories that deviance is perceived as insanity. The reality of the specific disability is ignored, and characters, motivated by fear and aversion, react in rejecting and punitive ways. Such terms as "a mental case," "tetched," "queer," and "loony" are indiscriminately applied to handicapped characters. An example from *Don't Take Teddy* is illustrative: "She shook her head and made a figure eight with her hand. . . . 'Why don't people like that wear a band on their arm or some thing so we can see.' "[72]

Irrational beliefs associate sin and evil with disability. The youth with the amputated leg in *The Namesake*[73] is believed to have the power of "the evil eye." However, all powers attributed to the handicapped are not seen as malevolent. Desirable qualities or abilities are ascribed to the disabled as deriving not from realistic bases but from mystical or wishful ones. In actual practice, the disabled are specifically taught to maximize intact senses, instruction that involves pragmatic procedures based on utilization of latent natural ability. This is of an entirely different order than the extraordinary power attributed to a deaf character in *The Silent Message*: "Handicapped people do seem to develop a sixth sense that others can't understand or explain."[74]

A corollary belief is that handicapped persons are uniquely in harmony with the natural world, unfeared by and able to communicate with wild creatures. Pleas, the profoundly retarded child in *A Crack in the Sidewalk*, is an extreme example:

> And Pleas was in tune with everything . . . as if he were a child of nature itself. . . . Once a little snake slipped through the grass beside him. He reached out and gently ran his hand along its back. . . . After a few days the birds hopped around him as if he were a tree planted, and a chipmunk came and ate the crumbs he dropped from his cookie.[75]

Unfortunately, even when these traits are projected as commendable or desirable, such attributed supernatural abilities tend to separate the disabled from the rest of humanity.

Roles Assigned to the Disabled Character

Personality and character are not the only elements used to construct a fictional person. The assignment of role is also contributory; particularly significant are those of hero or heroine, villain, and victim or outcast.

Hero or Heroine

In juvenile fiction, when the disabled are heroes or heroines, the presentation generally takes one of three forms: The protagonist is able to emerge victorious over the disability in the battle of daily life; the impaired character is able to perform courageously in a single act by ignoring or denying the reality of the disability; or the bravery is unrelated to the disability.

The most subtle manifestations of courage are those exhibited in the constant willingness to confront the everyday limitations of disability and persevere and endure despite them. Actions casually achieved by others are shown to call for great efforts by the disabled, who must disregard previous failures and ignore present pain. This form of valor is epitomized in *The Bates Family*[76] in which, without special pleading, the hero's uncomplaining acceptance of execrable but necessary working conditions illustrates conduct more admirable than any single spectacular act.

More theatrical than lifelike are actions such as Eytan's in *Other Sandals*.[77] Despite the agony caused by a crippled leg, he carries an injured companion to safety through the pitiless desert heat. His disagreeable disposition had isolated him from the social life of the community, but this humane and selfless act redeems him and becomes his visa to a more accepting world. The context in which such heroic acts take place often appears contrived, necessitating that the protagonist ignore or circumvent the disability.

Sometimes heroism is established independent of impairment. Tatlek, in At the Mouth of the Luckiest River,[78] ignores danger and becomes a peacemaker for his tribe, an action separated from his depiction as a disabled child. In these novels, the handicapped hero or heroine is courageous in ways indistinguishable from behavior of nonhandicapped heroic characters.

Villain

A very small minority of disabled characters is cast as malefactors, and of these, most are stage villains—their prostheses being mere props. Either a nonimpaired character or society tends to be assigned the villainous role, should one be required. Overt, aggressive and punitive acts continue to appear and be condemned in contemporary stories. Increasingly, reprehensible behavior against the disabled is seen in wider perspective. Both society and individuals are developed as culpable through indifference, apathy, unresponsiveness, or their sanctioning of violence.

Outcast or Victim

Heroes and heroines and villains are all active roles, but outcasts and victims are essentially passive ones. Although victimization may stem primarily from other sources, such as poverty or family disorganization, the vulnerability of a character is always increased by impairment. The extent to which the handicapped are abused ranges from name-calling to murder, but the most common form is social ostracism. The impaired boy in Take Wing[79] is unable to even discern that he is being teased. In other novels, by contrast, persecution may lead to total despair, resulting in suicide or pathological withdrawal.

Impaired characters satisfy the classical requirements for scapegoats, and it is not surprising to see them frequently cast in this role: They are readily identifiable, are usually powerless, and are unable to resist exploitation or manipulation. Auguste, the mute boy in Burnish Me Bright,[80] and Lovel, the crippled youth in The Witch's Brat,[81] are blamed for the natural disasters that occur and become the focus for the community's animosity. When a child is injured, the innocent retarded youth in *Hey, Dummy*[82] is automatically assumed to be the perpetrator and an enraged mob searches for him, crying for vengeance. This unwarranted presumption of guilt is a recurring pattern when the scapegoat role is used.

The outcast is a less dramatic but more common representation of victimization, and impairment is shown to be a factor in that status. Antagonistic reactions to exceptionality in juvenile fiction devolve from three major sources: Unimpaired characters are hostile to any evidence of nonconformity and the mere existence of difference is grounds for antipathy or hostility; the disability causes problems in communication or interaction that trigger rejecting responses; or the attitude of the disabled character is permeated with anger, self-pity, fears, or other similar components that inexorably lead to rejection or avoidance. Without provocation or justification, Jeff, in *Scarred*,[83] is elected to be the target for communal discharge of aggression. Neither his actions, conversations, nor other factors contribute to his initial outcast status. His persecution is based solely on the presence of an unobtrusive facial scar.

Most frequently, the isolate role devolves from actual aspects of the disability that lead to misunderstandings. In *David in Silence*, the neighborhood boys' inability either to comprehend the imperfect speech of the deaf boy or to make themselves understood by him generate feelings of suspicion, anger, and, inevitably, contempt. One child suggests that David may be mocking them: ". . . we've no way of knowing he hasn't been having us on." When a child sneaks up behind him and blows a blast on a whistle, another incredulously asserts: "He must have heard that . . . he must have." Often the observable behavior is misinterpreted, rationalizing and justifying the consequent exclusion: " 'Oh go on,' said the wicket keeper [in response to David]. . . . 'They always are peculiar, you know that.' "[84]

The attitude of the impaired person is sometimes cited as a cause of isolation. Fears of embarrassment, diminished feelings of manliness, and bitterness are attitudes typically shown to impede social intercourse. The outcast, according to this formulation, is primarily responsible for his or her own distress.

Proposed Solutions. Authors, directly and indirectly, suggest the means whereby the handicapped are enabled to achieve social acceptance. Some writers advocate society as the entity needing reformation and others see the responsibility of change contingent on modifications made by the disabled themselves. A small handful gloomily suggests the intransigence of this problem by replicating outcast scenarios, particularly in futuristic novels.

When discrimination is basically a xenophobic reaction, then the story may provide a formula for remediation generally accompanied by a sermon or two. Often the story is a microcosm of what is proposed on a larger scale. Discrimination against the handicapped is demonstrated to be injurious to the victim and perpetrator alike and the reader is helped to generalize from this object lesson to real social situations.

Other books suggest that proximity is the palliative. It is postulated that as encounters increase, children will come to look beyond the cloak of disability and discover a friendly, sociable, worthwhile companion. This hypothesis implies that knowledge and familiarity readily lead to acceptance.

The nature of the interaction should be closely examined since it is of prime importance. While some authors posit a coming together of equals, others project a dominant-subservient relationship. In a few stories, the disabled are seen as recipients of charitable acts, thus shaping the power dynamics of the interaction. In *Almena's Dogs*,[85] for instance, the handicapped students are identified as a "project" to be undertaken by the other children. A more egregious example occurs in *Flat on My Face* as the narrator describes her sister's current fad:

> But at supper she brought up the subject of human suffering again. I think Carla thrives on causes. . . . This was the first time something grabbed her from the United States. I have no idea what she plans to put her heart in after this C.P. [Cerebral Palsy] drive is over.[86]

> "Isn't there Something More we can do for the physically handicapped?" She was pleading with everyone at the table during the salad course. Nobody seemed to come up with any cures so she worried all through the meat loaf and green beans.[87]

The flippant language does not obscure the patronizing attitude toward the disabled, which is endorsed as a legitimate social posture. When the project is over, the recipient of the heroine's benevolence "gurgled his thanks," a demeaning description that emphasizes the differences not only in role but in the inequality in the relationship.

A major solution recommended to ease the loneliness derived from outcast status is affiliation with others similarly excluded from the social mainstream. In over one-fifth of these books, the authors advise an association with other isolates. The underlying assumption is that those who have themselves suffered social exclusion can empathize with others in analogous circumstances. Rennie, the crippled girl in *The Lion-hearted*,[88] becomes friendly with a lonely, obese girl whom she met at a concert. The overweight girl confides that she dedicated her songs to those "who spent their life on the outer fringe." A popular variation of this symbiotic theme involves an animal in the alliance. In *Three of a Kind*,[89] an orphan, an autisticlike child, and a tailless kitten form a mutually supportive, if unlikely, trio.

A more common formulation is that of an animal with the identical impairment as a human character who provides companionship or even inspiration. In the otherwise admirable *Ride the Pale Stallion*,[90] the ludicrous image of a one-legged eagle furnishes a model of adaptation and determination for the one-legged human counterpart. Lame blue jays, horses, and camels, as well as blind or diabetic canines, are part of the menagerie employed by writers to play similar roles.

These ploys do not really address the issue of outcast status, only an amelioration of its consequences. However, writers do speculate on some active ways in which the impaired individual might achieve prestige in the eyes of society. One recommendation put forth is for the disabled to do something valorous, saving lives for example, thereby winning the admiration of others. Numerous young heroes avail themselves of this technique for garnering acceptance. One book, *A Cry in the Wind*,[91] even manages two life-saving events performed by developmentally disabled grade-school children.

Where the disabled person's own attitude is projected as the barrier to acceptance, changing that attitude is considered vital. Some authors suggest that impaired characters be less self-preoccupied, initiate social overtures, and not anticipate rejection. Other writers, however, aver that society is too morally corrupt to ever be safe for those who are different. Even when the disabled behave in exemplary manner, or change their attitude, or simply keep out of the way, they will still continue to be abused.

Disability and the Structure of the Books

In addition to the content, the architecture of the story conveys certain attitudes about the disabled. McLuhan's doctrine that the medium not only delivers but shapes the message is applicable here. The first clue to perspective may appear in the title, and while some may be neutral, uninformative, or ironic, others express viewpoints by metaphorical content, connotation, or construction of those headings. Monbeck has commented on this irony in the selection of journal titles about the blind or on blindness, listing such names as *Lookout*, *Illuminator*, *Light*, *Beacon*, *Insight*, and *Outlook*.[92]

The practice of stressing absent elements is commonly found in juvenile book titles about the blind but it extends to other disabilities as well. Titles may hint that emphasis will be placed on hopeless or hopeful aspects, suggest a perspective by which the impairment may be perceived, or accent similarities or differences. Success is promised in *Triumph Clear*;[93] conversely, the ominous title *Dark Dreams*[94] cues the prospective reader that hopes will not be fulfilled. The presence of variants of "silence" in many story titles featuring deaf characters underlines the lack of communication possibilities and hints at the consequent loneliness. *Wheels for Ginny's Chariot*[95] implies, in its glamorizing of the wheelchair as a conveyance, that a serious treatment of mobility problems will not be forthcoming. *One of the Family*[96] and *A Different Kind of Sister*,[97] both titles for books focusing on retarded siblings, allude to different emphases.

In terms of structure, handicapped characters play the same literary (as opposed to character) roles as the nonhandicapped. That is, they are found as protagonists, antagonists, reagents, catalytic agents, and so on. A particular role they play, and one that exploits subliminal attitudes about disability, is that of a portent. Commonly, the handicapped individual is the focus of the story and a means for specifically and extensively examining the implications of impairment. *Light a Single Candle*[98] and the sequel, *Gift of Gold*,[99] follow a teenager from the first hint of impending blindness through medical treatment, remediative schooling, vocational training, and romance. Similar books are available in every major disability category.

Another common use of the disabled character is to provide a variation of a standard problem in other areas, that is, romances, sports stories, and mysteries feature a main or secondary character whose handicap complicates the plot. Occasionally, valid information or positive attitudes about disability are delivered throughout the course of the story. *The Runner*,[100] *The Secret Cowboy*,[101] and *The Golden Mare*[102] are basically horse stories featuring central human characters with impairments.

Frequently, exceptional characters serve catalytic functions. They precipitate the passage to adulthood of others, they alter moral perceptions and behaviors, and they provide insight into the self and the external world. Not infrequently, the impairment may also provide the means for resolving those crises.

Handicapped characters also act as reagents, illuminating the nature of other persons in the story. People are shown to be callous, sensitive, kind, or thoughtless through their responses to the disabled person. The changes in Jo's character correlate with alterations in her behavior toward Marcella in *Plague of Frogs*.[103] Jo is portrayed as insensitive and selfish at the outset but grows more admirable as her reactions to the slow-thinking girl become more compassionate.

Unlike the *literary* roles already discussed, in which the disabled and nondisabled may be used interchangeably, the role of portent derives specifically from the devalued status of the disabled. As a warning of ominous encounters, it exploits subliminal fears about the handicapped, associating disaster and disability. It is a use common in classical adult literature but unexpected here even in the diluted form in which it is generally found. Perhaps the most obvious instance is the seemingly chance encounter of the title character in *Simon* with a nameless boy in a wheelchair:

> He stared at the boy's jerky movements and turned his head away, uncomfortably, when the boy looked back at him. An odd uneasiness held Simon a moment. His neck felt prickly. He didn't like to look at people like that. . . . He had read once that some ancients drowned babies who were not perfect when born. Solved a lot of problems, Simon reflected. [104]

This early scene presages traumatic experiences Simon will have with "people like that" who will subsequently change his life, confronting him with crises that initiate his maturation.

The other major function, that of symbol, has been discussed extensively in other contexts. It is clearly possible for characters to play more than one important role.

The fate of the character and the resolution of the plot at the end of the novel leave the reader with certain feelings about the feasibility of resolving similar problems satisfactorily. Most of the books from the first two decades in this collection postulate a high degree of optimism about the ability of fictional characters, including the disabled, to cope with life's vicissitudes. These stories were concluded to conform with a view of a sunny future. Though this treatment persists, it seems a holdover from a more uncomplicated past.

During the decade from 1961 to 1970, there was a dramatic shift to less optimistic conclusions. The diminution in the number of roseate, fairy-talelike endings was part of a move toward pessimism, and almost 10 percent of these stories ended with such obviously worsened situations as reinstitutionalization, dramatically reduced functioning, or death.

In the subsequent years, catastrophic conclusions and ambiguous or mixed resolutions became commonplace, and these were not restricted to books written for older readers. To the depiction of physical, economic, and social problems were added stories that conceptualized tragedy in more complex terms. Some newer novels left the objective status of the characters unchanged, but might reveal a loss of hope or the forced abandonment of a greatly desired lifestyle.

Another sophisticated treatment of tragic endings emerged during the 1970s. The full devastating effect of events was projected beyond the conclusion of the book. This technique made more stringent demands upon readers, requiring their active extended cooperation for the book's message to be understood. *Ben and Annie*[105] exhibits both of these trends. Her friendship with Ben, which was the single bright and happy factor in Annie's life, is abruptly and irrevocably shattered by her well-meaning though misguided parents. This action terminates the book, but the effect on Annie—her inevitable return to isolation and loneliness—is the only possible result and will take place *after* the last page. Annie's physical deterioration is not at issue—it must proceed inexorably—but the elimination of the joy she experienced is total and immediate and characterizes the death of her spirit.

Role of Illustrations

Illustrations may be equal partners with the text, depicting and interpreting major aspects of the story; they may be mere adjuncts; or they may be of preeminent significance. The pictorial styles represented in this collection range from photographs and detailed naturalistic presentations to impressionistic ones. Highly realistic, near photographic drawings are not necessarily synonymous with good-quality illustration since artists are more than reporters—they are interpreters and commentators and must be free to respond in whatever medium and style they deem most appropriate.

While esthetic evaluation is outside the scope of this work, obvious poor quality requires comment. Some pictures are deficient in such basic components as proportion, perspective, composition, and color usage. The most ubiquitous fault, however, is blandness. Characters in too many illustrations have no individuality; their disabilities are ignored or minimized and there is no clue to personality provided in their depictions. The central character in *Show Ring Rogue*,[106] for instance, is sufficiently anonymous to be interchangeable with any found in a dozen other books. Other representations fortunately are individual, memorable, and affecting, providing moving visual images.

Many illustrations in the books in this collection are valuable in that they provide information, reveal character, interpret action, and reflect mood and attitude. *Howie Helps Himself*[107] and *Rachel*[108] are two picture books which introduce impaired characters. *Rachel* is the subtler work, presenting a very average child who is confined to a wheelchair. Comments about adaptations necessary to accommodate her disability are minimal and the emphasis is almost exclusively on those activities in which she can participate readily. Her disablement is not minimized and the postural adaptations required by her impairment are forthrightly pictured. The central message of both text and illustration is summarized in the final picture in which the handholds of her wheelchair can be located, only after careful scrutiny, in the very center of a page crowded with her schoolmates. It is obvious that that is precisely where she belongs. (See Figure 3.)

More ambitiously, *Howie Helps Himself*[109] visually explains the ramifications of cerebral palsy. The clear illustrations show the adapted educational environment Howie works in, the physical therapy apparatus and accoutrements he uses, and the adaptations Howie and his impaired classmates make. Beyond these tangible representations, the illustrations powerfully pull from the reader a sense of respect for Howie in his efforts to overcome his limitations. Particularly well portrayed

FIGURE 3. From *Rachel* by Elizabeth Fanshawe. Illustrated by Michael Charlton. Illustrations copyright © Michael Charlton 1975. Reprinted by permission of Bradbury Press.

are the frustrations that result from the inevitable dependence on others for satisfaction of simple needs and desires. One illustration shows Howie waiting with an obviously loving and concerned parent to be lifted into his adapted school bus. The regular bus pulling away in the background emphasizes Howie's exclusion and the wistful expression on his face reveals that he is very cognizant of this separation from other children. Lasker's skill in illuminating Howie's trials and successes is excellent. (See Figure 2.)

The illustrations in *From Anna*[110] show a typical "sight-saving" classroom from the 1930s and 1940s. Purposeful activity seems to be taking place in a supportive atmosphere. Anna appears busy and happy. Her low vision is neither exaggerated nor minimized, and the close inspection she must make of her work can be readily observed. That the teacher also wears glasses highlights the commonplace aspect of visual acuity loss and suggests that Anna's problem is one of degree. The portrayals in this work are optimistic, a quality not achieved through denial of the problem or avoidance of its importance. (See Figure 4.)

The Hayburners[111] and *A Dance to Still Music*[112] concern "invisible handicaps." Joey, the retarded man, in the former novel is depicted without condescension. His clothes fit loosely and are rumpled in keeping with his status as a farm laborer. His visage is open and guileless—too innocent and trusting for an adult—and he projects a naive enthusiasm. His appearance in the various illustrations emphasizes his wholly admirable qualities, and this, in concert with his innocence, beautifully supports the characterization presented in the text and hints at the paradox he embodies. (See Figure 1.)

There are no outward visual manifestations of Margaret's deafness in *A Dance to Still Music*. However, one particular poignant illustration reveals the loneliness and utter isolation she has felt since her sudden loss of hearing. The picture forcefully communicates the social implications of deafness. It is a portrait of her fears and concerns rather than of her physical appearance. (See Figure 5.)

Annie's despair is powerfully communicated in one illustration from *Ben and Annie*.[113] The realization that her only source of happiness has been irrevocably severed has overwhelmed her and the message that life without joy is also without value is faultlessly interpreted here. This picture is all the more effective in its contrast with a former illustration in which her unrestrained happiness at her friend's contrivance of a makeshift swing is revealed. The artist's skill in intensifying the emotional climax is a potent asset. (See Figure 6.)

In *Rachel*,[114] *Howie Helps Himself*,[115] and *A Dance to Still Music*,[116] disability is the central focus. When writers use handicapped characters to explore secondary social problems, value systems, and human rela-

FIGURE 4.   Illustration by Joan Sandin from *From Anna* by Jean Little. Illustrations copyright © 1972 by Joan Sandin. Reprinted by permission of Harper & Row, Publishers, Inc.

FIGURE 5.   Illustrated by Charles Robinson. Copyright © 1974 by Barbara Corcoran. From *A Dance to Still Music*. Used by permission of Atheneum Publishers.

tions, illustrations usually depict those characters positively. In too many other books, however, illustrations patronize, mock, or disparage disability.

Time[117] recently recounted the protest by a group of Japanese citizens against the portraits of the animal schemers as blind and crippled in a new edition of the classic story Pinocchio. In the revised version, the cat, faking blindness, is punished by actually realizing his disguise, and becoming blind and the pretense of a crippled leg by the fox is reformulated into an amputated tail. As retribution for their wickedness, the villains are doomed to live out their masquerade. Sufficient numbers of the Japanese public became incensed about this offensive treatment in both text and illustrations to pressure a local publisher to withdraw this edition.

This instance is not the first time Pinocchio has come under attack in Japan. One of the most vociferous critics condemned the illustrations in an earlier version, saying they "give the impression of the abjectness of disability and stress discrimination."[118] While this response may seem excessive, such casual, almost offhand disparagements can be instrumental in shaping the perceptions of children.

All societies encompass and express particular attitudes toward the disabled. One that is sensitive to the needs of impaired people will not support either incidental or deliberate insults and most assuredly will not present these images to their children.

FIGURE 6.   From Ben and Annie by Joan Tate. Illustrated by Judith Gwyn Brown. Reprinted by permission of Doubleday & Company, Inc.

Notes

A short form of reference citation is given here for those works that are cited fully and annotated in Chapter 5.

1. Joseph Carl Grund, *Beyond the Bridge*.
2. James Forman, *The Shield of Achilles*.
3. A. E. Johnson, *A Blues I Can Whistle* (New York: Four Winds, 1969).
4. Harriet May Savitz, *On the Move*.
5. Louisa R. Shotwell, *Roosevelt Grady*.
6. Sulamith Ish-Kishor, *Our Eddie*.
7. Elsie Oakes Barber, *The Trembling Years*.
8. Sally Watson, *Other Sandals*.
9. John D. Fitzgerald, *The Great Brain*.
10. Phyllis A. Whitney, *Secret of the Emerald Star*.
11. Betty Cavanna, *Joyride*.
12. Mary Canty, *The Green Gate*.
13. Clarice Pont, *The Immediate Gift*.
14. Margaret and George Ogan, *Water Rat*.
15. Lila Perl, *No Tears for Rainey*.
16. Jeanette Eyerly, *The Phaedra Complex*.
17. Susan Terris, *The Drowning Boy*.
18. Henry Treece, *The Dream Time*.
19. James Forman, *The Shield of Achilles*.
20. Laura Ingalls Wilder, *Little Town on the Prairie*.
21. Laura Ingalls Wilder, *These Happy Golden Years*.
22. Marguerite Harmon Bro, *Su-Mei's Golden Year*.
23. Cora Cheney, *Key of Gold*.
24. Ruth Wolff, *A Crack in the Sidewalk*.
25. John Neufeld, *Touching*.
26. Ivan Southall, *Let the Balloon Go*.
27. Barbara Rinkoff, *The Watchers*.
28. Roy Brown, *Escape the River*.
29. Judy Blume, *Deenie*.
30. Jean Little, *Take Wing*.
31. Bianca Bradbury, *Nancy and Her Johnny-O*.
32. M. E. Kerr, *Dinky Hocker Shoots Smack!*
33. Gunilla B. Norris, *The Top Step*.
34. Constance C. Greene, *The Unmaking of Rabbit*.
35. Harriet May Savitz, *The Lionhearted*.
36. Vera and Bill Cleaver, *Me Too*.
37. Kin Platt, *The Boy Who Could Make Himself Disappear*.
38. K. M. Peyton, *Flambards*.
39. Marilyn Sachs, *The Bears' House*.
40. Ella Thorp Ellis, *Celebrate the Morning*.
41. Louise Stinetorf, *A Charm for Paco's Mother*.
42. Clarice Pont, *The Immediate Gift*.
43. Judy Blume, *Deenie*.
44. Elsie Oakes Barber, *The Trembling Years*.
45. John Neufeld, *Touching*.
46. James Hamilton-Paterson, *The House in the Waves*.

47. Ella Thorp Ellis, *Celebrate the Morning*.
48. Jean Little, *From Anna*.
49. Edith Fisher Hunter, *Sue Ellen*.
50. Matt Christopher, *Long Shot for Paul*.
51. Phyllis A. Whitney, *Nobody Likes Trina*.
52. Babbis Friis-Baastad, *Kristy's Courage*.
53. Lou and Zena Shumsky, *Shutterbug*.
54. Joe Lasker, *He's My Brother*.
55. Kin Platt, *Hey, Dummy*.
56. John Neufeld, *Lisa, Bright and Dark*.
57. Kin Platt, *The Boy Who Could Make Himself Disappear*.
58. Alberta Armer, *Screwball*.
59. Adrienne Richard, *Wings*.
60. Beverly Butler, *Light a Single Candle*.
61. Kathryn Vinson, *Run with the Ring*.
62. Bill J. Carol, *Crazylegs Merrill*.
63. Elizabeth Stucley, *The Contrary Orphans*.
64. Kin Platt, *Hey, Dummy*.
65. Constance C. Greene, *The Unmaking of Rabbit*.
66. Lou and Zena Shumsky, *Shutterbug*.
67. Regina Woody, *Almena's Dogs*.
68. Shannon Garst, *Red Eagle*.
69. Alberta Armer, *Screwball*.
70. Richard Parker, *He Is Your Brother*.
71. Virginia H. Ormsby, *Mountain Magic for Rosy*.
72. Babbis Friis-Baastad, *Don't Take Teddy*, p. 38.
73. C. Walter Hodges, *The Namesake*.
74. Afton Huff, *The Silent Message*, p. 53.
75. Ruth Wolff, *A Crack in the Sidewalk*, p. 37.
76. Reginald Ottley, *The Bates Family*.
77. Sally Watson, *Other Sandals*.
78. Arnold A. Griese, *At the Mouth of the Luckiest River*.
79. Jean Little, *Take Wing*.
80. Julia Cunningham, *Burnish Me Bright*.
81. Rosemary Sutcliff, *The Witch's Brat*.
82. Kin Platt, *Hey, Dummy*.
83. Bruce Lowery, *Scarred*.
84. Veronica Robinson, *David in Silence*, p. 32.
85. Regina Woody, *Almena's Dogs*.
86. Julia First, *Flat on My Face*, p. 27.
87. Ibid., p. 93.
88. Harriet May Savitz, *The Lionhearted*.
89. Louise Dickinson Rich, *Three of a Kind*.
90. Gus Tavo, *Ride the Pale Stallion*.
91. L. Dean Carper, *A Cry in the Wind*.
92. Michael E. Monbeck, *The Meaning of Blindness: Attitudes toward Blindness and Blind People* (Bloomington, Ind.: Indiana University Press, 1973), p. 7.
93. Lorraine Beim, *Triumph Clear*.
94. C. L. Rinaldo, *Dark Dreams*.
95. Earlene W. Luis and Barbara F. Millar, *Wheels for Ginny's Chariot*.
96. Catherine Fowler Magee, *One of the Family*.
97. Pamela Reynolds, *A Different Kind of Sister*.

98. Beverly Butler, *Light a Single Candle*.
99. Beverly Butler, *Gift of Gold*.
100. Jane and Paul Annixter, *The Runner*.
101. Marjorie Rosevear, *The Secret Cowboy*.
102. William Corbin, *The Golden Mare*.
103. Susan Terris, *Plague of Frogs*.
104. Molly Cone, *Simon*, p. 8.
105. Joan Tate, *Ben and Annie*.
106. Patsey Gray, *Show Ring Rogue*.
107. Joan Fassler, *Howie Helps Himself*.
108. Elizabeth Fanshawe, *Rachel*.
109. Joan Fassler, *Howie Helps Himself*.
110. Jean Little, *From Anna*.
111. Gene Smith, *The Hayburners*.
112. Barbara Corcoran, *A Dance to Still Music*.
113. Joan Tate, *Ben and Annie*.
114. Elizabeth Fanshawe, *Rachel*.
115. Joan Fassler, *Howie Helps Himself*.
116. Barbara Corcoran, *A Dance to Still Music*.
117. "Nose Out of Joint," *Time*, January 10, 1977, p. 27.
118. Ibid.

5

An Annotated Guide to Juvenile Fiction Portraying the Handicapped, 1940–1975

This chapter contains individual descriptions of each of 311 books of juvenile fiction published between 1940 and 1975. The annotations are presented alphabetically by author's name, but access can also be obtained by consulting the Title Index and the Subject Index by particular impairment. Each annotation consists of a plot description and, when appropriate, excerpts from dialogue or narrative. The plot description is followed by *Analysis*, commentary that encompasses both interpretive and literary treatment, as well as some discussion of illustrations when pertinent. Since the focus of this book is on the treatment of impairment, this issue will receive the most attention, sometimes exaggerating its importance in the narratives. Stories are coded for reading level as follows.

Reading Level Designations

YC (young child); approximately 5–8 years old or in grades K–3. These children will need guidance in comprehending meaning and interpreting stories. They are relative newcomers to literature and have had limited personal experience. They may read simple stories by themselves but are dependent on pictures to carry part of the literary message. They may confuse fiction and life and believe that characters in books are real people.

MC (mature child); approximately 9–12 years old or in grades 4–6. These children have the ability to read more mature books. They have wider experiential backgrounds, both personal and vicarious, and are able to read books of over 100 pages keeping plot line and characters straight. Character identification is frequently strong, and loyalties to particular authors, genres, or content areas often develop. Their response is frequently excessive and approved models are inflated to heroic proportions. Children at this stage can begin to understand dissimilar life patterns.

YA (young adolescent); approximately 13–15 years old or in grades 7–9. Young adolescents have the ability to read more mature books. They have developed some sense of chronological time, so books of historical fiction can have meaning. They understand and are interested in boy/girl relationships, can perceive subtleties in human behavior. They are caught in the conflict of needing to conform to peer pressure while simultaneously developing their unique identities. By this stage, it is possible for them to understand and enjoy books using more sophisticated literary techniques, such as flashbacks, subplots, and nonomniscient perspectives.

MA (mature adolescent); approximately 16–18 years old or in grades 10–12. These readers can understand novels of considerable complexity. They are potentially responsive to ambiguities of human behavior as expressed in literature, to paradoxes, to multiple levels of meaning, and to philosophical, as opposed to pragmatic, approaches. They usually see themselves as mature and are interested in concerns of the adult world.

Any designation of reading level must of necessity be arbitrary. Obviously, children in any particular grade or age level will display tremendous variation in intellectual, social, and emotional maturity. We feel, then, that maturity level may be a better guide than chronological age to the ability of a child to understand a book. Approximate age and grade designations are included, but they are only general suggestions. It is entirely possible for a child reading on an eighth-grade level to exhibit maturity traits and interests of a fifth-grade or younger child. Conversely, extensive background information in combination with high interest can substantially elevate the level on which a child can comfortably read.

Following the reading designation is the *impairment designation*. If several impairments are listed, those disablements are a central or critical element in the novel. If the disablement is of secondary or peripheral importance, it (or they) is separated from the central disability or disabilities by a semicolon, and is introduced by the word "also." Some impairments are of minor importance and have been omitted in the *Disability* heading but may be mentioned in the text of the annotation. Most impairment groupings are self-explanatory except for General Health

Problems, which is a miscellaneous collection including unspecified impairments and such illnesses as cardiac disorders, rheumatism, and so on. The nine disability designations are: Auditory Impairment, Cosmetic Impairment, Emotional Dysfunction, General Health Problems, Intellectual Impairment, Neurological Impairment, Orthopedic Impairment, Speech Impairment, and Visual Impairment.

Alcock, Gudrun. *Turn the Next Corner*. New York: Lothrop, Lee and Shepard, 1969. 160 pp. Reading Level: MC
Disability: Orthopedic Impairment

Ritchie's father is in prison for embezzlement and the family's reduced circumstances compel a move to a small apartment in downtown Chicago. Ritchie intervenes in a fracas where two black boys attempt to hassle a third, who is disabled, twisting his wheelchair and throwing his books in the street. Slugger invites his would-be rescuer to his apartment in the same building and their friendship grows as they share Slugger's gym equipment. Although a fracture of his lower spine has left his leg paralyzed, Slugger is absolutely determined to eventually walk again. An operation provides some relief for Slugger and subsequently he can stand with the assistance of a leg brace. Ritchie, embarrassed by his father's situation, is panicky that the information will become common knowledge, and this fear is not greatly reduced when his father comes home on parole. When the boys search for Slugger's runaway kitten, one of the thieves taunts Ritchie with the observation that their fathers share the same parole officer. This so mortifies Ritchie that he loses the spirit to fight. When Slugger finds out, he says there will be no change in their relationship: He won't feel sorry for Ritchie since Ritchie did not feel pity for him.

Analysis. The theme of imprisonment is woven throughout the story: the real prisons for two parents as well as the kitten in the cage at the pound, the temporary prison of Slugger's chair, the economic and social prison of the ghetto, and the self-imposed prison into which Ritchie's predicament has locked him. Slugger's physical struggle parallels Ritchie's moral one. Slugger's response to his fetters is the most direct and healthy—he is not only resolved to escape but he makes continuous efforts to further his plan. The descriptions of his rehabilitation exercises are presented as are some of his problems in dealing with architectural barriers. Slugger is portrayed as a physical and competitive youth, but his weaknesses are revealed in his fears of losing a friend and in his bossiness. The sensitively drawn faces of the two troubled boys on the dust jacket are an excellent introduction to this upbeat, well-constructed, well-researched story.

Aldridge, James. *A Sporting Proposition*. Boston: Little, Brown, 1973.
206 pp. Reading Level: YA
Disability: Orthopedic Impairment

Scott Pirie is the son of Scottish immigrant parents who have been settled on poor scrub farmland outside a small Australian town. Scott used to accompany a neighbor child to school on the back of an old mare. One day the mare threw the child, who was killed, and the animal had to be shot. This left Scott five miles a day to walk to school. His parents, barely able to subsist, could hardly provide transportation. The settlement agency is pressured into providing a pony for Scott so he can get to school. Soon Scott and the pony, Taff, both half-wild, ornery, and fiercely independent, are inseparable. Suddenly the pony disappears.

Ellison Eyre owns a major ranch in the territory. His daughter, Josie, is paralyzed below the hips as a result of polio. Proud and independent, she avoids being seen in her wheelchair since she abhors the possibility of being pitied. Her father fixes a cart to which he harnesses a pony. She soon loves this pony, Bo, and spends much time driving alone, happily mobile.

The town has an annual agricultural show that includes racing events. Josie enters with her new pony for the "best turnout" event. Scott sees Josie's pony and knows it is his Taff. He tries to grab it but is restrained by Eyre and ejected from the fairgrounds. Soon after, Josie's pony disappears. Her father, outraged, makes the police charge Scott with theft, although the pony is not in his possession and cannot be found. Mr. Quayle undertakes the boy's defense and prevails upon Scott to produce the pony, which then is secured in the animal pound. Josie visits it every day, convinced it is Bo, and Scott feeds it, confident that it is Taff.

Mr. Quayle persuades the court that the pony might actually be Scott's and that the court's proper role is to determine whose pony it is and then return it to its rightful owner. Debate about proprietorship divides and electrifies the town: Some swear the animal belongs to Josie and others hotly claim it is Scott's. Mr. Quayle suggests to the court that the pony is the only one that can be relied upon to acknowledge its true owner. A corral is constructed for the pony through which it will emerge equidistant from Scott and Josie. Whichever one it goes to will be acknowledged as the true owner. Arrangements are made that satisfy the town's sense of fair play and appeal to its gambling instincts. The pony, vacillating, finally chooses Scott. It is clear that the pony is both Bo as well as Taff, having been caught by Eyre after it returned to a wild herd and tamed a second time. Josie and her father later visit Scott and

Josie asks if he will come with Taff to visit her home to which Scott agrees.

Analysis. A Sporting Proposition is an excellent, well-written, compelling and tightly constructed story with fine characterization and a strong sense of place. Josie, an arrogant, stiff-necked little girl, is never sentimentalized. Josie's independence and pride are carried over into her feeling about her disability. Although some of the townspeople pity Josie, and this colors their attitude about the Taff-Bo controversy, it is clearly an inappropriate and unnecessary response which she rejects. Aldridge skillfully contrasts the highly active impoverished boy with the immobile rich girl, refusing to romanticize either person or condition.

Allan, Mabel Esther. *Ship of Danger*. New York: Abelard-Schuman, 1974. 153 pp. Reading Level: YA
Disability: Auditory Impairment

Nella's father is purser on a cruise ship that is part of a financially shaky line. She is estranged from him but agrees to take her mother's place on a voyage to the Canary Islands. She meets Nola, the ship doctor's daughter, who lost her hearing in a bomb blast in Ireland. Nola, whose speech-reading skill is excellent, observes someone talking about a plot involving a bomb, and tells Nella. Nola is further persuaded of the accuracy of her perceptions when she is the object of an attempted poisoning. Along with Nella and Guy, a junior ship's officer, she surreptitiously follows the members of the cabal to a house on one of the stopover islands. When Nella tries to convince her father that something is amiss, he angrily rejects the "evidence" because it comes from Nola: "You mean you've based all this on something Nola . . . says she can lip read? Don't you realize that that poor girl has had a load of trouble, and is probably not far from a mental case?" Undaunted, after overhearing some sailors agree to meet at a house in Santa Cruz, the group tracks them down. They are observed, kidnapped, and drugged. Finally they are brought back to the ship, knowing that the ship is to be held for a million pounds ransom, but unable to do anything about it. During the hijacking, the young people, including Nola's boyfriend, Rufus, are taken to an island as hostages. With luck and a clever plan, they overwhelm their captors, ultimately trick the remaining conspirators, and save the ship as well as the fortunes of the shipping line. Nola and Rufus marry and Guy proposes to Nella.

Analysis. When Nola is first introduced, she is seen as restricted in her abilities and is distrusted and pitied. Nella presumes: "It must be a dreadful life. The more I think of it, the worse it seems. Nothing but blank, dead silence." But Nella soon learns the necessary adaptation to make to her new friend: "I had to make sure that she was looking at me before I spoke. But I was growing used to it and she didn't seem to mind if I put my hand on her arm and turned her toward me. And I'd already realized that she was highly intelligent and could be amusing, though I got the impression that her sense of humor was a little rusty." The perception of Nola by others changes through the course of the story. First people tend to respond in terms of stereotypes, but Nola forces them to rethink their initial reactions. The novel is fractionally better than the usual romance mystery, but the similarity of the girls' names seems unnecessarily confusing.

Allen, Elizabeth. *The Loser*. New York: Dutton, 1965. 128 pp. Reading Level: YA
Disability: Emotional Dysfunction

Dietz and her younger sister, Lee, live a conventional upper-middle-class existence in the Southwest. Dietz coasts through high school—dating, baton twirling, and ignoring suggestions by her teachers that she is capable of advanced academic work. Lee, however, finds life difficult and, in moments of despair, consoles herself by writing poetry. Dietz becomes intrigued with an asocial neighbor, Denny, and she believes his outright fabrications. Distressed by her failing grades and growing preoccupation with this boy, her parents discourage the friendship. Nevertheless, it is suggested that their relationship symbolizes the shucking off of Dietz's conventional behavior, the examination of issues of consequence, and the widening of her perspectives. When Denny admires one of Lee's poems, she gives him a copy. The three youngsters attend a poetry competition, discovering that Lee has earned an honorable mention. After it is announced that Denny's poem, "The Loon," has won first prize, Lee unaccountably dashes from the auditorium. Later, she reveals that the winning poem was actually hers. Dietz becomes less infatuated and more objective about Denny's irrational behavior, and is relieved at being able to interrupt their relationship during the summer when she will be working at a camp for handicapped children. Denny, perhaps deliberately, traps himself when the police are after him for drag racing, becoming upset when his father will not intervene and his usual tactic of blaming others for the consequences of his behavior fails. At last, Denny appears to recognize his need for help and has asked for the names of several psychiatrists. Dietz's father, optimistically and unwarrantedly, predicts that since the youth is bright and resourceful, he will probably be able to abandon his obsessive fantasizing.

Analysis. Certain familiar patterns emerge: The exceptional character interacts with the two major female characters so as to enable them to be more mature, sensitive, self-aware, and, in Dietz's case, less the mindless socialite. The characterization of Denny is particularly unsatisfying and incomplete. The reader never understands why the boy is a thief and compulsive liar or why he finally decides to seek psychiatric assistance.

Anderson, Paul. *The Boy and the Blind Storyteller*. Illus. by Yong Hwan Kim. New York: William R. Scott, 1964. 91 pp. Reading Level: MC
Disability: Visual Impairment

Following a trail of smoke, Au Sung, a young Korean boy, discovers an opening in some rocks that leads to a cave. To his surprise, he finds an ancient, blind storyteller inside. The two become very friendly and the old man reveals that he tells fortunes by detecting what people wish to hear and then predicting their desires. Au Sung returns many times to hear the tales he has come to love. The young boy asks his father to weave the storyteller some shoes as a present, but then decides he would rather give a gift that is truly his own, and that gift should be a story.

Analysis. The traditional function of the blind man as fortune teller finds odd expression in this tale. The old man is portrayed in both illustrations and text as eccentric and quaint, but is nonetheless deferred to. The dedication hints that the storyteller may be a synedoche for the Korean nation—strange to Western eyes, but worthy of respect. The children of the village are initially frightened by the blind man, as their parents expect them to be. As they know him better, imitate being blind, and learn how he is able to manage without sight, he becomes less mysterious and their fears recede. Despite the old man's confessed trickery as a prophet, Au Sung's decision to likewise be a storyteller suggests that he is a model worth emulating.

Andrew, Prudence. *Mister O'Brien*. Nashville: Nelson, 1972. 161 pp. Reading Level: MC
Disability: Orthopedic Impairment

Christopher Porter is miserable about his pronounced limp, the elaborate leg brace he must wear to support his underdeveloped leg, the patronizing way adults treat him, and his friendless existence. One day he encounters Mr. O'Brien, whose smile immediately and unwarrantedly heartens him. At school that day Penny Marshall sees Christopher and proffers her friendship. Penny is dirty, dishevelled, smelly, and, unsurprisingly, a social outcast. She becomes his only friend. Christopher visits Penny's home, which is as impoverished as the meanest Dickensian hovel. Her mother, poor but honest, works to support her large brood while Penny cheerfully struggles to cook and clean despite an outdoor latrine, no hot water, and mold growing on the walls.

Christopher's mother tries to persuade him that Penny is an unsuitable companion, but he becomes the girl's protector and determines to help her find a new dwelling. Some delinquents torment him as he leaves her home, but Mr. O'Brien appears, shouting such precepts as "Have fortitude! Be brave! At least you haven't got scurvy. . . . Endure! Struggle on against great odds!" This encouragement enables Christopher to face up to the four older boys and scare them off with no more than a fierce look. It soon becomes apparent that Mr. O'Brien is invisible to all but Christopher, whose reports at home convince his parents that their son is being trailed by a child molester. Evidently they are not conversant with the habits of guardian angels. Christopher locates an agency called REFUGE that helps needy families find new housing. He convinces himself that it will help Penny, and prepares to take part in its next fund-raising event—a walkathon. As a participant, he solicits sponsors who pay an agreed-upon sum for each mile he walks. Overestimating an eleven-year-old boy's ability to act with moderation, his doctors blithely override his mother's objections and give their permission. Christopher begins the journey, but soon his crippled leg develops huge blisters and painful cramps. Although in great anguish, he presses on. The pity of observers is degrading and he becomes angry at their clumsy attempts to be helpful. At his moment of greatest despair, Mr. O'Brien—"his usual cheery, rosy self, complete with cap and scarf, dazzling golden sweater, and single sturdy sneakered foot"—appears and energizes Christopher's will. He completes his ten-mile walk, only to find that REFUGE cannot help Penny.

A few days later there is a knock on the door. An old lady "with a sharp little hump between her shoulder blades" enters and offers to give Penny's family a new apartment. Mrs. Saloman is very rich, has no family, and gives money away to the deserving poor. She explains to Christopher: "I have a fellow feeling for you because of your leg."

Analysis. This book is a perfect disaster. The people are caricatures, events so unlikely as to be ludicrous, and writing style reminiscent of the cheerful improving little books of the last century. Some of the incidents are unabashedly banal, the Horatio Alger finale, for example.

The author seems confused about Christopher's need for crutches. At one point, he "wanted to get up and walk out of the room but he couldn't because he couldn't reach his crutches." This would seem to indicate considerable dependence; yet, at most other times, including during his ten-mile walk, he manages without them. Christopher's shoe and brace are described in some detail. These consist of three straps and two iron rods, the bottoms of which are screwed into a heavy surgical boot. The picture on the book jacket minimizes this, concealing the affected foot behind his other one and reducing the apparatus to insignificance.

The struggle of a child to overcome his handicap, find friendship, and assert a measure of independence and power is potentially a believable one. Unfortunately, in this book, although real issues have been conceptualized, fairy-tale solutions are proposed.

Annixter, Jane and Paul Annixter. Pseud. J. L. Comfort. *The Runner.* New York: Holiday House, 1956. 220 pp. Reading Level: MC/YA
Disability: Orthopedic Impairment; also general health problems

Since the death of his mother, Clem, known as Shadow, has lived on a ranch with his sick aunt and hardworking, horse-trading, taciturn uncle. Shadow, left with a slight limp after recovering from polio, works breaking in horses and training polo ponies. Whenever he has free time, he is preoccupied with watching the wild ponies that graze on the nearby mountains. He yearns to catch and tame one that he has named Runner. Runner is injured by some cowboys attempting to capture the herd. Shadow tracks the terrified colt, rescues it, and returns with it to the ranch. With love and patience, he breaks the colt, but one day it escapes the corral and returns to the mountains accompanied by Shadow's dog. In a few days the family will leave the ranch for their winter home and so Shadow searches desperately and unsuccessfully for the animals before he must leave the ranch. Runner and Poojer, the dog, living off their wits through the terrible winter, survive, despite hunger and attacks from wild animals. In the spring the family returns to the ranch and the horse and dog, lean and strong but badly mauled, soon appear. Shadow is astonished and overjoyed to see them, having almost given up hope. Runner is ruined as a show horse but his spirit, strength, and endurance ensure his value as a sire.

Analysis. Shadow is a misnomer since the youth is brave, intelligent, stubborn, and hardworking, qualities that he uses to overcome the aftereffects of polio and to participate fully in the arduous work of a farmhand. The disability is dealt with as just another of life's problems to cope with and overcome. The story of Runner and Shadow is a fast-paced, literate, exciting one about an animal and a boy who struggle and survive.

Armer, Alberta. *Screwball*. Illus. by W. T. Mars. Cleveland: World, 1963. 202 pp. Reading Level: MC
Disability: Orthopedic Impairment

Polio has markedly changed the course of Mike's life compared to that of his unaffected twin, Patrick. When finances oblige the family to move, Patrick, a natural athlete who has many social skills, is absorbed easily into the life of the new school. Mike not only has few friends but finds himself abused and harassed by the kids. Ambivalent when Patrick rescues him from fights, and resentful when he fails at sports or when his teacher unfeelingly derides his poor handwriting, he increasingly is truant from school. Duffy, a coach who is also the attendance officer, tries to give Mike advice and to help him socially, but to no avail. Mike has good mechanical skills and when Duffy gives the twins the rules for the soap box derby, he becomes excited about the project. Both boys build racers, but when they practice, Patrick inevitably wins, even though Mike's is the better constructed vehicle. Patrick generously oversees Mike's exercise program—a project that attempts to correct Mike's weakness in steering. Although they both win the first heat, ultimately the better workmanship in Mike's entry pays off, and Mike is a jubilant and grateful winner.

Analysis. In a nicely paced story, the author peers into the specially painful situation of one twin being disabled. Although this can be corrosive, the basic affection between the two mitigates against real jealousy. Armer explores Mike's feelings in depth and the reader can obtain some insights into his thoughts and emotions. One unusual inclusion is Mike's awareness of how he manipulates people with his handicap. The crippled boy's name is used oddly: Until he wins, Michael is called Mike; yet Patrick, the intact brother, maintains his full name consistently. Mike's other appellation, which describes his awkwardness at bat, forms the title for the book. The abuse taken by Mike is described vividly as is the cruel scene in the schoolroom where the teacher mocks his poor writing ability, ignorant of the connection between that and his crippled right arm. The dialogue in the novel is overly stiff, but the carefully designed scenes compensate and the result is a book with much realistic information about the social, emotional, and physical consequences of polio and a hero whose struggle is as much with himself as it is with the external world.

Armer, Alberta. *Steve and the Guide Dogs*. Illus. by J. D. Kocsis. Cleveland: World, 1965. 190 pp. Reading Level: MC/YA
Disability: Visual Impairment

This novel details initial failures and eventual success in training an animal to be a guide dog. Two incidental blind characters are included: the grandfather of Steve's friend, who runs a magazine stand and does wood carving, and the future owner of Steve's dog, who is a musician.

Analysis. Although there is some stereotyping in the occupations selected, both of these characters are developed very naturally and are portrayed as competent, self-employed, independent individuals who cope with their disabilities. Brotherhood, a minor theme in this book, emphasizes the need for better relations between whites and Native American Indians.

Arthur, Ruth M. *A Candle in Her Room*. Illus. by Margery Gill. New York: Atheneum, 1966. 212 pp. Reading Level: YA
Disability: Emotional Dysfunction

The Grenville family moves to Wales where Judith, who had always been the least congenial of the three daughters, turns openly hostile. She steals a doll with supernatural powers that her younger sister had found. The doll begins to exert its influence over Judith, who becomes completely ruthless. When Melissa, the oldest sister, approaches a cliff, she falls over it into the sea, and although she is rescued, her legs are paralyzed. Doctors are unable to find any medical reason for her inability to walk and suggest that her problem is purely psychological. Soon after, Judith runs off with Melissa's fiancé and is not heard from again until she returns home following his death. She brings with her a daughter whom Melissa raises while Judith pursues her obsession with art and becomes even more hateful in her relations with her family. When her daughter grows up, she marries a Polish citizen and they travel to his native land, where he becomes part of the Resistance. Hounded by the Nazis, he dies after the war as a result of the deprivations and suffering he endured. As the years pass and Melissa has no word from her niece, she despairs of ever hearing from her again. Frequently when alone she senses a ghostlike presence of a young girl. Deducing that this apparition may be the daughter of her beloved niece, she determines to regain the use of her paralyzed legs and search for the child. After more than a year of therapy, Melissa is at last able to walk. She succeeds in tracking down the girl, Nina, and returns home with her. Nina chooses to stay in Judith's old room where she discovers the evil doll. She too succumbs to the doll's power but, realizing the danger not only to herself but also to Melissa, frees herself by destroying the malevolent object.

Analysis. Melissa's hysterical paralysis and Judith's irrational behavior are both attributed to the powers of the wicked doll. One was an innocent victim and the other, at least at first, a willing collaborator. Once sufficiently motivated, the invalid was able to overcome decades of inertia and, through extensive therapy, to walk. The structure of a gothic novel such as this allows for the utilization of irrational events, so congruence with realism is irrelevant. Nevertheless, the linking of emotional dysfunction with evil forces is unfortunate.

Arthur, Ruth M. *Portrait of Margarita*. Illus. by Margery Gill. New York: Atheneum, 1968. 185 pp. Reading Level: YA
Disability: Emotional Dysfunction

Margarita is in boarding school when she hears of the death of her parents in an airplane accident. Her guardianship is assumed by her cousin, Francis, a kindly but aloof person who opens his home to her. She visits him in a little village outside London where his spiteful former governess, Miss Laura, expresses open hostility toward her. Margarita meets people in the village with whom she becomes friendly, particularly Giles, a painter; his wife, Martha; and their two young daughters. One of the girls, Stella, an autistic child, gradually begins to respond to Margarita's friendly overtures. Giles paints Margarita's portrait, which is viciously destroyed by Miss Laura. The cruel old lady sends Margarita on an errand by a route she knows to be treacherous. The girl is prevented from completing her mission by the ghost of a long dead dog, and her enemy, checking to see if her plan succeeded, is trapped by a washed-out bridge and drowns. Margarita returns to school, but is invited to her cousin's Italian villa when the term ends. She joins him there in an idyllic interlude. She hears from Martha, who reports that "Stella is slowly improving" and describes children at the clinic who are much more disturbed than her daughter. This intelligence leads Margarita to a major decision. "Suddenly with a blinding flash of insight, I knew what I wanted to be! I wanted to train to be a teacher, specially trained to work with mentally disturbed children, children like Stella." Margarita meets Francis' nephew, and after he is rescued from a terrible storm on the lake she realizes she loves him. She reveals her great secret: Her grandmother was a West Indian and she is consequently of mixed racial ancestry. He accepts this news with equanimity and tells her some day she will have to investigate this aspect of her heritage. A great burden is taken from her shoulders by this advice and she resolves "to weld together the two parts of me, the black and the white, into one complete whole."

Analysis. This formula gothic is complete with vindictive old ladies, portentious omens, ghostly canines, and family secrets. More dark deeds, dangerous encounters, and romantic involvements are hinted at, however, than actually transpire. In a few brief scenes some erroneous impressions about autism are promulgated. Stella's mother describes her daughter as "emotionally disturbed, mentally retarded." The doctors are reported to "hope she'll improve a lot," and while hope is not to be discouraged, implied expectations of great improvement are deceiving. Considerable betterment is hinted at over a short space of time, underestimating the resistance of the disorder to easy remediation. The disability functions in the story as window dressing, allowing the heroine to establish credentials as a compassionate, caring person.

Arthur, Ruth M. *The Saracen Lamp.* Illus. by Margery Gill. New York: Atheneum, 1970. 210 pp. Reading Level: YA
Disability: Orthopedic Impairment

This three-part segmented story is loosely connected through the successive appearances of a beautifully made lamp. It is first given by a Saracen captain to a fourteenth-century French girl who is unhappily married to an English knight. The girl has a prophetic vision of a girl in a chair with wheels. Several hundred years later, when faced with a loveless marriage, the new possessor of the lamp attempts to sell it and realize enough money to escape. The escapade is disastrous and the owner dies. The current heroine is recovering from a debilitating hip infection. She begins to communicate with the ghost of a long-dead former character. When she is persuaded to try to walk, her neurotic need for mystical communication lessens and her psychological and physical rehabilitation begins. The lamp is located and returned to its rightful place in her home.

Analysis. This pseudo-gothic tale is good in concept and unsuccessful in realization. The handicap, like the lamp, is a mere device to tie the characters and centuries together. Some information on rehabilitation and attendant psycholgical stress is presented; however, it is exaggerated for dramatic purposes. The strong, precise illustrations are disharmonious with the mystical tone and the conclusion seems neat and manufactured.

Baker, Margaret J. *The Bright High Flyer.* Illus. by Earle B. Winslow. New York: Longmans, Green, 1957. 113 pp. Reading Level: MC
Disability: Orthopedic Impairment

The Bennet family leaves London for their annual holiday. Deceived by an advertisement, they check into and then quickly out of a caravan camp disagreeably directed by Mr. Johnson. Stranded, they inquire about alternative accommodations and lease pleasant rooms from Mrs. Merit. Unfortunately, the landlady's daughter, Peggy Joyce, is unfriendly. She becomes particularly irritable when the Bennet children approach an old stagecoach named "The Bright High Flyer," which is stored in the barn. The three young Bennets picnic by a stream reputed to have curative powers. They decide the water actually has improved a cut on their dog and persuade each other that taking Peggy Joyce to the stream would restore the functioning of her arm, which had been debilitated by polio. Knowing she would resist, they kidnap her, blindfolding and gagging the terrified girl. They bathe her arm and force her to drink some of the water from the stream. She escapes and sick and hysterical from coercion and fear races home. Ashamed and chagrined at how their Good Samaritan intentions caused havoc, the children go to town to find a conciliatory present for Peggy. There they learn that the stagecoach originally belonged to an ancestor of Peggy's. Claws Johnson (so named because of the hook he used as a prosthesis) purchased the vehicle knowing some treasure was secreted in it, but still had not found it when he died. The contemporary Mr. Johnson from the caravan has been pressuring Mrs. Merit to sell him the coach. Almost ready to do so, she hesitates. After an abortive break-in, the children search the coach thoroughly and find a valuable diamond in it. The would-be thief, who is unmasked as the current Mr. Johnson, is revealed to be a descendant of the nefarious Claws Johnson. The Bennet children and Peggy are reconciled. They play together on a hillside where Peggy, seeing a snake strike at the dog, rescues the animal, using her damaged and formerly useless arm to do so.

Analysis. Claws Johnson's hook is merely a stage prop that adds modestly to his villainous stature. Peggy's last-chapter effort to use her arm underscores a popular attitude toward disability: One can instantaneously overcome handicaps by trying harder, a situation true in regrettably few instances. Peggy's disability contributes to her general grouchiness, but the children perceive this as passive acceptance of the disability and unwillingness to participate in her own rehabilitation. The plot is contrived, depending on farfetched, unlikely events and chance happenings. The characterizations are thin and the pacing unhurried—in short, a modest, forgettable story.

Baker, Margaret J. *The Sand Bird.* Illus. by Floyd Garet. Nashville: Nelson, 1973. 158 pp. Reading Level: MC
Disability: Auditory Impairment

The Minton children, including Nobs, who is deaf, buy a sand-filled glass bird who informs them of his ability to grant wishes. After several outlandish but unsatisfying ones, they light on the device of an imaginary uncle in Australia who bombards them with fabulous gifts. Complications and adventures ensue, but all works out well.

Analysis. Deafness is not Nobs' overriding characteristic; he is just a very normal boy who happens to be deaf. He deals with his hearing loss and his hearing aid with healthy matter-of-factness. The author convincingly re-creates a child's world and provides exemplary models for accommodation to the demands of the disability. The illustrations harmonize with both the content and tone of the story. The inter-weaving of ordinary child characters within imaginative situations pro-duces a delightful, unorthodox fantasy.

Barber, Elsie Oakes. *The Trembling Years.* New York: Macmillan, 1949. 237 pp. Reading Level: YA/MA
Disability: Orthopedic Impairment

During her first semester at college, Kathy Storm becomes desper-ately sick with polio. Weeks pass in pain, fever, and brief interludes of consciousness. Then paralysis sets in and she loses control over both legs and her right arm. When the danger of dying passes, the nurses leave her alone with her thoughts and fears for hours on end. She hears another patient being moved into the room across the hall. Max, now in his thirties, had polio as a child and is scheduled for surgery to attempt to straighten his underdeveloped legs sufficiently to permit him to walk. The two form a close friendship as they talk to each other across the hall. Max understands her despair and anguish and is able to pro-vide some solace and comfort. Kathy thinks constantly of the days when she had physical control and is filled with self-pity. It is the depths of the Depression and Kathy's brother is desperate for work. Over-whelmed by Kathy's mounting hospital bills, he tells her that walking the streets day after day searching for nonexistent jobs is also cause for distress; that other people have problems too. When Kathy is alone she calls out to Max to ask him what he does when he is angry. He tells her he draws. When she asks if that cures it, he tells her no—that's what he does but it doesn't change his anger. When Max visits her in her room for the first time just before he is discharged, she asks him if the worse is over or yet to come. He tells her it will get worse when she leaves and has to live as a cripple among healthy people.

When Kathy has recovered sufficiently, a physical therapist visits her to assess her muscle impairment. The physical rehabilitative process begins, but months pass with little change. One day a young man drops by. He is a frequent visitor to another patient on the floor. Much to her family's distress, he begins to visit Kathy regularly. They neither like nor trust him, but he perks up Kathy's spirits with his games and light chatter. He arranges for the woman he visits to give Kathy's family some money for Kathy's medical expenses. The woman explains that she often donates money to the poor and needy—in this case, Kathy. Kathy is humiliated, but too desperate to be proud. Soon after, her ben-efactor disappears with a check he had stolen from his mentor and some money he had taken from Kathy and her family.

Kathy is finally discharged from the hospital. Her former boyfriend, who has been able to find innumerable excuses for avoiding her, becomes intolerably inadequate. She begins a time of withdrawal and despondency, seeing her limitations contrasting painfully with the easy, unself-conscious movements of everyone else. Kathy decides to return to college and begins practicing walking. To do so, she must lean on someone for support and use her abdominal muscles to force her useless leg forward. One day, when her brother is late meeting her after class, she tries to walk by herself. She falls but is helped by Peter, a young man with whom she becomes friendly. When she, Peter, and her brother go sailing, the boat tips over and Kathy resists being saved, seeing death as a release from her unhappiness. She is rescued and gradually begins to accept the idea that "the older you grow the less important being lame will seem." Kathy finishes college and accepts Peter's proposal of marriage when she realizes that she can be of genuine assistance to him in his career and his life.

Analysis. The Trembling Years is a thoroughly satisfactory treatment of the physiological, psychological, and social ramifications of a severely debilitating disease. No effort is made to minimize or exaggerate the kind and extent of pain and functional impairment caused by polio. The hospitalization, treatment, and evaluative and rehabilitative procedures are accurately described. The familial stresses and dislocations are especially well presented, as is the portrayal of the boyfriend and his response to her illness. Showing him bound by conscience but avidly searching for a socially acceptable means of disengagement illustrates a painful but plausible eventuality. The only false note in this otherwise absorbing, informative, and refreshingly well-written book is the free gift of money that relieves the family's financial crisis.

Bawden, Nina. *The Witch's Daughter.* Philadelphia: Lippincott, 1966. 181 pp. Reading Level: MC
Disability: Visual Impairment

Perdita, who claims to have second sight, is the orphaned daughter of a woman who was ostensibly a witch. She lives with the housekeeper of the mysterious Mr. Smith on an island off the Scottish coast. A boat delivers a Mr. Jones, who comes to see Smith. Also aboard are a botanist's family, including Tim and his blind sister, Janey. Tim finds an unusual red stone, which he later learns is a ruby, in a cave and gives it to Janey. When their father goes to her room, he is viciously attacked by an unknown assailant and must be airlifted to a hospital on the mainland. The three children meet and discuss the puzzling behavior of Smith and Jones as well as the mysterious events surrounding some precious stones. They decide to meet again at the cave where Tim found the ruby. There Perdita shows them Jones' picture in a newspaper accompanied by an account of a jewel robbery in a store where Jones worked as a clerk. Tim concludes that the "theft" was a setup and the two men are the thieves. Later, when the children find themselves abandoned in the cave without a light, Janey is able to remember the way out and guides them to safety. The criminals are exposed and Jones is arrested, but his partner, Smith, drowns trying to escape. Returning to the cave, a cache of jewels is found. Perdita's farewell gift of rare flowers, the object of Janey's father's visit to the island, ensures the family's return.

Analysis. Stock characters and clichés abound in this nonetheless exciting story. The assertion that the blind have second sight, a claim made earlier by Perdita, is heard: " 'I know what's happening and I can't see at all,' Janey said triumphantly, 'So I've got second sight too.' " This is later explained as Janey tells Perdita what her scientist father has said about people who are blind or loners: "We've learned to see and hear things other people don't have time to, because they're always too busy just looking and playing. Dad says people like you and me—well—it's as if we'd grown an extra piece of ourselves that other people don't have." Despite a plot heavily dependent on improbable coincidences, the book presents a bright, attractive heroine whose blindness is no bar to her energetic involvement in adventures.

Beim, Jerrold. *Across the Bridge.* Illus. by Thomas Maley. New York: Harcourt, Brace, 1951. 183 pp. Reading Level: MC
Disability: Orthopedic Impairment, Visual Impairment

Jeff moves with his parents and his brother to a home in a poorer section of town. Their new neighborhood is in a factory district and the residents are predominantly Polish. Jeff, a loner, hopes to make new friends, but an encounter with some local boys results in the same teasing and mocking about his poor vision that he was subjected to in his old neighborhood. His mother, goaded by her family, bemoans the social and economic descent her new home signifies. She is particularly distressed at living among Poles, an ethnic group she considers decidedly inferior. Jeff makes friends with Sid, a boy his age, crippled as the result of some unspecified illness. They play together and cooperate in a venture selling newspapers. When a mutual friend is injured by a truck after she dashes into traffic, Jeff explains to his father that children must play in the street because there is no playground available. A proposal for a safe play area becomes a local cause and a petition presented to the city council to build a playground in the district is eventually approved.

Analysis. This is a simple story of vastly more innocent times. The teasing of Jeff because of his glasses seems excessive. Discrimination against those with physical or sensory impairments is paralleled with bias against ethnic minorities. When someone suggests people will buy papers from Sid because of his crippled condition, he denies the accusation and the opportunity is used to emphasize that performance is what really counts. The vocabulary and sentence structure make for easy reading. Characterization is weak and the plot unexciting. In sum, this is a modest story with a mild moral that asks for tolerance for any who differ from the majority.

Beim, Lorraine. *Triumph Clear*. New York: Harcourt, Brace, 1946. 200 pp. Reading Level: YA
Disability: Orthopedic Impairment

Seventeen-year-old Marsh Evans has been accepted at the Warm Springs Foundation in Georgia where she hopes to recuperate quickly from the effects of polio, expecting thereafter to study for a career in the theater. Her younger brother is sent away to boarding school so that her mother can devote all her time to Marsh's recovery. On the train to Georgia, she meets several other patients from whom she learns that her hopes for rapidly resuming her former life are unjustifiably optimistic. At the Foundation, she participates in swimming and physiotherapy, but little else. One night she sneaks into town with a few other patients to find some excitement drinking. The next time it happens she is caught and expelled. Chastened, she begs to be allowed to stay; the administration relents, but she is put on probation. Marsh soon plunges into the social life at the Foundation and even helps put on a play when President Franklin Roosevelt appears for one of his periodic therapeutic vacations. Her career goals are altered to more realistic levels and, upon her return home, she begins a relationship with a young man who appreciates her golden qualities.

Analysis. Triumph Clear is half adolescent romance and half paean of praise for Franklin Roosevelt. The dialogue is stilted and unlikely and cautionary imperatives, such as try harder, cooperate with authorities, don't judge people by appearances, and so on, suffuse the book. The treatment of polio is exaggerated. It is clear that a teenager who is able to take a train alone does not require the full-time attention of her mother to the point where her sibling must be sent away. There is some mildly interesting information about the Warm Springs Foundation, a center for polio victims earlier in this century, but it is not sufficient to breathe life into this tired tale.

Beim, Lorraine and Jerrold Beim. *Sunshine and Shadow*. New York: Harcourt, Brace, 1952. 182 pp. Reading Level: YA
Disability: Orthopedic Impairment

Deciding that an Arizona college would offer optimal climatic conditions after her bout with polio, Marsh Evans is excited when she is accepted there as a drama student. Budge, Marsh's new roommate, explains that her father wears a brace and when the Dean suggests the two would be compatible roommates, Budge agrees since, "I thought how wonderful everyone had been to Dad and it would be like paying them back a little bit to be a roommate to this girl." She meets another student on the way to class and they make a good acting team, but she remains true to her New York boyfriend. When Marsh visits him, he informs her that acting is an impractical vocation for her and she angrily leaves. In a pageant, she is given a large part that demands much physical effort, but despite her discomfort she refuses to withdraw. When her boyfriend visits, she finally acknowledges the validity of his criticism and thinks about redirecting her focus to stage design. He informs Marsh that his firm is transferring him to Arizona and they will be seeing more of each other.

Analysis. This cliché-ridden book does offer some minimal constructive information on the relationship between climate and mobility, and presents a glimpse of a successful businessman functioning in a wheelchair. Additionally, there is some exploration of the problems of reestablishing independence after a severely debilitating illness. The problem of overcompensation is superficially explored. Because of her disability, the heroine feels she must demonstrate competence in the very area of her weakness, as though she needed to prove that she was as good as anyone else. Some of the incidents, such as the rationale for the room assignment, portray stereotyped values that are never discredited.

Berry, Barbara J. *Just Don't Bug Me.* Illus. by Joe E. DeVelasco. Chicago: Follett, 1970. 125 pp. Reading Level: YA
Disability: Orthopedic Impairment

After his arrest with a gang of car strippers, Jonas is removed from an ineffective guardian's custody and remanded to the care of his Uncle Pete, a cowboy clown in a rodeo. Jonas feels he must repress all his feelings of affection. This feeling of vulnerability is an aftermath of the accident in which his parents were killed and he sustained a hip injury. Despite his uncle's friendly overtures, Jonas is either openly belligerent or coldly hostile. The youth rebuffs all offers of friendship, but accepts a job caring for some broncos, hoping to save money for his only wish in life—a shiny, blue motorcycle. When he first observes the hobbling gait of the rodeo hands, he believes that the other cowboys are mocking his limp, but slowly he comes to an awareness of the dangers and consequences of the job. As a result of recklessly accepting a dare, he becomes involved with a horse with whom he feels a kinship, perhaps because of their shared rebelliousness. One night, Jonas spots a haytruck afire in the stable where that horse is quartered and courageously drives it out before he collapses. When he regains consciousness, he alone is able to calm down the animal and lead it from the blazing building. Although the horse dies, Jonas realizes the pain he feels at its loss is partially compensated for by the happiness the relationship brought him. This insight helps him to expunge the fear of losing love and he is able to relate comfortably and openly with his uncle at last.

Analysis. The story is well written and fast-paced and has much insight into the actions and attitudes of a supercool delinquent. The novel looks beneath this pose to the painful fears underlying such behavior. When Jonas is in a setting where his peculiar walk is commonplace and not a mark of difference, he can let down his defenses enough to risk developing relationships again.

> Berry, Erick (pseud.). Allena Best. *Green Door to the Sea.* Illus. by author. New York: Viking, 1955. 192 pp. Reading Level: YA
> *Disability:* Orthopedic Impairment

Letty, sixteen, recovering from polio in Jamaica, has become passive, indecisive, and lacking in self-confidence. Nat, a boy tutored by Letty's mother, is an exemplary, determined, inventive youngster, and, using him as a model, Letty tries to overcome her dependency. Once, while trying to swim, she panics, but is saved by an ichthyologist, who fortuitously happens to be there working on a research theory. Letty ultimately uses a raft, walks on the sea bottom, and even paints underwater. Nat helps the researcher develop a tank so the fish can be sent to a research center and Letty becomes active to the point where she can walk unaided.

Analysis. This book, using polio as a device both to explain the heroine's attitude and as a vehicle for her growth, has little action and gives outlet to some stereotypes about Blacks. Two examples of sodden dialogue reflect Letty's thoughts: She thinks about her nurse, "Still to get along without Miss Dorothy, who had been with her as nurse and companion, counselor, crutch, and kindest and gentlest of friends for all these past months! To try and walk entirely by herself, to try to do everything for herself as she used to do! Letty felt the feeble tears begin to start." Later, she cleverly informs Nat's grandfather of her condition: "And if, thought Letty, after *that* blow you can snatch the sole toy from this poor little invalid che-ild, you cru-el man, your looks belie you. Any man with an expression so like the Great Stone Face must have a heart of custard." Readers looking for good writing, plausible characters, artistic quality in illustrations, and information about illness and rehabilitation had better keep looking.

> Blatter, Dorothy. *Cap and Candle.* Philadelphia: Westminster, 1961. 185 pp. Reading Level: YA/MA
> *Disability:* Auditory Impairment; also general health problems

Filiz is enrolled in the American Girls' School in Turkey. She thinks often of her young deaf sister, Esin, and how she patiently taught her to read and write. The occasional short letters of mostly nouns and a few verbs she receives from her sister give her much pleasure. Later, her own appendectomy and Esin's death from typhoid crystallize her decision to become a nurse. Reaching a compromise with her father, who believes nursing an unfit career for a decent woman and who has already made her betrothal plans, Filiz agrees to marry the man he has chosen if she can first go to nursing school. Her nursing training is arduous but rewarding and she proves herself an apt pupil and a brave and principled health professional. She returns home for her engagement party preparatory to her assignment to a remote mountain dispensary. After her husband is killed, the young Turkish woman decides to continue her career, and volunteers to work in a model village in the mountains. Filiz takes part in the difficult but useful community public health effort, but her advice is often discounted because of her youth and her single status. She encounters a young man whom she met as a nursing student and they begin to work as a team to bring a better life to the rural inhabitants.

Analysis. The author does not disguise the fact that this book is a tract, although it is somewhat more skillfully done than most. There are a number of disabilities and illnesses in the story which is unsurprising given this particular theme. Of special interest is the treatment of Esin, the deaf sister. It is she of the six girls in Filiz's family who dies of typhoid, and her death provides the motivation and rationale for the heroine's choice of occupation. "Oh, Esin, Esin, my dear, my dear! It is you who have given me my chance. You gave your life that I might show them what nursing means. You gave your life that Faruk might live. . . . Now I shall try to do for others what I would have done for you." That there is a supernatural cause-and-effect relationship is underscored: "It is kismet that little Esin's death paves the way for Filiz, who goes with her family's smiles at last to nursing school." Some information is provided on the primitive instruction Esin gets. Her language achievements, given her age and her sister's inexperience, are surprising but possible. The stilted language is typical of attempts to rephrase foreign speech for flavor and interferes only mildly in the flow of reading. Esin plays a small but critical role as the innocent sacrificial character whose death is essential for the realization of the heroine's goals.

Blume, Judy. *Deenie.* Scarsdale, N.Y.: Bradbury, 1973. 159 pp.
Reading Level: YA
Disability: Orthopedic Impairment

Her mother's ambition that she be a model is foiled when Deenie's poor posture and uneven walk indicate an orthopedic problem. Her doctor diagnoses adolescent idiopathic scoliosis, a condition that, if untreated, will lead to a permanent spinal deformity. Deenie's mother is nearly hysterical at the news. Deenie's orthopedist explains to her just what the condition means and prescribes a Milwaukee brace, a device she will have to wear for several years. Deenie finds the preparation of the body mold, which is necessary for the construction of the brace, an embarrassing experience and is distressed at having to wear so obvious and visible a prosthesis. Deenie decides she prefers surgery, a suggestion her doctor vetoes. When the brace arrives, it is clear she will need new, larger clothes to fit over it and this precipitates another minor crisis. Deenie previously had disdained anyone who appeared different, finding physical nonconformity distasteful. She had avoided any contact with a newsstand vendor whose spinal deformity she is now curious about and with whom she unsuccessfully tries to begin conversations. Deenie had found a girl in her gym class with eczema repulsive and secretly called her "Creeping Crud." A neighbor she had started school with was injured in an accident. "Now she wears braces on her legs and she's blind in one eye. I always feel funny when I pass her house—like I should stop and say hello—but then I think I better not, because I wouldn't know how to act or anything." Deenie, afraid she will be similarly rejected, wants to delay returning to school, but her father insists that she must learn to live with this new situation. Her fears that her social life will suffer prove unfounded when her friends, particularly the boy she is currently fond of, discuss her situation openly and matter-of-factly. Deenie is presented with forms for her parents to fill out so she can ride the special bus for handicapped students. Indignant, she throws the papers away, rejecting the label. A school administrator tells Deenie she had been talking with some of her teachers, "and they tell me you seem to be managing very well in spite of your handicap." Outraged, Deenie thinks, "How could she sit there and say such a thing to me! Did she honestly think I was handicapped? Is that what everybody thinks? Don't they know I'm going to be fine in four years—but Gena Courtney and those kids (the ones in the special classrooms) are *always* going to be the way they are now!" Deenie is invited to a party and wants to go without her brace, but her father adamantly refuses to consider the matter. As Deenie accepts this new development in her life, she learns that physical differences do not separate those who sustain them from the rest of humanity. One day she receives a letter from her doctor inviting her to a scoliosis clinic where his patients get together and share techniques for adjusting to their prostheses. Deenie looks forward to the meetings so she can get some answers to her questions: "I think I'll ask the other girls how they sit at their desks and if they got rashes too and if they all sleep flat on their backs and rip their clothes and worry about people looking at them wherever they go?" Deenie's acknowledgment and eventual coming to terms with her impairment are seen in her search for resolution to mundane problems as well as in her consideration of orthopedic work as a possible future career.

Analysis. This witty and delightful novel deals masterfully with how a young teenager copes with the sudden onset of a serious orthopedic difficulty. The portrait of Deenie as a child who, though never intentionally cruel, was insensitive to the needs of those who were different because of some physical disability is well drawn. The responses of other characters accurately reflect typical attitudes toward such problems. The father, eschewing theatrics, is concerned with how the condition can be remediated and unswervingly persists in doing whatever the doctors prescribe. He views scoliosis as neither cosmically motivated nor cataclysmic in its implications. The mother sees her ambitions for her daughter shattered and responds with the kind of excessive dramatics that her daughters and husband have fortunately learned to discount. Her sister and friends are concerned and accepting, but the teachers seem insensitive to Deenie's typically adolescent need not to be different and, more importantly, not to be labeled. Deenie herself, one of the most unforgettable characters in adolescent fiction, speaks for many readers, honestly voicing those fears and anxieties about disability that are so widespread and that, if not countered, lead to irreparable harm. In a memorable scene, Deenie subtly tells readers that handicapped individuals are people just like themselves: "This afternoon on my way to French, I didn't look away when I passed the Special Class. I saw Gena Courtney working at the blackboard. I wonder if she thinks of herself as a handicapped person or just a regular girl, like me."

Bonham, Frank. *Mystery of the Fat Cat.* Illus. by Alvin Smity. New York: Dutton, 1968. 160 pp. Reading Level: MC/YA
Disability: Intellectual Impairment

Ralphie, who is retarded, has a brother, Buddy, who is a lifeguard at the Oak Street Boy's Club. When Buddy is bitten by a rat, closing of the boys' only recreation center seems imminent. Their one hope is to obtain the bequest of a wealthy woman whose will stipulated that after her cat died, the remainder of her estate would go to the club. They suspect that perhaps the present animal, now 28 years old, is a ringer but they have no real way of knowing. The boys devise an elaborate plan to get a photo of the resident cat to compare with a picture of the original. Ralph is the one who realizes something is wrong in the photo and calls attention to some words printed backward. This clearly means that the markings on the cat are the reverse of what they should be. There is a confrontation and a mixup of plans, but finally the implication of Ralphie's insistence that there is an error pays off. After it becomes obvious that the original cat is dead, the perpetrators of the fraud are taken into custody before too much more of the estate money is siphoned into their pockets, and the boys can look forward to a rebuilt recreation center.

Analysis. This novel has idiomatic dialogue, fast pacing, a vivid sense of setting, and a strong brotherhood message, but it is seriously marred by its facile and contrived plot. Ralphie is the instrument by which the mystery is solved, but both his characterization and his functioning ring a false note. To presume that a person who is retarded, except for possibly idiot savants, sees the world in ways that are closed to others is to superimpose a mystique that is unsupported by either evidence or logic. In fact, the novel suggests that Ralphie may indeed be one of these unusual persons since he does have a prodigious, single-focus memory. Ralphie "came and went like smoke—saw all, knew all, though on a slightly different plane from other people. Sometimes, carrying his head slightly to one side, he seemed to peer at the world through a crack in reality, so that he saw things in a way others could not."

While the reader learns little useful information about retardation, the author's social message is of great value. Good sibling relationships are shown, Ralphie is portrayed functioning in the club, and the book's major theme—that people can get along despite their differences—is as valid about handicaps as it is about race or ethnic background.

> "For an M. R.," said Little Pie, "this kid shows a lot of class." Everyone laughed except Buddy who had an M. R. brother. He knew how people with good eyes made jokes about people who wore glasses, and how people who could hear well joked about "dummies" who could not. It was a sad fact of life. He seldom did anything about it unless someone . . . called Ralphie Dum-Dum.

Verbal and physical violence surfaces in the book, some of it tied in with negative behavior toward Ralphie. Violence is one of the techniques employed to sustain tension, an unnecessary ploy since the dangers involved in the solution of the mystery would suffice.

Borland, Kathryn, and Helen Speicher. *Good-by to Stony Crick.* Illus. by Deanne Hollinger. New York: McGraw-Hill, 1975. 138 pp. Reading Level: MC
Disability: Visual Impairment; also intellectual impairment

A fire has driven the Weatherhead family from their Appalachian home to a run-down area of Chicago. The rest of the family makes tentative adjustments, but Jeremy becomes a scapegoat in school because of his newness and rural innocence. Many of his social contacts with peers end in disappointment or in his victimization, and he dreams of returning to the haven of Stony Crick. He becomes friendly with Mr. Sherman, a blind teacher, who rooms in the same house. Jeremy, who was once bitten by a dog, keeps his distance from Baron, the seeing-eye dog. In the loneliness and chaos of his life, the teacher's apartment becomes an oasis, and in the course of the growing relationship, Jeremy learns about braille and how a guide dog functions. Re-echoing the first fire (in which a lame raccoon had alerted Jeremy), Baron's frenzied barking cues him that Mr. Sherman is in trouble. When an attempt is made to pull the unconscious man from the smoke-filled room, the dog guards him tenaciously. Jeremy screws up his courage and orders the dog to stay still. Ultimately, all are safe. In an abrupt, two-page ending, Jeremy's schoolmates, through a recounting of his adventure, now see him in an heroic context and it is implied that he is on his way to social acceptance by his peers.

Analysis. The disabled characters act as foils for Jeremy. He rescues Mr. Sherman and thus grows in stature. No explanation is given for the fire in the apartment, but this emergency provides the plot device by which the boy's classmates reevaluate him. The blind man's characterization is totally positive; he is friendly, patient, understanding, and vocationally successful. Jeremy's brother, Homer D., is retarded—an assumption extrapolated from numerous behavioral descriptions—but neither the parents nor the school acknowledge a problem nor attempt to remedy it. Jeremy's efforts to teach his seven-year-old brother to identify the letter "A" never succeed, but they do demonstrate Jeremy's persistence and loyalty, characteristics later reappearing in the rescue scene. The illustrations are exceptionally good, capturing the mood of the story. Those of Mr. Sherman and Homer D. are honest and attitudinally neutral. Homer D. is seen in one picture, probably realistically, at the edge of a group staring off into space, oblivious to the scene around him.

Enlivened by colorful colloquial speech, some overt brotherhood messages, and an out-of-the-ordinary plot, the story nonetheless suffers from its leisurely pace. The underdeveloped characterization and resultant lack of deep reader involvement diminish the quality of this sensitive, but flawed book.

Boston, Lucy Maria. *Treasure of Green Knowe.* Illus. by Peter Boston. New York: Harcourt, Brace and World, 1958. 185 pp. Reading Level: MC
Disability: Visual Impairment

Tolly learns the story of Susan, blind since birth, who lived in his great-grandmother's house over 150 years ago. We too learn that Susan's grandmother was convinced that Susan's visual loss was God's punishment, but that her father considered her blindness "not a defect but a mysterious charm." Tolly learns details of Susan's adventurousness, which include rescue from a burning house by a childhood black companion and her later marriage to her childhood neighbor and tutor.

Analysis. This low-key fantasy moves back and forth between centuries, with several scenes in which time barriers collapse and Tolly enters Susan's world. Some of the misguided adults view visual impairment from an irrational perspective but they are contrasted effectively with her two pragmatic teachers. Characters are defined and assessed in terms of their reactions to Susan's disability and this characterization generally dominates all their actions, limiting their plausibility. Susan herself is more patient and gentle than credibility will allow, but emerges as an interesting and likeable person. The story is a leisurely old-fashioned one, decorated with graceful language and a nostalgic feeling for a distant time and place.

Bothwell, Jean. *The Mystery Gatepost.* Illus. by Lilian Obligado. Eau Claire, Wis.: Hale, 1964. 159 pp. Reading Level: MC
Disability: Orthopedic Impairment

Quin is recovering from the effects of polio. A resident therapist massages his leg but his activities are still restricted. Quin's father has just purchased a pre-Revolutionary home in Westchester County, New York. There are no neighboring children to play with except for Marjorie, who is staying with her aunt, a local historian, while her parents are on vacation. The aunt is trying to clear up the deed for a house that a client wishes to purchase. The right to title of the house is clouded since the delivery of a "rede rose," a rent to be paid in perpetuity, was once not made. Quin and Marjorie explore his new home and by accident come upon a secret room. Imprisoned briefly, they are soon rescued by the local policeman. Confined to the house because of rainy weather and then a brief illness, Quin is anxious to be able to play outside again and continue his exploration. He discovers a tunnel that connects another hidden room to the front gatepost. Inside the post is a letter clearing up the mystery of the missing payment and the "rede rose" itself. While the children have been busy with their sleuthing, a romance has developed between Quin's widowed father and Marjorie's aunt, which will soon lead to marriage.

Analysis. Except for having to submit to therapy and being moderately restrained by a protective household, there is no indication in this unmysterious mystery story that recovery from polio is more than a minor inconvenience. Quin describes his leg as "gimpy" and declares he will not tolerate being called "Skippy" when he returns to school, but this is the extent of his problems. There seems no good reason for including a disability since the plot could have developed as well without it and no realistic reflection of the problem is included in the text or in the illustrations.

Bouchard, Lois Kalb. *The Boy Who Wouldn't Talk.* Illus. by Ann Grifalconi. Garden City, N.Y.: Doubleday, 1969. 74 pp. Reading Level: YC
Disability: Visual Impairment

Carlos has not made a good transition from Puerto Rico to New York City. The noise, the rapid pace, his loneliness for his relatives, and his inability to learn English are all so frustrating that he decides to stop talking altogether. His family and friends can decode his drawings and gestures but are unhappy at his decision. Carlos and his brother encounter Ricky, a blind boy, who is alone on the street and asks for help in getting home. Carlos goes with him, dismayed to discover his new communication techniques are useless with Ricky. When he inquires why Ricky can't see, the boy replies, "My eyes don't work." Carlos plays with him and decides he'll talk only to his new friend, but pragmatically includes Ricky's mother who is friendly and brings refreshments. Ricky exhibits his braille books and the two plan to go to a park that has a section where blind people can "touch all the plants you want." Carlos returns home and speaks.

Analysis. Ricky is portrayed realistically in terms of his abilities and limitations and is the model and facilitator for another child who needs adaptations to learn. Ricky takes the initiative and is imaginative and helpful. A slight but upbeat book, the writing is somewhat stilted, a frequent but patronizing convention in fiction with Spanish-speaking characters. At a very easy level, a child can obtain some useful information about blindness and some appreciation of the competence and potentialities of a blind playmate. The illustrations avoid any pictorial hint of vision loss in the child.

Bradbury, Bianca. *Nancy and Her Johnny-O.* New York: Ives Washburn, 1970. 150 pp. Reading Level: YA
Disability: Intellectual Impairment

Although Johnny Gill is five years old, he speaks only in one- or two-word sentences and exhibits the physical coordination of a much younger child. Thorough testing at a local clinic reveals that he is mildly retarded, a diagnosis his father heatedly denies. At large family gatherings, the subject of institutionalization for Johnny inevitably comes up—much to the distress of his immediate family. His older sister, Nancy, a senior in high school, adores her younger brother but cannot help resenting that her parents' lives seem to revolve entirely around Johnny. In nursery school, he seems to be doing so well that his mother insists on enrolling him in kindergarten despite his teacher's warnings that he is not ready for the experience. Her prediction is accurate: Johnny, unable to accomplish any of the academic tasks, becomes frustrated and disruptive and is finally expelled. Nancy is afraid to let her new boyfriend meet her brother, anticipating his rejection. Her fears are unwarranted, however, and she is relieved to find that he accepts Johnny unhesitatingly. Nancy's high school counselor had heard of her sibling's difficulties and encourages the family to locate other people in the community with similar problems in order to work together to provide adequate services for all retarded children. Mr. Gill has begun drinking heavily in an attempt to avoid confronting his son's limitations, but his wife has become active in the formation of a parents' group. The members receive permission to address the local PTA and seek its support. Mrs. Gill makes the presentation, and when questioned as to why she has a special interest, her husband rises to announce that they have a retarded child for whom they need help. The PTA endorses their efforts.

Analysis. Parental denial, pressures to institutionalize, sibling jealousy, and the need for concerted action to pressure communities for services are common problems of families that have retarded members, and these conditions are honestly and accurately delineated in this junior novel. Unfortunately, so many moral harangues are delivered— against alcohol and drug abuse, premarital sex, cruelty to retarded children—that the book is in danger of becoming a tract. Although the difficulties of raising a retarded child should not be minimized, a child with a 60 IQ should not create the problems herein described, which are exaggerated and magnified to the level of unbearable distress. The mother is pictured as so encumbered by her responsibilities that a day of shopping is a marvellous treat. If the father almost becomes an alcoholic because he cannot cope with a son who is retarded, then it should be clear that this is a problem of a weak personality and not an expected consequence of retardation. The melodramatic excesses of tone and event diminish the usefulness of this book in illuminating some facets of familial adaptation to the problem of an intellectually deficient child.

Branfield, John. *Why Me?* New York: Harper & Row, 1973. 233 pp.
Reading Level: MC/YA
Disability: General Health Problems

Sarah Freeman has diabetes. She broods over the injustice of having to cope with this condition and petulantly refuses to cooperate in taking insulin injections, sticking to a diet, or maintaining the necessary accurate medical records. Sarah's parents, unable to control her behavior in this or any other matter, agree to buy her a pony if only she will obey her doctor's instructions.

One day she takes her pony for a ride, passing a mineshaft in which a dog is trapped. After summoning help, she heads for home but collapses into a coma. Sugar would have prevented this but she recklessly and deliberately fed her supply to her horse. The dog is rescued and Sarah nags her parents to keep it, promising to follow medical orders faithfully. Not having learned anything about their daughter's integrity from the pony incident, they agree. Sarah continues to violate her dietary regimen and passes out in school. She reluctantly agrees to begin psychiatric treatment as suggested by her physician. In a gesture of contempt, on the way to her weekly appointments, Sarah purchases a candy bar, refusing to stop her self-indulgence even though the potentially damaging consequences are explained.

Soon Sarah begins to suspect that her dog is also diabetic. She shares her insulin, but her efforts to control the condition in the dog are based on guesswork. Returning home from school one day to find her dog in a coma, she forces sugar down its throat. She admits to having secretly given her own medicine to the dog. Later in the year, the dog goes into a coma again. A veterinarian is called, but the dog is too sick and soon dies. A few months later, Sarah gets a new dog, but unfortunately keeps her same old personality.

Analysis. Why Me? contains much clinically valid information about diabetes, including both physical and personality problems that may arise from it. However, when the author moves into the literary area, he is on shakier ground. Sarah is one of the most unpleasant and unappealing heroines to be found in current children's fiction. It would seem to be impossible to identify with such an obstinate, shallow, self-centered child. The didactic message is discredited since those promoting a rational response to the disorder (parents and physicians) are so ineffective.

Brink, Carol Ryrie. *The Bad Times of Irma Baumlein.* Illus. by Trina Schart Hyman. New York: Macmillan, 1972. 134 pp. Reading Level: MC
Disability: Auditory Impairment; also visual impairment

Irma and her father temporarily move to her great-uncle's house so that her father can assist in the management of the old man's department store. The uncle is invalided with gout and his wife has a serious hearing defect. "Aunt Julia never admitted that her hearing might be poor, but she deplored that fact that all the other people in the world were losing their voices." Irma has a bad habit of stretching the truth, which gets her into many scrapes. In order to make good on her fabrication that she has the biggest doll in the world, she steals a mannequin from her relative's store. Many problems ensue from this rash decision and the story chronicles her many ingenious and amusing attempts to put the problem right.

Analysis. Irma's adventures appear very contemporary and light-hearted, and young readers will undoubtedly nervously envy a fictional girl who may have carried out a common extravagant wish. It is in the use of disability as a plot device or emotional cues for pity or amusement that the story is open to serious criticism. The uncle's physical problem sets up the excuse for Irma's presence. The aunt is seen as someone Irma loved, "although it was almost impossible to talk sensibly to her. There were a number of gaps in their understanding of each other." Aunt Julia's hearing problem is exploited for its humorous value in the dialogue. The mistaking of lice for mice or monster for hamster is a rather sad substitute for wit: The girl protests, " 'No! No!' cried Irma. 'It isn't a mouse. It's a hamster. It doesn't have a *tail.*' 'Yes, I'm sure the biscuit must be *stale*,' said Aunt Julia, 'but there's no use screaming about it.' " Disability is further included in the theft scene. "With her arm around the dummy Irma walked right into the crowd and nobody seemed to notice her, nobody that is, except a near-sighted old lady who said, 'Dear child, has something happened to your little friend?' 'She hurt her foot,' said Irma. 'How kind you are, dear, to help her walk!' the lady said." Later, in the throes of conscience, Irma thinks about the fate of one of the employees. "He probably had an aged mother who sat in a wheelchair and maybe he had ten little brothers and sisters who would starve if he did not bring home his wages." The illustrations have the charm and wit the text aspires to but never achieves.

Bro, Marguerite Harmon. *Su-Mei's Golden Year.* Garden City, N.Y.: Doubleday, 1950. 246 pp. Reading Level: MC
Disability: Orthopedic Impairment

It is post-World War II China, and Su-Mei's town has been devastated by war, plunder, and blighted crops. Her father, Dwan-twei, born with a deformed leg, is the object of scorn by the villagers. When he returns to the village from the city and tries to share some of his agricultural knowledge with the other peasants, his suggestions are summarily rejected. However, his family follows his instructions and plants specially treated seed. Dwan-twei's wheat looks healthy but the other fields show evidence of blight. Su-Mei and her friends prevent the destruction of her family's crop, when one of the village men, frustrated by the evidence of his own unwise decision, plans to destroy Dwantwei's fields. The wisdom of Su-Mei's father is soon evident and he is now much honored. An educational revolution overtakes the town as a temple is converted to a school that all the children are obliged to attend. After they learn to read they will be required to spread literacy by sharing their new knowledge with the adults who had no such opportunity when they were young.

Analysis. Su-Mei's father is held in contempt because of his deformity except by his wife, who honors him for his good qualities. He is often described by the grandmother as "the twisted one" instead of by his name. At first, Su-Mei's attitude toward her father's infirmity is tied to its genesis; she feels that a war injury is somehow worthier of respect than a congenital deformity. As in many other books, the handicapped person is accepted when he achieves. Although the author extols certain components of the Chinese culture, many of her comments contain both subtle and overt bias and some descriptions of "quaint" behavior are condescending. The general style is upbeat, naive, and simplistic, typified in the author's assertion that no matter what government is in control, Chinese native life will endure unchanged.

Brown, Roy. *Escape the River.* Also published as *The River.* New York: Seabury, 1972. 160 pp. Reading Level: MC/YA
Disability: Intellectual Impairment

After the birth of Kenny, who is retarded, his parents were afraid to have any more of their own children, so they adopted Paul. With the father preoccupied with the problems of his marginal business and the mother busy with a new paramour, the boys are frequently unsupervised. Paul assumes total responsibility for the care of his brother. They meet Brad, an older boy who was recently released from reform school. He invites the brothers to join him in a plan that he predicts will earn them considerable money. Paul is convinced that their parents care little for them and is eager to collect enough cash to run away with Kenny, especially after their mother indicates she plans to marry her boyfriend and institutionalize Kenny. Brad's cover story sounds plausible but actually he has involved the boys in hiding stolen merchandise. The three boys load up a small boat and leave. Brad suggests that they get rid of Kenny and he and Paul become partners. A fight follows in which Kenny is pushed into the river. Paul jumps in after him and both boys are rescued by a police cruiser. Brad is captured and returned to custody, but Paul is given a suspended sentence and placed in his father's care. The father explains that he had never agreed to the mother's plan for Kenny, and that he hopes to keep both boys with him and become a more responsive and responsible parent.

Analysis. The action is sluggish in this unusual story of the corrosive effects of a disintegrating family. Kenny is described as brain damaged, and such manifestations as poor coordination, perseveration, lack of sense of humor, and uncontrollable fits of temper are not unexpected behaviors. The best aspect of this short novel is the portrayal of pressures on a caring and compassionate boy who sees his loved and dependent sibling all but abandoned by their parents. He feels compelled to provide what protection he can, and does become a towering model of brotherly love. The characters are well rounded, especially that of Paul, but the dialogue is uneven. Syntax unaccountably varies in Kenny's speech, and the content of Brad's language is sometimes out of character considering his background.

Brown, Roy. *Flight of Sparrows.* New York: Macmillan, 1972. 151 pp.
Reading Level: YA
Disability: Speech Impairment, Cosmetic Impairment, Emotional Dysfunction; also orthopedic impairment

Sprog, a runaway from a foster home, sees his meager possessions snatched by a limping mongrel. He trails the dog to his owner, a small, quiet masked boy. When Sprog reaches out to rip the disguise off, he finds that what he assumed was a mask is "warm, living flesh slightly rough and unreal to the touch." Homeless, Sprog follows the silent boy to a partially abandoned building where he lives. He moves in, and the two boys become more companions than friends, living parallel to, rather than with, each other. They are discovered by Scobie and Keith, escapees from a reformatory, who move in and take over. Scobie establishes himself as leader by beating up Sprog and providing them all with abundant stolen food. Scobie has stolen a key to a warehouse and plans to pressure the other boys into helping him steal the goods stored there. The warehouse is guarded by an old man with a wooden leg who spots the boys and, expecting trouble, alerts the police. Scobie is cornered but manages to stab one of the policemen before he is captured. Sprog then decides to move on alone, but, responding to a wordless plea from the mute boy, waits for his companion.

Analysis. The silent, scarred, nameless boy is a mysterious and wraithlike character who seems pitiable. The book is suffused with latent and overt violence. Scobie is portrayed as seriously disturbed—amoral, detached, purposefully or even casually violent—and is pathologically able to forget or ignore his own prior behavior. The action, alternating back and forth between the two sets of boys, is difficult to follow yet compelling because of the ever-present sense of imminent danger. This tale, in which the reader is confronted with strongly etched characters of unknown backgrounds, motivations, and futures, is ultimately unsatisfying. The characters' destinies seem momentarily important, even urgent, but then fade precipitously into oblivion.

Brown, Roy. *The Viaduct*. New York: Macmillan, 1967. 168 pp.
Reading Level: YA
Disability: Neurological Impairment

Phil's grandfather is gruff but kind, especially to his grandson, Phil. The old man is convinced that his genius forebear left an inheritance, which he wants to be certain goes to the boy. This brilliant inventor's diary and books have been found, but the grandfather's dyslexia has prevented him from deciphering the contents of these written materials. Phil and a confidant conceal the writings from a ne'er-do-well uncle intent on appropriating whatever he can. Phil eventually obtains help from someone who solves the mystery and confirms his grandfather's theory.

Analysis. Without the grandfather's problem and his concern and embarrassment about its possible exposure, there would have been no central dilemma. "Phil was quite unprepared for the hurt and humiliation the old man felt when his defect was discovered. Nor did he realize that it was possible to be quick-witted, yet word-blind." Thus the grandfather is portrayed as a capable, competent person who can calculate well but whose learning disability causes great difficulties. However, the author confuses this issue somewhat, suggesting that the inventor's books were in some kind of code, therefore making the grandfather's problem not totally necessary for the plot. The reader will not learn much about learning disability except how its presence generates ingenious artifices for camouflage and that the problem may persist throughout life. The pacing is uneven in this story, as Phil moves from the real world to that of his dreams about the past, but tension is sustained and the mystery is well done and neatly concluded.

Brown, Roy. *The White Sparrow*. New York: Seabury, 1975. 158 pp.
Reading Level: YA
Disability: Speech Impairment, Cosmetic Impairment

In this continuation of *Flight of Sparrows*, Sprog and his nameless, scarred, mute companion barely survive a London winter, finding shelter wherever they can. Finally they locate a refuge of sorts in a pile of stacked wood. Sprog, delirious from fever, loses touch with his surroundings; when he recovers, he is startled to find himself in a real bed in a heated room. His mute friend then becomes ill and Sprog hears him speak out for the first time, though in an indecipherable tongue. They are tended by Connie Angel, who locks them in their enclosure, but this proves no deterrent to Sprog, who comes and goes at will. He does occasional work for Mr. Angel, a junkman, and soon gives evidence of settling in to this new lifestyle. The silent boy, now recovered, becomes jealous. Chased by some children, he dashes off, disappearing near the docks without a trace. Sprog is restless and runs away, but soon is discovered and turned over to the police, who, at his request, notify the Angels.

Analysis. Not as compelling as its companion volume, *The White Sparrow* still commands reader involvement. Many threads are left hanging and the narrative remains more provocative than satisfying. For example, when Sprog brings his friend a mirror, the child's frantic destruction of it can be viewed as a rejection of his appearance or possibly a rejection of himself—either interpretation seems equally possible. The name "Angel" is not ironic, yet is certainly excessive and provides another disquieting unexplained factor. Most disturbing of all is the uncertainty of the mute boy's fate, leading the reader to anticipate a third book in the series.

Burch, Robert. *Simon and the Game of Chance.* Illus. by Fermin Rocker. New York: Viking, 1970. 128 pp. Reading Level: YA
Disability: Emotional Dysfunction

The shock of giving birth to a baby who soon dies devastates Simon's mother, and when she returns to their small-town Georgia home, she is unable to shake her depression:

> She sat motionless, not even blinking her eyes, and Simon, next to her was afraid she had stopped breathing. He was almost afraid to touch her, lest she topple out of the chair and onto the floor, all life gone, but he reached over and took her hand. "Daddy said that the baby died." Mrs. Bradley got up. Simon let her hand go, relieved that she was able to move. She stood in front of her chair a second, then said weakly, "Without a name," and walked through the room and out of the house as if she were sleepwalking.

Her withdrawal is so serious that she must be hospitalized. Mr. Bradley's rigid, distant relationship with his family is softened as he makes greater efforts during his visits to penetrate her passivity. Simon's older sister defers her plans to go to college and assumes the domestic responsibilities. However, when her boyfriend is killed in an explosion, she begins to imitate her mother's apathy. Thirteen-year-old Simon becomes alarmed and uneasy that such behavior should occur twice in the same family. His aunt assists the family and Simon tries to communicate to the adults that he and his father must take over the household responsibilities, allowing his sister a desperately needed respite. When the mother returns, she is functioning on a fairly adequate level and his father maintains his new, more pliant, open behavior. Most importantly, the crisis has made Simon look beyond his own needs to those of others.

Analysis. This well-written, sensitive tale stars an adolescent caught in an emotional web. While dealing with various forms of trauma—coping with the frightening behavior of his mother and sister and adjusting to the softening in attitude of his sanctimonious, overbearing father—the boy must also try to sort out his own inner conflicts, vacillating feelings, and the meaning of his often inconsistent acts. The use of interior perspective provides insight into the behavior and mood of this superior book about a family's response to the dysfunction of cherished members. The evocative and poignant illustrations contribute superbly to the story.

Butler, Beverly. *Feather in the Wind.* New York: Dodd, Mead, 1965. 243 pp. Reading Level: YA/MA
Disability: Emotional Dysfunction; also general health problems

Alex lives with her irascible, unreasonable father in a remote midwestern cabin in the first half of the nineteenth century. David comes to this lonely spot hoping to forget the errors he made as a physician and to locate his niece, Julie, whose father was killed by Indians. A blind amnesiac girl is named as the one he seeks, but he fears this identification is a ruse to unload an unwanted child. During an Indian uprising, Alex and Julie seek refuge in a fort where they become friendly, and then Alex teaches the child how to knit and sew. Regaining his confidence in his professional skill by ministering to the sick during an epidemic and ably assisting an expert surgeon, David returns to Julie and Alex. In a dramatic scene he subdues a man who has threatened to maim Alex's dog. This violent encounter precipitates the return of Julie's vision, since similar events took place when her father was killed. This recapitulation releases her from a psychic prison of amnesia and "blindness"—devices she used to erase her threatening memories of the past. Unquestionably, David, Julie, and Alex will soon be united in one happy family.

Analysis. The author has diverged from her interest in blindness to pseudo-blindness and the resultant sense of falsity diminishes her work. The condition of "blindness" is merely a contrivance useful in establishing the justification for the final climactic scene. The book is unnecessarily long, burdened with mixed stereotypes and confusing names. It contains much unnecessary violence and could have benefited from extensive editing.

Butler, Beverly. *Gift of Gold.* Illus. by Doris Reynolds. New York: Dodd, Mead, 1972. 278 pp. Reading Level: YA/MA
Disability: Visual Impairment; also intellectual impairment, speech impairment

A new department chairman tries unsuccessfully to discourage Cathy Wheeler, who is blind, from pursuing a career as a speech therapist. She refuses his suggestion that her aspirations be limited to working exclusively with blind people, and is further rebuffed when a parent expresses distaste for a blind therapist, requesting a replacement. Nevertheless, she experiences many satisfactions in her modest but active social life and in her professioinal growth. Most of her students make noticeable progress, but one developmentally disabled student dies. In a misguided attempt at kindness, a doctor tells Cathy she might regain some of her sight, but when she consults her regular physician, he is furious at this erroneous, cruel prognosis. Cathy evaluates her goals, accepts the permanent loss of her sight, considers an expanded career combining both special education and speech correction, and sloughs off an unsuitable boyfriend. Subsequently, a romantic relationship deepens with another young man who may soon be her husband.

Analysis. This sequel to *Light a Single Candle* is a standard adolescent romance complicated by the problem of Cathy's blindness. She is presented as a very normal, sensitive, intelligent student with the same needs and desires as her sighted friends. The insensitivity she encounters does not seem directed at her so much as it is a reflection of the general boorishness of some people. Although there are some cases of bias and undervaluation, generally this is an upbeat novel. Butler has developed a likeable, determined young woman with sufficient resources to adjust to her problems.

Butler, Beverly. *Light a Single Candle.* New York: Dodd, Mead, 1962. 242 pp. Reading Level: YA
Disability: Visual Impairment

Cathy Wheeler's sight is failing. She is diagnosed as having glaucoma, but despite surgery, loses all useful vision. A representative from the State School for the Blind visits her and insists the girl enroll for the next semester. Cathy is distressed at the woman's attitude and demeanor and decides not to attend. She begins school locally, but finds her social life has diminished drastically. Her former best friend avoids her, uncomfortable in her presence now that she is blind. When she can no longer rationalize his evasiveness, she decides to go to the State School, thereby hoping to avoid further rejection. The institutional experience is a nightmare. There are privileged cliques, poorly trained instructors, a spartan physical plant, and an atmosphere calculated to produce dependency. Cathy is miserable and wishes to return home, but her parents insist she stay for the remainder of the academic year. She does manage to learn some adaptive skills but is depressed by the faculty's contempt for her aspirations to attend college and be independent. Cathy's plan to attend her former school is disparaged and she is given dire warnings of failure. She decides to get a guide dog and is revivified by the entirely opposite perception of blindness she encounters at the training school. A former classmate offers to read to Cathy and conduct her around school. However, the offer is exploitative, and provides the girl with a posture of nobility and self-sacrifice. Frustrated at being victimized by one who pretended to be helping her, Cathy arranges to bring her dog to school. The administration allows her to explain the dog's function and solicit cooperation from the other students in not distracting the dog from its work. Cathy's new arrangement is a great improvement, allows her new freedom and independence, and permits her to develop friendships and to pursue an incipient romance. Another eye examination reveals she is permanently and irreversibly blind, but this assessment seems only a diagnosis, not a sentence.

Analysis. This story, which has as its exclusive focus the adjustment of an adolescent to her blindness, provides a wealth of information on practical, psychological, and social implications of vision loss. Braille instruction, writing technique, and learning problems and mobility training are explained, but the emphasis is placed on attitudes toward blind people. Social exclusion, the automatic assumption of inadequacy and dependency, and the exploitation by the sighted to inflate their own image, either by contrast or through postures of charity, are seen as particularly painful. The tone of the book is instructional and the characters not particularly well developed; it is fast paced and interesting, and, although not profound, is an honest and accurate novel.

Byars, Betsy. *Summer of the Swans.* Illus. by Ted CoConis. New York: Viking, 1970. 142 pp. Reading Level: MC/YA
Disability: Intellectual Impairment

Sara is a young teenager with a retarded brother, Charlie, whose condition resulted from an exceptionally high fever when he was three. Now Charlie "can be lost and afraid three blocks from home and cannot speak one word to ask for help." Also, "there were great parts of his life that were lost to Charlie, blank spaces that he could never fill in. He would find himself in a strange place and not know how he had got there." Although Sara's moods are volatile, she feels a tender love for Charlie, even though, like many younger siblings, he can be troublesome at times. However, when Charlie gets lost after Sara has taken him to see some swans, Sara forgets her own problems in a desperate need to find her brother. The police and the community join in the search, but Sara and a boy whom she had wrongfully accused of stealing Charlie's watch find the terrified child. After Charlie is taken home, Sara reflects on the depth of her affection for her brother. This experience is a cathartic release for her and she takes a significant step forward in her own maturation.

Analysis. Although there is some internal description from Charlie's perspective, this is essentially a beautifully written story about a sibling's love and responsibility and how mental retardation affects those feelings. The descriptions of behavior, such as the drawing of Charlie's self-portrait, are both tender and accurate. It is in just such vignettes that Byars' consummate skill is revealed. She can describe scenes revealing limitations in ways that reflect reality and avoid maudlin pity. At the same time, her descriptions of teasing incidents toward Charlie resonate with a vivid sense of reality. For example, Sara, not unashamedly, reports: "This nice little Gretchen Wyant didn't see me—all she saw was Charlie at the fence—and she said, 'How's the *retard* today?' only she made it sound even uglier, 'How's the *reeeeetard,*' like that. Nothing ever made me so mad. The best sight of my whole life was nice little Gretchen Wyant standing there in her wet Taiwan silk dress with her mouth hanging open." Much information about retardation can be extrapolated from incidents in Charlie's life, but more important is the feeling tone generated by the text and supported by the warm, touching illustrations. Charlie has his own modest literary identity, but his story function is to act as a catalyst in the clarification of values and establishment of self-identity of the heroine.

Canty, Mary. *The Green Gate.* Illus. by Vera Bock. New York: McKay, 1965. 134 pp. Reading Level: MC/YA
Disability: Visual Impairment

Eight-year-old Emily, who is blind, has been rescued by Aunt Alice from a house where she had been grossly neglected. Emily's benefactor teaches her to learn with her other senses and she gradually becomes less dependent and passive. Aunt Alice informs Emily that a tutor will soon come to initiate her formal education. Emily's solitary garden play is interrupted one day by Martha and soon they play together, a totally new experience for the blind girl. Martha reveals that the neighbors have been curious about Alice, whom Martha shrewdly discovers is blind too. Also living in the house is a visually impaired college student who plans to work as a special educator. Emily proves to be an apt pupil, and a host of good experiences gives Emily the impetus and strength to leave her protective environment and enter the difficult but troubling real world.

Analysis. This low-key pastoral story is a paean of praise, didactic in tone, of the benefits of intervention in the life of a blind child. Through rejection and isolation, Emily has become functionally retarded. Aunt Alice, personally aware of the effect of such neglect on independence, provides a supportive and nurturing setting. Early sensory training, uses of paraphernalia, and information about the activities of daily living are appropriately inserted. The illustrations are simplistic and unimaginative, but present a positive picture of the blind girl.

Carlson, Esther Elizabeth. *The Long Way Around.* New York: Rinehart, 1955. 244 pp. Reading Level: YA
Disability: Orthopedic Impairment

After high school, Enid decides that going to college would just perpetuate the rut she is now in—she would still be shy, unassertive, tongue-tied, and boyless. At her former high school she meets Brad, an ex-football player. He excitedly accepts a menial job, no longer able to aspire to sports stardom since polio rendered his left arm virtually useless. He agrees to work part time as an assistant coach at the high school while he tries to make up missed classes at college. The two meet and become good friends, but Enid's heart is elsewhere. In an explosive encounter, Brad's boss quits in the wake of team failures, but the subsequent investigation places Brad in a positive light. The resolution forecasts a two-year secretarial school for Enid and a romantic relationship for the two major characters.

Analysis. The constant concern over dating, clothing, and appearance is hardly surprising in this formula book. In true sexist fashion, the female character solves her problems by addressing her boyfriend's needs. The best feature of this dreary story is the presentation of the young man recovering from polio. His reduced agility requires a modification of vocational goals, but he swims, dances, plays tennis, and retains his image as a desirable and admirable person. The characters, though, are strictly caricatures; their social pairing is a cliché.

Carol, Bill J. *Crazylegs Merrill.* Austin, Tex.: Steck-Vaughn, 1969. 155 pp. Reading Level: YA
Disability: Orthopedic Impairment

While passing by a football game, Gene Merrill catches an out-of-bounds pass and is tackled. Coach Lenardi takes Gene on as a replacement despite Gene's obvious limp. The boy learns that the invitation was fake, intended to embarrass the other players. The coach finally admits this, but challenges Gene to prove his worth by playing. When the recruit comes to practice, he meets hostility, especially from Townsend, the quarterback. Gene becomes a star because of his excellent ability to catch, a skill he learned from Skip Wittington, a black quarterback. Both his parents and his new girl friend, Barbara, disparage this friendship and to please his girl, he accedes to her racial bias. He is conscience-stricken and ashamed, and later apologizes to Skip. Townsend informs Merrill that he has hidden behind his infirmity, making him an easy target for the teasing of others. Gene instantly sees the validity of the charge, especially since it is said in the locker room where truth traditionally hangs out. Gene keeps winning, he and Townsend are now friends, people's biases melt after the most modest of encounters, and Gene's nickname has earned a respectful rather than a pejorative connotation.

Analysis. This book is a series of set pieces typical of the sports story genre. The message about brotherhood—don't discriminate against Blacks or the disabled—seems ironic in a story replete with sexist clichés. The action proceeds at a fast clip, but people behave in ways that lead to easy and neat resolutions rather than in keeping with what is known about real behavior. The plot device of using a coach (especially one whose name echoes the conviction of winning at any cost) to exploit a handicapped adolescent as a means for shaming his team is offensive. The implication is that, although the exploitation seemed brutal, it really rebounded to everyone's benefit. The delivery in this book of the traditional exhortation to try harder implies that sometimes people accept greater limitations than necessary by assuming inadequacy instead of developing latent competencies. This perception, inaccurate when dealing with more serious incapacitating disabilities, has some validity within the context of this story.

Carpelan, Bo. *Bow Island.* Trans. by Sheila LaFarge. New York: Delacorte, 1968. 140 pp. Reading Level: YA
Disability: Intellectual Impairment; also general health problems

Johan spends his eleventh summer with his parents in a small fishing community facing Bow Island. He meets Marvin, a retarded young adult resident with whom he becomes friendly. Johan, frequently thinking about Marvin, is troubled about why people have such limitations and seeks information, interpretation, and comfort from his parents. He encounters two islanders who care for Marvin: Soder, who has a heart attack, and Nora, Marvin's loving, joyful, sensible sister. Johan also has several encounters with Erik, a cruel local boy who taunts and mocks Marvin. This distresses Johan, but he does not have the courage to intervene and then feels guilty for his cowardice and disloyalty. Johan is both attracted to Erik for his skill and repelled by his meanness. However, when Erik tricks Marvin and ties him to a tree, Johan releases him and the two go off to a cave. Johan is hurt there and Marvin summons help, and by his appropriate action, repays Johan in kind.

Analysis. This is a delicate, gentle, lyrical story, leisurely and unhurried. The characters are seen in relief against the foggy, remote Scandinavian seacoast as though in an old film or a recalled dream. Although Marvin has real corporeality, he also personifies the mysteries of life with which humanity must come to terms. Nora is contrasted with Erik, as good is contrasted with cruelty and as caring is opposed to victimization. Marvin has had his share of problems, but he is also portrayed as having valuable competencies—he fishes well, handles his boat skillfully, and is brave, overcoming his fear of the impending storm when he seeks help for Johan. The nature child theme recurs but this is the only cliché in an unusual, masterful novel.

Carper, L. Dean. *A Cry in the Wind.* Independence, Mo.: Herald, 1973. 128 pp. Reading Level: MC
Disability: Intellectual Impairment; also orthopedic impairment

Tom Farrish is in serious trouble. He is failing in school and faces expulsion. Caught by the constable in what appear to be some minor misdemeanors, he is threatened with reform school. The only alternative seen by the principal is assignment to a special education class. Apparently this is a response more to his misbehavior than to his educational needs. Tom, classified as a retardate, nonetheless manages some remarkable feats: He beats up a bully and intimidates his cohorts, discovers the culprit who vandalized his school, and braves a snowstorm to save a bus driver's life. This heroism inspires a local philanthropist to arrange for a new home for Tom's family. Tom is not the only retarded hero in town. Lonnie, his friend, rescues Tom's sister from a well.

Analysis. The efforts of Mr. Montgomery, Tom's teacher, to establish rapport are certainly imaginative. When they first meet, he says: "Say, Tom, I've got a double-barreled shotgun that needs some repairs. I'll bring it Monday and you can work it over for me." This seems a pedagogically innovative approach to a child classified as retarded and described by his principal as a "strong candidate for reform school."

Without regard for either coherence or probability, all problems approach solution by book's end. Tom's status as a solid citizen is firmly established, the principal apologizes for his early attitude and offers to help the family on moving day, and Tom's mother has been transformed from the woman who slaps Tom in greeting to one who agrees with him that, "It takes a heap of livin' in a house t' make it home."

Cardboard characterization, endless clichés, and an improbable resolution come together in an effort at inflating the image of retarded children. This is so incongruent with reality that the message is drained of believability and thus is counterproductive.

> Caudill, Rebecca. *A Certain Small Shepherd.* Illus. by William Pene duBois. New York: Holt, Rinehart and Winston, 1965. 48 pp. Reading Level: MC
> *Disability:* Speech Impairment

On a "freakish night in November," an Appalachian woman dies in childbirth. Her son, Jamie, grows up and, except for his speech, which consists of grunts, every other developmental milestone shows him to be typical. Nevertheless, he is pitied by the townspeople, teased by the children, and only reluctantly accepted into school. He is given the part of a shepherd in the Christmas play and is heavily involved in the role. An impending storm causes some fear that the production, which will take place in the community church, may have to be called off. Two strangers come to Jamie's house and take shelter in the stable where the woman gives birth. Later Jamie goes to the church to give an orange to the newborn and is thereafter able to speak—an event which is perceived as miraculous.

Analysis. This story cannot be evaluated on a conventional literary basis since it is obviously a religious parable. The lack of useful speech is not seen to have functional, structural, or traumatic origins and its restoration has no rational basis. Instead, it serves as a device to mark innocence and belief rewarded.

> Cavanna, Betty. *Joyride.* New York: Morrow, 1974. 222 pp. Reading Level: YA/MA
> *Disability:* Orthopedic Impairment; also visual impairment

Since Susan has been lamed by polio, her high school friends, now greatly preoccupied with boys, see her as asocial and involve her less and less in their activities. She becomes restive and opposes her family's urgings to become a teacher. Although Susan has some interest as well as considerable talent in art, she conceals this ability. She is racked by jealousy of her friends' activities and tries to fade into obscurity, but gradually allows herself to be drawn into debating and artwork on the newspaper. She becomes excited by her involvement in a debate on the Scopes trial and becomes friends with a Jewish boy whose house is later burned by the Ku Klux Klan. She observes some friends charting their own course in life and others who are trapped by circumstance and accident. Susan finally gets a grip on herself, determines she must assert her independence despite her disability, and decides she will go to art school on a scholarship.

Analysis. The title of this novel is ironic in terms of the tone of the story, the setting, and the painful decisions and assertions the heroine must make. Assisting Susan in her maturation is her growing awareness of the social dangers of overzealousness and prejudice and the personal dangers of irresponsible or purposeless behavior. Susan is treated as less than a person in several instances. Her friends' exclusion of her from their pleasures is more thoughtless than deliberately mean, and the family's attempt to superimpose their will on her future is highly infantilizing, although presumably done with the best motives. The story suffers greatly from a sense of distance and a lack of tension or involvement.

Cheney, Cora, *Key of Gold.* Illus. by Paul Galdone. New York: Holt, 1955. 127 pp. Reading Level: MC
Disability: Orthopedic Impairment

Edward Norris, recently recovered from polio, moves with his parents to a Florida key were his father plans to help him recover the use of his affected leg through water therapy. The key is deserted except for an old fisherman and his grandson, Lemmy. Edward and Lemmy become friends and Lemmy brings a wheelbarrow for Edward to get around in. Edward reads about pirate treasure and becomes convinced that there may be some nearby. Dora is the name of the key, which the boys learn is a corruption of Cayo de Oro, or Gold Key. Edward does not regain the use of his leg as expected. The doctor suggests that he may be experiencing "an hysterical condition," hypothesizing that his desire to walk is so intense that it results in a psychological block that is counterproductive for his recovery. The physician forecasts that a shock "will make him forget himself some day and he will begin to walk involuntarily." A hurricane hits the island and leaves what appears to be a wrecked ship in its wake. When the others go to investigate this tempting hulk, Edward, frustrated at being left behind, gets up as predicted and hightails after them. A treasure chest is found on board and the old Spanish pistol it contains is donated to a local museum. However, the real treasure is the restoration of Edward's ability to walk.

Analysis. The premise that too great a desire to walk is its own preventive is specious at best, and the idea that trauma is a curative for disability does not seem to diminish in popularity despite the lack of supportive evidence. The plot is contrived and the characterizations shallow. This is a superficial story that offers little information about infantile paralysis. The illustrations do depict the leg brace but in a sketchy manner.

Cheney, Cora. *The Peg-Legged Pirate of Sulu.* New York: Knopf, 1960. 109 pp. Reading Level: MC
Disability: Orthopedic Impairment; also general health problems

Long ago, Ping lived on a Philippine island. Tempted by an older boy, Manuel, to go diving for shells, he irresponsibly leaves his lame grandfather home alone. However, when he sees their caribou wandering loose, he leaves his companion's shells to capture the animal. Returning home, he is ashamed to discover that he was not there when the old man needed help. Stung by Manuel's accusation of theft, he returns to the beach where he stowed the fragile treasures, and he sees odd tracks and the remains of the shells, boiled for their food content. Ping decides to reduce his guilt feelings and make a Christmas star for his beloved grandfather, who is too weak to attend church. Hoping to trade some of his own shells for paper for this project, Ping returns to the beach where he encounters a pirate with one leg. He recalls the legend his father told him of a wicked peg-legged pirate thrown overboard by his shipmates. It is the same pirate, who now claims he had been jettisoned because he had reformed, a result of his conversion after being forgiven by a holy man whom he had mortally wounded. Giving Ping some coins, he demands that the boy take a message and a cross to Brother Francisco. Ping returns from town with the paper for his project but with the news that the monk is dead. After urging the pirate to consult his wise grandfather, Ping hears the old man tell the one-legged man to seek asylum in the church. He leads the convert there, guided by the light from the star made for the grandfather. Ping is commended for his bravery and intelligence and returns home happily.

Analysis. The peg leg is clearly a pirate cliché and serves no real purpose except for its costume effect. The old man is portrayed as kind and wise, but again his disability is a prop, a device to advance the plot on several occasions. The story has some intermittent moments of tension, but its base is a simple moral tale peopled by cardboard characters.

Chipperfield, Joseph E. *A Dog to Trust; The Saga of a Seeing-Eye Dog.* Illus. by Larry Toschik. New York: McKay, 1964. 181 pp. Reading Level: YA
Disability: Visual Impairment

While Ralph is sketching one day in rural England, he sees Marian Ash on a runaway horse. Ralph bravely saves her, but is kicked by the animal and subsequently blinded. He is persuaded to return to the country where, in gratitude, Marian and her father, a dog breeder, care for him. After a dog, Arno, proves his intelligence, he is sent to Guide Dog School to ultimately lead Ralph, and in this capacity ably proves his worth. Gradually Ralph becomes aware that a modest amount of his light perception has returned, but Arno unfortunately gets an eye infection and the dog's vision deteriorates rapidly. The villagers, assuming that Ralph no longer needs help, want him to give Arno to a young motorcyclist who lost his sight after a collision. Ralph is reluctant to tell people about the dog's virtual blindness. When the youth is killed, the locals become enraged and attack Ralph and Arno, who successfully retreat to a cottage, which Ralph barricades. Finally, the crowd is placated and order restored. Ralph is now convinced that he must not be so detached and uncommunicative.

Analysis. The writing is cliché-ridden, mawkish, and melodramatic. These excerpts are typical: "The very mention of the words guide dog brought before her vivid imagination the lifetime servitude such a dog would be required to give. For such a one there would be no more play, no more racing over the hills . . . only a pattern that must be unchanging as the months went by, until the years finally brought the frost of age. . . ."; and "She had recognized only too surely the twilight path the dog must tread in the future." The book's main focus is the animal, and, not unexpectedly, treatment of human characters tends to remain mostly superficial. The author apparently feels the dog has given up "as much by losing his freedom as the man by losing his sight," and the illustrator provides no close-up of Ralph—only showing the young man in one distant shot. The most dismal moment occurs when Marian, the love interest, finds "joy and pity mingled in her as she realized how deeply the golden days had imprinted themselves on the mind of a man who could not see." There is no indication that the writer thinks pity inappropriate. Neither is there a feeling that the hostile actions of the crowd were to be condemned out-of-hand as evil. Rather, the blame is transferred to Ralph—his reticence caused him to be a victim. Ralph's improved vision in exchange for the dog's loss seems contrived and excessively dramatic and contains a suggestion of payment or price. The frequent references to "dogs of darkness" not only are inaccurate but are also highly offensive, evoking unwarranted and ponderous emotionalism.

Christopher, Matt. *Glue Fingers.* Illus. by Jim Venable. Boston: Little, Brown, 1975. 48 pp. Reading Level: YC
Disability: Speech Impairment

Billy Joe refuses to play football with a team because he is afraid he will be mocked when he stutters. Coach Davis of the Apple-Jacks asks him to join his team because he is such an outstanding pass catcher. Billy Joe's older brothers point out that speech is not an essential part of football. Convinced, he signs up, catches a key pass, and runs for a touchdown. The coach congratulates him and the boy realizes that the roar he hears is a cheer, not a taunt, from his teammates.

Analysis. Glue Fingers is a particularly heavyhanded delivery of a standard sports story message: It's not who you are, but what you do that counts. Since the initial crisis is contrived, the story is implausible. Billy Joe's lament: "Who would want a stuttering kid for a friend?" seems unwarranted and self-pitying. Despite its faults, the focus on play action may yet attract some readers willing to overlook the unlikely story line.

> Christopher, Matt. *Long Shot for Paul.* Illus. by Foster Caddell. Boston: Little, Brown, 1966. 151 pp. Reading Level: MC
> *Disability:* Intellectual Impairment

After Glenn and Judy learn from physicians about their brother Paul's intellectual impairment, they become very helpful and supportive. Although they can do little about improving their thirteen-year-old brother's academic work, now at second-grade level, they make plans to teach him basketball. They hope this will give him a skill he can enjoy and perhaps reduce the loneliness he endures. Practice goes fairly well and Paul likes the recreation center, though few people speak to him. A neighborhood boy, Benjy, joins them but is discouraged from playing with Paul because Benjy's mother considers the retarded boy's behavior contagious. Finally, the sympathetic coach gets a uniform for Paul, and, despite his poor performance—fouling, traveling, making a basket for the other team(!)—the man continues to play him for short periods. In contrast, the team members completely ignore Paul on the floor and in the locker room. Discouraged, Glenn decides he will concentrate on teaching his brother foul shots, a gambit that pays off when Paul's two free shots tie a game. After the subsequent win, Paul is congratulated on his contribution and is somewhat more accepted by his teammates.

Analysis. Long Shot for Paul is a simple book but it has unusually strong attributes, once the unlikely proposition is accepted of a family's surpise at being informed that their thirteen-year-old son's behavior is due to developmental disability. Paul's mistakes are credible ones, but the evidence that he can succeed in a competitive game underscores the fact that an individual may do poorly on tests or other intellectual tasks, yet be physically very proficient. Christopher wisely refrains from having an unrealistically upbeat ending, and the introduction of a coach more interested in his players than in winning at any cost is refreshing. Standard in terms of literary qualities for this genre, the book offers a plausible hero, some valid information on a child with retardation, useful and helpful models, and accurate reflections of community beliefs.

Christopher, Matt. *Sink It, Rusty.* Illus. by Foster Caddell. Boston: Little, Brown, 1963. 138 pp. Reading Level: MC
Disability: Orthopedic Impairment

Rusty is an avid basketball fan, but because of his post-polio condition participates only as a referee. Alec Daws, whose own sports career was stopped short when his hand was mutilated, sees the boy practicing alone and encourages him. Rusty accompanies his friends on a hike. When a trapped rabbit is released and demonstrates functional use of its leg, unsurprisingly the stage is set for the duplication of this event in the human central character. Alec gives Rusty opportunities on the court, but the body contact and frenzied action are too much for him. He learns how to adapt by working on precision shots and in this role becomes a contributing member of the team. Although Alec is no longer an active basketball player, he successfully sublimates his personal goals through those of the team.

Analysis. Since this book is designed for sports buffs with presumably heavy psychological investment in physical prowess, it is especially useful to portray to this audience a hero who achieves even though he is not physically perfect. To show Rusty's adult counterpart in several romantic scenes is inappropriate and probably unappreciated by this audience, nevertheless, it adds to the healthiness of the depiction. Rusty confronts pity, exclusion, and the expectation of failure—all exacerbated by his own sense of hopelessness about being a valuable player. His parents try to deal with his unhappiness through an unsatisfying ploy, pointing out to him that there are many people left in far worse condition after having had polio. *Sink It, Rusty*, on balance, is a useful book—straightforward and unpretentious with honest, unflinching illustrations.

Christopher, Matt. *Stranded.* Illus. by Gail Owens. Boston: Little, Brown, 1974. 117 pp. Reading Level: MC
Disability: Visual Impairment

With only his dog Max for a companion, young blind Andy Crosset explores the small island he manages to reach after being shipwrecked. Andy falls off a cliff into the sea but Max rescues him. The two narrowly miss being attacked by a barracuda. Max encounters another dog and a fight breaks out. The strange dog's owners appear and take both dogs away in their boat, unaware that Andy is on the island. The Coast Guard arrives to rescue Andy, who is reluctant to leave without his pet. The sailors return later to look for Max, who has managed to escape his captors and swim back to the island. Max, Andy, and his parents are eventually reunited.

Analysis. The story line enables Andy to prove to his overprotective mother that he can manage under the most arduous of circumstances, but if *Stranded* is an attempt to develop an heroic blind character, the improbability of the events negates the intent. Credibility is strained to the utmost when Andy's dog responds to such commands as "take me to a small tree" and swims from island to island across a navigable body of water and when a hungry shark passes up a couple of good meals in the form of Andy and Max! Not much information about blindness or real insight into procedures required for coping with the problem is revealed. The disability merely serves as a device to set up the plot and to create some tension in an otherwise bland tale.

Cleaver, Vera and Bill Cleaver. *Me Too.* Philadelphia: Lippincott, 1973. 158 pp. Reading Level: YA
Disability: Intellectual Impairment

Lydia and Lorna are twin twelve-year-old sisters. Lorna, retarded, walks in "a queer limp way with her head pulled down to one side although there was nothing wrong with it or any part of it physically." Her speech is highly idiosyncratic, frequently consisting of unintelligible phrases. Lydia (whose head, according to her father, is "stuffed with brains") acts as her sister's protector and tutor. Hoping that her father will return again, although this last abandonment she fears may be permanent, Lydia tries to teach her sister enough to be acceptable to him. She works with Lorna all summer, but the dimensions of the task are enormous. Their neighbors display a wide spectrum of constructive, deleterious, even mystical, attitudes toward Lorna's disorder; Lydia is pained and angry when their attitude is rejecting. Finally, she is relieved of the responsibility for the total care of her sister by a housekeeper and Lorna's return to a special educational setting. Lydia abandons the fantasy of her father's return and begins to accept the idea that some aspects of her life are beyond her control.

Analysis. The chronicles of Lorna's behavior, especially her erratic speech patterns, upon examination are somewhat off-target descriptions of reality. And while Lydia is a perceptive child, the contention that she could know that the composer whose music she heard was going through an ordeal when he wrote it is highly unlikely: "Deaf and still able to write music like that. How was it she knew beforehand the music hadn't come from any normal person?" However, the Cleavers are in top form in terms of pacing and style and the deceptively simple novel makes some sophisticated demands on its readers, asking them to consider the philosophical aspects of love, its limitations, and its contradictions. Some existential and religious questions are raised and some shocking insights into people's responses to stress are effectively presented.

Cleaver, Vera and Bill Cleaver. *The Mimosa Tree*. Philadelphia: Lippincott, 1970. 125 pp. Reading Level: YA
Disability: Visual Impairment, Neurological Impairment

The Proffitts, driven off their North Carolina backwoods farm by poverty, travel to Chicago seeking work and a better life. The father, who is blind, remains inside their apartment while the others seek work. The mother gets a job as a hotel domestic, but soon deserts the family. Marvella, fourteen, finally finds a job with a pawnbroker, while her younger brother, initiated into street life by neighborhood boys, steals. The children learn about welfare from a friend and, although Marvella quits her job to be eligible for this relief, the payments never start and the family is overwhelmed with the red tape of bureaucracy. Their friend, Mario, has epileptic seizures, but his indifferent mother ignores his medical needs. The neighborhood children pool their money from purse snatchings and take him to a doctor. Once there, he unaccountably races from the consulting room, has a seizure, and dies. Innocent of the connivances and wiles of the big city, the Proffitts are easy prey for various confidence schemes. They pay for purchases that never arrive, are misled by an employment agency, and unknowingly take jobs that involve stolen goods. When Marvella sees one of the neighbors push his mother into the path of a bus, it is the last straw and she knows she must return home before the family is further corrupted. The imaginary mimosa tree, described to her blind father in the hope it might make him happy, she now knows could never exist in such harsh soil. Frightened, she drives nonstop back to their farm where they are all welcomed home by caring neighbors.

Analysis. Although the writing is good and the story involving, the contrast between the unrelieved evil of the big city and the supportiveness of the country seems excessive. The blind father is totally passive with little discernible personality or character, and is considerably more incapacitated than blindness alone would explain. The mimosa tree is fragile, representing beauty and hope and therefore doomed to extinction in the slum. The gang's thievery is shown as arising from necessity rather than avarice; hence their concern for Mario is credible and perhaps the prime outlet for their humanity. His seizures are described in great detail as is the helpful response of his friend. His slothful mother, the admixture of poverty and the slum, the physician's insensitivity to the impractical treatment he prescribes all foretell that

Mario, like the mimosa tree, is designed not to survive in such an inhospitable environment.

> Clewes, Dorothy. *Guide Dog*. Illus. by Peter Burchard. New York: Coward-McCann & Geoghegan, 1965. 159 pp. Reading Level: YA
> *Disability:* Visual Impairment; also cosmetic impairment

Medical training is expensive, so Roley takes on a job of delivering preholiday mail. A dog jumps at him from a professor's house and he loses consciousness when a bomb in the package he is delivering explodes. An ophthalmologist advises him that he is permanently blind and that he should learn braille and change his vocational goal to the field of physiotherapy. He is cheered by a nurse he meets at the hospital; a newly close friend, Steve; and a constable interested in the bomber. After his initial reluctance to rely on a dog, he is finally convinced when his guide dog saves him. Constable Sutton has been laboriously tracking down clues and is convinced the offender will try again. Although the criminal cleverly manages to get into the educator's house disguised as a telephone repairman, the policeman suddenly recalls the disfiguration of the evildoer and hastily returns to toss out the phone rigged like a bomb. The criminal is apprehended and Roley is pleasantly startled to discover that the nurse wants to be his girl friend.

Analysis. A fast-paced mystery, *Guide Dog* also includes extensive information about adjustment to blindness, the origins of guide dog training, and other historical data. Although the writing bogs down somewhat during these didactic interludes, the presentation is well made and unusually enlightening. The psychological information is even more useful, especially in the blind youth's painful scenes of taking stock and planning for the future. The facial scarring of the criminal is the weakest aspect, although essential to his detection by the police. Roley's shock about his condition is shared with the readers, and this experience binds them together as they see him struggle and mature in his difficult quest for a meaningful life.

> Cone, Molly. *Simon*. Illus. by Marvin Friedman. Boston: Houghton Mifflin, 1970. 102 pp. Reading Level: YA
> *Disability:* Intellectual Impairment, Visual Impairment

Simon is a friendless young man experiencing an extremely distressing and traumatic adolescence. He engages in Walter-Mitty-like daydreams and avoids communication with his parents. They are distressed and Simon is the cause of much worry, fighting, and anger. He frequently escapes to a deserted lot used by the community as an unofficial rubbish dump. There he sits alone daydreaming in an abandoned car, which he pretends is his private cave. Julia, a ten-year-old retarded child who lives in his neighborhood, has no friends her own age and is the butt of many local pranks. Simon pretends that he cannot see her, but when he finds her one day in his haven, he becomes terribly angry. He drags her home and yells at her housekeeper to keep the child away from him. Simon discovers that a storm had toppled a tree on "his" car, entangling a blind man in its branches. Realizing he must help free the man, he is nevertheless disturbed by the experience. Investigating a strange sound, Simon sees Julia with a dog collar and leash on, chained to her porch. She is surrounded by the neighborhood children, who are jumping around, barking, and making fun of her. Simon unfastens her collar and, one boy, upset at having his "sport" interrupted, attacks Simon, wrestling him to the ground. When the police are called and the crowd disperses, Simon returns home—physically and symbolically— knowing he has done what decency and maturity require.

Analysis. The handicapped characters are never fully developed. Their literary function is to serve as the machinery for the civilizing of Simon. The boy's behavior, while bizarre, is essentially estranged rather than sick. He has several false starts in striving for an identity. His most absorbing daydream concerns the rites of passage of certain American Indian tribes in which the would-be braves face and overcome perils. Having behaved nobly in the two experiences with disabled persons, Simon has established his right to adult status in similar fashion. Initially, Simon had been upset and hostile to any indication of imperfection. Unsure of himself, he displaced his uneasiness on those people who reminded him of his own vulnerability: "He had read once that some ancients drowned babies who were not perfect when born. Solved a lot of problems, Simon reflected."

This strange and unsettling book, while exploring the problems of an alienated youth, depicts some cruel and vicious attitudes toward the disabled. Although the author strongly and unequivocally disavows those values, the incidents are haunting and ultimately disturbing. Sentence structure and content are incongruent: The former is suitable for a young reader, while the latter, involving extensive use of symbolism, suggests the need for a more sophisticated audience. The sketches neither adequately interpret the text nor generate interest in the story.

Corbett, Scott. *Dead before Docking.* Illus. by Paul Frame. Boston: Little, Brown, 1972. 134 pp. Reading Level: MC
Disability: Auditory Impairment

A recent operation has restored almost all of young Jeff Wister's hearing, and he is now ready to return to his parents' home in South America. Self-assured and confident, he has no concerns about traveling alone on an ocean liner. Just before boarding, he chances upon a man in a phone booth. An accomplished speech reader, Jeff observes the man speaking and interprets his words to be: "Don't worry! I tell you it's all set, he'll be dead before they reach port. Our friend knows his business." He considers the possibility that he may have misunderstood, but decides to do a bit of sleuthing just in case. There are only eleven other passengers, so the would-be detective soon knows all the likely suspects. One woman learns that Jeff reads lips and inadvertently informs the conspirator, who realizes the lad may have understood the revealing conversation and waits for an opportunity to silence the boy. The man seizes him, but luckily Jeff has his tape recorder with him on which he had previously recorded the blast of the ship's whistle. He presses the play button and the tremendous booming sound that results so startles the hard-of-hearing criminal that he releases Jeff. Rescuers are alerted and the nefarious schemes are undone.

Analysis. All but the most nondiscriminating and credulous mystery fans will be put off by the outrageous manipulation of events in this tale. The description of the way in which speech reading takes place is very informative and understandable and therefore normalized. However, to build an entire story on the ability to interpret the speech of a stranger, closed off in a phone booth, when the speaker is looking away from the boy, is to set up a superhuman situation. It is this exaggeration that diminishes Jeff's credibility and decreases the ability of the reader to comprehend how deaf people understand oral speech.

Corbin, William. *The Golden Mare.* Illus. by Pers Crowell. New York: Coward-McCann, 1955. 122 pp. Reading Level: MC
Disability: General Health Problems

Because of such aftereffects of rheumatic fever as chest pains and dizziness, Robin's activities on his family's ranch are highly restricted. He cannot attend school and so obtains his education from library books his father brings him. After receiving the physician's approval, his father permits him to ride a very old mare named Magic. Upset about his son's fantasizing behavior, Robin's father teaches him to shoot, believing that such manly skills will counterbalance his more passive preoccupations. The winter that Robin is ten, there is a violent snowstorm and he is left alone with his mother when the others go off to feed their stranded cattle. Robin's mother falls and then faints from the pain. Believing her leg is broken, he rides for help to a neighbor. On the return trip, Magic rears, dropping the boy from her back into a snowdrift. Spotting a cougar's shadow, he calls Magic to his side, and, gaining courage, aims and shoots just before he feels the pain that signals the loss of consciousness. He is found near the dead cat and has new respect from his more active brothers. When Magic becomes critically ill,

Robin dreams about an idyllic land where his horse can become immortal. His brothers take the animal away the next night hoping Robin will believe it escaped to the dreamed-about paradise. The boy suspects that his brothers are trying to spare him the pain of his horse's death and is comforted by both the hope that his dream may come true and the fact of his brothers' love.

Analysis. Since Robin is patronized by his brothers because of his delicate physical condition and unfit for school and its attendant friendships, Robin has only the old horse for a companion. The restrictions necessitated by the seriousness of his disorder are accurately described, but the boy's rather grand achievement strains belief. The lyrical ending is consonant with antecedents in the story but unique in horse stories for this young an audience. Idealized action drawings are completely harmonious with Robin's perceptions of a creature larger than life.

Corcoran, Barbara. *A Dance to Still Music.* Illus. by Charles Robinson. New York: Atheneum, 1974. 192 pp. Reading Level: YA
Disability: Auditory Impairment; also emotional dysfunction, general health problems

The sense of isolation that deafness often imposes is exemplified in the narrow boundaries of fourteen-year-old Margaret's lonely life in Florida. She recalls with longing her former life in Maine, filled with music, caring friends, and fond relatives. This is counterbalanced by thoughts of her father's desertion, her mother's disinterest, her difficulty in maintaining friendships, and the fear she might now commit the kinds of social errors her deaf grandfather did. Resenting the suggestion that she attend a school for the deaf, Margaret starts to hitchhike back North. Diverted from her trip to minister to an injured fawn, the girl and a friendly passerby, Josie, take the deer to Josie's houseboat where the two are given refuge. Margaret's association with Josie, although nonverbal at the outset, thaws Margaret's fear of being ridiculed. She finally takes a chance on speaking and, with relief, unburdens her problems to the older woman. Josie brings Margaret a book about deafness and introduces her friend, a physically handicapped teacher (presumably developing the concept of identification through shared disability). This woman tells her about a day school where deaf students are taught by a technique that multiplies communication skills. Margaret has an encounter with another isolate, a "wild" woman who lives in the swamp. After some frightening collisions in which both misunderstand the other's motives, the woman saves Margaret from a potentially deadly snakebite. Eventually, contact is made with Margaret's mother, who is relieved to transfer major responsibility to Josie, and agreement and support are given for a plan for Margaret to join a retraining program—a symbol of her exit from solitude.

Analysis. The optimism implied in the title, that joyful response is possible despite deafness, is a key to the theme. The heroine's frustrations, her pitiful schemes, and her fears and memories are exquisitely portrayed. Margaret's perseverance and unresentful acceptance of her inadequate mother give her real stature. The techniques the guilt-ridden mother uses to blot out the memories of her neglect that contributed to her child's deafness are vividly recounted and evoke a pathetic but believable character. Josie, the stalwart individualist, is somewhat less credible in the role of a loving but undemanding person who creates a climate in which Margaret is able to abandon her unhealthy defenses. The hermit woman, the deer, and Margaret are depicted as innocent societal victims, who, though damaged, still survive.

Information about deafness, such as the frequent presence of chronic residual buzzing and the ineffectiveness of hearing aids for nerve deafness, should add to the reader's understanding of this disability. Robinson's haunting illustrations in tandem with Corcoran's beautifully etched delineation of Margaret compassionately explore the social and emotional ramifications of deafness in this unusual and moving story. (See Figure 5.)

Corcoran, Barbara. *The Long Journey.* Illus. by Charles Robinson. New York: Atheneum, 1970. 187 pp. Reading Level: MC/YA
Disability: Visual Impairment; also emotional dysfunction

Laurie's grandfather finally acknowledges concern about his rapidly diminishing vision. His fear of officials and public institutions preclude Laurie's attendance at school and his hospitalization to remove his cataracts. The old man sends her on horseback across Montana to find Uncle Arthur, her only other relative. Laurie is attacked twice by a religious fanatic and has many other harrowing adventures on this trip, discovering that the world is more complicated and threatening than she had imagined but also kinder than she had expected. When she tracks down her uncle, she finds he has remarried and wants to adopt her. Her grandfather eventually consents to surgery and the family plans a permanent reunion.

Analysis. The story is irrevocably damaged since all action results from a single totally unbelievable event: The old man is unwilling to make a phone call, electing instead to send his young granddaughter alone across dangerous country. The grandfather is drawn as loving but eccentric. Her uncle's casual dismissal of the man who attacked and terrorized Laurie seems callously mindless: "He's peculiar, a little touched in the upper story. But he's harmless." Her uncle's lack of concern expressed in this evaluation appears to contradict the portrait of a caring, concerned relative. Very little information is given about vision loss or adaptation to it. Neither characterization, plot, nor problem is up to the author's usual standards.

Corcoran, Barbara. *A Row of Tigers*. New York: Atheneum, 1969. 165 pp. Reading Level: YA
Disability: Orthopedic Impairment

Jackie is a sensitive, noncomforming young girl trying to maintain her individuality in a brutal, unfeeling, violence-prone community. Morose about her deceased father, she runs away from her ranch home. By chance, she meets Gene, a Hollywood publicist whose curved spine has resulted in a misshapen body and diminutive stature. Gene is kind and gentle, qualities widely at variance with those more commonly displayed in the community. The two are ready victims of the many destructive, competing forces they encounter. The town Jackie lives in is volatile and pistol-happy. When Gene accompanies Jackie to her school, some rowdy students tease him and attempt to touch the hump on his back. Outraged, Jackie bloodies one attacker's nose. Gene, pleased at her ardent defense, tells her he is used to being teased, but Jackie explains that since he is her best friend she had to fight for him. In a climactic scene at the dump, which had been her refuge, the town derelict, another friend of Jackie's, is shot and wounded—one more instance of the mindless, reckless turbulence that suffuses the community. Gene, to Jackie's great joy, decides to stay and enter in a partnership with a ranch hand who had once worked for her father. The unlikely friendship is mutually satisfying: Gene finds a new direction for his life and Jackie is able to sustain the direction she had already chosen. When they return to the dump, they play an old slot machine and a row of tigers, symbolizing winners, appears.

Analysis. All of Jackie's friends are social outcasts, and the casual violence that is directed toward them is very powerful—as if fate had given approval for them to be easy prey. The dump, where much of the action takes place, is an apt metaphor. Gene emerges as a substantial person—at the beginning cynical, tired, yet courageous; at the end, his perception of himself as automatically excluded from love, strenuous physical activity, or friendship has been greatly moderated. Corcoran's writing is sensitive and imbued with obvious as well as subtle humor, vitiating the many scenes of violence. The portrayal of Gene is not fully satisfying, but the scenes where he is treated patronizingly as if he were a child, the attack scenes with Jackie, and the episode where he is invited to be a partner on a ranch are tellingly done. The illustrations of

Gene are perfectly realized, informative, and warm but not sentimentalized.

Corcoran, Barbara. *Sasha, My Friend.* Illus. by Richard L. Shell. New
York: Atheneum, 1972. 203 pp. Reading Level: YA
Disability: Orthopedic Impairment, Neurological Impairment

Hallie meets John Penny, an aggressive, unpleasant lout whose sister, Birdie, has been confined to a wheelchair since the age of seven
when she had polio. Birdie, who is also subject to epilepticlike seizures,
spends much of her time alone in this isolated part of Montana. She
welcomes Hallie's friendship, but becomes distressed when Hallie
takes Sasha, a wolf cub, for a pet and John threatens to shoot it. When
his sister's pet lamb is killed, the boy insists that Sasha is responsible
and sets a trap in which the animal is caught. Hallie must destroy her
pet to end its suffering, but when John moves to take the pelt, Hallie
threatens to shoot him. Convinced that she is serious, he retreats, and
she buries Sasha. Returning home to find her father very ill, she assumes the responsibility of harvesting the trees, and with the Pennys'
help, the job is completed. Her father regains his strength and, deciding that his daughter needs more social contacts, plans to send her away
to school for the next term.

Analysis. Birdie is a real character, not a cardboard abstraction:
"She was quite broad in the upper part of her body but her legs hung
limp and were pitifully thin. She had a wide smiling face, very pale,
with a high forehead." Though passive and weak, Birdie is seen skillfully maneuvering her wheelchair, dealing forthrightly with her tough
brother, ignoring her father's ponderous pity, enjoying her pet, taking
pleasure from her lovely voice, and even participating in the logging
operation to a very limited extent. Her parents' attitudes and values are
understandable. Though highly protective, their concerns seem consonant with the dimensions of her impairment. Her lack of schooling,
the social deficiencies deriving from the isolated rural setting, as well as
the multiple disabilities, all contribute to her unusually immature perspective. The story is low-key, more disjointed and less satisfactory
than others by the same author, but still offering multidimensional
characters and a well-told tale.

Corcoran, Barbara. *The Winds of Time.* Illus. by Gail Owens. New
York: Atheneum, 1974. 164 pp. Reading Level: YA
Disability: Neurological Impairment; also emotional dysfunction

Since her father had abandoned his family to pursue a career as an
artist and her mother has been reinstitutionalized, Gail's social worker

has made plans for her to be placed in her uncle's care. She resists these arrangements since she neither likes nor trusts him, but he arrives ready to take her to his home. On the drive there, he tries to pat her knee, is scratched by Gail's cat, and loses control of the car. Gail escapes, finding a refuge in the home of an old woman; her son, Sonny; and her great-grandson, Christopher. Sonny has had a stroke and is partially paralyzed but still plays the piano and has learned to compensate somewhat for the lessened functioning of his hand. The family asks few questions and graciously accepts her presence. The sheriff and her uncle come after Gail, but her father also arrives in response to a letter and announces his intention of resuming his daughter's care. The old woman hires him to tutor Chris and satisfactory arrangements are made that will permit Gail to retain her new friendships.

Analysis. Gail's mother's emotional disorders precipitate the events that unfold in this story. While little information about the woman's problems is presented, the impact on an already unstable family structure is shown. Sonny's family has adapted to his impairment, and his attitude of persistence in maximizing his intact abilities is a reasonable and healthy response The characterizations, especially that of Gail, are good, but the plot is strained and the conclusion particularly weak. The fine drawings are compatible with the carefully created mood of the text.

Courlander, Harold. *The Son of the Leopard.* Illus. by Rocco Negri. New York: Crown, 1974. 55 pp. Reading Level: MC
Disability: Orthopedic Impairment, Visual Impairment

The people of Adi Keritoha believe in the reincarnation of souls, so when babies are born their former identity is divined and the names they once used are restored to them. Almost 500 years previously, the men of this tribe revolted against their hated chief, Wolde Nebri, and killed him. When the wise men report that a new child has been born who is the returned spirit of Wolde Nebri, the boy is shunned by all until finally he is stoned and banished from the village. Angry and restless, he searches for meaning in life. Wolde Nebri encounters a blind prophet who predicts he will fail three trials until, through sorrow, he will triumph in the fourth. The failures occur, but the final promised victory eludes him. He then meets an old musician whose "legs were shrivelled and dead." Asked how this occurred, the bard reveals it "happened through knowledge." When young, he "sought knowledge of medicine and magic" and stole a potion to find it. He was very successful but consequently was deprived of the power of his legs. Wolde Nebri says he would gladly make the same sacrifice. He is given a powder, which he takes, and then returns to his village. After falling asleep, he awakens to find that his legs "were as two sticks of wood. They felt no pain, neither would they move." The villagers flee from him and, abandoned like his namesake, he wanders through the countryside paying for food with his music. Upon meeting the fortune teller again, he upbraids him, saying, "Three times I failed, but where is the victory that comes from grief?" Told that his victory lies within, he is satisfied and continues his wandering in peace at last—no longer known as Wolde Nebri, Son of the Leopard, but as the Brother of the Harp.

Analysis. This modern story, derived from Ethiopian sources, recalls themes common to the legends of many peoples. That suffering must precede peace and contentment and that a heavy physical price must be paid for knowledge are found in the Odin myth, among others. The blind seer echoes another popular folk device, suggesting that to see truly one must look beyond what the eyes reveal. The woodcuts are handsome and in keeping with the tone, style, and simple power of the text.

Crane, Caroline. *A Girl Like Tracy.* New York: McKay, 1966. 186 pp.
Reading Level: YA
Disability: Intellectual Impairment

Nineteen-year-old Tracy is severely retarded. Her overprotective mother refuses to let her daughter do more than take care of her own personal needs. As a result, Tracy is frequently bored and sneaks out of the house to look for excitement. Kath, her sister, must hurry home from high school each day to supervise Tracy when their mother leaves for work. At church, Kath meets Alex, who tells her he expects to be drafted soon, but when he returns from service he plans to attend college. He presents a marked contrast to so many of her friends who appear to be drifting and aimless. Kath comes home from school one day to find her mother ill. The woman is hospitalized and this experience makes her confront the idea that some day she will no longer be able to watch over Tracy. The mother informs Kath that one day her sister will become her responsibility. Overwhelmed with feelings of frustration at the immensity of this burden, Kath decides to run away and gets as far as the basic training camp where Alex is stationed. But she returns home without seeing him, fearful that she would be cheapening their relationship. She implores her mother to take Tracy to a workshop sponsored by the Association for Retarded Children. Reluctantly, her mother agrees and is surprised to find a place where her daughter can learn social skills and receive vocational training. Alex comes home on leave to find a much improved family situation and his girl friend planning to get a job so she can save money for a college education.

Analysis. This book seems more a reminder of the rewards that come from adhering to middle-class values than a literary effort. Those who espouse planning for the future, working hard, and going to college are good. Those who drop out of school, have no clear direction, and chase after momentary pleasures are not. The characterization of Tracy is inadequate and contradictory. Her only distinguishing trait seems to be her oft-referred to prettiness. The sheltered workshop in which Tracy is enrolled is posited as a panacea for all her familial, social, and vocational problems. The plot proceeds in a leisurely manner, providing little excitement.

Cunningham, Julia. *Burnish Me Bright.* Illus. by Don Freeman. New York: Pantheon, 1970. 80 pp. Reading Level: MC/YA
Disability: Speech Impairment; also general health problems

Auguste is a gentle, vulnerable orphan who is mute, and is treated harshly by his unfeeling foster parent and abused by children when he is allowed to attend school. The stage is set for tragedy by M. Hilaire, a retired mime, who explains why Auguste is victimized: The "enemy is anyone who is different. They fear the boy who can't speak, the woman who lives by herself and believes in the curative powers of herbs, the man who reads books instead of going to the cafe at night, the person like me who has lived in the distant differentness of the theater. They are not willing to try to understand, so they react against them and occasionally do them injury. I say all this to warn you." The iconoclastic Hilaire finds an apt apprentice in Auguste. Although the boy does make friends with a few children, adults become very suspicious. After contact with Auguste, a sick child becomes healthy, a brat becomes tolerable, and a mad dog is "bewitched" into calmness. Despite these benevolent acts, when things go badly, the villagers conclude that some evil presence is at work. They stone a dog to death and then turn on Auguste. He flees from the enraged mob to the now dead Hilaire's old house, which is set afire. Later, after the fire is out, a child views the boy in burnt clothing pantomiming in the ruins. Hilaire's image is conjured up in a mirror, Auguste repeats a ritual recapitulation of their pantomime lessons, and the image disappears. As Auguste bids goodbye to his friend, he takes his mentor's medal and leaves the town.

Analysis. Although the theme of the book is protest against demands for conformity, the message is weakened by the very intensity of the antihumane actions of many of the characters. Stoning an animal to death, plotting a similar fate for the hero, and setting fire to a house in an attempt to immolate the boy are heavy images for the young reader. These images are especially emotionally devastating because of the author's great skill with language:

The crowd swerved as if on a turntable. Mesmerized, they watched the boy disappear up the road. Then someone shouted, "After him! He's the devil!" Released and wild as a wolf pack, they charged after him. After, they set fire to the house. "The boy's inside," a man answered. And as if his statement commenced a contagion of shame, the crowd began to dissolve, to back off. It turned and started up the road in retreat.

Avril leaped onto the terrace but the solid heat of the flames repelled her. She wished desperately she were in there with her friend, a part of his agony, his death. Alone, she looked upward. There on the roof, his arms outstretched like an eagle about to skim into space, stood Auguste. The distant whiteness of his face seemed to her to be illuminated by another light than the fire. Then, like a vision, he vanished.

Although later the villagers acknowledge that what was done was wrong, this awareness is so skimpy and colorless in comparison to the descriptions of violence that the condemnation of evil recedes and the images of aggression and brutality remain. Partially counterbalancing the effects of this frightening text are the sketchy illustrations that beautifully characterize Auguste's waiflike, ephemeral nature. The mute boy is depicted as an innocent child of nature.

Cunningham, Julia. *Dorp Dead*. Illus. by James Spanfeller. New York: Pantheon, 1965. 88 pp. Reading Level: MC
Disability: Emotional Dysfunction

After Gilly's grandmother dies, the bright, lonely ten-year-old is sent to an orphanage. He builds an invisible barrier between himself and the rest of the world, concealing his ability with a mask of stupidity and isolating himself totally from any intimate social contact. He is sent to a foster home run by an obsessive, compulsive ladder maker, Kobalt, a man as hard and unfeeling as his name. Gilly at first adjusts to the reassuring order and structure but soon realizes that Kobalt means for him and a dog, Mash, to die. He and Mash escape, seeking refuge in a stone tower in the woods where a mysterious hunter once promised him help. There is a confrontation when Kobalt follows the boy whom he violently attacks with his hammer. Fortunately, Gilly and Mash emerge victorious and return to the village where the boy writes on the door his misspelled defiant epithet, "Dorp Dead."

Analysis. This chilling, surrealistic book delivers a tale deceptively simple in plot. The allusions, incomplete images, and insinuated meanings combine with an ominous sense of impending doom. That the writing reveals fine craftsmanship is undisputed; it is the structure, concept, and chaotic values that suffuse the book that generate a sense of uneasiness. The evil man is shown performing apparently motiveless acts. The reader has no knowledge of antecedents or purpose and so can make no sense of Kobalt's behavior. Why does he plan to kill Gilly and the dog? And why is the particularly gruesome fate of hammering them to death selected? Is the black-garbed nameless man a hunter as he claims, or does he represent Gilly's own courage, or Death, or is he some undefined savior? How does he know Gilly is in danger and why should he care? The pathetically crude pejorative that terminates the book is an inadequate piece of defiance to a hostile world and a would-be murderer. The misspelling is dramatic but makes no literary sense since it is no longer the device Gilly uses to conceal his ability and is apparently done without deliberate intent. The excellent illustrations evoke a powerful sense of horror for Kobalt and superbly communicate an image of a man out of control.

Cunningham, Julia. *Far in the Day*. Illus. by Don Freeman. New York: Pantheon, 1972. 98 pp. Reading Level: MC/YA
Disability: Speech Impairment; also general health problems

Auguste, a waiflike mute, wanders into a small, scruffy circus. He meets Billyboy, whose father owns the outfit and whose mother has died of tuberculosis. He is greeted variously: " 'Must be an idiot,' grunted Madame Creel, her eyes, pouched by fat, somewhat satisfied, as though they were feeding on the helplessness of a stranger"; the clown, Tallow: "I like you. . . . Dumb or not, I like you. Maybe because you're stupider than I am"; and Jimsey: "You can't understand one word in fifty and you may well be daft in the head—far in the day is what my grandmother would have called you—but . . . you seem to care." None of the derogatory labels is true—Auguste is a gentle, intelligent soul and a gifted mime. He soon discovers that Madame Creel has some sort of power over Billyboy and is able to force him to steal whenever they stop near a town. Exhausted by these surreptitious efforts and his increasingly debilitating tuberculosis, Billyboy dies. Unfortunately, the unscrupulous woman believes that Billyboy had given some jewels to Auguste and spitefully takes the boy's only keepsake. When she is drunk, Auguste is able to retrieve it. She calls the police and when they will not shoot Auguste, she attempts to kill him herself, but misses the boy and hits a horse instead. Finally, her villainy is revealed, and the boy is freed of her evil manipulations.

Analysis. The sketchy illustrations are satisfying visually and do communicate some feeling of Auguste's fragility and the insubstantiality of circus life. The labeling in the story is very unfortunate. If the villainous Madame Creel calls the mute boy an idiot, that is one thing, since she is evil personified and is eventually punished. However, to have positively portrayed characters think of the hero in such stigmatizing terms is confusing for the young audience to whom this story is addressed.

The story, a sequel to *Burnish Me Bright*, is replete with brutal, senseless violence—a horse is shot; there is an attempt to murder the hero; and Billyboy, a victim of a distracted, neglectful father and an exploitative woman, dies. This pervasive mayhem does not instruct or illuminate, rather it threatens and demeans.

Curry, Jane Louise. *The Change Child*. Illus. by Gareth Floyd. New York: Harcourt, Brace, 1969. 174 pp. Reading Level: YA
Disability: Orthopedic Impairment

In sixteenth-century Wales, Eilian, a lame, impoverished serving maid, is startled when Rastall, a cruel but wealthy young man, hints she will soon be his bride. Distressed and frightened, she returns to her parents' home to find that during her absence their economic circumstances have improved considerably. Her father is pleased to see her but her rejecting mother is angry at the girl's sudden reappearance. Eilian is secretly hurried off to her grandmother's home where she can hide from Rastall, who plans to marry her so that he can claim title to the family's newly acquired wealth. The grandmother is the leader of a band of outlaws who lives by plundering the countryside. She schemes to sacrifice Eilian to bribe the law into leaving her people alone. The old woman, although apparently loving, leads her granddaughter into a trap that, had it succeeded, would have delivered the child into Rastall's hands. The conspirators, however, are all betrayed and many are killed or wounded. Eilian is seized in the confusion and taken to a strange, opulent land, which is the dwelling of the Fair Folk. Eilian is told a legend of a lamed man, a gifted singer like herself, who once dwelt with the Fair Folk. He was slain and his wife, grief-stricken, cursed the fairies, warning them that one of her descendants would be the fateful instrument of their destruction. Eilian's appearance signals the fulfillment of the prophecy: the Fair Folk are destroyed and their kingdom is consumed by fire. Only the king's son, who decides to live with mortals, and Eilian, who returns to her family, escape.

Analysis. Eilian's lameness is a signal that she has been singled out for a special destiny. Echoing ancient Celtic folklore, this contorted and jumbled tale moves back and forth between fantasy and naturalism. Confusion over action, locale, and time frame is disorienting and diminishes the reader's concern and involvement. Ostensible facts, behaviors, and interpretations that exist simultaneously appear to be both true and not true. For example, her mother's suspicions that Eilian is not a "natural" child are correct and yet false since the girl lives both a normal and a magical life. She is a real person, a reincarnation of an ancestor, and an agent of destiny. The grandmother is a natural person and she may or may not be one of the Fair Folk.

The essence of each major person's character is revealed by his or her response to Eilian's crippled limb. Rastall's sadistic and deliberate injury to her foot exposes him as a brute. Her mother's minimization of Eilian's problem identifies her as callous and selfish. The grandmother's gentleness and tenderness establish her credentials as a kind and loving person, despite her later desperate sacrifice of the child. Although there is some discussion of the pain associated with her condition, the impairment essentially serves a mystical purpose.

Davies, Peter. *Fly Away Paul.* New York: Crown, 1974. 213 pp.
Reading Level: MA
Disability: Emotional Dysfunction

Each time Paul runs away from the boys' home in Montreal, he is forcibly returned and brutally beaten. His mother has the boy believing she is making every effort to have him live with her, but in truth, when she does remarry and must choose between Paul and her new husband, she does not choose Paul. Every friend Paul makes is lost to him: One is redeemed by his family and moves away, one dies tragically, and the last is forbidden to see him. The brutality, sadism, and sexual exploitation the defenseless boys endure at the institution cause several whose tragic lives have already made them especially vulnerable to resort to desperate means to find relief. One commits suicide. Paul makes a final desperate attempt to escape, is almost foiled, but manages to elude his pursuers and board a train for Toronto.

Analysis. Fly Away Paul is an unbearably brutal tale of unrelieved physical and psychological abuse. Even though Paul escapes at the end, the permanence of his freedom is questionable and the scars he has accumulated can never be eradicated. The causes of the emotional disorders the boys exhibit are clear: An absence of love is abetted by both deliberate and casual mistreatment. The author makes clear his feeling that such acts can only occur if society is indifferent to the fate of its helpless members. The story is powerful, almost intolerably so, and the unrelieved anguish makes it painful to read.

de Angeli, Marguerite. *The Door in the Wall.* Illus. by author. Garden City, N.Y.: Doubleday, 1949. 121 pp. Reading Level: MC
Disability: Orthopedic Impairment

With thirteenth-century England as the setting, this tale describes how Robin, crippled by an unspecified illness, is rescued by Brother

Luke, who takes him to recuperate at the castle of his father's friend. Dubbed "Crookshanks" by the other boys, he learns to carve, make harps, swim, read, and use crutches. Certain that he would not be caught during the siege at the castle, Robin bravely slips out, crosses an icy ravine, and sets up the signal for the assault. Soon after, the forces of the king are able to subdue the enemy and Robin's sovereign knights him. His father, now released from the king's service, embraces him and "nothing was said of crutches or of misshapen legs." Nevertheless, Robin is uncertain of his father's opinion of him: "Mind you not that I must go thus, bent over, and with these crutches to help me walk?" His father gravely replies, "The courage you have shown, the craftsmanship proven by the harp, and the spirit in your singing all make so bright a light that I cannot see whether or no your legs are misshape [sic]." He is welcomed back in his own family as warmly as young readers will take Robin to their own hearts.

Analysis. The author carefully prepares Robin for his ultimate heroic role and this is intrinsic and not superimposed. His rehabilitation is gradual, natural, and believable. Although there is an unpleasant, descriptive nickname and some teasing, Robin ultimately achieves respect and even envy by his peers: "You can go twice as fast as we can, on those seven-league boots of yours." He fulfills the admonition that one should make the best of what one has and be ready when the doors of opportunity are opened. The tender, detailed pictures promote the image of a disabled boy who is an esteemed, attractive, and well-deserving hero.

DeJong, Meindert. *Journey from Peppermint Street.* New York: Harper & Row, 1968. 242 pp. Reading Level: MC
Disability: Auditory Impairment, Speech Impairment

Siebren is a young Dutch boy living in a small coastal village. His grandfather stops by on his way to visit a dying sister and Siebren is allowed to accompany his grandparent. They have a number of adventures and finally arrive at the remote home of his aunt and uncle. The grandfather and aunt continue the journey, leaving the frightened boy to stay with his huge unknown uncle, who is deaf and mute. The uncle, also named Siebren, writes him a beautiful, gentle, somewhat self-mocking note, and the boy knows he has nothing to fear. An exciting productive fishing experience cements their friendship.

Analysis. Uncle Siebren is clearly a heroic figure and demonstrates both gentleness and strength. He communicates gesturally and by writing. His muteness is a terrible inconvenience, but only that. Knowledge of it inspires awe in young Siebren but this is quickly replaced by affection. The writing is typical DeJong, but the bluntness of the uncle is startling: "Do you think your deaf-and-dumb uncle would let a dumb animal suffer like that—he dumb himself?" The author's use of "dumb," meaning mute, is now archaic but other images are more positive: "They were talking—Aunt Hinka and Uncle Siebren—their eyes fixed on each other. Their fingers must be making letters, and words were flying. Oh, it must be wonderful to make your fingers talk!" *Journey* is a story full of loving, affectionate adults in which the deaf-mute uncle is unexceptional, and of young Siebren, a lad of innocence and unbounded affection.

DeJong, Meindert. *The Wheel on the School.* Illus. by Maurice Sendak. New York: Harper & Row, 1954. Reading Level: MC
Disability: Orthopedic Impairment

Legless Janus lives in a small Dutch village where six children are engaged in searching for a wheel to use as a nesting base to entice storks to settle in their town. Janus is perceived of as the local bogeyman and the children are afraid of him and generate fantastic tales about him. But thanks in large measure to the man's ingenuity, two townspeople are saved, some storks are rescued, and a wheel is readied for the great nesting birds. Janus' image of himself as a competent, social person grows concurrently with the town's changed perception of him from an ogre to a vital and valued community member.

Analysis. The story is folksy, gentle, and old-fashioned. Sendak's illustrations beautifully complement the story and portray Janus in warm terms. The tale reveals the escalating hostility caused by rejection and counterrejection. Mutual antagonism gives way to self-respect and reciprocal affection as Janus joins in the common goal. DeJong says that all—the old, the young, the poor, and the disabled—are useful and needed by the community.

de Trevino, Elizabeth Borton. *Nacar, the White Deer.* Illus. by Enrico Arno. New York: Farrar, Straus, 1963. 147 pp. Reading Level: MC
Disability: Emotional Dysfunction

When Lalo was four years old, he saw his house burn down, but his cries of warning were insufficient to save his mother or her newborn child. Since that traumatic event, he has not spoken one word. Nacar, a white deer, captured in the Philippines, has been given over to his care. Under the boy's loving and skillful protection, the animal had developed into a beautiful mature creature. The viceroy decides to give the deer to the king of Spain and directs Lalo to accompany the animal on the ocean voyage. The king is pleased with the gift. He decides to declare a holiday, release the deer in the forest, and proclaim a hunt for the purpose of killing the noble creature. Lalo is incensed at this threat to the beloved animal and yells out to save Nacar. " 'Our Lady opened your throat because your heart is good,' said the king. 'I consider it a miracle.' " The King promises Nacar will be protected and Lalo can forever live close to it. The boy has one final request. " 'Speak,' said the King. 'I will give you what you ask.' 'Could I learn to sing? Could I learn to be a chorister in the churches?' " The request is, of course, granted.

Analysis. Nacar, the White Deer is a religious story that uses a mute character to demonstrate the power of human and divine love. Even though information about disability is peripheral to the story, yet in delivering the religious message, some myths about the disabled are promulgated. Most notable is the portrayal of Lalo as a true child of nature. In essence, although he could not speak, he could communicate and was one with the animal world, for example: "I have been told about a little Indian boy who is a goatherd and who seems to have some magical understanding of animals" and "The boy did not go up to the animal at once, but stood a little distance away, adjusting his breathing to that of the deer's." The story, read on one level, asserts that the youth's mutism was the result of early trauma and an equally emotional condition is generated by the incipient death of the deer, in a sense shocking him out of a state of psychic mutism. Although this could conceivably occur, this story must not be read literally. The remission of impairment is simply a literary convenience to dramatize a tale of marvels.

Dickinson, Peter. *Heartsease.* Illus. by Nathan Goldstein. Boston: Little, Brown, 1969. 223 pp. Reading Level: YA
Disability: Intellectual Impairment; also orthopedic impairment

It is after the time of the Changes in the near future in England. Margaret, hearing a groan from a rock pile where a witch has just been stoned, concludes the person must still be alive. With the help of a retarded youth, Tim, she hides the man in a barn, offbounds because it contains the engines that ostensibly have been banished in this antitechnological age. To divert the parson, Mr. Gordon, and his cohorts who are searching for an evildoer, Margaret tells them about noticing a lame cat that said "hello." The posse immediately deduces that the witch has changed into a cat, but when they cannot find it, instead kill a bird with a broken wing. When Margaret overhears the parson's suspicions that Tim might be a witch, she becomes alarmed for his safety. The young people decide to try to escape with the wounded man by tugboat through a series of canal locks, now rusty with disuse. Secretly they make their plans and, with maps and instruments taken from abandoned boats and the overhaul of the boat's simple engine, they are optimistic about reaching the sea. The group concocts a cover story to explain the surreptitious movements, but the evil parson has been alerted that some forbidden act is in the wind. Margaret, astride her horse, works the canal locks and bridge openings as the boat is pulled through them. The parson, whose crippled condition has so worsened that he must be transported in a litter, has nonetheless assembled a gang of cronies who plan to trap the escapees at an upcoming bridge. Through the use of a bull to divert the hostile townspeople, the complicated plot succeeds, and the boat chugs through the last barrier on its own engine. Enraged, the mob attacks them and Margaret escapes an axe tossed at her by jumping on the passing boat. Although the others escape to Ireland, Margaret returns to live in the home of her relatives.

Analysis. The proposition that technological and political repression go hand in hand is suggested here. Although this story is cast in the future, one has an uneasy feeling of recycled history. Echoes of Salem are heard in the suggestion that manifestation of disability, even in nonhuman creatures, is incontrovertible evidence of evil. Equally chilling is the concept that suppression of nonconformity will continue in the future and that victimization of the handicapped may be public policy in future societies. The interplay of these issues provides a gripping story that is marred by such flaws as fuzzy motivations, the contradiction of the oppressor of the disabled being safe, although crippled himself, and an ending illogical in terms of antecedent events. Tim, while not developed as a major character, is portrayed as valued by his sister and able to play a significant role in the group's escape to freedom.

Dickson, Marguerite. *Bramble Bush.* Illus. by Ruth King. New York: Longmans, Green, 1945. 270 pp. Reading Level: YA
Disability: Visual Impairment

Family financial problems keep Mary Elizabeth from attending college. When a new family moves to town, she becomes friendly with Ruth, the blind daughter. Since an accident two years ago in which she lost her sight, Ruth has become totally dependent, even letting others wash and dress her. Mary Elizabeth embarks on a concerted missionary campaign to reinvolve Ruth in life and so takes her on walks, invites her to dinner, and accompanies her to concerts. Their mutual friend reawakens an interest in music and Ruth resumes her practicing. A New Year's party is planned to provide more social experiences for Ruth and in this it succeeds. A general musical competition is held and although the blind girl does not win, she is awarded an honorable mention as one who "in spite of a heartbreaking handicap, gave us last night a performance we shall long remember for its excellence." Ruth, buoyed by her friends, her rewarding experiences, and a sense of confidence, is now ready to resume a full life and enrolls in a school for the blind. Before Ruth enters, she and her two friends are involved in an automobile accident. Although the others are uninjured, Ruth suffers a concussion and is rushed to a local hospital. When she regains consciousness, she finds her sight has been restored. Everyone is overjoyed and all agree it has been a remarkable year.

Analysis. The attitudes expressed toward blindness in this particularly inept attempt at literature are naive and misleading. Mary Elizabeth's uncle remarks—"And blind people, they aren't always unhappy . . ."—inadvertently suggesting that unhappiness is their norm. The general tone is condescending and patronizing: "She's an attractive looking girl, isn't she?" one character asks. "Yes, she is. And it seems so awful to be like that all her life," another responds. When referring to some deaf-blind students, a teacher portentiously says, "And now we have six children here who are being led out of silence and darkness to understand the world about them." To provide a neat climax and happy resolution, the myth of the instantaneous curative powers of a blow to the head is revived. It is at once ludicrous, erroneous, and offensive.

Donovan, John. *Remove Protective Coating a Little at a Time.* New York: Harper, 1973. 101 pp. Reading Level: YA
Disability: Emotional Dysfunction

When Harry's parents bring him home from summer camp, he sees that his mother's behavior is strange, aloof, and withdrawn. During the days before school begins, Harry plays alone in the park where he encounters Amelia, an eccentric old woman. Accompanying her home to a condemned building, he is entertained by her biographical reminiscences and her unorthodox, highly pragmatic philosophy. Amelia survives principally through panhandling, with her diet occasionally enriched by pigeons attracted and deceived by her bird-feeding ploy. Harry's mother becomes increasingly unstable. Her sessions with a therapist are not productive and she is admitted to a psychiatric hospital, but is able to visit her family briefly at Christmas. On a visit to Amelia's home, Harry finds a large mongrel with a severely deformed leg in residence. Later, Harry sees the dog roaming the streets and by spring the wreckers have leveled Amelia's home.

Analysis. The increasing instability of Harry's mother is sketchily, though convincingly, developed through episodes that interpret the vacuous life she feels she now leads and her attempt to resurrect happier more fulfilling teenage days when the excitement and flush of youth made everything seem not only possible but assured. Finding her lifestyle so much less than her inflated Hollywood dreams, she retreats. As she makes tentative steps back to recovery, she still must borrow her psychiatrist's words, finding her own efforts inadequate to explain and interpret her behavior to herself and others. Her seemingly irrelevant life is contrasted with that of the casual, practical Amelia whose rootless, amoral lifestyle provides an emotional oasis for Harry. The story concludes on a note of optimism as his mother initiates the painful reconstruction of her life. This canny, cynical, sophisticated book is basically a coming-of-age story in which Harry encounters various lifestyles, beliefs, and crises that demand of him more complex, mature responses.

Duncan, Lois. *Ransom*. Garden City, N.Y.: Doubleday, 1966. 188 pp. Reading Level: YA
Disability: Orthopedic Impairment

Dexter, now seventeen, lives with his bachelor uncle, a reluctant guardian who is away on business much of the time. After a bout with polio at twelve, the musculature on his right side remained underdeveloped and, although he has learned to ski and write with his left hand, the youth retains a residual limp and the social status of a loner. His school bus is hijacked and Dexter and several others are transferred to a lonely mountain cabin. There are many complications attendant on obtaining ransom for each person, which create problems for the kidnappers. In an aborted escape attempt, Dexter is wounded. Despite his protests, one of the girls, Jesse, removes Dexter's jacket to give first aid and notes his physical condition. Helpless, he complains she is staring at him, but she silences him with a kiss. One kidnapper is killed in a road accident and the others are eventually captured. The abduction experience affects several family relationships. One naive boy's admiration for his ne'er-do-well brother diminishes to a more accurate critical assessment, and a girl's inflated affection for a selfish father is replaced by respect for her brave stepfather whom she had disdained and rejected.

Analysis. Ransom is a crisply written adventure story. There is reasonably good character development and the perceptions, aspirations, and conflicts of adolescence are ably used to substantiate the credibility of the plot. Although Dexter is the only hostage who gets shot (and such behavior is too frequently directed against the disabled in books), in this case it is a most likely event given the sequence of the story. He is the one who engineers the escape plan and at the end is seen as a romantic figure by a girl who up to that point also had been portrayed as a loner. Their blossoming relationship provides the low-key romantic interest of the tale. After the wounded young man is kissed, his abrasive query is, " 'You're sorry for me, is that it?' His voice began to harden. 'You don't have to be. If you think you're going to play the fairy princess, going around kissing cripples to turn them into. . . .' " Jesse angrily protests, taking Dexter's comment as a criticism of her life and beliefs. "I've heard symphonies written by blind composers and seen cathedrals designed by dying artists, and none of them were cripples, none of them! It's bitterness that makes a person a cripple, bitterness and meanness and smallness! It's an emptiness inside them, not anything to do with their bodies!" Dexter relaxes, relieved by the observation that she does not consider him handicapped but simply a young man she admires. Except for this obvious and excessive sermon, the message that value resides in character, not body structure, is delivered effectively.

Ehrlich, Bettina. *A Horse for the Island.* Illus. by author. New York: Harper, 1952. 213 pp. Reading Level: MC/YA
Disability: Emotional Dysfunction

The Tarlao family purchases some land on a tiny Italian island. The oldest son, Benedetto, "lost his speech at the age of three when a fire in their home caused him great fright and his temporary removal to the house of an unkind old aunt inflicted much distress on the child." He shows no other signs of stress, is a kind and patient boy, and helps his hardworking family by fishing and working the land. While delivering produce in the lagoons, he meets Margherita with whom he instantly falls in love. During a terrible winter, he dreams she is calling to him to save her, and he harnesses his horse to find her. His younger brother, Toni, tries to stop him, but Benedetto cries out and explains his mission. The boy is deliriously happy at hearing his brother speak after years of silence and, though worried for his safety, assists him. Benedetto drives the horse across the frozen waters and returns with the desperately sick girl to the hospital where the nuns nurse her back to health. His mother and the townspeople consider his restoration of speech a miracle. When Margherita is strong enough and has assembled a proper dowry, she and Benedetto are married. They grow older and have children. Through technology, their world changes as the little island is invaded by progress, but, since human nature does not change, they stay much the same.

Analysis. A single traumatic incident is seen as causing Benedetto's muteness, but leaves him with no other psychological scars. The lack of speech is a contrivance—introduced so that it could be retracted, creating a dramatic moment. Necessity causes him to abandon his world of silence as precipitously as he entered it. This simplistic view of events results in a cozy, warm, but not very profound, pastoral story.

Elkins, Evelyn. *Chuck, a Story of the Florida Pinelands.* Philadelphia:
Lippincott, 1948. 211 pp. Reading Level: MC
Disability: Orthopedic Impairment, Emotional Dysfunction, Visual
Impairment

Infantile paralysis has left Chuck with damaged leg muscles and a
terrible fear that he will never be able to walk again. His doctor is confident that the boy will acquire full functioning with sufficient exercise.
Hoping to tempt his nature-loving son, Chuck's father brings home
small objects, including a baby skunk, from his hunting trips. Chuck's
mother tells her son that if he wishes to keep the animal he must be
responsible for its care and feeding. So motivated, the boy gets out of
bed and eventually recovers completely. Chuck's brother, recently
home from service in World War II, is in a deep state of depression,
unable to work or concentrate on anything. When Chuck accuses him of
withholding his badly needed ability to contribute to the family's support, he realizes the truth of the charge and pitches in immediately with
the family chores, improving his mental health in the process.

The announcement that a blind cousin plans a visit to the farm at
first fills the family with apprehension. Their fears prove unfounded
when the cousin manages in this totally new environment without any
apparent need for assistance at all.

Analysis. The individual chapters, brought together in this volume,
were originally published separately. The resultant lack of continuity is
only one of the structural problems. More serious is the lack of con-
gruity between the characters described and any possibility of real-life
similarity. The painfulness and difficulty of regaining the use of damaged muscles are honestly portrayed, but the cure is too precipitous and
complete to be convincing. The brother's depression is equally subject
to total and nearly instantaneous remediation. In attempting to demonstrate how well a blind person can function, adaptation is so minimal
and effortless that Elkin leaves the impression that no serious limitation
exists at all—a thoroughly misleading inference.

Ellis, Ella Thorp. *Celebrate the Morning.* New York: Atheneum, 1972.
177 pp. Reading Level: YA
Disability: Emotional Dysfunction

Fourteen-year-old April lives with her mother in a small California
town. The woman, a gentle, romantic dreamer, has become increasingly detached from reality. She no longer does housework or cooks and
her nocturnal meanderings into town have provoked warnings by the
concerned sheriff to April to keep her mother under closer watch. Fermine, a neighbor, wishes to marry her mother. April both resents his
intrusions into her life and depends on him as the only stable, trust-

worthy, and unwaveringly supportive adult she knows. When her mother becomes physically ill and her behavior more erratic, their welfare worker arranges for the woman to be hospitalized. April's mother wanders out of the hospital and when finally located is brought back, but soon thereafter transferred to an asylum. April's visit to her in this new setting is terribly traumatic. The girl refuses to return, and when Fermine pressures her, she reveals that at the end of her last visit, the nurse mistakenly thought it was she, not her mother, who was the patient. April is fearful that if she goes back, the authorities mistakenly will confine her there. Fermine comforts the distraught child, swearing he would never allow such a thing to happen. April accompanies her friends to a fortune teller who predicts the girl's troubles will pass. Trusting in Fermine, and more self-confident, she is able to visit her mother again. Relieved of the total burden of her mother's care, she appears able to begin to build a life for herself.

Analysis. This portrait of the emotionally dysfunctional woman may help to challenge some stereotypes about mental disorders, shedding light on the difficulties experienced by the friends and families of such people. The mother is presented as a poetic, forgetful woman, whose perceptions are so selective, whose behavior is so irrational, and whose judgment is so poor that she cannot function out of a totally protective environment. There is no way she can accept parental responsibilities, and, in effect, the roles of mother and child have been reversed. April and Fermine, loving and unswervingly loyal to her, are dramatically contrasted with the father who deserted the family, but who remembers April's birthday only with extravagant presents. The character of the social worker presents a vehicle whereby commentary on the inadequacy of social services is pointedly made. The portrait of a child who has to cope with the ramifications of such serious problems is expertly drawn. Characterizations are good but the story itself lacks a defined structure, a clearly felt climax or a satisfactory conclusion.

Ericsson, Mary Kentra. *About Glasses for Gladys.* Illus. by Pauline Batchelder Adams. Chicago: Melmont, 1962. 31 pp. Reading Level: YC
Disability: Visual Impairment

Gladys is a third-grade student, picked on by her classmates because of her myopia. She follows the school nurse's suggestion to have her eyes tested and discovers that glasses enable her to function much better in school as well as relieve her of headaches.

Analysis. Much information about vision testing and its importance is presented yet the content is comprehensible by young children. Difficult vocabulary is eased by syllabified words. The narrative is flat and

unimaginative, typical of quasi-fiction, but the illustrations are pleasant.

Essex, Rosamund. *Into the Forest.* New York: Coward-McCann,
1965. 156 pp. Reading Level: MC/YA
Disability: Visual Impairment, Auditory Impairment, Orthopedic
Impairment

Into the Forest is a Christian allegory of the search for salvation.
Wystan, blind; Bridget, lame; and Hadrian, deaf, have been orphaned
by the Great Destruction. They have tried to avoid the roving bands of
scavengers who steal and rob the vulnerable. They encounter Ted and
Sally, who are invited to join them in their search for the World where
they will be safe. Ted takes over the role of leader from Wystan, but he
leads them astray. They encounter (St.) Christopher, who returns them
to the proper path and directs them to the home of Mrs. Hospitality
where they are refreshed and replenished and sent on their way. The
perils increase and each of the travelers is separately threatened and
barely escapes and, with each other's assistance, survives. At the moment of greatest despair, Christopher appears once more and leads
them to the crest of the mountain from which they can see the golden
beautiful land they seek.

Analysis. The disabled characters symbolize humanity's imperfections that hamper the search for redemption. Despite the extended descriptions, the impairments are not seen or meant to be real, so no
information or attitude toward them is significant in terms of real-life
counterparts. The violence and trickery they encounter are not so much
directed at them as disabled, but as people with symbolic blemishes.
The impairments are strictly metaphorical, that is, all people are blind
to the way, deaf to the message, and so on, that would lead them to the
promised land.

Eyerly, Jeanette. *The Girl Inside.* Philadelphia: Lippincott, 1968. 186
pp. Reading Level: YA
Disability: Emotional Dysfunction; also general health problems

Christina's life has been a series of tragedies. Her parents died, she
was sexually molested, and her false presumption of responsibility for
her father's fatal accident led her to attempt suicide. After transferring
to a juvenile home, she meets Mr. Keller, who becomes her foster father. She moves to the Keller home and helps with their son, Davy.
Everyone has a hard time adjusting to the new situation, and Christina
gives in to much self-absorbed contemplation. In her new school she
encounters Clay, an attractive student; Barbara, his vindictive girl
friend; and an obese girl whose offer of friendship she rebuffs. Clay has

managed to get hold of her school files, and tells her he admires her for her strength in coping with the trauma in her life. Her respite from trouble is brief and she becomes frightened when she observes that the man who once attacked her is nearby. She is further devastated when Mr. Keller dies and she overhears his widow implying that she had contributed to his fatal heart attack. Inevitably, her depressed state is reflected in her school grades, and her low spirits become of serious concern to her friends, especially to Clay. After the young Keller boy falls down the stairs, she again contemplates suicide despite predictions that he will recover. Christina is given a letter by the overweight, lonely girl that reveals her intent to commit suicide. Rushing to her, Christina finds that the girl has changed her mind and this fact gives Christina the courage to abandon her own intentions to kill herself. Finally ready to begin rebuilding her life, she seeks help from a doctor whom she discovers is Clay's mother.

Analysis. One tragedy relentlessly follows another in this soap opera. As is typical of this genre, events move inexorably downward, holding the reader's interest by the sheer outrageousness of the heroine's misfortunes. Descriptions of pressures that led to her suicidal attempts and of the hard, brittle protective veneer she developed are the most credible aspects of this unlikely tale. However, the crises are so overblown and the solutions so neat and simplistic that no insights into the problems of stress can be gleaned from this story.

Eyerly, Jeanette. *The Phaedra Complex.* Philadelphia: Lippincott, 1971. 159 pp. Reading Level: YA/MA
Disability: Emotional Dysfunction

Laura Richards lives with her wealthy, divorced mother in New York City. Her mother marries Michael, a well-known correspondent, who successfully pressures his new wife to quit working. Laura and Michael develop a turbulent relationship in which a mutual attraction is disguised by overt hostility. Soon Laura's mother begins to exhibit distressing behavior. No longer involved in stimulating activities, and jealous of her husband's unconscious but obvious fascination with her daughter, she becomes slothful, withdrawn, argumentative, and depressed. Laura comes home one day to find her mother has attempted suicide. It is questionable whether she can completely recover from the effects of the overdose of pills she has taken. Her psychiatrist explains to Laura and Michael that they are living out a variation of the Phaedra myth and this has contributed to the mother's illness. Laura encounters a former boyfriend who had become jealous of her relationship with her stepfather. Now it appears, since both he and Laura will be going to school in New Hampshire, their friendship will be rekindled and the unseemly attraction between stepdaughter and father surrogate will be terminated.

Analysis. Hints of incestuous attraction are exploited in this shallow novel. Nothing in the story related to emotional dysfunction is credible. Neither the onset, development, nor facile explanations yield insight or compassion. To use the Phaedra complex as a title when it is an inaccurate description of the relationship—as the psychiatrist says, a "variation" of the Phaedra myth—is an example of the literary carelessness typified in the story.

Faber, Nancy W. *Cathy at the Crossroads.* Illus. by Howard Simon. Philadelphia: Lippincott, 1962. 190 pp. Reading Level: MC
Disability: Intellectual Impairment

Cathy, a lonely and insecure child, had been distressed at her father's plans to remarry. The child rebuffs all the attempts of Barbara, her stepmother, to establish a warm relationship. Neither the woman's efforts to decorate Cathy's room, nor her encouragement and approval of the child's participation in the school play, nor her hospitality toward Cathy's friends breaks through the child's reserve. Barbara begins to receive late night calls that necessitate leaving the house. One day she returns home very ill with pneumonia and Cathy suddenly realizes how important her stepmother is to the family. After Barbara's recovery, another urgent call is received, but this time the inquisitive Cathy trails her parents to a special school. There she sees a girl lying on the ground talking to Barbara, whom she calls "mother." The girl is taken to a hospital and Barbara tells Cathy that the sick child is her daughter, Anne, who is retarded, a fact she had never mentioned because of Cathy's hostility to the marriage. Cathy, realizing that her unpleasant behavior was shameful and unwarranted, now welcomes both Anne and Barbara into her life.

Analysis. Of the many faults of this story, the most deplorable is the totally erroneous impressions conveyed about the behavior of retarded children. Anne is shown to exhibit developmental abilities widely discordant with usual expectations. She can read and write—advanced, demanding skills—but uses only one color when she prints and is too uncoordinated to throw a ball, activities requiring only primitive gross motor and perceptual skills. Despite such low-level coordination, plans are made to send Anne to a vocational school where, "She'll learn to make things with her hands—perhaps even to type," an unlikely projection for a child with such ascribed limitations. The story is contrived and the characterizations unconvincing.

Faber, Nancy W. *Cathy's Secret Kingdom.* Illus. by Howard Simon. Philadelphia: Lippincott, 1963. 183 pp. Reading Level: MC
Disability: Emotional Dysfunction

Intrigued by rumors about a haunted house, Cathy goes there and discovers instead a private haven where she can write undisturbed. Her talent has been affirmed in a junior high school writing contest in which her essay on happiness as one of the greatest gifts wins first prize. Cathy is convinced that her retarded stepsister, Anne, could learn if she really wanted to, and, disdaining the views of the parents and educators from Anne's special school, begins to teach her to do such things as ride a bike. When Cathy convinces Anne to attend a dance, a new phase of her rapid rehabilitation begins. Dismayed when she finds that the old house she has come to think of as her secret "kingdom" is to be sold, Cathy is reassured that happiness is not in a place but in one's heart.

Analysis. Below the harmless platitudes are several dubious story elements. In the antecedent story, *Cathy at the Crossroads*, Anne was described as retarded. In this book this is shown to be a pretense, although "her blue eyes held a strange, empty expression. It was a not-glad, not-sad, not anything sort of expression. . . . Anne was learning little, doing nothing." Despite an evaluation by professionals and by her mother that Anne "didn't develop like other little girls," a teacher whom Cathy consults who has had no close contact with Anne blithely asserts, "She *is* as smart as anyone, Cathy. Because Anne isn't what we call a true retardate. I think the whole thing will turn out to be emotional." The girl's behavior is undoubtedly due to separation anxiety, the teacher explains. Such an interpretation, based on the most casual of contacts, is totally unwarranted. It uses the terminology of psychology to give credence to a ridiculous plot resolution. Additionally, emotionalism runs rampant throughout the story: "The money from selling this house will help my husband take care of mentally ill children who need his help"; when Cathy wins the prize, "No one said what was in all their minds: Cathy had been given so much; Anne, so little." Youngsters reading this book may identify with Anne and feel equally bereft.

Fanshawe, Elizabeth. *Rachel.* Illus. by Michael Charlton. Scarsdale, N.Y.: Bradbury, 1975. unpaged. Reading Level: YC
Disability: Orthopedic Impairment

In a sense, Rachel's story is that she does not have a special story. She is a very young average looking child who must use a wheelchair. She participates fully in school, and has a full and loving family life and friends who like her company. She enjoys life hugely and ignores whenever possible the inconvenience of her means of travel.

Analysis. As a work of quasi-fiction, this deceptively simple book is a gem. The heroine's portrayal, without hint of pity or condescension, is beautifully crafted. As in books for beginning readers, illustrations are of prime importance and Charlton has risen marvelously to the task. His last illustration, where the viewer cannot readily find Rachel in a crowded room, makes a powerful statement about the common humanity of all children. (See Figure 3.)

Fassler, Joan. *Howie Helps Himself.* Illus. by Joe Lasker. Chicago: Whitman, 1975. unpaged. Reading Level: YC
Disability: Neurological Impairment

There are many things Howie cannot do. He cannot skip or run or write his name. He walks with difficulty and needs a wheelchair to travel. A special school bus with a hydraulic lift picks him up daily. What he wants more than anything is to learn to maneuver his wheelchair independently. Finally he succeeds, and his father, who has seen his triumph and appreciated the effort involved, shares his elation.

Analysis. Packed into this slim portrayal of Howie's achievement is an extraordinary amount of information about the problems of daily living associated with cerebral palsy. Holding small items, dressing and feeding himself, and playing most games are activities that Howie has not yet mastered. In addition, the discouragement resulting from aspirations far outstripping ability, and the frustrations that are the inevitable concomitants of dependency, are made clear to even the young reader. When the illustrations depict classroom scenes, manifestations of Howie's emotions, or the loving quality of his family's relationships, they are excellent. Howie's posture and positioning of limbs, so characteristic of cerebral-palsied youngsters, are forthrightly shown. One picture contrasts Howie and his mother quietly waiting for his special bus with other children energetically running off to catch theirs. This effectively points out his feelings of isolation. However, when Lasker resorts to symbolization, he lapses into clichés, for example, soaring birds and golden sunsets.

The writing is strained and choppy, similar to that found in basal readers. There is no true plot, rather a string of scenes that culminate in Howie learning to manage his wheelchair. Despite the more active or outgoing aspects of his character, such as liking to learn, play ball, or make friends, Howie is initially characterized as a passive, somewhat undistinguished child. The considerable value of the book lies in its honest, accurate, and direct presentation of the problems of a severely physically handicapped child. As a discussion guide, this book is useful with disabled as well as nondisabled youngsters. (See Figure 2.)

Fassler, Joan. *One Little Girl.* Illus. by M. Jane Smyth. New York: Human Sciences, 1969. unpaged. Reading Level: YC
Disability: Intellectual Impairment

Laurie can do many things, but adults are concerned about her learning rate. She has a psychological examination and the report reveals that she is a slow learner but well adjusted. Laurie feels better when her positive attributes are considered.

Analysis. This well-meaning book of quasi-fiction suffers from a lack of focus as to its appropriate audience. Both the sketches and the text appear directed toward adults who read at the second-grade level. Except for some illustrations where she looks sad, Laurie is pictured in positive terms.

First, Julia. *Flat on My Face.* Englewood Cliffs, N.J.: Prentice-Hall, 1974. 95 pp. Reading Level: MC
Disability: Neurological Impairment

Laura Loring, a sixth-grader, is dissatisfied with her lack of popularity. One day she babysits for George, a boy with cerebral palsy who is confined to an electric wheelchair. Overcome by mutual admiration and a shared passion for baseball, they instantly and improbably become fast friends. Laura arranges to take nine-year-old George to a local baseball game, an act that promotes her attractiveness in the eyes of the school hero. George is overjoyed to hold a bat for the first time and the event is preserved by the local school photographer. When George mentions that the other children at his special school also like the sport, Laura embarks on a project to bring them all to the next Little League game. The complex logistics having been solved, the curious community shows up to view the unusual guests as well as the contest. Laura's sixth-grade class bestows a bat, ball, uniform, and certificate naming George an honorary member of the league. He "gurgled his thanks."

Analysis. The characters and the ostensible humanitarian goals of the plot lack depth. George is the device by which Laura's innate benevolence is demonstrated, her popularity achieved, and the crossover from a tomboy to a mothering "feminine" role is begun. To state that cerebral palsy is a disease, to treat her contact with George as the personification of a mission, to provide him with dialogue and then give him a "gurgling" speech in the climax, to have instant proof of his character by physical appearance—all this is bad enough. But to make the climax of the book a circus spectacle where the town appears to watch the "unfortunates" enjoy themselves is highly offensive and sabotages the author's presumably benign intent.

First, Julia. *Getting Smarter.* Englewood Cliffs, N.J.: Prentice-Hall, 1974. 89 pp. Reading Level: MC/YA
Disability: Visual Impairment

Rona considers the news that she needs glasses as the final blow to her shaky self-appraisal. Her mother, in a burst of raised consciousness, leaves her husband's delicatessen, and of necessity is replaced by Rona. Demoralized by people's reaction to her glasses and determined to use the money she earns for contact lenses, Rona hopes to attract the attention of a would-be boyfriend. An attempt to make additional money selling greeting card verses fails and the purchase must be delayed. When she waits on some college students, Rona notices that one has a white cane. Jerry is very casual about his blindness, but Rona is nervous and turns away from him. Jerry gently informs her, "With this din in here, you have to speak fairly loudly, because I can't read lips, you know." When she looks at his eyes, she notes: "The difference was there was no expression in them. The happy or sad look that you see in people's eyes wasn't there. They were sort of blank." She muses, "Golly, he talks about his affliction as if it doesn't bother him at all." She reports to her best friend, "It's so strange. I mean, he's like regular. You'd never know." A heavy plain girl with glasses, who is clearly the girl friend of Jerry's handsome friend, comes in, and Rona is dumbfounded. She shares the insight with her girl friend that she no longer desires contact lenses since external appearances are really not important.

Analysis. Rona is portrayed as a teenager preoccupied with some prototypical crises and emerges as a barely credible, if not overly bright, character in this pedestrian novel. The blind youth is used in a routine manner to provide perspective for the less seriously but similarly affected person. Jerry's characterization is shallow but very upbeat and he is seen as a person coping socially and academically.

Fitzgerald, John D. *The Great Brain.* Illus. by Mercer Mayer. New York: Dial, 1967. 175 pp. Reading Level: MC/YA
Disability: Orthopedic Impairment

Tom is a ten-year-old boy, a non-Mormon in a predominantly Mormon small town in Utah before the turn of the century. Tom's moniker, "The Brain," is earned when he cunningly uses his wits in money-making deals or in getting revenge on a teacher, although he sometimes employs them for higher motives. Tom's father, a newspaper editor, convinces an itinerant Jewish peddler to open a store in town. However, the mercantile business is essentially a religious monopoly, and when customers are obliged to purchase from their coreligionists, the stranger's business fails. Too proud to reveal his poverty, the Jew starves to death and the townspeople only then realize they were not sufficiently interested in the problems of one they perceived as an outsider.

Tom's friend, Andy, steps on a nail and the subsequent infection is so pervasive that the leg must be amputated below the knee. Andy is depressed at his inability to do the many things he once took for granted and makes some desperate and ridiculous suicide attempts. The Great Brain analyzes Andy's strengths and teaches him how to compensate for his deficiencies using his wooden leg. Tom's instructions are so good that Andy is able to provide a crucial home run for their baseball team. Tom's return of a construction set he conned out of one of his followers heralds the beginning of the Great Brain's reformation. He further astonishes observers when he gives back the profits he made on numerous deals. His brother sums it up: "And so it came to pass just a week before Christmas . . . a miracle took place in Adenville, Utah. The Christmas spirit arrived at our house early and with the help of a boy with a peg leg made a Christian out of my brother."

Analysis. The dominant thread that permeates this seriocomic story is the responsibility and resultant obligations of brotherhood. Lack of concern or compassion toward outgroup representatives is dramatized in the incident involving the Jewish peddler, and echoed in the harassment of Basil, the son of a Greek immigrant. Although Andy's characterization is credible, he also performs a specific function in relation to the hero: As Tom assists Andy in regaining self-confidence and physical mobility, so Andy is the instrument for Tom's transformation. Below the surface banter, poor self-image, physical and psychological distress, and the fear and reality of inadvertent social exclusion are sensitively explored. The writing is crisp and stylish and humanistic messages are delivered in a subtle and low-key manner. The otherwise charming and supportive illustrations do not show the disabled boy even though his rehabilitation is critical to the resolution of the plot.

Forbes, Esther. *Johnny Tremain.* Illus. by Lynd Ward. Boston: Houghton Mifflin, 1943. 256 pp. Reading Level: MC/YA
Disability: Orthopedic Impairment; also cosmetic impairment

In the years just preceding the American Revolution, Johnny Tremain is apprenticed to a Boston silversmith. Mr. Lapham has become so absorbed in his religious ruminations that he neglects his trade. Johnny is his most talented worker, but the boy's pride, skill, and obvious lack of deference earn him the disapproval of his master and the hostility of the other apprentices. A wealthy customer places an order, but it cannot be completed on time unless work is done on the Sabbath, a practice

Mr. Lapham refuses to countenance. His wife, concerned about the family's declining fortunes, persuades Johnny to carry out the work in secret. One of the resentful apprentices sabotages a crucible of molten silver so that it spills on Johnny's hand, causing excruciating pain. Desperate to hide evidence that any work was done on a holy day, no doctor is called, and only inadequate remedies are tried. When the pain subsides, and the extensive burn heals, it is clear that Johnny's hand is too badly injured for him to continue in his chosen profession. Out of work and shaken by the reactions to his disfigurement, he recalls his dead mother's instructions to use a silver cup as his unassailable credential to establish kinship with a wealthy family. He is accused of stealing the vessel and, although acquitted, is deprived of this valuable memento through trickery. He encounters a young man who helps him find a job on a newspaper and initiates him into revolutionary activities. He meets Sam Adams, Paul Revere, John Hancock, and their coterie of followers who will be instrumental in establishing the independence of the young country. From Dr. Warren he learns it is not too late to correct the damage done to his hand and he happily discovers that his mother came from a wealthy family to whose properties he has a legitimate claim.

Analysis. The feeling that the patriots were embarking on a dangerous, costly, but glorious adventure is vigorously conveyed in this exciting novel. Johnny's injury is viewed as divine punishment for breaking the Sabbath, a view of disability as punishment then commonly held. It is clear, though, that this perception is that of the characters in the novel, and not one the author accepts. In fact, the quality of various people's characters is reflected almost perfectly in their reaction to Johnny's hand. Mrs. Lapham considers Johnny useless: "That's worse than anything I had imagined. Now isn't that a shame! Bright boy like Johnny just ruined. No more good than a horse with sprung knees." The spoiled Lapham child now finds him repulsive: "Don't touch me! Don't touch me with that dreadful hand." The cowardly and inept apprentice is pleased, glad that one superior to him has been reduced in station. Cilla, the kind and sensitive Lapham child, is concerned and solicitous of Johnny's feelings. The compassionate doctor offers his skill and time to restore functioning, suggesting that the boy might be able to return to his craft. The actual physical adaptations Johnny must make are not nearly as significant as the array of attitudes expressed toward his disability. The illustrations do not show his hand at all but otherwise picture the youth in strongly positive terms.

Forman, James. *The Shield of Achilles.* New York: Farrar, Straus, 1966. 211 pp. Reading Level: MA
Disability: Orthopedic Impairment; also general health problems

The fight between Greek and Turkish factions for dominance of Cyprus forms the backdrop for the story of young people who find themselves actors in a turbulent drama. Eleni is sent to Athens to pursue her art studies. She is worried about her mother in a tuberculosis sanitorium where she is receiving inadequate care and about her friends whose loyalties are with different factions. She stays with her uncle whose injuries from World War II are regarded as badges of honor. Eleni is not prepared for the extent of his disablement and is at first repulsed to find that both his legs have been amputated. She grows increasingly fond of him, and just before she returns home, buys him a wheelchair with the last of her money. Seeing this as an act of pity, the uncle is furious. Unwittingly, she has attacked his pride by this innocent gesture. The two are reconciled before she leaves and the uncle sells the chair, continuing to propel himself in a cart he had adapted for this purpose. Eleni returns home to devastation. One of her friends who has become fanatical kills one of the others. Eleni reveals his hiding place to the British soldiers and he is killed too. Overwhelmed, she swims out to sea planning to drown, but at the last minute changes her mind. She signals a boat to save her and returns home to try and rebuild her life.

Analysis. *The Shield of Achilles* is a powerful antiwar polemic that speaks against the destruction of lives and bodies. The fanatic's name, Phaeton, is reminiscent of the mythic character whose attempt to control the fiery chariot of the sun resulted in devastation of the earth. Phaeton's guerilla tactics are portrayed as similarly destructive. His first act involves an explosion that leaves a little girl without hands, as fighting in a previous war left Eleni's uncle legless. The volatile reaction and fierce pride of the veteran show he feels he has lost not only his mobility but also his manhood. His wounds also consign him to poverty since he must live on an inadequate pension plus the meager sums he makes from peddling cards. How disability affects self-perception and how it can result in economic deprivation are well developed. The story is complex, highly symbolic, well-written, and overwhelmingly somber. In a large sense the novel deals with nationalistic as well as personal obsessions.

Frick, C. H. *Five against the Odds.* New York: Harcourt, Brace, 1955. 210 pp. Reading Level: MC/YA
Disability: Orthopedic Impairment

After months of therapy following polio, Tim Moore returns home with crutches and a leg brace. A former basketball star, Tim bitterly forbids anyone even to discuss the subject in his presence. His brothers are both on the high school team, but their ragged playing is contributing to the team's losing streak. Realizing he is to blame for making his brothers feel guilty and distraught, Tim shows up at the next game, demonstrates his change of heart, and helps initiate a turnaround in team morale. The example of his grandfather with whom he lives and who lost a leg in World War I, and the chance encounter with a seemingly independent armless boy, convince Tim that he can adapt to his disability. Through a combination of persistence, chance, and clever deduction, he solves a crime and identifies the criminal. For clearing his name, the wrongly suspected man gratefully rewards Tim with $3,000, the money to be used for college expenses.

Analysis. The focus of the story is the basketball court with extensive descriptions of fast and exciting game plays. In the context of this absorbing story, Tim's feelings of despair about exclusion from the activity that was so important to him are readily understood. Like so many sports stories, though, the action is paramount, plot events contrived, characters stereotypical, and the message delivered with lack of subtlety.

Friermood, Elisabeth Hamilton. *The Luck of Daphne Tolliver.* Garden City, N.Y.: Doubleday, 1961. 239 pp. Reading Level: YA
Disability: Orthopedic Impairment

During World War I, the Tolliver family, consisting of the parents and nine children, move to a house they inherit in a small community in Indiana. The father is a junk dealer who is helped in the business by Poll, his oldest son, until the young man enlists. Daphne, although still in school, takes over many of her brother's responsibilities when he leaves. Jim, a classmate, has had polio and is bitter about the severe limp that remains. Amy Tolliver, similarly stricken, has no use of her legs at all. Through helping Amy learn to swim, Jim begins to dwell less on his own unhappiness. Encouraged by the initial rewarding experience, he begins giving swimming lessons at the YMCA and slowly metamorphoses from a withdrawn boy to an outgoing, less self-absorbed one. A doctor examines Amy and prescribes exercises, including the continuation of swimming. Finally, he fits her with braces and crutches, enabling her to begin the long, slow process of learning to walk. Poll had one leg amputated as a result of his war wounds, but he returns to take up his former responsibilities. Daphne, now relieved of this heavy work load and excited about the remarkable rehabilitation of her friend and her sister, decides to enter nursing school.

Analysis. The Tollivers are a warm, happy, supportive family relentlessly engaged in good works. Despite the excessive sentimentality and the impression that Amy is a direct descendant of Tiny Tim, treatment of the many disabilities is straightforward and without bathos. The dominant attitude, reiterated in numerous instances, is that disabilities pose limitations, but within those restrictions there remains much that can be done and the disabled person and his or her family should address this with matter-of-fact dispatch.

Friis-Baastad, Babbis. *Don't Take Teddy*. Trans. by Lise Sømme McKinnon. New York: Scribners, 1967. 218 pp. Reading Level: MC
Disability: Intellectual Impairment

Mikkel worries that "they" will take his retarded older brother away and "imprison him" somewhere. He is very protective of Teddy, harboring some mild resentment at having to give up some of his own needs for him but basically loving his sibling. Depending on the circumstances, he becomes combative or embarrassed when other people react badly to Teddy. One day, he becomes so involved in his ball game that he forgets to monitor Teddy's actions. There is a scuffle, and Teddy throws a stone at Mikkel's opponent, splitting his lip and loosening some teeth. Mikkel is afraid that this could be the excuse to lock Teddy up and he decides to run away with his brother to their uncle's mountain cabin. Their journey through the Norwegian countryside is often arduous and exhausting. On a train ride they meet a sympathetic teacher who eventually makes arrangements for Teddy's education. After the two boys recover from pneumonia, an aftermath of their flight, Teddy is enrolled in a school for retarded children. Mikkel is resentful, but when he sees the school and his brother's pleasure in being there, he is convinced it is the right move.

Analysis. This superb book provides in excellent detail an insider's view of the daily agonies a loving child feels when his brother is disparaged and reviled. The ignorance and abuse reported in a straight, matter-of-fact way are shocking:

> Once the police had called on us because some neighbors complained that Teddy had frightened their children.
>
> That's what they said. But it wasn't true! Their children had teased Teddy, tormenting him and prodding him with sticks. He'd tried to run away, but the children had run much faster of course.
>
> They ran in front of him and around him and behind him, making a horrible noise. A couple of grownups came out and asked them if they were afraid of Teddy. Was he frightening them, perhaps?
>
> "Yes," the kids said.

There are only occasional interludes where characters treat the two boys with concern or, as Mikkel prefers, exactly like everyone else. The author recaptures these scenes with an ear tuned to the fidelities of speech and action. Teddy is a very low functioning boy, and we get little interior knowledge of him. The book is not without some missionary intent—a plea for such day schools as provided placement beneficial for both the family and children with Teddy's limitations. The teacher is almost too good to be true. Her approach of dealing head-on with an explanation of retardation, despite the use of outdated terminology, is marvelously refreshing. Despite minor flaws, *Don't Take Teddy* is a literate, sensitive novel whose powerful impact remains long after the book is finished.

Friis-Baastad, Babbis. *Kristy's Courage*. Illus. by Charles Geer. Trans. by Lise Sømme McKinnon. New York: Harcourt, Brace, 1965. 159 pp. Reading Level: MC
Disability: Cosmetic Impairment, Speech Impairment

Seven-year-old Kristy comes home from the hospital still carrying the scars from a serious auto accident as well as the related problem of unintelligible speech. She returns to school, unprepared for the taunts and mockery that greet her. Her mother's absence in a hospital with a new baby, combined with the lack of anyone with whom to share her confusion and pain, propels her back to a kindly friend in the hospital. A physician concludes that the problem is more psychological than physical, explains the nature of the difficulty to Kristy's father, and prescribes a fake bandage that will elicit sympathy rather than revulsion. The doctor's prognosis is correct and the bandaged girl is received warmly when she returns. However, she realizes that she cannot continue the pretense and removes the bandage. By now, the children have become accustomed to her condition and she is no longer the object of their teasing.

Analysis. This beautifully delineated and sensitive story is presented in a very matter-of-fact way. The pain of playground taunts is credibly portrayed, and in overcoming them Kristy emerges as a strong, resolute child. The emotional power of the central character and of the events is diluted by the sketchy illustrations, which are almost cartoon-like and avoid any visual presentation of the girl's cosmetic problem. One outstanding incident in the story involves Kristy's veto of the physician's gloomy assertion that sympathy must precede acceptance of one who is markedly different. Kristy's courage includes a large measure of common sense.

Garfield, James B. *Follow My Leader*. Illus. by Robert Greiner. New York: Viking, 1957. 191 pp. Reading Level: MC
Disability: Visual Impairment

When a firecracker explodes, eleven-year-old Jimmy loses his sight. Fortunately, he meets a dedicated rehabilitation worker who teaches him braille and how to use his cane, encouraging Jimmy's friends to participate in these learning experiences. At the outset of his recovery, the boy is extremely hostile and depressed but his adjustment is exceptionally rapid and complete, marred only by an immutable hatred for the boy who blinded him in the firecracker accident. He is accepted at leader dog school, and in the process of working his dog, learns to be forgiving. Jimmy begins to participate in many activities, including selling papers and Scouting. Hiking is difficult for him but through great effort he manages to keep up with other troop members. On one trek, some Scouts get lost but, thanks to Jimmy's dog, they are able to find their way back to camp. The dog's skills are further demonstrated when he saves the boy who blinded Jimmy, an antecedent to their eventual reconciliation.

Analysis. Despite linguistic clichés and attitudes toward Jimmy by various adults fostering his dependency, this story has much appeal, perhaps because it generates a sense of drama. His rehabilitation is incredibly idealized, as he improbably exclaims when he hears he will get another mobility aid: "A white cane! I'm an insect, an automobile, a clock, and now I'm a drum major. Okay, what else?" Later he joyously says about his new cane. "Oh, boy! . . . I'll be like Sherlock Holmes. I'll see things the rest of the gang never notice." Dialogue aside, the book's value is clear: Extensive information about blindness combined with the easy level of the presentation make for a useful and affecting novel for young readers.

Garfield, Leon. *Black Jack.* Illus. by Anthony Maitland. New York: Pantheon, 1968. 243 pp. Reading Level: YA
Disability: Emotional Dysfunction; also orthopedic impairment

By sheer coincidence, Tolly becomes enmeshed in the skullduggery of Black Jack, a notorious criminal the hangman mistakenly thought was dead. The two form an uneasy symbiotic alliance: The giant villain determines to hang on to Tolly and the optimistic lad naively hopes to dissuade Jack from his life of crime. In one violent episode, Tolly meets Belle in transit to Dr. Jones' Madhouse. The unhappy girl has been banished there to conceal her emotional condition from her sister's fiancé. During the escapade, Jack disappears and Tolly is left with the young woman on his hands. A traveling medicine man, cunningly seeing an opportunity to exploit Belle's condition, agrees to give them transportation. Black Jack also joins the caravan, living with a troop of midgets from whom he unsuccessfully tries to steal. Tolly's influence on Belle is beneficent; she becomes more alert, more coherent, and regains her memory. Black Jack tricks her into entering the asylum, but later, remorseful, he rescues her. Tolly and the now-recovered Belle are happily reunited.

Analysis. This delightful, picaresque tale races along pell-mell resulting in love and innocence conquering evil. Belle's condition is regarded variously with fear, embarrassment, compassion, and plans for exploitation. The medical charlatans and the shameful madhouse vividly come to life, reminding the reader of their modern counterparts. Superstitions related to this condition appear in beliefs of familial susceptibility, in prophecies of the doomsayer, and in claims for elixirs with curative powers. Maitland's superb illustrations of the midgets and of Belle are gently etched; those of the young woman are particularly full of affection. The impaired characters never lose their dignity despite the breakneck speed of events in this romantic and amusing novel of nineteenth-century England.

Garfield, Leon. *Devil-in-the-Fog.* Illus. by Anthony Maitland. New York: Pantheon, 1966. 188 pp. Reading Level: YA
Disability: Emotional Dysfunction

Eighteenth-century England is the setting for this unusual mystery adventure. Sir John Dexter, in a paroxysm of paranoia when his own son, George, dies, conceals the death and devises a plot to keep his brother, Richard, from obtaining the family fortune. His elaborate plan includes informing a lawyer that his brother has kidnapped the baby and suggesting that a fraudulent child should be kept in readiness so that if his brother should not return the child, another could be brought forth and claimed as his own son. Thus he could prevent Richard's presumed profit from the abduction. The son of an itinerant actor is provided an annual allowance and ultimately, at thirteen, is brought to the manor for a showdown. In an exciting but convoluted resolution, Sir John attempts to shoot the youth, but a defective gun explodes and that, coupled with a heart condition, finishes him. The relieved widow and Richard inform the boy that he was an innocent actor in the ill man's insane schemes.

Analysis. Garfield has embedded in his high adventure novel a rather old-fashioned perception of mental illness. Sir Dexter is essentially seen as villain rather than victim, but in the explication, he is portrayed as a captive of his own irrational motives.

Garfield, Leon. *Smith.* Illus. by Anthony Maitland. New York: Pantheon, 1967. 218 pp. Reading Level: YA
Disability: Visual Impairment; also orthopedic impairment

A twelve-year-old orphan, known as Smith, works the London streets as a pickpocket. After the boy lifts a wallet from a man named Field and conceals himself to check its contents, he sees two men knife his victim, search fruitlessly through the man's papers, and leave angrily after being joined by a limping cohort. Hoping to decipher the document found in the wallet, Smith pleads unsuccessfully with people to teach him to read. On the verge of being discovered by the cutthroats, the lad encounters Mr. Mansfield, a blind justice of the peace. The man's daughter, Meg, promises to instruct him, although she has second thoughts when she sees him rummaging among her father's papers, where a housekeeper has mistakenly placed his document. Mr. Billings, who is courting Meg, accuses Smith of stabbing Field, and despite his denials, the boy is clapped into jail. Fearful about Mansfield's safety, Smith plans to escape through the ventilation system and warn him. Seeing the murderers in waiting, the resourceful boy revises his scheme, leaving the prison by concealing himself under the hoopskirt of his sister. The intrepid boy, determined to take matters into his own hands, whisks the blind man out of his carriage and hides him just before an ambush, which results in the shooting of the coachman. Reflecting on his actions and the magistrate's implacable position on crime, Smith at first considers his rescue of the old man ill-advised. Trying to unravel the meaning of all these seemingly inexplicable events, Mansfield asks him to read the key document, and they are disappointed to learn it only contains instructions to a servant. In a churchyard confrontation, all the conspirators assemble and the justice overhears evidence of Billings' involvement in the scheme. Smith deduces the secret Field was hiding, the evildoers are foiled in their final desperate attempt to kill the old man, Smith earns a princely sum for his assistance, and the magistrate learns the value of tempering justice with compassion.

Analysis. This rousing complicated adventure tale engrosses the reader to the very end with its vivid sense of setting, its extraordinary characters and style, and its headlong, nonstop movement. The blind magistrate is not only literally unable to see but he also lacks vision figuratively as well. His rigidity is the very quality that prevents him from administering justice with mercy. He is easily deceived by surface appearances of events, thus is unable to penetrate to the core of a problem and find an equitable and fair solution. His change of perspective, in Garfield's masterful hands, provides marvelous irony. The only lapse is the use of the criminal's limp, a device for readily identifying one of the villains. The exciting pen and ink illustrations are a welcome bit of lagniappe to an already stirring tale.

Garfield, Leon. *The Sound of Coaches.* Illus. by John Lawrence. New York: Viking, 1974. 256 pp. Reading Level: YA
Disability: Orthopedic Impairment

On a dark and windy night, a coach stops at the Red Lion Inn on its route to London. There an infant is born to a young woman who dies in childbirth. The baby is immediately adopted by the childless coachman and his wife. The Chichesters lovingly raise Sam and proudly teach him their trade. One day a stranger, frantically trying to force the already full coach to stop for him, angrily shoots Chichester as he rides by, leaving him permanently paralyzed. Young Sam takes over the route but, on his first run, overturns the vehicle. His foster father is overcome with anger and grief so the lad leaves home to seek his fortune. He becomes the protege of Daniel Coventry, a vain, arrogant, unscrupulous but gifted actor who separates the innocent boy from a sizable amount of his money. When he searches the boy's room for the remainder, he comes across a pistol that, along with a ring, was the entire estate left to Sam by his hapless mother. Coventry shows Sam that he owns the matched mate to the elaborately decorated weapon and the two realize that they are father and son. Coventry now develops the boy's acting skills in earnest. Sam shows considerable talent, but his father seizes every opportunity to upstage his son. From a chance encounter with another traveling troupe, Sam learns that his adoptive father is in failing health and dangerously depressed. A performance is scheduled into the Red Lion Inn where the Chichesters now reside. Sam is anxious to be reunited but, ashamed of his neglect of the couple who loved him so freely, is fearful of his reception. When Coventry appears on the stage, Chichester recognizes him as the villain who had shot him and the actor is overcome with dread at seeing his victim. Sam's performance is an unqualified success; Chichester, proud of his adopted son, does not mention Coventry's role in his injury; and Sam's neglected paramour arrives at the inn pregnant and ready to marry Sam.

Analysis. With his usual verve and dash, flavored by more than a little irreverence and cynicism, Garfield has created a witty, amusing romance. Mr. Chichester's injury is a bald contrivance initiating the train of events that lead to the dramatic, ironic, sentimental, and, given the genre, inevitable denouement. Although the disability is an unblushingly obvious device, the scenes involving the coachman's altered abilities and lifestyle are credible.

Garst, Shannon. *Red Eagle.* Illus. by Hubert Buel. New York: Hastings House, 1959. 145 pp. Reading Level: MC
Disability: Orthopedic Impairment

A young Sioux, called Lame Foot because of his club foot, has also suffered from what was presumably tuberculosis. His peers are extremely competitive and, since Lame Foot seldom wins, he has a low opinion of himself. He is loved by his family and is adopted as a nephew by a wise man, Grey Owl, a considerable honor. Grey Owl instructs him to avoid self-pity, to counter his peers' taunts with laughter, and to learn how to swim, a sport in which his foot will be no hindrance. These tactics are effective, as he builds up his strength and defuses the teasing. His nemesis, Crow Boy, continues to harass Lame Foot, sabotaging his efforts to prove himself competent and mature. During a ritual of contemplation and search for destiny, he is inspired by a red eagle and rejects what had been selfish reasons for seeking success. Eventually he captures the great bird and adopts a new, esteemed, and deserved name—Red Eagle.

Analysis. The story is a simple one with a simple message: There is no disgrace in failing, only in not trying. As in many books, a connection is made between strength or physical competence and leadership. The young Indian boy is disparaged for his imperfect physique, but once he proves himself, his companions can see beyond the impairment to the qualities the wise man had noted all along. The illustrations portray Red Eagle as strong and heroic but avoid depicting any hint of disability.

Gold, Phyllis. *Please Don't Say Hello.* Photog. by Carl Baker. New York: Human Sciences, 1975. 47 pp. Reading Level: MC
Disability: Emotional Dysfunction

When the new family moves into the neighborhood, it is apparent that something serious is wrong. Eddie Mason's behavior is incomprehensible and he will not speak except in a kind of moan. The questions of the neighborhood children provide the opportunity for an extended discourse on autism, Eddie's condition. The children visit his school and their parents visit his home, opening the way for further explanations. By the end of the year, some improvement in the boy is noticeable. Mrs. Mason attributes this to the program in his school, his maturity, and the support of the neighborhood children.

Analysis. Probably the most understandable explanation of autism available for children, this book still remains unsatisfactory. The very complexity of the syndrome and the extreme oddness of the behavior may render the subject inherently incomprehensible to the immature audience for this book. The analogies and explanations that satisfy the children in the book are unlikely to pacify their real-life counterparts: "You know . . . the human body is in many ways the most amazing and complicated machine there is. And just the way something wrong with a real machine can keep it from working right, some parts of a person's body can wrong. With autistic children something did go wrong, and nobody yet has been able to discover what it is." In effect, nothing has been explained. The tone, as indicated by the title, is also inappropriate. A plea for compassion is undoubtedly less effective than a simple declarative statement explaining that autistic children cannot control their actions and require protection, socialization with other children, and a degree of tolerance for their bizarre behavior. The book contains literary lapses: "He hardly ever spinned himself around any more"; and the writing, though accurate, is mechanical. The photographs are excellent and mitigate the patronizing tone of the narrative. The book's best qualities are the honesty and directness with which it tackles a very difficult subject.

Goldfeder, Cheryl and James Goldfeder. *The Girl Who Wouldn't Talk.* Illus. by Cheryl Goldfeder. Silver Springs, Md.: National Association of the Deaf, 1974. unpaged. Reading Level: YC
Disability: Auditory Impairment

Robin, a deaf girl, grew up unaware of communication skills. She is given hearing aids but they are not sufficient. The young girl is unhappy at first when she is sent to a school for the deaf, but after she learns signing, she has the basis for conceptualization and language and is no longer sad. An alphabet in American Sign Language is appended.

Analysis. Despite good intentions, this promotional book has little to recommend it. Most educators of the deaf support total communication, but only manual instruction is stressed here. The text is printed in capital letters in clumsy verse. The authors' efforts at rhyming lead them to absurdities and misrepresentations. Robin, frustrated at being unable to communicate, abandons her attempts at speech: "INSTEAD SHE WOULD PONDER / THE LOOK OF A FACE, / OR THE GENTLE BEAUTY / OF A BUTTERFLY'S GRACE." In a later verse, the difficulties of manual communication are grossly minimized: "HER HANDS LEARNED TO TALK / QUICK AS A WINK! / AND AS HER HANDS TALKED, / HER MIND LEARNED TO THINK!" The title, implying willfulness rather than a lack of instruction, is misleading. The drawings are amateurish and occasionally ridiculous, as in the illustration of young Robin contemplating the structure of the atom and the formula for relativity.

Goodsell, Jane. *Katie's Magic Glasses.* Illus. by Barbara Cooney. Boston: Houghton Mifflin, 1965. 43 pp. Reading Level: YC
Disability: Visual Impairment

Katie is a five-year-old who likes to play with her friends, but her visual problem causes her to see everything in a blur. When she takes a medical examination during kindergarten, her physician discovers the impairment and sends her to an ophthalmologist, promising that she will have magic glasses soon. In nervous anticipation, Katie tries on her father's, but almost becomes ill and decides she doesn't like glasses. However, when hers arrive, Katie's world takes on new precision and clarity.

Analysis. This story, actually quasi-fiction, is hampered by its being written in rhyme. The text offers information about physical examinations and how responses to visual problems cause social misperceptions. The delightful illustrations marvelously portray the scruffy heroine and her foggy, fuzzy, preglasses state.

Gray, Patsey. *Show Ring Rogue.* Illus. by Sam Savitt. New York: Coward-McCann, 1963. 157 pp. Reading Level: MC
Disability: Orthopedic Impairment

Her bout with polio has left Sheila with a slight limp and an unpleasant disposition. She resents the brace and special shoe she must wear and is careless about the exercises that would restore her former mobility. Her father takes her from their Hawaiian home to consult a specialist on the mainland who recommends that she change her attitude, spend the summer away from her too indulgent and undemanding parents, and "take up horseback riding" as a means of regaining proper function in her weakened foot. She remains with a friend of her father's who is a horse trainer and begins her unusual therapy. Resentful and uncooperative at first, she thaws slightly when she finds a horse that she feels is unappreciated. Since being gored in a bull ring, it has been unreliable, distrusting men and shying in the presence of noisy crowds. Despite the trainer's reluctance, Sheila works with the horse, helping it to overcome its fears and turning it into a model, prize-winning animal. In the process of reclaiming the creature, Sheila recovers control of her weakened leg and abandons her self-pity.

Analysis. Because residual impairment was so slight, the reported recovery does not seem unbelievable, although the therapy prescribed does seem too good to be true. There is considerably more information in this bland effort about training horses for show than about recovering from polio. Characters are stock, dialogue uninspired, and the ending predictable. The unremarkable illustrations give no indication of the prostheses that the heroine so bitterly resents.

Greene, Constance C. *The Unmaking of Rabbit.* New York: Viking, 1972. 125 pp. Reading Level: MC
Disability: Speech Impairment

His father deserted the family when Paul was a baby and his mother is busy pursuing a life of her own, so eleven-year-old Paul lives with his grandmother. Paul has no friends in the little town where he lives. The local bully calls him "rabbit" and tries to make him the butt of jokes. Paul stutters when he is anxious and this a source of embarrassment for him. He almost goes along with a group break-in of an empty house in a misguided effort to have some friends. Eventually the grandson of a neighbor becomes Paul's first real friend. Paul's next visit to his mother and her new husband convinces him that his real home is with his grandmother whose love combines responsibility with deep affection. In the least likely incident in the book, his antagonist meets him after class one day with an apparently sincere offer of friendship. Paul's life is taking a positive direction at last.

Analysis. The plot moves well and the characterizations are good, although Paul's social problems are presented and solved on a surface level. His speech problem is presented as one among many minor negative physical attributes that identify him as a potential victim and a loner. Some insight into situations that exacerbate tensions and intensify speech dysfunction is provided. Moreover, the frustrations that must accompany the inability to communicate like everyone else are equally well dramatized.

Griese, Arnold A. *At the Mouth of the Luckiest River.* Illus. by Glo Coalson. New York: Crowell, 1969. 65 pp. Reading Level: YC/MC
Disability: Orthopedic Impairment

Tatlek, an Athabascan Indian, lives in Alaska near a tribe of Eskimos. His mother is unhappy about his weak, pronated foot, but Tatlek feels good about himself, and is encouraged by his grandfather's assertion that a yega, a good spirit, is looking after him. The medicine man provokes Tatlek often, since in tribal lore, there is a tradition for the greatest shamans to be born with "weak bodies," and he is concerned about eventually being replaced. The medicine man has worked out a profitable scheme for himself, based on excluding Eskimos from trade. He connives to convince his tribe that Eskimos must be killed, and a war party is formed. Tatlek, attempting to intercept them, miscalculates and encounters the advancing Eskimos with trade objects, not war materials, in their dogsleds. Tatlek confronts the provocateur, who attacks the boy with a knife, but the man is overcome and bound in the sled. Tatlek returns to the tribe with an account of the shaman's perfidy, but is disbelieved. He challenges the medicine man's yega to harm him but nothing happens. The boy says that if his power is stronger, he will be able to return with the Eskimos as friends. He does this and this act presages his future career as the medicine man for his tribe.

Analysis. The story moves along well, punctuated with strong, intense illustrations that give a marvelous sense of the harsh realities of the environment. Disability as a mark of favor occurs again in this story. Tatlek is shown as an inventive child and the community rejects him, not because of his misshapen foot, but because he challenges tradition by his innovative trapping technique. He knows that he has problems but also feels he has compensations, sensibly competing in games like wrestling where he knows his foot will not be a hindrance, and using the sled as a resting place for his disabled foot and employing the unimpaired one for the more strenuous work of pushing. Tatlek is an admirable hero representing, in a low-key manner, a child who is different but deals with this difference in a natural, pragmatic fashion.

Griffiths, Helen. *The Mysterious Appearance of Agnes.* Also published as *Witch Fear.* Illus. by Victor Ambrus. New York: Holiday House, 1975. 160 pp. Reading Level: YA
Disability: Emotional Dysfunction; also neurological impairment

In a German forest in the year 1540, Josef finds a child alone in the woods and brings her to the local priest. She is given to Klaus and Wilhelmina to raise in an attempt to help assuage the grief of their own daughter's recent death. The child, named Agnes after the dead girl, is mute and half wild, unresponsive to either her new mother's unwavering love or her stepfather's uncomprehending wonder at her presence. Adults shun her and the village children stone her for sport. Her only interest is in a cat caught in a snare that she rescued and cares for. One day strangers arrive in town. They are the survivors of a village whose homes and fields were plundered and whose neighbors were killed by soldiers and bandits. One of them tells Josef of a witch who was hanged seven years ago and who left behind a child just the age Agnes was when she was found. The two spy on the child and see her playing with the cat, clear evidence to them of witchcraft. The stranger tries to make Agnes' stepparents pay for his silence and, when they refuse, he denounces the child. Klaus, confused and frightened, tries to kill the cat, which he somehow considers responsible for his problems. He manages to stab it, but the animal scratches him and escapes. Agnes faints and he carries her home to find the townspeople, stirred to fear and brimming with violence, assembled and waiting for them. Agnes is turned over to the priest, who decides to hold a trial, confident that God will provide some sign. The wild accusations against the silent girl are heard in this unruly travesty of a court and are supported by the weak and cowardly Josef. Suddenly, a man steps forward to protest and is turned on by the hysterical mob, but the priest insists he be heard. He explains that Agnes, the child of his unmarried daughter, was secretly given to Lena, the murdered "witch," to be raised. Lena was subject to epileptic seizures and was feared by her ignorant and superstitious neighbors. The child had watched the woman she thought was her mother tortured and hanged and he, to his shame, had done nothing to save either. He is believed, and the outraged listeners now redirect their mindless fury toward the accuser whom they beat unmercifully. Agnes, now totally withdrawn and seemingly oblivious to all events, is returned home. The cat, whom her mother had saved, somehow believing any hope for Agnes was inextricably linked to the animal's survival, recovers. Its playfulness and persistence finally draw a response from Agnes, and Wilhelmina dares hope the child may yet recover.

Analysis. The portrait of the girl, whose response to intolerable trauma is psychic mutism and disengagement with human contact, is convincing. Conditions of sanctioned abuse of the disabled by a community of ignorant, gullible, and vengeful people, for whom those who are different become an inevitable target, are vividly recreated. Essentially this is a story of the persistence of love and faith over seemingly insurmountable odds, despite lack of reinforcement, support, or response. Excellent illustrations add to the skillful characterizations and a superb creation of mood contributes to a unique and disturbing book.

Griffiths, Helen. *The Wild Horse of Santander.* Illus. by Victor G. Ambrus. Garden City, N.Y.: Doubleday, 1966. 182 pp. Reading Level: YA

Disability: Visual Impairment

Physicians have informed Joaquin's father that the blindness that followed his son's illness might someday be cured. Joaquin's health improves daily in the small Spanish village where he lives and he develops an almost obsessive love for a newborn colt, Linda. His grandmother, not realizing the impact of her story, tells him of a magic horse who grows by being taken to a mountain top. Joaquin collapses in attempting to duplicate this feat, and Linda brings him home. The boy is afraid that an upcoming operation to restore his sight may damage the magic of their relationship. Joaquin disconsolately takes the animal to another stable to prepare for their first separation in years and the horse's mean temper comes to the fore. Linda escapes with another colt and together they manage to damage property and cleverly avoid capture. The neighboring men determine to kill Linda and recapture the valuable colt. Joaquin is recovering from his successful surgery and has not been told of his mare's wild behavior. When his jealous sister reveals the men's terrible plan, Joaquin rushes out to find the beloved creature. The two see each other, and in a flash the horse's recollection of its former blind master returns and it rushes toward him. In a wild, shocking convulsion of action, the mare is shot while the stunned boy looks on. After Joaquin goes through a period of mourning and has received a new horse, he realizes that Linda belonged to a world he no longer inhabits.

Analysis. Although the author mentions that a newspaper article inspired this novel, the feeling tone of the story is mythic. In an engrossing blend of reality and illusion, the stage is set for an uneasy journey: The doctor's prediction, the grandmother's tale of a magical odyssey, the almost human qualities of the wild horse all prepare for the inevitable moment when the elements of a perfect love relationship are changed. When the boy is blind, he truly believes that the horse has a mystical dimension, and the two share an emotional world from which the sighted are barred. But the author suggests that such an idyllic world cannot last. The major event after the boy recovers his sight is the death of the horse—the terrible cost of his symbolic rebirth. The various family reactions to blindness are plausible and a strong plea is made for learning independence, although the boy is described as having "that kind of sixth sense." Complemented perfectly by the tone of the illustrations, this brooding, dark story moves inexorably to its fatalistic ending.

> Groshkopf, Bernice. *Shadow in the Sun.* New York: Atheneum, 1975.
> 182 pp. Reading Level: YA
> *Disability:* Orthopedic Impairment

Thirteen-year-old Fran, visiting her aunt, accepts a job as a paid companion for Wilma, who is partially paralyzed and confined to a wheelchair. Wilma's volatile behavior ranges from generosity to self-pity and Wilma's father, absorbed in his work, is oblivious to her needs. He has divorced her rejecting mother and is awaiting the birth of a new baby by Wilma's young stepmother. Fran is disheartened by Wilma's offensive behavior, but tries to understand the contributing factors and respects the adjustments and adaptations that Wilma has made. In that spirit, with a few somewhat reluctant teenagers, she arranges a party. Wilma concludes that she has been invited out of pity and is jealous that one of the boys, Jack, clearly likes Fran. Wilma's feelings of rejection have been compounded by the birth of her stepsister (whom she stated she hoped would be born crippled) and her father's neglect and preoccupation. In her anger, she accuses Fran's aunt of homosexuality. Despite her compassion for Wilma, Fran, shocked, runs away. Wilma has an accident with her wheelchair and is rescued by Jack and hospitalized. Wilma's father is furious at Fran for leaving his daughter alone, but Fran tells him that it is his own rejection and infantilization that are really destroying Wilma. In an implausible conclusion, both Wilma and her father in flashes of insight agree to restructure their lives into loving behaviors.

Analysis. The clumsily handled lesbian theme is a bald device used to convey the message that everyone is "handicapped" in some way and that one must be evaluated by the sum of all characteristics, not a single one. The writing is wooden and contains much lecturing. It is when the author deals with the central theme and substance of the novel that she is on stronger ground. When she concentrates on the behavioral sequelae of the condition, rather than the handicap, the author provides an excellent, probing picture of the ambivalence of love and hate in the family. The academically disciplined but behaviorally immature Wilma is described as compulsively hurting others as she feels she has been hurt, covering her ineffable longing for love and affection with spite and one-upmanship. Inability to communicate, especially about disability-related matters, is extensively examined by the author and is a critical element in the progression of the plot. Wilma's trap, only partially self-made, of wanting to join in the adolescent romance scene and being barred by her physical and personality handicaps, is an apt and realistic addition to the novel.

Grund, Joseph Carl. *Beyond the Bridge.* Trans. by Lucile Harrington. Boston: Little, Brown, 1968. 143 pp. Reading Level: YA
Disability: Cosmetic Impairment; also orthopedic impairment

Fritz Hartman is called to his father's deathbed to hear a ghoulish confession. The father cathartically recounts his World War II days as a German pilot engaged in wanton killing. His conscience haunts him and even his mutilated hands are not adequate punishment to expiate his guilt. He makes Fritz promise that he will try to atone for his father's vile acts. After his father's funeral and a passing encounter with a one-legged woman, he sees young children entranced by war toys in a display, and breaks the store window in a convulsion of anger. He realizes violence is not the answer to war and begs for some time to earn money to replace the glass. Several people at his school and others anonymously compensate the storekeeper. Fritz contacts the families of Allied soldiers and gains insight into others' feelings about war. With the guidance of his teacher, he improves his work and plans to become a teacher and work with other intellectuals on plans for world peace and reconciliation.

Analysis. The goal of the guilt-ridden pilot is a microcosm of the goal of the writer: to atone for the horrors of German atrocities and to use the medium of the book to build international contacts with young people who can work constructively together for pacific goals. Disability tied to expiation is clearly seen in the portrayal of the father with missing digits from both hands. He sees his lost career as a musician as well as his impairment as symbolic but inadequate retribution for his unthinking cruelty. The plot is overly neat and the writing is somewhat choppy, but this may be due to the translation. The message—a hard sell for forgiveness and cooperation—is crystal clear.

Hall, Lynn. *Sticks and Stones.* Chicago: Follett, 1972. 220 pp. Reading Level: YA/MA
Disability: Intellectual Impairment

Tom Naylor has just moved with his mother to a small town in Iowa. Floyd Schleffe, a slovenly, lonely, retarded boy, hopes Tom will be his friend and eagerly but clumsily pursues a relationship, but Tom tries hard to discourage him. When Tom becomes friendly with Ward, a homosexual, Floyd seizes the opportunity for revenge and restoration of his damaged ego. As Floyd spreads false rumors of Tom's homosexuality, he not only rationalizes the rejection he experienced but also enjoys a few rare moments in the limelight. Scorned by his schoolmates, treated with contempt by the coach, and barred from participating in a statewide music competition because of the accusations, Tom's self-image is shattered and he begins to doubt his masculinity. Distraught by the events, his schoolwork suffers and he finds he is failing. The combination of anger, frustration, and desperation leads to an auto accident in which Floyd is killed and Tom hospitalized. While confined to bed, he thinks over the tragic events of the year, realizes he has been victimized by rumormongers, and decides he must control his own destiny despite community pressures. When Ward is finally allowed to visit him, Tom greets him warmly.

Analysis. Although never specifically labeled, the description of his intellectual and social functioning identifies Floyd as mildly retarded. This categorization appears intended to increase the distastefulness of this character and to emphasize further the differences between the very attractive victim and the contemptible accusor. The story moves well with good control of tension, although the conversations seem artificial and contrived and the characters drawn in extremes. The central theses—the wickedness of gossip and social abuse of homosexuals—are powerfully presented. It is unfortunate that the villain is drawn from another equally abused outgroup; the pleas for compassion for homosexuals are made at the expense of the retarded.

Hamilton, Virginia. *The Planet of Junior Brown.* New York: Macmillan, 1971. 210 pp. Reading Level: YA/MA
Disability: Emotional Dysfunction; also general health problems

Junior Brown, black, musically gifted, and extraordinarily obese, lives with his mother, a neurotically possessive woman. His only young friend, Buddy Clark, lives in the basement of an abandoned building where he shelters two young runaways. This compassionate youth is one of a number of "Tomorrow Billys" who teach such homeless youngsters how to survive on their own. When they are independent enough, he will abandon them as he has their predecessors, and take on the care of others. Buddy and Mr. Pool, the janitor, have constructed in a hidden room in their junior high school a model of the solar system to which they had added a tenth planet named in honor of Junior Brown.

Neither of the two boys attends classes anymore; instead, they wile away the school days unmolested in this room. Junior takes piano lessons from a woman who has an imaginary relative living with her. Mrs. Peebs won't allow Junior to touch her piano, which has been viciously damaged, but occasionally, when not too overwrought, does allow him to beat out the rhythm of his lessons on a tabletop.

Junior's piano at home has had all the wires removed so that the sound will not annoy his mother. When Mrs. Brown discovers a painting Junior has made, she is aghast at the images and their symbolic meaning and destroys it immediately, further diminishing her son's already tenuous ties to sanity. After the boys are finally caught playing hookey, Junior Brown leaves his home and meets Buddy, and the two enter their sanctuary for the last time. Mr. Pool dismantles the solar system and then Junior takes Buddy with him to his last piano lesson. Mrs. Peebs is in a state of terror over the imagined relative she insists is on her couch. Junior accepts her fantasy for his own and removes the nonexistent person, but, in doing so, severs his last link with reality. Buddy takes Junior to school where Mr. Pool advises him that Junior will need eventual hospitalization. The custodian states that first Junior requires some breathing time, an interval without pressure. They take Junior and Mrs. Peebs' invisible relative to where Buddy lives with his homeless boys, a haven they rename "The Planet of Junior Brown."

Analysis. This powerful, haunting, troubling book contrasts sanity and madness, endorsement and rejection of life, commitment to others and absorption with self. The treatment of Junior Brown's retreat from reality is paradoxical: It is a response to an oppressive, uncaring world and yet it embodies a surprising innocence. Mrs. Peebs surrounds herself with objects, trying to compensate for a life of losses. Her barely manageable fantasy life substitutes for a totally unmanageable real world. Mrs. Brown is victim and victimizer; her asthma and loneliness (her husband is perpetually due home, but never manages to arrive) trap her and simultaneously are the devices she uses to control her son. Hamilton chronicles the inexorable progress and contagion of emotional stress. Buddy's characterization makes an assertive statement presenting a caring, loving alternative to social trauma. A well-constructed plot, superb characterizations, and fine, tight, compelling style are blended in this extraordinary story.

Hamilton-Paterson, James. *The House in the Waves.* New York: Phillips, 1970. 157 pp. Reading Level: YA/MA
Disability: Emotional Dysfunction; also cosmetic impairment

A land of fantasy provides the setting wherein fourteen-year-old Martin overturns his psychological pattern of retreat, acting out his inchoate wish for rescue from the emotional fetters that lock him into his own isolated world. Dr. Smedley is unsuccessfully treating the boy, who has been placed in an institution by the courts. The doctor, hoping to halt an obsessive involvement with birds and shells and to intervene in his growing alienation, sends him to a hostel for multiple-problem children near the seashore. There he meets Miss Brunt, a dedicated nurse, and begins narcotherapy. He discovers a plea for help written in an ancient style and, believing it comes from the sea, decides to locate the writer, Will Howlett. His mind gears up for the project and he runs away to an old town (presumably circa 1600) where he is told that Will died the year before, but that Will's "mad" uncle still lives in an old house by the water's edge. The uncle, the lower half of his face covered by a mask, invites Martin in. However, his behavior alarms the boy, who leaves. Martin knows Will is really inside and identifies with the young prisoner, perceiving the menacing uncle as the embodiment of all the jailers in his own life. Martin becomes alarmed at the severity of a storm, noting that the sea is undermining the foundations of the house, and is afraid that his alter ego will be unable to escape. The boy sneaks into the house, meets Will, but is now also trapped. Exultant, Uncle Jeremiah informs Will that he has almost completed his experiment to turn lead into gold, but Will is unimpressed. Will explains that he is an orphan and had been an apprentice in alchemy to his uncle. By now the water is flooding into the rotting house. The boys barely escape their place of confinement in time, and they see the man's scarred face, which he claims was damaged during his experiments. The boys depart just as the house is destroyed by the rising waters, and Will asks Martin to be his friend. Martin wakes up in the hospital where the psychiatrist tells him he has been asleep for the past 48 hours. The nurse takes him to the scene of his "experience" and together they work out its meaning. Martin is able to throw away his talisman fossil shell, a relic of his psychotic past, and Miss Brunt reflects on the thanklessness of her job, except for "recaptures" like Martin.

Analysis. The author superbly re-creates the hospital and staff, imperfections and all, and writes knowledgeably about therapy and treatment. The separate worlds Martin lives in are sensitively etched and a close feeling with the withdrawn boy is promoted in the reader. Unlike many dream solution conclusions, the reader does not feel cheated. The story is beautifully crafted, full of startling images: "He gradually unfurled in the warmth of his new surroundings, like a tight bud timidly wondering whether spring was just a confidence trick." An upbeat ending encourages hope that regaining contact with reality for the seriously disturbed may be realized.

Hark, Mildred, and Noll McQueen. *Mary Lou and Johnny*. Illus. by Taylor Oughton. New York: Watts, 1963. 228 pp. Reading Level: MC
Disability: Visual Impairment

Mary Lou moves into Johnny's neighborhood and also into his world of blindness. She meets his mother and grandfather, who have learned braille; Mr. Fiorelli, a recently blinded engineer who lives in the apartment next to Johnny's; and a dog given to Johnny by the police. Mary Lou becomes interested and involved in the subject of blindness and she volunteers to help children who are blind; but she is oppressively helpful and is asked to leave. The two children try to help their neighbor but he fails and becomes even more depressed. However, Mr. Fiorelli gets a dog and eventually completes the guide dog training curriculum. The animal saves him from a potentially dangerous fall through an elevator shaft. Mary Lou learns how to be more selective in her assistance efforts and is reinstated in her volunteer job. Mr. Fiorelli, planning a new career as a drummer, thanks the children for giving him the inspiration to redirect his life. During the celebration all agree that everyone has handicaps in life that must be overcome.

Analysis. The story is a painless, if wooden, primer on information about the young and old who are blind. The book, long for this age group, contains discussions about braille books, special education and educators, guide dog training, fears of the newly blinded, functions of an association for the blind, family adjustments to visual loss, the necessity for independence, and the heavy reliance on other senses in relearning. Perhaps the best feature is the sense of normalcy with which Johnny's family treats him. The pictures are realistic and ably complement this textual treatment. The writers acknowledge their gratitude to professionals who have provided relevant background, and this factual accuracy permeates the book. *Mary Lou and Johnny* is both an account of the ordinary domestic adventures of two friends and a compendium of information on blindness for the young reader.

Harnden, Ruth. *Next Door*. Illus. by Marvin Friedman. Boston: Houghton Mifflin, 1970. 166 pp. Reading Level: MC/YA
Disability: Emotional Dysfunction

Since her best friend moved away, Sandy has felt abandoned, angry, and defensive. The house next door where the girl had lived is now occupied by Greg, a high school boy who appears to be a loner. One day, Sandy meets Greg at a fair and, after they talk about some Irish wolfhounds, he agrees to drop her off at a nearby kennel. Because he is unable to leave her there after they discover no puppies are available, he reluctantly allows her to accompany him to a psychiatric hospital where his mother is a patient. Greg is distressed that Sandy has discovered his secret because he believes that people overreact when they learn about his mother—convinced that anyone requiring hospitalization must act in bizarre or dangerous ways. The young girl suggests that instead of hiding his mother's state, he try to explain it. Relieved at her interest and rational reaction, he reveals that his mother would often misinterpret events. She would take inconsequential incidents and magnify their meaning and importance until she was unable to cope with the problem. Greg shares his feelings of anxiety and self-doubts about having to suddenly assume the adult role in his family. Further, he confesses that for a while he had even blamed his mother for her confused state and had considered running away. His mother's problems raise in Sandy's mind the fear that her own mother could be similarly affected—a response likely in a young child. Unable to digest these new and confusing thoughts, Sandy consults her grandmother, who says she's happy that neighbors are living next door and is confident her grandchild will feel more comfortable once she meets Greg's mother. Sandy's distant friend invites her to visit at Christmas, but the puppy she hopes for will be ready for its new home by then, so she decides to remain at home instead.

Analysis. Action is minimal in this low-key story of an adolescent coping alone with adult responsibilities, the result of his father's absence and his mother's inability to manage. The presentation of emotional dysfunction as a misperception and misinterpretation of events, resulting in excessive or inappropriate responses, is a reasonable one considering the age of the child to whom it is addressed. Sandy functions as a catalyst initiating a recitation and interpretation of events that explain the mother's erratic behavior and Greg's adaptations. Characterizations are the best literary feature of this uneventful, slow-paced novel.

Harnishfeger, Lloyd. *Hunters of the Black Swamp.* Illus. by George Overlie. Minneapolis, Minn.: Lerner, 1971. 94 pp. Reading Level: MC/YA
Disability: Orthopedic Impairment

In prehistoric times in North America, Man and his family leave their companions to live alone. Armed with the most primitive weapons and with only his careless and disrespectful son to help him, Man tracks and kills a grizzly bear. Man is seriously wounded in the struggle. The responsibility for their lives is now the boy's. Abandoning his childish self-absorption, he attends to his father's injuries as well as he can. He assists in the hunt with strangers from another tribe. At the celebration and feasting that follow the successful kill, the tribal shaman, Hunchback, retells an important myth—a story almost identical to the Noah/ Gilgamesh legend—that reiterates their moral code and authenticates their historic origins. Boy's contribution to the hunt is acknowledged and he is given a new name that affirms his adult status. The tribal chief generously decides to help Man return to his family. Boy returns home with his father, enlightened by the words of the shaman and matured by his recent experiences.

Analysis. The focus of this story is a compelling evocation of primeval days, ably abetted by the dark and brooding illustrations. Though the physically impaired medicine man is not central to the story, he is portrayed as an esteemed and pivotal figure in the tribe, tying the people to their roots and their meaning. This story replicates mythical and historical models in presenting the shaman with a physical impairment.

Harnishfeger, Lloyd. *Prisoner of the Mound Builders.* Illus. by George Overlie. Minneapolis, Minn.: Lerner, 1973. 141 pp. Reading Level: MC/YA
Disability: Orthopedic Impairment

O-Tah-Wah's deformed leg is considered a curiosity by his enslavers, the mound builders, an Indian tribe that esteems such a disability. He meets another captive and they plan an escape. When a priest dies, the two slaves accelerate their preparations, since it is clear that O-Tah-Wah will be selected for burial with the man's corpse because his unique body structure is considered a desirable attribute for one who will serve the medicine man in the afterlife. The plotters use various ruses and finally escape their relentless captors. In an epilogue, it is clear that the two courageous Indians settle by O-Tah-Wah's river and found a great nation.

Analysis. This talented author pushes aside the fog shrouding North America in prehistoric times, using the disabled hero as the presumed eponymous creator of a great tribe. The blurred illustrations aptly recapture the setting but give no indication of an orthopedic problem. The hero's leg, dubbed "Lazy One," causes him difficulty in being an effective hunter and oddly increases his jeopardy by its reverence among his captors. The Indian's arm muscles, highly developed to compensate for his disadvantage on the hunt, are a decided asset in the escape. O-Tah-Wah—lonely, strong, loyal, tenacious, volatile, and somewhat lumbering—emerges as a flawed but heroic figure of the past.

Harris, Rosemary. *The Bright and Morning Star*. New York: Macmillan, 1972. 254 pp. Reading Level: YA
Disabilty: Auditory Impairment

In Ancient Egypt, the fever and convulsions of a young boy, Sadhi, resulted in temporary paralysis followed by deafness and mutism. His mother, following a sign, takes him to the king's palace where he is given to Hekhti, the court architect, healer, and seer, for an evaluation. Sadhi is gradually weaned from his mother's overprotective care, and as he becomes more proficient in manual communication, his tantrums diminish. Under the pretext of discussing Sadhi's condition, Hekhti informs his ruler that a powerful priest is plotting against him. The coup is highly successful, but the seer is able to escape. Ignoring the rebels' attempt to use Sadhi as bait, the loyal healer sneaks back into the palace and using sign language sends a secret message with the deaf boy. A counterplot to rescue the king and restore him to the throne is successful, although Hekhti dies of poison. Sadhi's voice returns after a sojourn to Imhotep's tomb but there is no indication of a similar miraculous remission of his deafness.

Analysis. This historical fantasy is narrated by an observant cat, a clue to the detached tone and extraordinary nature of the events that ensue. Nevertheless, *The Bright and Morning Star*, the third book in a trilogy, is a fast-moving story and credible within the context it has established. The mentor, Hekhti, uses instructional techniques similar to those used in teaching sign language today, and Sadhi's remarkable change from a tyrant to a reasonable person able to communicate his needs and feelings is both plausible and valid. Deafness has an important function in many elements of the story. The character of the boy himself is less well developed. A reference to the king's "madness" is made but it appears to be a transitory event. There is some superstitious speculation about the impairment: "The heavens rule us when we're born, and someone like Sadhi had a star eclipsed at birth" and "Evil spirits inhabit him, and prevent his hearing and his speech." In one remarkable scene vividly recalling the Hellen Keller-Annie Sullivan confrontation, Hekhti asserts his domination over the boy, and the beginning of a breakthrough to communication and mental health is made possible.

Heide, Florence Parry. *Sound of Sunshine, Sound of Rain*. Illus. by Kenneth Longtemps. New York: Parents Magazine, 1970. unpaged. Reading Level: MC
Disability: Visual Impairment

The sister of the young black, blind, unnamed narrator leaves him to play by himself in the park as she continues on her way to study. The boy plays quiet, private games, entertaining himself by identifying the sounds around him. When he hears the bells of the ice-cream truck, he walks to the curb where the vendor refuses his money: "Guess what? . . . Every tenth kid wins a free ice cream bar, and you're the lucky one today." Leaving his truck, Abram joins the boy on a park bench and describes the shabby park in the most favorable light—the debris and litter "and all those things lying around are like flowers," and lucky people, like themselves, don't have to depend just on their eyes to be aware of things. On successive days they meet and Abram continues to share his view of a benevolent world with his young friend. One day as the boy returns home with his sister, they stop at a store where she is the target of racial slurs. The girl is angry; her brother tries to comfort her, telling her that Abram says color doesn't matter. This only serves to anger her more and she lashes out: "What does he know? Is he black, your friend?" That night the boy is troubled by nightmares. The next day it is raining so he cannot go to the park, but he tells himself: "Tomorrow it will be a nice day. Tomorrow my sister will feel better and I will go to the park and find Abram. He will make my balloon as good as new. Now I walk over to the window and lean my head against it. The rain taps its song to me against the glass, and I tap back."

Analysis. This lyrical novel does not limit itself to describing the world that the narrator knows but attempts to help the reader understand *how* he knows it. The world is absorbed through tactile, auditory, olfactory, and gustatory senses: "My mother's voice is warm and soft as a pillow. My sister's voice is little and sharp and high, like needles flying in the air . . . his voice [Abram's] is soft and kind as fur." "I put my feet on the floor and feel the cool wood and curl my toes against it." "I breathe on the hot chocolate so I can feel it on my face coming back warm." The sister's impatience and unhappiness find an outlet in her insensitive treatment of her brother: "My sister thinks because I cannot see that maybe I cannot hear very well, and she talks loud to me, and soft when she does not want me to hear, but I hear." "I make sure I have buttoned all my buttons the right way, or my sister will be cross and maybe not have time to take me to the park." The young woman's distress stems at least in part from the prejudice that victimizes her and produces anger that she then displaces onto her brother. Abram, oblivious to skin color, tells the child that color does not matter. The sister knows that society has insisted that color does matter—it may even be what matters most. The story, both simple and sophisticated, communicates on several levels. The brilliant, vibrant colors and the striking composition of the illustrations beautifully complement the poetic text.

Henry, Marguerite. *King of the Wind*. Illus. by Wesley Dennis. Chicago: Rand McNally, 1948. 175 pp. Reading level: MC
Disability: Speech Impairment

A colt, born in the stables of the sultan of Morocco, is cared for by a mute stableboy named Agba. He is selected by the sultan to accompany the animal to Versailles where it will be given as a gift to the king of France. The captain defrauds the sultan and the horses that are delivered to the king are in such bad condition that they are assigned to heavy work. Agba discovers that his horse, Sham, was sold and finally locates the animal hauling loads for a cruel carter. The Moroccan boy faithfully follows the horse as it becomes the property of some kindly English Quakers, then an indifferent innkeeper, and finally the evil Slade, who is a heartless horse breaker. Agba, erroneously accused of horse theft, has no voice to defend himself. He is rescued from jail and goes with Sham to become a stableboy for the Earl of Godolphin. Sham is eventually restored to health but again is assigned as a workhorse. Only Agba is aware of the nobility and talent of his charge. The Earl's plans for horse breeding are thwarted when Sham mates with a brood mare originally selected for another steed. Furious, the owner banishes the horse and stableboy until the new colt proves to be an excellent racer. Ultimately, Sham's progeny reflect their racing bloodline and their purses save the Earl's property, initiating the breeding of the great Godolphin Arabian horse strain in England.

Analysis. Agba's lack of speech is double-edged: It keeps him from socializing, which, in turn, keeps others away from him. He is so isolated that his compatriots are even unaware that he cannot speak. The author provides much insight into his feelings and presents a youth who accepts events and tries to make the best of them. Excellent illustrations in color and black and white show Agba in positive or neutral portrayals. As the boy was different, so was the horse: At birth it was believed to have the "evil sign" and later the groom remarks on his crest, "tis almost a deformity." The crippled sultan has a cleft lip although this does not impair his speech. "His eyes were hidden by heavy folds of eyelids, like a camel's, and his lips were thick and slit in two, and there was a big hump on his back." At one point, the groom's speech was typical of a stutterer when under stress. "He was so nervous that he could not control his stammering. 'Y-y-y-you, Ag-g-g-ba. Y-you lay a fresh l-l-litter of st-st-straw in the new m-m-mare's stall. And w-w-wash out the mang-g-ger.' " Later, however, "there was not the slightest hesitation or stammering in Mister Twickerham's speech. It was as if he had wound up his words into a ball and now had only to unwind them." Agba, the hero, is positively depicted in the text of this well-written, fast-paced novel. The author suggests that the boy's lack of human interaction was mitigated by his relationship with the animal he lovingly cared for: "The golden bay was tended all his life by a boy who could not speak. He left for Morocco the night his horse died. Without any words at all he made me understand that his mission in life was fulfilled."

Heppner, Elizabeth. *Inky: Seeing Eye Dog.* Also published as *Inki.* Illus. by Tom O'Sullivan. New York: Macmillan, 1957. 135 pp. Reading Level: MC
Disability: Visual Impairment

Jonathan's father is released from a Korean prisoner-of-war camp and returns to his family farm. His optic nerve has been atrophying and he soon loses his sight completely. The pup Jonathan has been raising is trained as a seeing eye dog and is eventually assigned to his father.

Analysis. The biblical origin of the expression "seeing eye" is noted by a visiting minister: "The hearing ear and the seeing eye, the Lord hath made even both of them." This reference leads to the articulation of the upbeat message of the book—although people may have difficulties, there are ways to surmount them: "For our blind—well, we have dogs like Inky here. Inky will someday be the seeing eye for someone who will be in desperate need of her." The plot of this well-intentioned but bland effort is without surprises and the characterizations are familiar.

Hodges, C. Walter. *The Namesake.* Illus. by author. New York: Coward-McCann, 1964. 269 pp. Reading Level: YA
Disability: Orthopedic Impairment; also emotional dysfunction, general health problems

In the wake of the violence that racks England during the period of the Viking invasions, Alfred, a young orphaned boy, has his injured leg amputated. He has a vision in which he is commanded to present a harnesslike device to the king, whose name he bears. The boy has many perilous adventures as he tried to fulfill his mission, and successful at last, he is finally accepted in the king's retinue where he learns to read and write. He is under King Alfred's formal protection as his personal historian and dutifully records the royal strategy and exploits. A substory concerns the martyr Edmund whose disciple, Esdras, becomes the fiery spirit of English vengeance. The zealot accompanies King Alfred into battle but subsequently has his tongue amputated and becomes highly irrational. Young Alfred is captured, escapes, and rejoins his sovereign, and eventually the Vikings sue for peace.

Analysis. This is an exciting, bloodcurdling adventure, definitely not for the faint of heart. The battlefield is the predominant setting, and so pain and suffering permeate the narrative. In some cases, young Alfred's disability is dealt with cruelly, but the times were brutal and hostility and exploitation were pandemic. Hodges shows an array of historically representative attitudes toward the one-legged boy. One of the refugees comments somewhat enviously, "A beggar could do well for himself like that. Going from one fat monastery to the next upon one leg, that's the way to live!" Contrarily, the young orphan is treated with pity by the Vikings, and when the other refugees are forced into the water, he and the women and children are exempted. " 'Not thee, thou little one-leg,' . . . and he smiled and patted me on the back." The superstitious attitude of the peasantry is exemplified when the youth happens upon a woman who "cried out and made the sign of the cross upon herself and the child, and for better measure thrust the child away into the shed and locked the door, for fear I would put the evil eye upon it." Ashamed, young Alfred tries to conceal his disability with a long gown, "but its loose folds were an encumbrance against the crutch; neither could I wear it when riding a horse, . . . so I soon gave it up, and contented myself to be seen for what I am." The battle scenes are overly long and somewhat confusing, the medical problem of the king is not clearly defined, and the imagery of the dream is not adequately developed. However, the momentum of the story and the courage of the young disabled hero demand the reader's attention. The dramatic illustrations boldly confront the disabilities, and their starkness adds greatly to the impact of this powerful historical novel.

Holland, Isabelle. *Heads You Win, Tails I Lose.* Philadelphia: Lippincott, 1973. 159 pp. Reading Level: YA/MA
Disability: Cosmetic Impairment, Orthopedic Impairment

Melissa Hammond has a crush on Ted, the neighborhood Adonis, a boy with few brains and less charm. Ted is happy to exploit her academic talent, but has no romantic interest. When Melissa shares her disappointment with her mother, she is advised to lose weight in order to be more attractive. Mrs. Hammond is a "molder of avant garde opinion and Father is her dedicated opponent." He is a sarcastic, bitter conservative; she is shallow, skinny, and alcoholic. The Hammond home is an armed camp with Melissa's excess weight providing ammunition for both sides.

The high school play for the year is "Antigone." Mrs. Ainslie, the drama coach, asks Joel Martin to read Creon's part. Joel, who has a cleft lip, lives with his father; his mother's situation is unclear. Melissa reads well, but does not look the part she would have to play, so Miss Ainslie suggests a diet, a recommendation not unheard before. Claire caustically explains that Melissa is a compulsive eater, whereupon Joel cleverly and sarcastically puts her down. Melissa decides to use her mother's diet pills to get started on her weight loss. After school the students exchange unpleasantries, but Ted turns nasty advising Joel to shut up or he'll split his mouth open for him again—a telling thrust since the usually sharp-tongued Joel blushes and is speechless.

There is another dreadful, hate-filled dinner at home that night; Melissa loses her temper and rushes out of the house. By the time she returns, her father has moved out and her mother has consumed an impressive quantity of liquor. Melissa takes enough of her mother's diet pills to have an uncontrollable high. She meets Joel and the two encounter Miss Ainslie, who insists that Mrs. Hammond be informed of her daughter's condition. She is so advised, but is too drunk to understand what she is being told. Melissa, on her doctor's advice, goes to her father's office where his secretary and purported mistress informs her that his leg, shattered when he was in the air force, has been causing him severe pain and he will soon face major surgery. Father and daughter discuss how they inadvertently and unintentionally have hurt each other. He accompanies Melissa home to help her cope with his wife's drinking. Both realize this is only a temporary move since there is no salvageable marriage relationship.

Analysis. Although the father's limp is briefly mentioned at the outset, this attribute is easily overlooked in his bitter, belittling dialogue. When there is a need to "humanize" this unpleasant person, his disability is resurrected. It appears that the condition is used to rationalize his behavior and his pain provides the catalyst for contact between father and daughter. Melissa feels pleased with herself, having taken the initiative for this and "Joel, with his ex-harelip, would understand." The discussion of the lip scar reverses and polarizes her opinions of the two boys. It simultaneously signals Ted's boorishness and Joel's vulnerability in one of the most moving but painful scenes in the book. Although the scene is brief, the author uses the confrontation to show how Ted's brutal blow isolates and demoralizes his victim. His intuitive thrust effectively illustrates how a wound, apparently dormant, can still cause pain. The exposition of the latter problem is by far the more credible of the two.

Holland, Isabelle. *The Man without a Face.* Philadelphia: Lippincott, 1972. 159 pp. Reading Level: MA
Disability: Cosmetic Impairment

Gloria has decided to remain at home, a crushing blow to the plans of her fourteen-year-old brother, Charles. Aware that an entrance exam to a boarding school he had already failed through negligence was his only passport away from his sister's spiteful, vicious tongue, Charles desperately searches for another chance to retake it. His younger sister suggests he ask McLeod, a recluse the locals have named "the man without a face," to tutor him. Unhappy, but having no other options, Charles asks him, and the former schoolteacher consents. McLeod sets rigorous conditions: three hours of tutoring each day followed by three full hours of homework. Any failure to comply will terminate the arrangement, he declares. Charles resentfully and grudgingly agrees and keeps his schedule a secret from all but Meg. His mother and Gloria are suspicious but involvement in their various romances keeps them too preoccupied to pursue the issue. Despite the academic pressures heaped on him, his abhorrence of the tutor's burnt and scarred face, and the aloofness of McLeod's behavior, Charles comes to admire and respect the older man. Charles, who remembers little of his own father, develops a complex relationship with McLeod—part father-son, part mentor-pupil. His mother announces her impending marriage, her fifth, to a long-time friend. Gloria leaves to visit her father, sister Meg is off to camp, and Charles, ostensibly under the care of a neighbor, spends most nights home alone except for a stray cat he lets have the run of the house. Gloria returns home unexpectedly to find the cat has messed her bed. Her boyfriend kicks the cat down a flight of stairs, and when Charles comes home he finds the animal is dying. He is devastated and runs to McLeod for solace. The process of consolation leads to a sexual encounter. The next morning Charles is angry and guilt-ridden. McLeod refuses to accept responsibility as instigator of the incident; he wishes to discuss it and keep the boy from exaggerating or misinterpreting its significance.

Charles readily passes the entrance examination, but is haunted by thoughts of his tutor. The boy hitchhikes to McLeod's home, but finds it deserted. He discovers a note addressed to him in which the hope is expressed that Charles will have resolved his anxieties about their relationship. His new stepfather finds him there, informs him McLeod has died of a heart attack, and tells Charles he must decide whether or not to return to school. At last understanding that he must be responsible for his own decisions and their consequences, Charles goes back to his studies.

Analysis. The tragic disfigurement of McLeod, which helps to isolate him from the community, is the result of an accident in which a young boy was killed. McLeod was driving while intoxicated and was sent to jail for two years, but this penalty did not expiate his guilt. It is hinted that plastic surgery would improve his appearance, but he keeps the scars as a kind of mortification or penance for his fatal negligence. In this instance, the branding produced by fate is not obliterated as it could be. Holland develops sensitive, complex, and paradoxical threads with great skill and adroitness.

Holman, Felice. *Slake's Limbo*. New York: Scribners, 1974. 117 pp.
Reading Level: YA
Disability: Visual Impairment

Thirteen-year-old Aremis Slake is myopic, a condition as well as a metaphor for his life—vague, fuzzy, and unfocused. No longer held by the relationship with his one friend, a retarded boy who died in an accident, Slake abandons his home with an indifferent aunt and his dreary existence as the butt of pranks. He hides in an abandoned section of a subway where he uses the washrooms, survives on the leftovers in coffee shops, and is unexpectedly launched in a newspaper "business" when a man gives him some money for a used newspaper the boy has reassembled. For several months Slake lives underground, furnishing his "home" with refuse left by travelers. This hermitlike lifestyle is comfortable for Slake, a timid, fearful boy who is alarmed by direct encounters. His panic is manifested as a feeling of a bird trapped in his chest, crying piteously and fluttering its wings to escape. He sweeps up in a luncheonette and is paid off in meals, experiencing for the first time what it is like not to be hungry. One day, he reconstructs some glasses from discarded frames and lenses and, by luck, improves his vision slightly. As his life develops structure, however unorthodox, and as he gains confidence, his surroundings come into sharper focus. Slake is able to achieve a miniscule but warming feeling of power as he shares some food with a rat and realizes the creature is as terrified of him as he is of life.

Slake reads in the paper of an accident in the subway tunnel and is petrified that the subsequent investigation for repairs means the end of his safe, cloistered, but independent life. He runs out on a track with a sign saying "stop" and fortunately is seen by a conductor. The motorman picks up the collapsed boy, who is taken to a hospital where plans are made to send Slake to a juvenile home. But with his newly provided clothes and glasses, Slake takes over the direction of his life and leaves to find his own future. "He didn't know where he was going, but the general direction was up."

Analysis. His limbo, oddly enough, is liberating rather than imprisoning. Slake's hibernation enables him to find the focus necessary for his growth. At last he relinquishes underground security for the risks of the open, lighted world, signaling his conscious acceptance of the challenge that life holds. The short interior contrapuntal story of the conductor and his obsessive fantasy of herding sheep in Australia instead of the human sheep he transports in New York seems too obviously appended to the story, distracting from the painful progress of Slake's odyssey. Although the symbolism of myopia is obvious, the story tension, the tight, skillful writing, indeed the whole compelling conceptualization, are anything but ordinary.

Holman, Felice. *A Year to Grow.* New York: Norton, 1968, 100 pp.
Reading Level: YA
Disability: Intellectual Impairment

Narrated in the first person by fifteen-year-old Julia, this slim novel recounts a year in her life at an inhospitable, austere boarding school. She is unable to relate to her withdrawn roommate, Nora, or to most of the staff, who are distant, formal, and deficient in knowledge about adolescent needs. Julia's only sustained linkage involves a male instructor on whom she develops an unrequited crush and an incipient relationship with the one relaxed, involved teacher on the staff who is subsequently dismissed. Julia ponders the teacher's prediction that something will happen to release the dam she has erected between herself and the world. During a compulsory afternoon walk, Julia turns her ankle and drops out, resting at a neglected, overgrown cemetery across the road. Everyday thereafter, she uses a stratagem to return to this refuge. She sets herself to the tasks of pulling weeds and righting fallen gravestones. She is joined by the retarded son of the director of the boarding school. They spend long afternoons just sitting or walking companionably together. Jimmy does not speak but communicates his contentment especially when Julia reads to him. They become very fond of each other and Julia gains a sense of purpose and connectedness through this relationship. One day Jimmy stops coming. Three weeks later, never having returned, he dies. Julia realizes that she is "a real person in the real world, and had loved and been loved, been bereaved, and had grown, with great pain and pride, in a sunny field of buttercups, and Queen Anne's lace, and dead children."

Analysis. The story is a moving, coming-of-age mood piece. The retarded youth is known only inferentially. He is spoken of in frightening terms by everyone except Julia, who comes to know him as a tender, gentle man, also reaching out for some human contact, some communication with a caring person. Although there is a recurring pattern of real or wished for intimacy followed by withdrawals, it is unfortunate that the final withdrawal is the death of the retarded character; however, dramatically and in terms of the story context, it is logical and inevitable, foreshadowed by their encounters in the cemetery. Jimmy never emerges as a well-defined character, yet the dimension of his loneliness is clear. His central function is as a propellent to more maturity and self-assurance for the central character. Essentially this is a story of aborted communication and lack of knowledge, ironically redressed through the retarded and mute character, who, although unable to communicate conventionally, was able to do so through friendship and companionship.

Huff, Afton. *The Silent Message*. Austin, Tex.: Steck-Vaughn, 1970. 186 pp. Reading Level: MC/YA
Disability: Auditory Impairment, Speech Impairment

Heather Carter, recently recovered from an operation that partially restored her hearing, visits her cousin, Jinks, on her ranch in New Mexico. She is alarmed to find that another cousin, Jasper, is sought by the FBI, suspected of stealing scientific secrets. It dawns on Heather that the mysterious package, containing some surprisingly ugly beads that arrived just before she left home must have come from her fugitive cousin. Heather visits a place she and Jasper used to frequent, unaware that she has been followed by a federal agent. In saving her from a rattlesnake, Jasper reveals his hiding place and is arrested by the agent. Jasper had been injured in an automobile accident 15 years earlier and has been mute since then—a fact oddly unnoticed by Heather and not mentioned by anyone else. In the process of unraveling the mystery, the ability to lip-read allows her to communicate with her cousin. The beads he had sent her contained microdots with information that convincingly clears Jasper of the charges and leads to the capture of the real spy.

Analysis. Although some information proffered about auditory disability is useful and valid, particularly that pertaining to problems of sound distortion attendant upon hearing loss, other statements are erroneous or misleading. The assertion by one character—"Handicapped people do seem to develop a sixth sense that others can't understand, or explain"—although compatible with popular thinking, is patently ridiculous. Several situations are at least questionable: The heroine does not realize a favorite cousin is mute; and the hearing-impaired character has had speech problems requiring long periods of therapy even though hearing loss occurred in adolescence, after speech and language have developed and usually stabilized. While such unlikely situations could conceivably occur, the reader should not be asked to accept them on faith. The writing is standard for the genre, strictly escape literature, and never intended to withstand intensive scrutiny.

Hunt, Irene. *No Promises in the Wind*. Chicago: Follett, 1970. 247 pp. Reading Level: YA/MA
Disability: Orthopedic Impairment

The familial tensions at home caused by the Depression lead Joey and Josh to run away and become part of the army of homeless boys who survive as best they can by living off charity or odd jobs. The brothers hitch a ride from a compassionate truck driver, who leaves them at a carnival in Baton Rouge where he suspects there may be work. They enjoy a brief interlude of steady work and regular meals during which they come to know some of the sideshow people. Edward C., one of the dwarfs, befriends the boys and offers them some of the affection they so desperately need. Blegens, another dwarf, is vicious and gossipy, impervious to the pain of others. When fire destroys the carnival, the boys move on, searching for the truck driver who helped them. Joey becomes very sick and almost dies but is discovered and cared for by generous strangers. Josh begins to realize the consequences of the financial pressures that not earning enough money to feed his family placed on his father. Further, he discerns that the trouble between them was largely caused by economic desperation. Josh feels an overwhelming need to return home, and the boys are reunited with their grateful parents.

Analysis. Even though the disabled characters have minor roles in this beautifully crafted book, their depictions are excellent. The two dwarfs are dissimilar in characteristics: One is a minor villain, the other a gentle, caring person. Their disparate personalities are obviously independent of their impairments. Good characterizations, an outstanding sense of historic events, and skillful use of language combine in this admirable book that vividly reports on the terrible human suffering that resulted from the Great Depression.

Hunt, Irene. *Up a Road Slowly.* Chicago: Follett, 1966. 192 pp. Reading Level: YA
Disability: Intellectual Impairment, Emotional Dysfunction

After the death of her mother, seven-year-old Julia moves to the home of her Aunt Cordelia. This austere, demanding woman, who is also the teacher in the rural, one-room school, tries to impose some structure on the life of her impetuous, headstrong niece. One of the students at school is Agnes Kilpin, a filthy, abused, retarded child. The other children try to avoid her but their teacher will not allow them to do so. Julia, who is the prime focus of Agnes' desire for attention, finally develops an elaborate lunchtime ritual in which Agnes is elected "queen" and must hold court during the noon recess in lonely isolation. When Aunt Cordelia catches on to their game, she is saddened, but resignedly permits it to continue. Julia plans a birthday party and her aunt insists Agnes be included. The girl hotly refuses, and when an ultimatum is delivered, Julia chooses not to have the party rather than invite the loathed girl. Soon after, Agnes becomes ill. Aunt Cordelia visits her and is appalled at the evidence of neglect and squalor that she finds. When Julia is invited for a ride in a friend's elegant little carriage, her aunt insists she deliver some cut flowers to the sick child. Furious but unable to resist the woman's demands, she goes. The sight of the dying child so upsets Julia that she returns home in acute distress. That night Agnes dies and Julia is remorseful. Her cynical uncle, Cordelia's brother, disparages her contrite behavior: "You know very well that if this Kilpin girl could approach you again, as moronic and distasteful as she was a month ago, that you'd feel the same revulsion for her." Although recognizing the truth of his cruel remarks, she intuitively understands that his insight encompasses only a partial perception of reality.

When Cordelia was young she was in love with a man, but demands of her family kept her from joining him when he went away to complete his studies. He returns now with his wife, a once-talented musician whose delusions and irrational fears have reduced her to a helpless, childlike state. Somehow, she sees Cordelia's brother as her protector and the selfish, solitary poseur responds to the unhappy woman's needs, soothing her when she refuses anyone else's attentions. She increasingly retreats to her private world and soon dies. Julia remains with her aunt through high school, slowly coming to appreciate and internalize the woman's rigid but compassionate moral code.

Analysis. The children reject Agnes more on the basis of her complete lack of social skills and her repulsive physical condition rather than her slow functioning. She can be easily manipulated, though, and with a mixture of guilt and relief, they find a way to exclude her. The aunt insists on compassion, not out of any special regard for the child, but from an understanding that she is being victimized by her environment. Further, Cordelia operates from an unbending belief that all people must be treated humanely. This same attitude permeates her response to the woman who returns with the man she had once hoped to marry. The writing is literate and the characterizations and setting especially well crafted. The author expresses an ethic that contrasts laxness with an unbending sense of responsibility and a demanding moral code and somehow manages to make the latter choice seem the only desirable one.

Hunter, Edith Fisher. *Sue Ellen.* Illus. by Bea Holmes. Boston: Houghton Mifflin, 1969. 170 pp. Reading Level: MC
Disability: Intellectual Impairment; also general health problems

Sue Ellen, a retarded child, is almost eight years old. There are also five other siblings, an illiterate father with a drinking problem, an invalid cranky mother, and a home that reflects their poverty. Sue Ellen is transferred from her former class where she was making little progress to a new class and placed under the care of the exemplary Miss Kelly. The teacher has a high school student, Polly, who assists her in class. Polly becomes interested in Sue Ellen; she is very pleased with Sue Ellen's progress but is distressed when growth is not constant. Miss Kelly assures her that this is to be expected and continues to note improvement both academically and in attitude as Sue Ellen thrives on the activity-based curriculum. The class has an auction and the proceeds ensure that Sue Ellen will have a two-week vacation. The local priest obtains some household goods for the destitute family, Sue Ellen's mother returns from the hospital, and the future looks somewhat improved.

Analysis. Although Sue Ellen functions as a retarded person (she can only correctly identify blue and red), it is quite clear that her impoverished home condition, with its attendant lack of food, affection, and opportunities for language development, has contributed heavily to her inability to learn. The teacher's innovative techniques, style, and relationship to her students might well be required reading for any educator. There is some name calling that is handled well. Sue Ellen's former unsympathetic teacher is contrasted with the too-good-to-be-true Miss Kelly. The writing is simple and there is little in the way of excitement to move the story line along. The illustrations are exceptionally sketchy and visually unsatisfying. The strongest virtue of this upbeat book is its depiction of how concern and pedagogy have a crucial impact on a child's ability to learn.

> Hunter, Mollie (pseud.). Maureen Mollie Hunter McIlwraith. *The Stronghold.* New York: Harper & Row, 1974. 259 pp. Reading Level: YA/MA
> *Disability:* Orthopedic Impairment

Coll, eighteen, has sustained a leg injury since the Roman invasion of Scotland when his parents were killed and he was brutally injured. News has circulated that another raid is imminent, and various plans for resistance are proposed. Rivals for authority in the tribe see this new external threat as an opportunity to seize power. Coll, now a foster son of a tribal leader, has designed a fortification that he thinks could resist the most powerful attacks of the more skilled and better armed Romans. His plan, at first rejected, is tried in desperation. The daughter of the tribal chief announces her willingness to marry Coll. The alliance is criticized, for Coll would then be in line to succeed to leadership of the tribe and "how then could the tribe survive with only a cripple to lead them?" The argument is refuted by pointing out that Coll's other qualities are more important. A stronghold is built from which the invasion is repelled. Coll's supporters are vindicated and his design for fortification becomes the key element in their defensive strategy.

Analysis: The boy is developed as a fully rounded person, gifted in some areas, but naive and inadequate in others. The presentation of the treatment of Coll's disability has historical validity. The violence, endemic at the time, was certainly the cause of many disabilities and the response to it was likewise credible. The disability causes pain and impedes his functioning and is an important but not the overriding factor in his life. Political factions tried to use Coll's impairment to attack his credibility and reduce his influence. The tale has the ring of historical truth, with a large, though well-developed, cast of characters and a compelling rush of action and intrigue.

Ish-Kishor, Sulamith. *Our Eddie.* New York: Pantheon, 1969. 183 pp. Reading Level: YA
Disability: Neurological Impairment, Orthopedic Impairment, Emotional Dysfunction

Eddie Raphel's father is headmaster in a Hebrew school for poor children. Although he is respected by his students, at home he is considered a tyrant, putting the welfare of his pupils before that of his own family. Most of his time and energy is zealously devoted to the school. When home, the old man is inconsistent, flies into uncontrollable rages, and claims the air and his food have been poisoned by enemies. The physicians describe this as paranoia, although one claims it results from a bicycle accident that created pressure on the brain. None of the doctors is able to diagnose or explain the cause of Mrs. Raphel's spinal problem. However they do suggest an impossible prescription, namely, not to work so hard. She does have some assistance from Ada, a household helper, who has problems of her own—an exploding stove left her face badly disfigured. Eddie, now fifteen, obtains a clerk's job but is fired for thievery. Soon after, on a stair, his leg falters and the hot water he is carrying scalds him so severely he must be hospitalized. Mr. Raphel is becoming much worse, and the family decides his only hope lies in going to America. Once there, he takes another low-paying job and neither the family's fortune nor the father's disposition improves much. When an appeal is made to him to take Eddie to a neurologist, he refuses, saying the boy's limp is simply a sign of incompetence and such errands are exclusively a wife's responsibility. This heartless comment is underscored by his wife's desperate physical condition: Now unable to even walk, she has become a semi-invalid. Eddie's physical condition worsens and multiple sclerosis is suspected. Although the surgeon is reluctant to operate, he finally does, warning Eddie that the procedure may be fatal. Eddie, feeling he has no option, agrees to the surgery and the doctor's gloomy prediction comes true. Mr. Raphel, more contrite and decidedly tardy in attending to his family's needs, grieves over the loss of his son and finally assumes some of the household responsibilities.

Analysis. The portrayal of the excesses of pathological behavior is especially effective and, although the reader will be shocked and ultimately repelled by Mr. Raphel's increasingly irrational conduct, there is some feeling for him as a man caught in a web, even though it is of his own making. Great compassion is generated for Eddie as well as for his mother. They are depicted as victims of the father's paranoia and disinterest, of painful and debilitating illnesses, and of conditions of poverty so extreme as to preclude adequate health care. Although the characterizations are vivid, the tone is one of unrelieved gloom and agony.

Jewett, Eleanore M. *The Hidden Treasure of Glaston.* Illus. by Frederick T. Chapman. New York: Viking, 1946. 307 pp. Reading Level: YA

Disability: Orthopedic Impairment, Emotional Dysfunction

In 1171, a knight leaves his son, Hugh, in the care of the monks at the Glaston Monastery as he flees his home. Hugh, weak and lame, is a disappointment to his father, who had hoped for a son capable of being a warrior. Hugh, happily absorbed in his training as a scribe, is befriended by Dickon, who shows him a secret underground tunnel filled with forgotten religious artifacts. Hugh learns that Joseph of Arimathea had once brought the Holy Grail to Glaston from where it had disappeared. The story of the Grail is inscribed in an old book in the abbey, but some crucial pages have been removed. The boys discover that an allegedly "mad" hermit periodically visits their secret cave. Bleheris, whose erratic behavior sometimes distresses the boys, enters into a tentative alliance with them as they all pursue leads to the whereabouts of the Grail. The hermit finds a sword he is convinced is Excalibur and predicts that Hugh will find the Grail. However, Hugh asserts that Bleheris might be the chosen one, since "folks think anyone whose mind is not right is especially beloved and protected by God." Hugh becomes lost in a marsh, prays, and is told in a vision that he must dig in the churchyard. He does so and the graves of King Arthur and Guinevere are found. The reigning king and queen journey to the monastery to celebrate the discovery. After their departure, Hugh discovers that the book about the Grail is missing and, suspecting a certain culprit, frantically rides in pursuit of the royal party. He is stopped in the forest and given a message for the king about his son's planned insurrection. Hugh delivers the warning and, returning without the book, discovers the monastery is on fire. Hugh races into the burning church where he has a vision of the Holy Cup in the flames. Bleheris is dead, but the boy is able to pull one of his teachers to safety. Although Hugh has gradually been getting stronger during his apprenticeship, he becomes completely healed at the moment he perceives the sacred image. Plans for rebuilding are underway when Hugh's father returns and, seeing his son restored, states he will take the boy with him to Jerusalem. Hugh declines, deciding to remain with the monks since only he knows the full story of the Grail and has an obligation to record and preserve it.

Analysis. The Hidden Treasure of Glaston is a well-written, interesting, historical adventure with a strong, but not overbearing religious message. Hugh's limp, his youth, and his kindness all establish his credentials as an innocent, hence one worthy of receiving the message. The other character singled out for his piety is "mad," and the prediction that the vision will probably be seen by fools or children comes true. Bleheris dies, Hugh is cured, and the youth's dedication to a religious life is intensified. The illustrations are appropriate, but not outstanding. They fail to give any indication of the boy's impairment, although Bleheris' portrait provides evidence of his distraught mental state.

Jewett, Eleanore M. *Mystery at Boulder Point*. Also published as *The Mooncusser*. Illus. by Jay Hyde Barnum. New York: Viking, 1949. 281 pp. Reading Level: MC/YA
Disability: Visual Impairment; also emotional dysfunction

Kathleen Maclain, a blind child, and her family move into a house where a "mooncusser" (a person who lures ships to their doom) once lived. According to rumor, when neighbors caught the ghoulish wrecker guiding ships to the rocky shore so he might salvage the cargo, they ran him out of town. One foggy day after Marty and her buddy, Mike, have become friends with Kathleen, the three encounter a mysterious stranger, who Marty is convinced is the ghost of the mooncusser. Kathleen learned to row a boat, but in the fog she and Marty become disoriented and land near a cottage housing an old woman and the stranger. She tells the children about the man who is her son: "He didn't do no harm to nobody, but he talked to himself constant, and took to broodin' and starin' and the neighbors got uneasy." During a storm the man reappears, rescuing Marty as well as his own mother, but subsequently dies. The rumors about the stranger are revealed to be untrue and the children discover he has been a victim of community misperceptions. Kathleen's house was destroyed by the storm, and she moves with her family to Marty's house. Marty's father is a widower and Kathleen's mother is a widow, and the two soon decide to marry.

Analysis. Minimal information about blindness is presented, such as the need to maintain furniture in fixed positions for ease in moving through a house safely. But the implication that braille books are the only source of learning for the blind is misleading, and the mother's lack of stress on academics for a girl presented as a good student is accepted without condemnation. Although Kathleen is ultimately portrayed as a strong and able person, there is substantial manipulation to achieve this end. Marty's dog has a limp, prompting her to assert that she will love him all the more since he is handicapped—a remark that sets up a climate for acceptance of Kathleen and admiration for her courage in dealing with "the weight of her affliction." She is unpalatably oversold: "Quiet and quick, she moved easily about the house now that she had become accustomed to it, helped in household matters and sang as she worked, loving everybody and so dearly loved by them all"; "She could play the flute with remarkable sweetness of tone . . . all day long she would be busy and happy over one thing or another"; and incredibly, "When one is blind, everybody, *everybody* is so kind! I can hear voices change when folks speak to me, harsh unpleasant, ugly voices soften up a bit, and I can feel the kindness sticking right out of people. I don't believe anybody in the world would do any harm to a person who is blind."

The emotionally disturbed stranger is seen from three perspectives: as a target of community ignorance and hostility, as suffering from his mother's overprotection, and as a hostage of his own delusions. The major characters have no distinguishable personalities, the incidents are contrived, and the writing is flat. The illustrations tend to be static and show Kathleen with vacant eye sockets.

Johnson, Annabel and Edgar Johnson. *The Black Symbol.* New York: Harper & Row, 1959. 207 pp. Reading Level: YA
Disability: Visual Impairment

Blind since childhood, Steve was used as a beast of burden by his father, until Dr. Cathcart buys him for fifty dollars and trains him to be a strongman in his traveling medicine show. Meanwhile, Barney runs away from a ranch after he overhears his aunt and uncle say that his father is dead. Hoping to come across news that his parent still lives, he too joins the doctor's caravan and is assigned the responsibility of Steve's care. Doc has warned Barney that the blind man is unstable, but after an initial period of difficulty they grudgingly come to like each other. Although the boy is at first loyal to Doc, he soon realizes that the older man is a fraud, palming off his worthless concoction as an elixir. Barney begins to understand the ramifications of blindness and is empathic with Steve's anger about being imprisoned in the traveling wagon. In a series of events revealing how evil the itinerant huckster really is, Barney finds out that his father is alive, escapes, and finally locates his father who decides to bamboozle the con man and rescue Steve. Pretending to be naive, the father cleverly exposes the charlatan to the crowd and the caravan is destroyed in the melee that follows. When Steve is rescued, he, another escapee, Barney, and his father join together in a copper mining partnership.

   Analysis. The book is a nonstop roller coaster of a story, a heady collection of innocents, villains, and heroes. While these are stock characters to some degree, they take on flesh and bone in the dialogue and in the headlong rush of this complex story. Steve is an unique character and, in his sagacity, bravery, and resistance to oppression, he takes on a strength over and above his acting role as the strongman. There is much violence and cruelty in this adventure tale, most of it directed at Steve who, despite both verbal and physical abuse, remains indomitable.

Jordan, Hope Dahle. *The Fortune Cake.* New York: Lothrop, Lee and Shepard, 1972. 160 pp. Reading Level: YA
Disability: Intellectual Impairment

   When Jenny Jonsonn's parents leave for Europe, she stays with her Aunt Hertha and cousins, Tracy, 16, and Dawn, 12, who is retarded. Jenny, fond of the younger child, has been her tutor since the "schools couldn't give her the special attention she needed, and Aunt Hertha had scoured the state for help, with no luck." The four leave town to vacation at a lake, which becomes increasingly deserted as summer comes to an end. Jenny plans to be a special education teacher, and the daily practice with Dawn helps them both. When she briefly returns to her city home, Jenny discovers that a rock with a threatening note has been thrown through the window. The police deduce that the warning is the work of an escaped prisoner once sentenced by Jenny's father. Jenny and Dawn are alone in the cottage when a young stranger enters, claiming to be a convicted murderer. He intends to hold the girls as hostages, bartering their lives for his imprisoned brother's freedom. Jenny proceeds with Dawn's daily instruction, hoping to keep the child calm and unafraid. Her lessons surreptitiously include clues indicating where their captor plans to take them and Jenny hides the incriminating paper in a birthday cake she is baking for her cousin. Jenny's boyfriend and cousin decipher the clues and locate the deserted farm where the girls are kept prisoner. Jenny feels that their kidnapper is not the villain he appears. The young man admits that his wicked behavior is deceiving—he is not as bad as he seems. He has only been attempting to cover up his brother's crimes, and this evidence (!) of basic decency will lead to a complete review of his case.

Analysis. Assertions and insinuations in this story about various aspects of mental retardation are misleading. Wisconsin, where the story is set, has many public, private, and parochial special schools that provide extensive high quality services for retarded children. The active parent advocate groups and government agencies have been responsive to the needs of this population, so the suggestion that the state has been "scoured" for help and none was available strains credulity. Jenny claims that she has read a few books about retarded children and reports "they seem to differ," a statement simultaneously obvious and irrelevant. The depiction of Dawn demonstrates little knowledge of the learning behavior of those with intellectual deficiencies. She is presented as unable to express herself verbally, yet can do so in writing, a reversal of usual developmental growth. Certainly a child who is just learning her colors could scarcely write a 99-word letter that contains words like "tomorrow," "fortune," "whistle," and so on, nor could she compose sentences initiated by adverbial clauses. The retarded child is merely used as a device to alert the reader to sinister developments and as a means to precipitate the rescue. Also, she provides the heroine's vocational goal: "Working with Dawn has made me decide that I want to teach retarded children after college." The writing is undistinguished, and little tension is generated by the romance or the slight suspense in this story.

Jupo, Frank. *Atu, the Silent One.* Illus. by author. New York: Holiday House, 1967. unpaged. Reading Level: YC
Disability: Speech Impairment

In the time before recorded history, there lived a young African bushman named Atu, who could not speak. Atu learns the ways of the hunter but can only communicate through gestures and drawings. One night, after a great hunt in which an elephant is killed, the men celebrate by feasting and telling stories about their exploits. Atu disappears, but is found on a hillside drawing the story of the hunt so vividly on some rocks that the very stones speak for him. Atu becomes a great hunter and, although mute, the graphic chronicler of his tribe's feats.

Analysis. Mythlike, this simple story echoes the theme of achievement in one's area of loss. Unlike many historical tales, the hero is never an outcast who must achieve to be valued. Atu is loved and respected as a child and, although his skill is greatly prized and admired, his ability is never a justification for acceptance. The simple, stylized illustrations support the positive image of a tribal member contributing to the community through his originality and artistic ability.

Keats, Ezra Jack. *Apt. 3*. Illus. by author. New York: Macmillan, 1971. unpaged. Reading Level: YC
Disability: Visual Impairment

Two young brothers, inside their apartment house on a rainy day, hear music and decide to see if they can find where it comes from. They trace the sounds to an apartment where a voice orders them to come in. Too frightened to refuse, they see a blind man and his harmonica as they enter. The children are astonished at what the blind man can learn about the world through his hearing and what he can say about it through his music. Enchanted, they ask him to accompany them on a walk the next day; joyfully he accepts.

Analysis. The muted, but lavish colors of the illustrations portray an exciting, wonder-filled world of which the blind man is a part. The children's awe and mistaken impressions about visual loss are briefly explored. Apprehension is replaced by a desire for friendship as information and interaction supplant ignorance and fear. The deliberate ordinariness of the title underscores an important point: The blind are our neighbors. The writing has clarity, simplicity, and punch—a top-notch introduction to the meaning of impairment.

Kerr, M. E. (pseud.). Marijane Meaker. *Dinky Hocker Shoots Smack!* New York: Harper & Row, 1972. 198 pp. Reading Level: YA/MA
Disability: Emotional Dysfunction

Dinky, daily growing more obese, is relentlessly stuffing a cat, Nader, into a similar state. Mrs. Hocker, on a perpetual search for causes, is currently focusing all her attention on a rehabilitation program for drug addicts. She gives only the most cursory attention to her daughter and her niece, Natalia, who has just returned from a therapeutic center for schizophrenics. Tucker, former owner of Nader, asks Natalia to go to a dance and a foursome is arranged that includes P. John Knight. He and Dinky join Weight Watchers together, and as Dinky begins to lose weight, her obsession with physical abnormalities diminishes also. Mrs. Hocker, shocked at P. John's archconservative political views, ejects him and interferes with Natalia and Tucker's growing relationship. Natalia retreats to the compulsive rhyming typical of some schizophrenic patterns and Dinky to the refrigerator, her obsession, and her defensive cynicism. The night that Mrs. Hocker is to be honored for her marvelous contribution to the community program for ex-addicts, her daughter sprays "Dinky Hocker Shoots Smack!" over walls surrounding the banquet hall. The Hockers finally hear the message and acknowledge Dinky's desperate need for their attention.

Analysis. The shocking Day-Glo title traps attention at the outset, and the attentive, sophisticated reader is thereafter treated to witty writing, clever dialogue, unconventional plot, and superb characterizations. The portrayal of Natalia is excellent. The genesis of her problems arising from the death of her parents and her therapeutic treatment at the Renaissance School is briefly but compassionately touched upon. Her response to having a desirable and attractive boyfriend and then having him banished is presented in a comprehensible and empathic manner. Natalia has better and worse days and the parallel between her emotional state and Dinky's self-destructive and erratic behavior as a result of parental indifference is not hard to draw. The story strongly suggests that mental health is a position on a continuum: Under pressure, Natalia requires her specialized school and compulsive rhyming and Dinky turns to Sara Lee. This is a superbly satirical book, with marvelous insight into the well-to-do urban scene and the inner world of struggling and troubled adolescents.

Kerr, M. E. (pseud.). Marijane Meaker. *Is That You, Miss Blue?* New York: Harper & Row, 1975. 170 pp. Reading Level: YA/MA
Disability: Emotional Dysfunction; also auditory impairment, visual impairment, speech impairment, general health problems

Flanders Brown, the narrator in this story, has been sent to an Episcopal boarding school after the dissolution of her parents' marriage. Because of her asthmatic condition, Flanders is assigned to the dormitory reserved for students with health problems. Sharing these quarters with her is Agnes Thatcher, who is deaf and mute. Miss Blue, the faculty adviser, insists on viewing Agnes' disability in the most mawkish terms: " 'Isn't that sad, dear?' she said. 'Jesus allows our afflictions to test us, but we sometimes forget 'His will be done' when we see the stricken'." The more pragmatic Flanders finds such an approach distasteful: "I didn't take to the idea of God or Jesus treating whoever He felt like treating the same way a vivisectionist might treat a stray dog, testing someone's faith the way the dog might be tested for the physical side effects of a new drug." In the clique-bound school, Agnes, beautiful and wealthy, is sought after by the most society-minded girls. A blind date is arranged for her with a boy who is literally blind and Agnes is furious at what she intuitively knows would be perceived as a sideshow. Miss Blue, an excellent science teacher, becomes increasingly obsessed with her religion. She is convinced that she has direct personal encounters and conversations with Jesus. This religious preoccupation is highly embarrassing to the administration, which decides to dismiss her. The irony of the situation is not wasted on Flanders whose cynicism increases daily. Some of the students are contemptuous of Miss Blue, but a few are compassionate, seeing no reason for her to leave, although none of them supports her out of personal regard. Flanders is surprised to find that when Miss Blue was a college student, she was attractive and popular. The young girl wonders how her teacher could have descended to her present unhappy, friendless state. Flanders and a few friends, without authorization, give Miss Blue a painting belonging to the school as a going-away present. This is done out of sympathy with her dismissal and in protest at the administration's callousness. At Christmas vacation, Flanders visits her mother and soon after leaves the school for good to stay with her. Although she loses track of her former friends there, Miss Blue remains indelibly in her memory.

Analysis. The key to Flanders' maturation is her ability to view people and events in a multiplicity of ways, understanding that they can contain contradictory, seemingly irreconcilable, qualities. As Flanders is able to set aside preconceptions and initial impressions and, in the case of her relationships with her parents, her own hurt, she perceives the world more accurately and compassionately. The tragedy of Miss Blue's abandonment of reality for her delusional world is neither romanticized nor overdramatized. Rather it causes Flanders to speculate about how a once attractive and popular person could be reduced to a helpless and ineffectual condition. Agnes, hardly the stereotypical shy and withdrawn deaf-mute student, is seen objectively as a tough, self-assured, aggressive person. The author's skill and adroitness—most apparent in the vignette involving Agnes and her "blind date"—guide the reader to the understanding that no single perception can ever provide more than a fractional view of reality. Although the conclusion is flat, this unusual and demanding novel is incisive, witty, and challenges stereotypes.

Key, Alexander. *Escape to Witch Mountain.* Illus. by Leon B. Wisdom, Jr. Philadelphia: Westminster, 1968. 170 pp. Reading Level: MC
Disability: Speech Impairment

Tonio and his mute sister, Tia, orphans, undeservedly have bad reputations and are taken to a detention home. They have only hazy recollections of their origins but are convinced that their roots are somehow tied to the unusual starred box Tia still retains. The girl communicates with others in writing but with her brother by telepathic means. Tonio, also strangely gifted, has the special power of psychokinesis. A stranger, claiming he is their uncle, arrives at the institution, but Tia senses that his purposes are nefarious, and the two children, with the help of a clergyman, hide. After a series of perilous adventures, they find themselves ascending Witch Mountain. They deduce that they came from another planet and have skills that the evil man and his cohorts want to harness. The two children narrowly elude their pursuers, returning in an extraterrestrial vehicle to their homeland. Ironically, on their planet, Tia's muteness is commonplace. It is those who must resort to using their voice for communication who are considered handicapped.

Analysis. There is much violence in the story, but the fantasy format diminishes its potency. Although conceptually imaginative, the story suffers from its loose development. Because of the presentation, little information about mutism can be gained; however, the turnabout—defining a handicap by a particularized perspective—is startling and suggests that "handicap" is not an absolute but can be situationally defined.

Klein, Gerda. *The Blue Rose.* Photog. by Norma Holt. New York: Lawrence Hall, 1974. unpaged. Reading Level: YC
Disability: Intellectual Impairment

Jenny, retarded, is much loved by her family, but has trouble with her peers because her behavior seems inappropriate to them. Although her parents are concerned about her future they still enjoy the present happiness she brings them.

Analysis. More a plea for pity than a coherent story, *The Blue Rose* is replete with unsupported assumptions, misunderstandings, and misinformation. Jenny is unrestrainedly likened to lower forms of animal life and even to plants. Characteristics that are incorrectly attributed to animals are also claimed for the child. "You know, when a kitten loses its tail, it is said to gain sharper ears," the author authoritatively reports. Too many people concentrate on the disability (the lost tail) and neglect the compensatory strengths, it is implied, but what compensation Jenny has is neither suggested nor explained. Unabated, the comparisons continue: the child responds to "sounds we never hear" like fish who "have a language and music of their own"(!); she is hampered in her tasks like a short-winged bird for whom "flying is very hard"; and, finally, having seemingly exhausted the animal kingdom, she is like a blue rose, rare, and therefore to be especially cherished. The style of writing is reminiscent of primers with their short, choppy sentences and therefore the intended audience would seem to be young children. The images are so sentimental that an older population would seem more receptive to such devices. Presumably, the purpose of this book is to promote the understanding of retardation among very young readers by providing a model to which children can relate. However, instead of concentrating on comprehensible similarities, connections, or positive portrayals, the publishers have employed dark, confusing photographs containing Jenny often staring off into space. Similes are employed, such as that of the rare blue rose, that are conceptually difficult for youngsters and largely meaningless to them. Thus, instead of humanizing or warmly interpreting this condition, this novel depersonalizes retardation, creating distance from, rather than identification with, Jenny.

Klein, Norma. *It's Not What You Expect.* New York: Pantheon, 1973. 128 pp. Reading Level: YA
Disability: Emotional Dysfunction

Carla and Oliver, teenage twins, embark on the unlikely enterprise of running a restaurant for the summer. The mother of Letty, who works as a waitress for the twins, has been institutionalized on numerous occasions. Letty is concerned that her parent may be a source of embarrassment, yet wants acceptance for her. When the twins visit Letty's home, they find her mother's behavior strange, in conflict with their stereotyped thinking about mental patients. Her actions are neither threatening nor bizarre, rather more inappropriate and seemingly not responsive to observable stimuli. The girl friend of the twins' older brother decides to have an abortion. Carla blurts out this news to her mother, who tells her that she had undergone the same experience as a young woman. Carla is surprised to find she is comforted by this intimate revelation. Her father, having left the family in search for himself, returns, evidently having worked through his problems.

Analysis. This articulate yet disjointed novel concerns a variety of contemporary social problems—separation, extramarital sex, abortion, and, peripherally, emotional stress. Although Letty's mother is a minor character, her role offers the opportunity to examine briefly some common misperceptions about emotional dysfunction. The woman's behavior, withdrawn and reflective, confounds the adolescents' expectation since she seems more frightened than frightening.

Knight, Ruth Adams. *Brave Companions.* Garden City, N.Y.: Doubleday, 1945. 215 pp. Reading Level: YA
Disability: Visual Impairment

Tom Talbert has worked with dogs all his life and his expertise is put to good use in training animals in the K-9 Corps during World War II. In a military maneuver on a Pacific island, Tom is saved by a dog but loses his eyesight in the action. He becomes very depressed after a number of unsuccessful surgical operations. He is temporarily reunited with a pup, Joey, but must leave him when he returns to the States. Tom has drifted into a state of apathy and passivity so profound that he is unable to be properly rehabilitated. A friend finally takes Tom to the seeing eye school where Joey is now in residence. Tom enrolls as a student and Joey becomes his dog. The experience revitalizes him and it is clear that his life has taken on new meaning and direction and that, though blind, he can continue his work with the animals he loves.

Analysis. At least one-quarter of this story describes in great detail the rehabilitation process for the newly blinded who plan to use seeing eye dogs. This is done in a concentrated, highly informative manner and much attention is given to the adaptations needed by the blind. The inclusion of a blind chemist is an oddity, but all other portrayals of the vocational competencies of those without vision are well done. Tom's agony about his vision loss is probed when a friend comes to visit him. "Take a good look. This is the first stage. Next time I'll have a tin cup and a fistful of lead pencils." "Cut that out," said Marvin, genuinely shocked. "What else is there for me?" Tom burst out. "What else is there for me ever again? A blind man, tapping along with a cane?" As can be noted, the writing is of the pulp variety, but it is a fast-moving adventure story crammed full of information about the emotional and rehabilitative needs of the blind. The deliberate ethnic slurs leveled at the Japanese people are highly offensive. The publishing date indicates the book was written at a time when Japan was an enemy of this country and such unrestrained attacks were commonplace. This information explains but hardly justifies its occurrence.

Koob, Theodora. *The Deep Search.* Philadelphia: Lippincott, 1969. 188 pp. Reading Level: YA
Disability: Intellectual Impairment

Dee Fontaine quits her high school drama club and ends her participation in sports so she can hurry home to look after her severely retarded ten-year-old brother, Paul. Their father has left home, refusing to return unless Paul is placed in a special school. The mother resists, interpreting her son's condition "as an act of God to punish her or make her a better person." The guidance counselor to whom Dee turns for help suggests that remediation may be possible since "strides have recently been made with assisting such children by speeding up their own attempts at programming. It's a kind of neurological patterning."

The only person able to communicate readily with Paul is Petey, a five-year-old girl who lives nearby. One day after the two play together, Paul returns home alone. Search parties are assembled and sinister accusations are leveled against the boy. The belief that he has harmed her spreads unchecked because he is unable to explain her disappearance.

Dee believes that her brother may be able to help, and tries to get him to communicate, confidently engaging him in play. He keeps crushing the structures she builds out of blocks, symbolically depicting the cave-in that trapped Petey. Paul leads his sister to the cave where he played with his young friend, but the interior landslide that trapped her also prevents her rescue. Dee's boyfriend remembers an incident that occurred when he was hunting last year, which, upon reflection, suggests the possibility of another access. He and Dee retrace his steps and uncover the entrance to an adjacent cave and the little girl is ultimately freed. Galvanized into motion by the harrowing experience, Paul's parents decide to arrange for a special teacher for their son.

Analysis. The Deep Search presents simplistic explanations and convenient resolutions for a highly complex problem. The counselor specifically denies being knowledgeable about mental retardation yet, sight unseen, unhesitatingly diagnoses Paul's problem and prescribes a course of action. His disclaimer of competence is unwittingly and unintentionally proven correct. Paul is described as functioning on a low intellectual level, yet the scene with the blocks has him interpreting symbolically what he is unable to express concretely—a perfect reversal of the usual sequence of cognitive functioning. The mother is presented as a neurotic, misguided woman. Her initial assumption that her son is a symbol of punishment or a means of salvation is never adequately discredited, even though she belatedly does consider addressing his educational needs. No criticism is made (except a brief comment by Dee) of the concept of a handicap being God's punishment or for the inanity of teaching a child two languages when he is having difficulty with one. The major roles that Paul plays are those of spoiler and innocent victim. The destructive effects of overemotionalism in individual characters and in the community toward mental retardation are effectively portrayed.

Lasker, Joe. *He's My Brother.* Illus. by author. Chicago: Whitman, 1974. 40 pp. Reading Level: YC
Disability: Neurological Impairment

A young boy lovingly chronicles the plentiful problems in the life of his brother, Jamie, who is learning disabled. Jamie's difficulties occur in school and on the playground. They arise from rejection by his peers and from his academic failures. This is balanced by support provided by his sensitive parents who value him for what he *can* do as well as what he is.

Analysis. He's My Brother projects an honest picture of this impairment, and, within the framework of quasi-fiction, is well written. The author urges recognition of the differences between learning disabilities and mental retardation. However, some of the behaviors depicted—poor coordination and perseveration—and some concomitant consequences—frustration and social rejection—could be part of the life of a child from either group. The image of sibling affection, the exploration of frustration, and the accuracy of information presented make this book an excellent interpreter of learning disabilities for the very young reader. The illustrations support the text and make it easy to identify with Jamie and his brother.

Lawrence, Mildred. *The Shining Moment.* New York: Harcourt, Brace, 1960. 187 pp. Reading Level: YA
Disability: Cosmetic Impairment

Since the height of her ambition is to be a beauty queen, the facial scarring she suffers as the result of an automobile accident is devastating to Janey. Ashamed to meet her friends, she retreats to her grandmother's home in a small town where she is almost unknown. Janey takes a job on the local newspaper, becomes involved in several town projects, and changes from a flighty, shallow, self-centered individual to a more serious, community-spirited person. By the time her injuries have healed and her scar has faded, she realizes that beauty is more than skin deep.

Analysis. In view of the fact that the heroine's scar fades and all but disappears within a year, her response—leaving home, covering her face with a scarf, sitting with her scar averted, and favoring lowered lights—seems almost hysterically excessive. The temporary nature of her disfigurement seems to contradict the message that appearances are not terribly important since when she emerges as a wonderful new person, she is once again a beauty. This shallow story is a conventional romance which stresses the redemptive value of misfortune.

Lawrence, Mildred. *The Touchmark.* Illus. by Dianne Hollinger. New York: Harcourt Brace Jovanovich, 1975. 186 pp. Reading Level: MC/YA
Disability: Orthopedic Impairment

Abigail (Nabby), newly orphaned, lives in pre-Revolutionary Boston and longs to be apprenticed to a pewtermaker. She is engaged by Master Butler, a master pewtermaker, but only as a servant and companion for his crippled daughter, Emily. Nabby is astounded at Emily's drawing skill and obtains paper for her. Through wit, agility, and brazenness, she manages to assemble a crude mobile chair for Emily, obtain scarce tin, and transport messages and even bullets for the patriots. Her general heroics include modest spying activities as well as creating a diversion so Paul Revere could make an undetected harbor crossing.

Master Butler semigrudgingly allows both his daughter and Nabby to assist him in his workshop.

Analysis. The Touchmark is responsive to the call for feminist hero- ines. However meritorious this objective, the characterization seems a posture rather than a valid representation. The cause of Emily's immo- bility is not stated; presumably it was poliomyelitis that left her legs "useless" and "dangling" and killed her twin brother. The young girl's disability is central to the story, since the wheeled-chair is used as a device to deliver contraband. Although unconvincing in some of its assumptions—a very demanding father allows Emily to work in pewter after seeing only one example of her work—it nevertheless provides a historically flavored novel about a disabled girl who learns to fight against overprotection and self-pity. The illustrations nicely simulate drawings similar to those Emily makes and are a valuable addition to a modest book.

Lee, Mildred. *The Skating Rink.* New York: Seabury, 1969. 126 pp.
Reading Level: YA/MA
Disability: Speech Impairment; also orthopedic impairment

Tuck Faraday is a loner, vulnerable, an outsider in his own family. He refuses to talk in school and is the object of derision because of his speech impairment and poor social skills. His stutter, apparently trig- gered by the trauma of his mother's drowning, causes him to withdraw from peer contacts and he seriously considers dropping out of school. His life as a drudge on a marginal farm in rural Georgia offers no pros- pect of pleasure or reward. Tuck hangs around an ice-skating rink that is under construction. Pete Degley, the owner, who is no longer able to perform, offers to teach Tuck how to skate, hoping he will be good enough to perform as a skating partner with Mrs. Degley. Tuck prac- tices in secret and his unflagging effort pays off. His debut is a success, and Tuck is thrilled at his own achievement and delights in his im- proved status in the little community. The fifteen-year-old is astonished to receive $100, a concrete token of his ability, which he generously gives to his father for the family's welfare. The bleakness and wretched- ness of Tuck's life to this point recede before his achievements in the most glamorous arena in town.

Analysis. When Tuck is in situations of stress, particularly in scenes with the father, his problem is exacerbated. When he works with Pete and Lily Degley, who are sensitive and supportive, his speech is clearer and more comprehensible. His growing confidence and decreasing con- cern with self, coupled with the smooth physical motions of his skating, all could work to decrease the body tension associated with this dis- ability. Lee sensitively illumines Tuck and the process of his growth as he improves his self-image and his speech. This recently achieved control of his body parallels his increasing mastery of his speech, symbolizing his coming of age. The story is strong and unique with a memorable and sympathetic hero.

Lee, Robert C. *It's a Mile from Here to Glory.* Boston: Little, Brown, 1972. 150 pp. Reading Level: MC/YA
Disability: Orthopedic Impairment, Cosmetic Impairment

Sixteen-year-old Early is painfully self-conscious about his short stature, but compensates for it by his athletic ability as well as his sheer physical pleasure in running. When Jimmy, a boy who retains some facial paralysis after an undefined illness, teases him, they fight. Oddly enough, the dean suggests track exercise for punishment and when the coach sees Early's skill, he quickly invites him to join the track team. After a false start and another fight with Jimmy, Early begins to win in competitions. In a motorcycle accident, Early is badly hurt and despairs of ever walking again. A hardheaded physical therapist persistently and effectively deals with both his severe physical damage and his depressed mental state. A crisis occurs on their dairy farm when the hired hand fails to show up. Jimmy asks for the job, claiming he cannot get a job because of his face. Desperate for help, the boy hires Jimmy who is exceedingly grateful. At story's end, Early has qualified for the state meet and Jimmy has learned those social skills required for acceptance and has gained greatly in self-confidence.

Analysis. Extravagant use of coincidence characterizes the simple plot line, but no more so than is commonly found in such sports stories. Readers can learn about the painful process of rehabilitation for damaged leg muscles and for an equally impaired will. The psychological freedom to accept others after being accepted oneself is neatly developed in both young major characters. The unpleasant but frequently found use of a pecking order among those who are rejected is briefly, but effectively, vignetted. Jimmy's unpleasant behavior is seen not as a consequence of his facial disfigurement, as he asserts, but from his social deficiencies.

Lee, Virginia. *The Magic Moth.* Illus. by Richard Cuffari. New York: Seabury, 1972. 64 pp. Reading Level: MC
Disability: General Health Problems

Maryanne is dying of a heart defect. Earlier surgery has been ineffective and she is confined to bed, too weak even to eat a full meal by herself. After her father explains to the family that Maryanne will leave them soon, the children, particularly five-year-old Mark-O, work through the meaning of Maryanne's life and what her impending death implies. The parents try to interpret their daughter's death in terms of the eternal cycle of life and their belief in an afterlife. When the children are bidden to say their farewells, they see a moth released from its cocoon just as their sister dies. Attempting to cope with his grief, Mark-O plants a seedling, which he will nurture and think of as his Maryanne Tree.

Analysis. The Magic Moth chronicles a loving family's efforts to come to terms with their distress over the loss of a child. The story is compelling and tragic without being maudlin. The dialogue is authentic and the writing extremely sensitive. Handsome line drawings effectively convey the family's sorrow and perfectly complement the text. The story provides some symptomatic signs of serious cardiac dysfunction, but the dying process and its aftermath, not the impairment itself, are stressed. Except for the unfortunate choice of an insect to represent the dead child's spirit, the story avoids sentimentality.

L'Engle, Madeleine. *Camilla Dickinson.* Also published as *Camilla.* New York: Crowell, 1965. 282 pp. Reading Level: MA
Disability: Orthopedic Impairment

Camilla is upset about her parents' tumultuous marriage and unburdens herself to her friend, Luisa, who exchanges confidences about her own battling parents. Camilla seeks both relief from the tension at home and an outlet for her own adolescent cravings for affection as she becomes close to Luisa's brother, Frank. They have many intellectual interests in common and the two have lofty discussions about God, life, and death. After Frank affirms how precious life is, they go to see his friend, David, a legless, badly wounded war veteran whose life is lonely and painful. Camilla is not put off by his plight and often comes to see him by herself. The invalided young man is ambivalent about his visitor, since he is attracted to her yet aware of the futility of pursuing a deeper relationship. On one occasion, he throws off restraint, kisses her passionately, then, embarrassed, terminates the encounter. They remain friends, although she regrets she was not first kissed by Frank with whom she is now infatuated. Her parents become reconciled and plan to send her off to a boarding school, and Frank leaves with his father for the Midwest. She feels desperate and abandoned but knows she will survive.

Analysis. Although the veteran has a minor role quantitatively, it is a double-barreled one: David is a flesh-and-blood person whose agonizing needs for contact the reader is forced to share; he also represents the indomitableness of life. He is a survivor against the odds and, although in chronic physical and emotional pain and bitter and cynical, he struggles to believe in life. David assumes the role of sage traditionally assigned to the disabled. He "liberates" Camilla's thoughts about life and is a catalyst precipitating her self-insight. The writing, though highly literate, is somewhat ponderous, but those scenes involving David are vivid, sensual, and unforgettable.

L'Engle, Madeleine. *The Young Unicorns.* New York: Farrar, Straus & Giroux, 1968. 245 pp. Reading Level: YA
Disability: Visual Impairment

Emily is blinded by a laser beam when she inadvertently intrudes upon a thief seeking the formula for effectively harnessing this powerful energy source. Her father, a renowned social scientist, leaves her in the care of the Austin family when his work takes him to Europe. Dr. Austin has resumed the research in the laboratory where the attack took place, recently becoming excessively absorbed in his work and increasingly withdrawn from his family. Emily, a gifted pianist, is tutored in her school work by Dave, a hostile and suspicious former member of an adolescent gang, who has an abrasive but affectionate relationship with the girl. The men responsible for the injury to Emily have been plotting to seize political power by using the laser as a means of mind control. Thus far they have been foiled in their scheme by Dr. Austin's rigorous guarding of the formulas that regulate the power of the laser gun. The plotters plan to kidnap his children, thereby forcing his compliance with their plans. Dave is deceived into turning Rob, the youngest Austin, over to them. Emily knows something is amiss and insists that one of the Austin girls take her to the cathedral, which she suspects holds the answer. She is discovered, but her companion escapes and lights the candles in the chapel as a signal of distress. Just as the villains are about to turn the laser on Rob, Dave disconnects the light cord, grabs Rob as the room is plunged into darkness, finds Emily, and the three enter the tunnel that promises escape. In the darkness, the plotters are helpless, but Emily is able to retrace her steps through the labyrinth, finally guided to safety by the sounds coming from the cathedral organ. The police arrive and capture the kidnappers, who are led by the actor brother of the dead bishop. He had assumed the churchman's disguise as an ideal cover for his wicked schemes.

Analysis. Against the backdrop of a vast New York City cathedral, the author sets up a battlefield on which conflict between critical ethical issues is joined. She insists that there are moral imperatives that force individuals to choose freedom or suffer repression, opt for discipline over self-indulgence, seek out reality and not be deceived by illusion, and continually renew their trust despite suspicion, deceit, and even betrayal. Emily, her talented, resourceful, and indomitable protagonist, is the embodiment of these values. Although admirable, her virtues are not exaggerated, and by contrast she is also stubborn and impatient. The girl's blindness is used as a literary device to initiate and resolve the key events in the plot. Her friends react reasonably to her blindness, providing the assistance she needs, but neither give pity nor make allowances. Her piano teacher refuses to let her give a concert: "You are too young for a concert. You would be not only a child prodigy, you would be a blind child prodigy, and people would say, 'Isn't she marvelous, poor little thing?' and nobody would have heard you play at all." Although the moral messages are strong, they are delivered more as arguments for consideration and reflection than as sermons to be accepted on authority, and as such are an acceptable addition to the tense, action-packed adventure. Puns and word play, so rare in juvenile fiction, provide relief from the sober, ethical questions and the compelling tension of the plot. But the mental discipline inherent in this particular type of humor reinforces L'Engle's obvious support for rational, intelligent approaches to life's activities.

Lenski, Lois. *Corn Farm Boy*. Illus. by author. Philadelphia: Lippincott, 1954. 179 pp. Reading Level: MC
Disability: General Health Problems

Dick lives on a farm in Iowa owned by his uncle but which his father runs. The boy tries to be active in farm life but his rheumatism and general weakness interfere. The family is excited by the purchase of a new tractor and the introduction of contour plowing. They allow Dick to drive the vehicle even though he once fell off, but his legs soon become numb and he begins to get dizzy. He catches the flu and, with swollen joints and achy limbs, is very uncomfortable. The physician, alarmed about Dick's heart, advises no school, bed rest, and then crutches. The boy despairs of ever becoming a farmer, and decides to capitalize on his interests and abilities with animals and become a veterinarian.

Analysis. This lethargic, low-key story features a family with warm, caring feelings toward their son. He is not idealized but is presented as a very average boy who adjusts reasonably to his difficulties. Dick's health problem is originally identified as rheumatism, but is later referred to as rheumatic fever—a carelessness in labeling that could be confusing to young readers. The symptomatology would indicate that the described restrictions on Dick's behavior were appropriate, but the proposed vocational choice of veterinary work seems incompatible with the child's limitation. The impact of impairment on functioning in a physically demanding environment is clearly delineated, although psychological ramifications are glossed over.

> Lenski, Lois. *We Live in the South.* Illus. by the author. Philadelphia: Lippincott, 1952. 128 pp. Reading Level: YC
> *Disability:* General Health Problems

Seven-year-old Evelina is a poor, quiet, shy black girl with an enlarged heart. She frequently complains of chest pains and likes to stay near her mother, retreating to her bed when loud noises upset her. Numerous consultations with doctors prove useless and a $1.98 "heart tonic" is equally ineffective. Evelina is afraid and her mother refuses to send her North with her grandmother to a "good doctor." Neither the girl nor her mother discusses her problem with her siblings or neighbors, which results in both hurt feelings and no accommodation to her physical needs (for example, the playmates will not slow down the jump rope for her and she collapses). Evelina goes to the hospital but returns.

Analysis. The tale, a typical Lenski slice-of-life nonstory, is a segment of a four-part collection of stories of various children in the poverty-stricken rural South. The dialect, tone, and illustrations attempt to add a feeling of realism and compassion. The fraudulent prescription and the fruitless visits to doctors' offices until money runs out are instructive incidents, but the implications might be bypassed by a young reading audience. Most useful is the presentation of insensitivity by her companions to Evelina's hidden handicap and the mixed presentation of the heroine.

> Levin, Betty. *A Griffon's Nest.* New York: Macmillan, 1975. 346 pp. Reading Level: MA
> *Disability:* Speech Impairment; also general health problems

Two children, through the agency of a magical sword hilt, travel back through time to the seventh century where they encounter Nessa, a mute Pictish girl. She leads them through a series of harrowing adventures, finally returning them safely to the present, whereupon she transforms herself back into a seal.

Analysis. This conclusion coincides with the author's prologue in which the passing of the Pictish culture is mourned. Nessa, representing that culture in her inability to communicate, also leaves no message and vanishes into the sea without a trace. Nessa should therefore be considered solely in symbolic terms rather than assessed as a palpable human character.

> Levine, Edna S. *Lisa and Her Soundless World.* Illus. by Gloria Kamen. New York: Human Sciences, 1974. 40 pp. Reading Level: YC
> *Disability:* Auditory Impairment

Lisa is a young girl whose undiagnosed deafness causes many problems. When her true difficulty is determined by a physician, a plan to assist her is mapped out and the implication is made that, by specialized training, Lisa will progress both academically and socially.

Analysis. The illustrations and text are both well done and provide good background on the hearing and speaking processes. The simple story line promotes empathy and understanding without being maudlin. A minor quibble is that finger spelling is suggested as an alternative if a child is not a good speech reader, whereas now most authorities support total communication approaches. Nevertheless, this quasi-fiction book has great utility as an introduction to the importance of hearing. The story line is a palatable vehicle for reaching young readers with this information.

Little, Jean. *From Anna.* Illus. by Joan Sandin. New York: Harper, 1972. 201 pp. Reading Level: MC
Disability: Visual Impairment

The Solden family, disturbed by events in Nazi Germany, move to Canada where the five children enroll in school. Anna, the youngest, does not do well in social or motor activities and so acquires the unwelcome nickname "awkward Anna." She believes she is unattractive and rejected by her mother. The children had not previously visited a physician, but are now required to do so. The doctor discovers Anna's vision problem, and she is sent to a special class for children with reduced visual efficiency. She is assigned to a gem of a teacher who selects a curriculum that lures Anna into gratifying encounters with reading. Through a climate of acceptance and approval established by the teacher, the children readily accept their new classmate. Although her self-image is low and she has had few experiences in social interaction, Anna makes friends. The Christmas present she creates for her family demonstrates her improving visual and tactile skills and signals her new status as a child of creditable accomplishments.

Analysis. One of the best of Little's books, *From Anna* ties in some large social themes with a very insightful examination of the physical, social, and emotional behavior that may emerge as a consequence of impaired vision. The author is right on target with her many descriptions of the family's actions and reactions to Anna's problem. The importance of freedom to speak is bracketed loosely with the ability to read—both essential to being a whole person. A brief but accurate description of a classroom typical of that time period is evoked by the charming illustrations. Although there are several teasing episodes, the book is essentially a gentle, positive one. The change in Anna's status from victim to achiever results from remediation of her problem. This novel asserts that providing comprehensive assistance to children with difficulties has implications far beyond the classroom. (See Figure 4.)

Little, Jean. *Mine for Keeps.* Boston: Little, Brown, 1962. 186 pp.
Reading Level: MC
Disability: Neurological Impairment, General Health Problems

Having only attended special schools, Sal is unnerved at the prospect of attending a regular one. Although she has adjusted well to the adaptations cerebral palsy has necessitated, her parents feel she must learn to function in a less sheltered environment. Her new friend, Elsje, is a Dutch immigrant whose brother, Piet, has not been able to attend school since a debilitating bout with rheumatic fever. Sal's family brings her a dog and she asks Elsje's help in training the animal. Piet is contemptuous, saying a "kreupel" could not possibly instruct a dog properly. Elsje, concerned with her brother's unhappiness resulting from the isolation and physical restrictions necessitated by his illness, organizes an informal dog training school, hoping to help Sal and prove to her brother that people with impairments can be successful. The dogs improve under Elsje's tutelege, but instruction stops after she becomes ill. When the children visit her with their dogs, the teacher asks if any of the pets can do tricks. Sal says that only Piet's dog is able to perform, and the reluctant boy is pressured into demonstrating his animal's proficiency. The children's obvious admiration breaks through his protective reserve and he now is able to accept their friendly overtures.

Analysis. The physical and psychological adaptations necessary when leaving a protected environment for an unadapted one are capably explored in this novel. Realistic attitudes and honest concerns of the exceptional child, as well as the implications and rationale for family decisions, are expressed. Little brings immediacy and honesty to Sal's adjustment in a regular class:

> She had to get her crutches stowed out of the way, and then undo the kneelocks on her braces and get turned around so that her feet were under the desk instead of sticking out blocking the aisle. The lock on her left brace jammed. Sally tugged at it angrily. Her fingers, stiff with tension and damp with perspiration, slipped on the smooth steel. She wiped her palm on her skirt, gave one more tug, and the lock clicked open. Her knees bent. She swung her feet under her desk and sighed thankfully.
>
> Never had she noticed how much room she took up or how much noise she made, doing this simple thing. Never before had it seemed to take such a long time to get it done. But then, this was the first time she had ever done it in a schoolroom where others weren't doing it too.

Piet's inability to speak English and frustrations arising from his weakened condition are effectively conveyed. Characterization and dialogue are excellent, and despite a clumsily contrived ending, the book holds interest, provides accurate information, and features an admirable, substantial heroine.

Little Jean. *Spring Begins in March*. Illus. by Lewis Parker. Boston: Little, Brown, 1966. 156 pp. Reading Level: MC
Disability: Neurological Impairment

This sequel to *Mine for Keeps* has Sal recede in importance to be replaced by her younger sister. Brief vignettes of Sal's accommodation to her disability convey positive, low-key impressions of a child reacting matter-of-factly to problems created by cerebral palsy.

Little, Jean. *Take Wing*. Illus. by Jerry Lazare. Boston: Little, Brown, 1968. 176 pp. Reading Level: MC/YA
Disability: Intellectual Impairment

Laurel realizes that her brother, James, is different, but her efforts to communicate her concerns are ignored by their parents. Laurel overprotects her seven-year-old brother, dressing him, changing his wet bedsheet, and taking him to and from school. The need to care constantly for James causes problems for Laurel, particularly since she has little time and thus little opportunity to develop her own social skills. Fortunately, an aunt comes to stay in the house when Laurel's mother is hospitalized, and responsibility for James' care is removed from the young girl's shoulders. When Laurel tries to tell a new friend about mental retardation, she is rebuffed. The girl misinterprets the discussion, thinking it is related to her own sister who is severely retarded. Ultimately, the aunt's assertions that her nephew needs special help are confirmed by the report from the psychologist, which recommends that James attend a special classroom "with other boys and girls with intellectual handicaps, taught by a teacher specially trained to help such children learn." Unfortunately, their neighborhood school, like many others, is insensitive to this boy's plight. "Laurel had known for a long time that school was bad for James. He was growing more and more certain that he was no good. More and more often he came home listless and dull or angry at everyone. . . . 'There's one problem,' Dad said bitterly . . . 'we have Special Education all right . . . but they don't take any child into the special classes until he is nine years old.' 'But James is only seven' . . . Laurel breathed . . . 'that would mean he'd have to fail twice more before he got help. That can't be right.' "

Analysis. Take Wing is crammed full of information about retardation. Both family problems relating to denial and community problems of unresponsiveness are seen as destructive to James' growth. The difficulty of discussing retardation of a sibling is sensitively examined, and

Laurel's ambivalent relationship toward James, protective and loving but also resentful, is honestly presented. Through a mutual sharing of their "secrets," which can now be discussed openly, the girls realize that their situations are not unique. One of the strongest elements of the book is the description of the boy's learning problems, and these are accurately and explicitly portrayed.

Lofts, Norah. *Rupert Hatton's Story.* Illus. by Anne and Janet Grahame Johnstone. Nashville: Nelson, 1972. 136 pp. Reading Level: MC

Disability: Orthopedic Impairment

Rupert Hatton is the son of English boarding school owners. Uncle Flowerdew, an aging schoolmaster whose arm was left stiff and weak from an old wound, has a violin he keeps in his room but which he can no longer play. From the first time he holds it, Rupert becomes obsessed with the instrument. His father unreasonably forbids any contact with it, but Rupert secretly develops proficiency in its use. When Danielli, the great violinist, gives a concert in their little town, Rupert steals into the hall to listen. Afterward he rushes home, returns with his own violin, and plays for the virtuoso. Danielli acknowledges the boy's gifts, but cynically advises another profession less subject to heartbreak. When Rupert attempts to return unnoticed to his own home, he finds his parents and Uncle Flowerdew waiting. His father angrily commands Rupert to destroy the violin. Refusing, Rupert falls protectively over it. His father, in an uncontrollable rage, strikes out with his cane, breaking Rupert's collarbone, killing Uncle Flowerdew, and smashing the instrument. The next morning Rupert leaves home with "one arm, two shillings, and a smashed violin." He travels toward London, faints from delayed shock, is rescued by some peddlers, and has his bones amateurishly set. When sufficiently recovered, he doggedly tracks Danielli down and plays for him again. The pain is unbearable; Danielli realizes something is drastically wrong, examines Rupert's shoulder, and realizes it was badly set. The boy's bones are broken and reset, his reconstructed violin is returned to him, and he is launched into a successful musical career.

Analysis. The apparent lesson of this tale is that art is a cruel taskmaster, demanding single-mindedness of purpose and sublimation of all other needs. Rupert must pay for his gifts through his own pain and the pain he causes others through his callousness. Uncle Flowerdew is the kindest, most compassionate person of the boy's youth. The old man's disability is seen as evidence of his fragility, but seems to serve little other purpose. Lofts' style is crisp and she manages to convey some feeling of life in eighteenth-century England. Her message, however, seems odd and presumptuous for the age group most apt to read this book.

Lowe, Patricia Tracy. *The Different Ones*. Indianapolis: Bobbs-Merrill, 1965. 153 pp. Reading Level: MC
Disability: General Health Problems

After Mark's parents have been killed in a plane crash, he is taken to live with the Wilsons, former friends of his father. Their own son, Chris, who has had rheumatic fever, is overprotected by his mother and a disappointment to his sports-loving father. His mother has contaminated the boy with her fears and he is too immobilized by them to take part in any reasonably appropriate activities. His father's senseless insistence on more assertive physical activities is equally inhibiting. Chris is the butt of neighborhood teasing, led by Buff, a local bully. Buff is shown to be struggling with problems of his own, and this revelation opens the way to friendship between him and his former victim. Mark, the orphan, and Chris, the physically handicapped child, realize that Buff too "is different than other kids." Their "differences" are seen to make them special, but Mark observes that everyone is, in a sense, different.

Analysis. This simplistic book makes much of a tired truism: Each person should be treated as an individual with respect for his or her unique qualities. The characterizations are flat and the outcome of the plot can be predicted from the first chapter.

Lowery, Bruce. *Scarred*. New York: Vanguard, 1961. 160 pp. Reading Level: YA
Disability: Cosmetic Impairment

When Jeff's family moves, he becomes an object of ridicule in his class at the new school to which he has transferred. The scar from his cleft lip is the subject of endless taunts and jibes and he is either ignored or pointedly excluded from every social and sports activity. His weak and ineffectual teacher makes occasional attempts to curb the cruel harassment, but her ineptitude generally makes things worse. Willy, an esteemed member of the class, has never participated in the abuse, and one day he deliberately and conspicuously includes Jeff in their game. Hostility diminishes slightly and Jeff is tolerated on the periphery of school events. The two boys share an interest in stamp collecting and, one day at Willy's house, while Ronald, a particularly antagonistic boy, is there, Jeff inexplicably and compulsively steals some of his only friend's treasured stamps. When Willy notices they are gone, he asks to search the visitors and, while Ronald permits it, Jeff hotly refuses, insisting such an action would be a breach of friendship.

Soon the rumor that he is a thief spreads throughout the school and the tolerance he had almost attained turns to unalloyed contempt. Confused, unhappy, and disgusted with himself, Jeff sees no way to escape the dilemma he has created. He is afraid to return the stamps since that would prove the accusations correct and ensure his permanent exclusion. He hesitates and his opportunity slips away when the stamps he had hidden in his shirt pocket are inadvertently washed and destroyed in the laundry. Frustrated and despairing, he lashes out at his family, particularly his adoring younger brother, who is confused and hurt by this rejection. Jeff hides the remaining stamps in a paper belonging to Ronald and returns them to Willy. Willy concludes that Jeff was innocent all along and attempts to resurrect their friendship. Relief is mixed with uneasiness as the guilt Jeff feels at this further deception and betrayal renders him unable to accept this reprieve. On Easter, Jeff's brother, hoping to recapture some of the closeness he enjoyed with his older sibling, begs for an explanation of his aloofness, but is rebuffed. Hurt, the child runs to his mother for comfort, but trips and falls down the basement stairs. An ambulance is called and he is rushed to the hospital, but dies the next day. Months later Jeff finds an Easter egg his brother had hidden in the secret hiding place among his stolen stamps. It carries the message: "I love you," and Jeff considers, "Maybe that was what God was, after all."

Analysis. The relentless, unwavering brutality toward Jeff seems outrageously excessive even when seen through the eyes of the victim. Every stranger Jeff encounters reacts to him solely on the basis of his scar, a mark represented so faintly on the dust jacket that it could be almost overlooked. While teasing for such a minor problem is not uncommon, to project a community conspiracy is literary overkill. Equally arbitrary is Jeff's irrational behavior in the stamp theft. But most intolerable is the conclusion that the boy's scar was the agent that set in motion events that led to his brother's death. The conclusion is as fuzzy as the narrative is overwritten. The tone of this novel is so obsessive that initial concern about the central character evaporates.

Luis, Earlene W., and Barbara F. Millar. *Listen, Lissa! (A Candy Striper Meets the Biggest Challenge).* New York: Dodd, Mead, 1968. 144 pp.
Reading Level: YA
Disability: Intellectual Impairment

Melissa's eleven-year-old brother has a friend, Artie, a boy his own age who is severely retarded. Unable to provide the care he needs at home, his parents make plans to send Artie to a training school. Melissa's Candy Striper organization visits the school and is elated to find beautiful grounds, spacious, attractive facilities, a dedicated, loving, and competent staff, as well as delicious food in the cafeteria. Although she lacks any basis for judgment, Melissa is confident that the institution will provide superlative care. Her brother, however, sees this placement as a device for abandoning his friend and makes plans to foil the plot by running away with the boy. The escapade is a catastrophe, Artie almost drowns, and the boys return home discouraged. Melissa learns about a therapeutic procedure known as patterning and hopes it may help Artie. The boy's doctor rejects her prescription but suggests the therapy might be suitable for some other local child, and directs Melissa to schedule volunteers to implement the program. Melissa's boyfriend, previously petulant about her absorption with her various good works, is inspired by her example and benevolently arranges for his swimming team to give lessons to retarded children. Artie is heard from and, unsurprisingly, is thriving in the institution. This intelligence leads his mother to the Panglossian observation that: "Things have a way of working out for the best in the long run."

Analysis. Under the guise of concern for the retarded, various insidious messages are delivered. The authors project a Hollywood version of an institution for the retarded and a society that instantly mobilizes its energies for the interests of the retarded. That this is a never-never land is abundantly clear to any adult who reads a newspaper. To a youngster, resolution of such a serious social problem seems remarkably simple, and it is in this context that a serious disservice is done. Entering an institution is not without trauma. To promote a medical rehabilitation program that is in disrepute is audacious. To suggest that a doctor would select a therapeutic program from a teenager's suggestion is almost as credible as the assertion that the food in the institutional cafeteria is delicious. More important, young readers may conclude that exile of a retarded child is a desirable, even preferred option for a family.

Luis, Earlene W., and Barbara F. Millar. *Wheels for Ginny's Chariot.* New York: Dodd, Mead, 1966. 205 pp. Reading Level: MC
Disability: Orthopedic Impairment; also auditory impairment

As the result of an injury, Ginny, bright, young, and athletic, is now fettered to a wheelchair. Cut off from her former companions by her mandatory attendance at a special school, Ginny is further alienated from those friends by her sulking and bad temper. Due to the unflagging dedication of the teachers and the limitless appeal of her fellow students, Ginny begins to realize that a rewarding life is possible despite her impairments. Suffused with missionary zeal, she tutors, reads, instructs, and inspires. Not surprisingly, she is considered for student council and is able to find peace and happiness ("In such blithe and gallant company it was impossible for Ginny to feel depressed") with her old as well as her new friends.

Analysis. Neither plot, characterization, setting, theme, nor style of this book could withstand the mildest critical scrutiny. The qualities of the disabled children and their teachers are so inflated as to make any attempts at comparisons with real-life counterparts ludicrous. This missionary effort plods along without an unpredictable turn, the setting surpasses the idyllic, and the messages, offensive in their self-congratulatory tone, match the other components in superficiality and lack of subtlety. The dialogue particularly displays gross insensitivity toward the disabled. Mrs. Moyer (the principal) is on an outing with some children. Although the school is a hodgepodge of children with various disabilities, in this instance, four children, grouped on the basis of auditory impairment, are gathered. "The little deaf and hard-of-hearing children squealed when they saw Mrs. Moyer, and she laughed at [!] their attempts to tell her about things they had seen."

This same thick-skinned woman responds modestly to a teacher's praise for influencing Ginny's new perspective in this novel's typical sodden prose:

> I'm glad we were able to help her see what a mistaken attitude it is. If only more people who take that attitude could be reached! If only these children could be accepted everywhere as they are here—as children first of all and as handicapped children secondly. Sometimes I wonder if this feeling of pity which is so overdone and so strong on the part of many people will ever change. It discourages me to think that it may not. Of course, I know that Ginny's case is a phase through which all handicapped people pass. At first they feel anger and resentment, then self-pity, then pity for the other handicapped, and finally, if they're lucky, acceptance. They may become temporarily or even permanently stopped at any phase, but the only one through which they may gain happiness is acceptance. Which is true of all of us, handicapped or not.

Lyons, Dorothy. *Dark Sunshine.* Illus. by Wesley Dennis. New York: Harcourt, Brace, 1951. 244 pp. Reading Level: YA
Disability: Orthopedic Impairment

Polio has left Blythe listless and self-absorbed. As she begins to participate in family and outdoor life on the Arizona ranch where the family has moved, she loses her self-pity and takes herself less seriously. Horseback riding and other physical exercise also have a salutary effect. A wild mare named Dark Sunshine is captured and Blythe's slow movements in taming the animal appear to have a calming effect. When school resumes, she hears about a scholarship, which would add considerably to her family's low financial situation. Blythe knows that she could compete on the basis of school activities, leadership, and scholarship, but the athletic requirement of "a sound mind in a sound body" will automatically exclude her, and the voice lessons she craves become an unreachable dream. Determined to earn the scholarship, she enters an endurance contest but is disqualified when she goes for emergency medical attention for another competitor. Her Good Samaritan efforts are considered and she wins the scholarship in spite of the breach of regulations. She is able to discard her crutch and gain the attention of an agreeable young man who congratulates her on her accomplishment: "You're wonderful—but I've known it all along, now will you go to the dance with me? You can lean on me for a crutch." "Oh, will I, Jerry! I've just discovered I don't really need one—but you'll have to remember to twirl me on my left leg."

Analysis. This dialogue typifies the lightweight manner in which the disability is treated. Good family models are provided and the adaptations Blythe requires are reasonably portrayed. Not a profound story and burdened with artificial dialogue and a too-good-to-be-true heroine, it is nonetheless fast paced, and likely to appeal to Western fans.

MacIntyre, Elisabeth. *The Purple Mouse.* Nashville: Nelson, 1975. 108 pp. Reading Level: MC
Disability: Auditory Impairment

Hatty is surrounded by a family of assertive achievers, but deafness has made her shy and hesitant. She can hear amplified sounds, loud noises, and, unless there is interference, can follow conversation by lip-reading and extrapolating content. In an accident, the white mice her brother is using for an experimental get loose and, in the confusion of recapturing them before her cat does, Hatty drops one in a beaker of indelible dye. Spotting a birdcage in a gift shop, she considers it the perfect place for a lonely mouse who has initially been isolated, then attacked by the others, presumably on the basis of its vibrant, newly purple fur. She impulsively agrees to work there to pay for the expensive object. When she tells her brother about the accident, he is elated at the effectiveness of the dye, improbably exclaiming, "The greatest," which Hatty misinterprets as "the waste." Justifiably concerned that her impaired hearing will embarrass her at the gift shop, she persists, inspired by the mouse. At first, she does well as a salesgirl, but when the store becomes busy, her impairment creates confusion. Hatty tries to cheer up her mother, who is facing dismissal from her job. She advises her parent to model her behavior after that of the tenacious rodent, and inspired by the intrepid creature, the woman ingeniously manages to get a better job. Following a lead for marketing her brother's dyes, Hatty temporarily gets lost, but she overcomes her panic, confident that the future will be as bright as her pet mouse's coat.

Analysis. Although there is an attempt at brittle cleverness to match the artificiality of Hatty's mother's editorial work on a recherché magazine, the characters are dimensionless, the dialogue trite, and the conclusion corny and incomplete. The presentation of the mouse—"He's a marvelous personality too. And so sensible! He doesn't know what it is to be frightened or discouraged"—as savior and inspiration for the family is an unmitigated disaster. The book's only value lies in illuminating how partially received communications create problems in many aspects of a hearing-impaired person's life.

Magee, Catherine Fowler. *One of the Family.* New York: McKay, 1964. 210 pp. Reading Level: YA
Disability: Intellectual Impairment

On the night of her high school graduation, Sally Rockwell's brother is born. He is a baby with Down's syndrome. The doctor and family minister convince the father that it would be best for everyone if the baby were placed in a nursing home until room can be found for him in an institution. Sally spends that summer at a camp and is surprised to find a camp for exceptional children located directly across the lake. She is amazed at the high level of functioning of the young campers she is able to observe, some of whom have the same genetic disorder as her infant brother. When Mrs. Rockwell returns home from the hospital, she is persuaded it would be better never to see her new son. Reluctantly she accepts the decision forced on her, but sinks into a deep depression. At college, Sally fulfills her sorority's community service obligation through volunteer work at a school for retarded children. Meanwhile her parents have changed their minds and retrieved their son from the nursing home despite dire warnings of ruined lives. Sally is threatened with expulsion from her sorority because of the shame of having a retarded child in the family. She only becomes more militant in her championing of retardation, speaks up at a public hearing on providing schooling for seriously retarded children, and starts an organization called "Siblings of the Mentally Retarded." The housemother, ashamed of this association, asks for Sally's pledge pin back, but is overruled by the sorority sisters who support Sally.

Analysis. Superficial and silly, *One of the Family* is a message thinly papered over with a story line. This is unfortunate since some aspects, such as the common conspiracy to push for instant institutionalization of the disabled newborn, require sensitive elaboration. Negative attitudes toward retarded children, though endemic in society, are presented in such extreme form that they seem more absurd than deleterious. This is echoed in the treatment of the presentation of the retarded children, who scarcely appear in the story except as adorable creatures. These children unfortunately become depersonalized as objects or causes in a hard sell for compassion.

Mathis, Sharon Bell. *Listen for the Fig Tree.* New York: Viking, 1974. 175 pp. Reading Level: YA
Disability: Visual Impairment; also emotional dysfunction, speech impairment

In the year since Marvin Johnson was killed, his widow has alternated between long periods of despair punctuated by brief intervals of pretended delusion when she talks as though he were still alive. Drink offers no escape from loneliness as self-pity overwhelms her. Muffin, her blind sixteen-year-old daughter, is torn between love for her mother and resentment at being forced to assume all responsibilities for the two of them. Mr. Dale, a neighbor, has been a surrogate father and has instilled in Muffin both personal and racial pride. He insists that she always dress attractively and walk with assurance. Her crowning achievement will be the beautiful dress she is making for her first Kwanza, an African festival. Ernie, her boyfriend, feels she is too absorbed with trivial concerns about how she will look and that she neglects the human essence of the celebration. Its true meaning, he feels, is to be found in the love and interdependence of people, in Muffin's case, particularly in her relationship with her mother. Muffin finishes her dress and leaves for Mr. Dale's apartment to get his approval, but she is attacked and almost raped on the way. Another neighbor, a mute, elderly man, fights off the assailant but is badly beaten in the process. Mr. Dale arrives, comforts her, takes her to the hospital, and then home. He makes her a new dress and also presents her with a silver cane with "strut" embossed on it in braille. Muffin goes to the Kwanza with Ernie, and the warmth and support she feels there make the true significance of the festival clear. When Muffin returns home to find her mother has been drinking again, she puts the bottle away, saying it will no longer be necessary. She will accompany her mother to the clinic until the woman is well.

Analysis. Black origins, consciousness, pride, identity, religion, and family are the foundations of Muffin's future, but first she must reconcile seemingly contradictory elements in her present life. At first, Muffin's mother seems contemptible, more obsessed with her own loss than responsive to her daughter's needs. But, viewed differently, she is a person whose life has been shattered and who must rely on her daughter for support. The mute neighbor, at first, seems suspicious and incomprehensible. His silence was considered strange, but although cast as an outsider, he demonstrates his bravery and sense of responsibility through his courageous defense of Muffin. Mr. Dale emphasizes the importance of her appearance: Her exterior should reflect a self-assurance and pride she must feel. The message on her cane is virtually a command. Ernie will not let her settle for appearances alone, and as she focuses her thoughts of the festival on the dress she is making, he insists she "see" beyond it to the meaning not only of the celebration but of her life. Muffin is portrayed as overcoming the limitations of circumstance and drawing on her own strength, the concern of friends, and the survival skills of her heritage. Mathis has used her impressive literary skills to portray an admirable, indomitable heroine.

Micklish, Rita. *Sugar Bee.* Illus. by Ted Lewin. New York: Delacorte, 1972. 195 pp. Reading Level: MC
Disability: Visual Impairment

A shy, sensitive, black girl lives with her parents in a ghetto. Stephanie (Sugar Bee) tries to counteract the baseness of her surroundings through poetry. As a reward for her writing talent, she spends a week on a farm in Pennsylvania and meets Rosemary, a blind girl. Sugar Bee is first shocked and then repelled by Rosemary's blindness, but the two girls painfully and tentatively air their individual feelings of being different. Rosemary becomes fond of a sickly and ugly lamb she calls Beautiful but which ultimately dies. The girls undergo an unpleasant name-calling experience, and Rosemary finds herself as unable to repeat the racist epithet as Sugar Bee is to pronounce the word "blind." When Sugar Bee's week is up, Rosemary gives her a sprig of rosemary and an artificial egg containing a lamb. Sugar Bee ponders the experience on her way home, reflecting that if Rosemary could find love and beauty in her restricted world, so could she.

Analysis. Micklish carefully chronicles the meeting between two children, each a victim of social exclusion. She proposes the blind girl can be a model for the black girl. Rosemary not only teaches her friend about habilitation but, more importantly, how to deal with educational problems, socially imposed limitations, and consequent psychological trauma. In the unfolding relationship, Sugar Bee is able to look with greater clarity at her own biases. This insightful experience gives her the strength to perceive her own life from a new and optimistic perspective. Rosemary is presented as a credible character struggling against loneliness and rejection with much determination. The story excessively simplifies the ramifications of prejudice and social exclusion, but on an elementary level shows how self-regard and internal strength can diminish their destructive impact.

Montgomery, Elizabeth Rider. *Tide Treasure Camper*. Illus. by Isabel Dawson. New York: Ives-Washburn, 1963. 122 pp. Reading Level: MC

Disability: Visual Impairment

An accident at five years of age virtually erased Betsy's vision. However, after a corneal transplant she was able to see with the help of heavy lenses. Her condition was so fragile and uncertain that it precluded parties, picnics, traveling, camping, and even schooling. Her mother had agreed to allow her to go to Tide Treasure Camp and had promised not to tell about her bleak past. Betsy's lack of knowledge creates many problems. Some thought she was a snob, others considered her insensitive, overprotective, or, worse, a nonconformist. Her cabin mate has even started a Hate Betsy Club, and the counselors also become angry at her when she takes out a boat without permission. However, defections in the club occur when she does not snitch about the harassment and when her ineptitude is revealed in an overnight cookout. Although she has ingeniously tried to conceal her medical past and the resultant inadequacies, a treasure hunt with written clues proves her undoing and she is compelled to confess that she cannot read. When the counselor divulges to the other campers that Betsy was unable to use her eyes in the past and that she was determined to succeed on her own without revealing her secret, she is cheered.

Analysis. Tide Treasure Camper implies falsely that formal education is not available to the blind child unless she goes to school. Certainly, records, radio, and home teaching are readily available to the child who cannot leave home. It is inconceivable that a mother such as Betsy's would not provide extensive passive but highly supervised activities with other children, such as doll play or listening to stories, which require little or no active movement but which would have provided the socialization skills Betsy lacked. From this utterly protective background, it is difficult to conceive of a character with the heroine's characteristics, such as tenacity and independence. That a girl with her lack of visual experience would win a painting prize is also illogical. She is not commended for her ingenious ways of coping with problems but instead is gently chided. The presentation of a visually impaired character too proud or too stubborn to ask for assistance has become a cliché and its presence here is not unexpected. Despite such literary and logical lapses, the book manages to project a doughty heroine and provides food for thought about misconceptions of the disabled and pressures for conformity.

> Mulcahy, Lucille. *Magic Fingers*. Illus. by Don Lambo. New York: Nelson, 1958. 124 pp. Reading Level: MC
> *Disability:* Visual Impairment

Natachee and her blind grandmother, Namby, still live in the pueblo. The old woman recollects better days when she made ceremonial bowls for the village and her husband had been governor of the community. To earn money, Namby and Natachee locate good clay, and make several pots of outstanding quality, which are sold at high prices. Lupe, another potter, is furious and circulates a rumor that Namby has used witchcraft in the making of pottery. Lupe is ultimately revealed as a thief and Namby is vindicated.

Analysis. Magic Fingers is a gentle little story with a positive portrayal of Indian life and customs. The old grandmother is shown somewhat larger than life—skillful, wise, of good memory, and able to compensate readily for her visual loss. At a simple level, Namby illustrates how a person whose disability has mistakenly been perceived as necessitating passivity and retirement can regain former status when the impairment is bypassed. The charge that a person who has a disability must use supernatural means to achieve is exploded despite the seeming contradiction of the title. The stereotypical illustrations show the old woman with eyes narrowed, but this may be more an interpretation of heritage than of disability.

> Musgrave, Florence. *Merrie's Miracle*. Illus. by Mary Stevens. New York: Hastings House, 1962. 157 pp. Reading Level: YA
> *Disability:* Orthopedic Impairment

The Hilliard family moves from Connecticut to Ohio during the first half of the nineteenth century. Their daughter, Merrie, has an intermittent limp. She stumbles when mountain climbing or going to the well, but fortunately never on the dance floor. Thus, although her limp offers the opportunity to demonstrate her determination despite physical hardships, it does not interfere with a glamorous image. Making a living is difficult on the new land and, despite the demands of work, Merrie finds ample opportunities for adventure. She learns of the evils of slavery when she meets a girl whose family is active in the Underground Railroad. After winning an oratory contest, she is distressed at a schoolmate's accusation that the award was given out of pity, but soon becomes convinced that the charge was only made out of jealousy. A neighbor's son seeks to marry her. Dismissing her fears that her lameness might be a barrier to their happiness, her fiancé asks: "why worry about separate pieces when the whole picture is so good?"

Analysis. This simple, simplistic adolescent romance includes the message that people should not be judged by externals, nor should they yearn for what cannot be. The story is so moralistic and contrived that lessons about both slavery and abuse of those who are handicapped seem to be mere padding. Thus, Merrie's lameness never is believable; it is sporadically mentioned and then forgotten. It seems to appear whenever dramatic tension or evidence of her determination is needed.

Naylor, Phyllis. *Jennifer Jean, the Cross-Eyed Queen.* Illus. by Harold K. Lamson. Minneapolis, Minn.: Lerner, 1967. unpaged. Reading Level: YC
Disability: Visual Impairment

By the time Jennifer Jean is four, one of her eyes has turned inward. In addition, as her visual acuity deteriorates, she squints and tilts her head. She is teased, but confounds her oppressors. She is skeptical when one friend tells her he had eye surgery to correct a similar problem. When the girl reminds her mother that everybody is different, the mother responds that when the difference causes trouble and is remediable, one should take action. Jennifer Jean first gets a patch, next glasses, later eye exercises, and then she is ready to enjoy kindergarten.

Analysis. In this book a feisty, determined little heroine is found. When the neighborhood children tease Jennifer Jean with the unpleasant chant in the title, she doughtily responds: "I'm Jennifer Jean, the Cross-Eyed Queen, and if I blink three times you'll turn into a toad." This would startle the taunters and they "would be quiet for awhile in case she meant it." The author gives some notion of the discomfort that results from the rehabilitation process and the simple pictures accurately depict Jennifer Jean's condition.

Neufeld, John. *Lisa, Bright and Dark.* New York: Phillips, 1969. 125 pp. Reading Level: YA/MA
Disability: Emotional Dysfunction

Lisa Shilling is afraid she is losing her mind. She seems to be two different people—the old Lisa, gregarious and outgoing, and the new Lisa, distrustful, moody, and uncontrollable. Lisa pleads with her parents for assistance, but neither parent responds to her pleas. Lisa's friends try to help, but the girls' understanding of mental problems is naive and faulty and their support grossly inadequate to the dimensions of the dilemma. The school counselor and teachers, though asked, also will not actively intervene to confront the problem, despite the fact that Lisa's behavior in school becomes increasingly bizarre. After she attempts suicide twice, her parents finally arrange for her to get psychiatric help.

Analysis. The novel condemns the denial and passivity of significant adults in Lisa's life and contrasts them with the commitment and involvement, although amateurish and insufficient, of her girl friends. The most significant element of the story may be that Lisa's friends do not abandon her even though her behavior is frightening and non-conforming. Neufeld writes in a compelling, dramatic manner, with characterizations that are vivid and strong. The descriptions of the behavior of an emotionally distraught person are excellent—simplified yet believable.

Neufeld, John. *Sleep Two, Three, Four!* New York: Harper & Row, 1971. 159 pp. Reading Level: YA/MA
Disability: Orthopedic Impairment, Visual Impairment

It is 1984 and all the totalitarian, repressive images that year connotes have come to pass. Squads of young toughs, under the guidance and protection of the government, vandalize the homes of citizens and terrorize the occupants. One young man, D. J., suffering pangs of conscience, decides to leave the squad and join the underground. He and some freedom-loving friends capture the squadron unit leader, who later escapes. Their lives are in danger but, before fleeing, they return to a house to rescue Freddy, a young boy with a deformed foot. Freddy's family had been able to conceal his impairment up to now, but since the law requires that the physically imperfect be removed from society, D. J. knows that the boy will soon be betrayed and is thus in jeopardy. The youths at first successfully elude the squads sent to capture them. Frannie, a black girl who had escaped from one of the ghettos where non-Caucasians are confined, joins their group and leads them to the cave where Raph, a near-blind Indian, has been hiding out for years. He lives near a prison in which Robin, a friend of Freddy's, is incarcerated. They plan a daring rescue and succeed in bringing Robin out safely, but Freddy is killed and another of the group is injured. The young people realize they must quickly move on and they leave, determined to make contact with other resistance groups. Raph remains to bury Freddy and care for the injured Gar. As they depart, "Raph felt their footfalls above his head and wished he had been able to see them, to see them really clearly, just once before it was too late."

Analysis. This futuristic morality tale proclaims that any society that demands unanimity and conformity destroys its finest people. D. J., an independent thinker; Frannie and Raph, ethnic outcasts; and Freddy and Raph, physically imperfect, are courageous, intelligent, and noble. Freddy's disability is the stigma that marks him for exile, but it also emphasizes the heroism he displays in uncomplainingly keeping pace with his companions. Although Freddy dies, his condition of disability is transferred to Gar, thus symbolically pointing out its continuity. Raph cannot see what is close to him (the present) but has a clear vision of distant things (the past and future). The action is fast and exciting, but the characters are stereotypes. The writing is free of subtleties, and the anticonformity theme overwhelms all other elements.

Neufeld, John. *Touching*. Also published as *Twink*. New York: Phillips, 1970. 119 pp. Reading Level: MA
Disability: Neurological Impairment, Visual Impairment

Harry Walsh, sixteen, returns home from school to meet his new stepsister, Twink. Twink is severely afflicted with cerebral palsy, and despite having prepared himself psychologically to be accepting, Harry is almost overcome. In order for Twink to communicate, one must anticipate what she intends to say and supply her with cues, which she then indicates are right or wrong.

Harry asks Ellie, Twink's mother, about her, and this question serves as the impetus for the unfolding of Twink's story. Her parents placed Twink in a special school when she was two. Leaving the child was traumatic for Ellie, even though the school was bright and cheery and Twink did not seem dismayed. Twink had her first visit home when she was eight. Those accomplishments that seemed so significant to her immediate family were regarded with pity or distaste by outsiders. Her first school had been run efficiently by dedicated personnel, but when it closed she was transferred to one that was disastrous. The staff was poorly trained and turnovers were frequent. Vital equipment was lost and the instructional program was virtually nonexistent. Twink regressed, but when the director of the school was confronted by her parents and berated for his poor management, he threatened to expel their daughter. With no available options, they backed down. While they desperately searched for another school, Twink's physical condition began to deteriorate alarmingly. Twink heard about some experimental surgery and her parents finally located a Dr. Fry who was engaged in such work. The procedure he recommended terrified them, but Twink insisted on trying, although she was terribly afraid. The operation was even worse than their expectations, but initially there seemed to be some slight improvement. Her vision occasionally blurred, but the doctor dismissed this development as a temporary aftereffect of no special consequence. In the aftermath of a second operation, Twink lost mobility control: where she had been flexible, now she was rigid. Because of the damage sustained by her optic nerves during surgery, she lost her sight permanently. Her parents, heartbroken and outraged, brought charges against Dr. Fry and succeeded in having his medical license revoked—a Pyrrhic victory since Twink was now irremediably damaged. Dr. Fry was contemptuous and unrepentant, challenging them: "Well, how do you expect us to learn if we don't experiment?" Twink's father died and she moved to a residential facility. The title signifies Harry's realization that he never touched Twink during his visit home and touching is the one clear sign of acceptance.

Analysis. Touching is an angry, bitter, essentially hopeless story. Twink and her parents are engaged in a doomed battle with incompetent, uncaring, selfish, and self-righteous people whose avowed intent is to help others, but who carelessly or cynically exploit Twink for their own purposes. Her final expression of hope at book's end provides the ultimate irony; there is no case for optimism. This brutal look at situations that can and have existed in society exposes how severely handicapped people are abused. The story is devastating and emotionally draining.

Ney, John. *Ox Goes North: More Trouble for the Kid at the Top.* New York: Harper, 1973. 274 pp. Reading Level: MA
Disability: Orthopedic Impairment

When Ox's parents depart for their assorted exotic vacations, they deposit their reluctant son at an exclusive boy's camp. His cabin mates are Lattimore, a savvy kid, and Campbell, "a nervous mess." Campbell tells the two boys that his parents are dead and his malevolent grandparents, the Shreckers, having adopted him, are scheming to arrange for his psychiatric commitment so that they can control his sizable inheritance. The panicky boy is too terrified to resist his guardians when they remove him from camp. Ox and Lattimore, now convinced Campbell was telling the truth, decide to save him. The Shreckers, wealthy and politically powerful, have intimidated everyone in town except Dacoolah Tompkins, a cynical, tippling ex-actress who becomes the boys' ally. The boys concoct a rescue mission, baroque in its conceptualization and implementation, but Dacoolah decides to act on her own. She confronts the Shreckers in their own home, waving some sticks of dynamite and demanding Campbell's release. Dr. Shrecker, confined to a wheelchair, is unable to corner or subdue her. When he refuses her demands, she orders Campbell and the servants to evacuate the premises. She ignites the explosives, killing herself and the power-mad old couple. Dacoolah has left a note explaining that the evil the Shreckers embody must be stopped at any cost and she is willing to pay whatever price is necessary. With his persecutors dead, Campbell's fears are allayed, the other actors in the drama reflect on Dacoolah's message, and return, sobered, to their former occupations.

Analysis. The lighthearted tone of this witty, clever, outrageously funny novel abruptly changes to a somber, weighty one as the moral issue of the individual's responsibility in combating evil—even to the extent of using violent means—is introduced. The community, over-awed by Shrecker's wealth and power and cowed by his unscrupulous machinations, is co-opted and collaborates in its own exploitation as well as in the abuse of an innocent. The characterization of Shrecker echoes that of Dr. Strangelove—physically, psychologically, and politically. His disability appears to be intended to add to the image of villainy and to justify Dacoolah's easy dominance in the confrontation.

Noble, Iris. *Courage in Her Hands*. New York: Messner, 1967. 190 pp.
Reading Level: YA
Disability: Orthopedic Impairment

It is 1815 and Malinda's father, a sea captain, leaves her at Fort Ross on the California coast when he departs in search of furs for his trading company. The Russian commandant of the fort is not pleased to have a fragile girl unused to the harsh conditions and nonconversant with Indian ways remain with him. Malinda is surprised at the authority and strength of the man despite his peg leg. "Peg-legged sailors were common in Boston. . . . Their wooden legs had a way of making them seem feebler and less manly. It was not so with the Commandant. He stood on his as if it were a staff of office." Malinda is entrusted to the care of Nahomen, an Indian woman, whom she at first fears but soon learns to love and admire. When the portrait she sketches terrifies the woman, Malinda tries to make amends. News of her husband's death convinces Nahomen that she is the victim of evil powers and she becomes deathly ill. Malinda nurses the Indian woman back to health and this action, combined with her heroic rescue of her fiancé from Spanish soldiers, causes the commandant to regard the girl with respect.

Analysis. Commandant Kuskov is presented as a strong and domineering man whose wooden leg does not affect his physical powers or military standing. Although there is some historical basis for the story, specific events are so unlikely as to be unbelievable and characterizations are flat.

Norris, Gunilla B. *The Top Step*. Illus. by Richard Cuffari. New York: Atheneum, 1970. 102 pp. Reading Level: MC
Disability: General Health Problems

Mikael, demoralized about his asthma, is caught between his mother's protective concern and his father's opinion of him as a weakling who gives in too easily to his illness. His problem, however, is real: "His breathing was ragged and labored making Mikael so tired he could hardly do anything." Mikael's ambition is to go on Sunday walks with his father; he feels that he will be big enough as soon as he is able to jump off the top step of their porch. Trying to excise his fear of physical effort and to dispel his father's contempt, he foolishly jumps from one ice floe to another in the partially frozen river. Days of chills and fever are the consequence of his predictable immersion. After recovering, he receives a pair of walking shoes from his father. At last Mikael is able to describe his feelings and worries to his father during a tiring but comforting walk.

Analysis. Slow pacing, an absence of real tension, and superficial characterizations minimize involvement in this story and leave the reader unconcerned with the hero's fate. The illustrations, however, are superb, particularly one in which the boy overhears his father's true opinion of him. Descriptions of the asthmatic attacks are accurate, effectively communicating the emotional component of the illness. The image of asthma as a bird trapped inside Mikael's chest seems farfetched and discordant though. Surprisingly, no criticism seems to be leveled at the father's machismo drive for his son, despite the obvious emotional pain and physical danger his attitude engenders.

Norton, Andre. *Scarface.* Illus. by Lorence Bjorklund. New York: Harcourt, Brace, 1948. 263 pp. Reading Level: YA
Disability: Cosmetic Impairment; also orthopedic impairment

An orphaned cabin boy called Scarface has a feared but dependent relationship with Captain Cheap, a cruel pirate who preys on ships in the West Indies. The pirate alludes to the boy's mysterious past and hints of his intention to use the youth as a tool for an unspecified revenge. The boy, whose treatment since he was disfigured has been extraordinarily harsh, is befriended by a one-armed sailor who teaches him to be an expert fencer. Scarface's ship sails to Barbados where a prisoner, Major Cocklyn, is taken. Cheap orders Scarface to pretend to assist the major while secretly inveigling from him plans of his own ship's purposes. Scarface sees this as an opportunity to escape from the hated captain but his plan is foiled. After the major disappears overboard, Scarface is taken prisoner and severely beaten. Part of Cheap's devious plan is underway as envoys from Sir Robert, the island's governor, board and insist on taking Scarface ashore for interrogation. A battle ensues in which Cheap escapes and the major, who was presumed dead, assists in Scarface's rescue. Although originally charged with serious crimes, the youth is pardoned and employment is found for him as an instructor for Sir Robert's nephew, Francis. The two are out of the house when they discover the pirates are nearby. Scarface sends the lad for help, but the boy is captured and when Scarface attempts a rescue, he too is seized. The pirate ships are raided and all aboard are condemned to be hanged. Cheap, thinking that Scarface is dead, gloatingly informs the governor that the lad is his long lost son. But it is the captain who dies, and Scarface, now reunited with his father, who lives.

Analysis. Scarface is an old-fashioned historical adventure of derring-do that includes such standard genre items as mistaken identity, names with character clues, harrowing last-minute rescues, and the ultimate triumph of justice. Scarface's disfigurement in no way impairs his functioning and, in a sense, provides the defect that keeps him from too great perfection. There is much violence and bloodshed, but it is all presented in the exotic, unrealistic, romantic fashion required by the genre.

Nourse, Alan B. *The Bladerunner*. New York: McKay, 1974. 245 pp.
Reading Level: MA
Disability: Orthopedic Impairment

Billy Gimp, an orphan, lives at the beginning of the twenty-first century and works as a "bladerunner," a supplier of medical equipment. He works with Dr. Long, whose official position is in a government-run hospital, but who uses Billy to help him in his underground practice. Since the riots, the government has totally taken over health services. Because sterilization is a requirement for hospital care, many people shun legitimate channels, compelling many physicians, like Long, to lead double lives. Both the doctor and Billy are under suspicion, and the youth has been required to wear a "responder," which monitors his whereabouts. Long convinces a colleague influential in the government that an influenza epidemic is imminent and that unless preventative treatment is arranged, meningitis will be rampant: People will not accept government protection unless the sterilization requirement is suspended. Their hand forced by the crisis, the authorities agree. Billy is sent to spread the word via the other bladerunners. Despite a superhuman effort, the boy collapses before he is able to reach all his contacts, but he is instrumental in averting a major catastrophe. Billy has been resentful of Dr. Long: The man never followed through on his promise to find an orthopedic surgeon to operate on the boy's foot. Furthermore, he treats Billy simply as a source of supplies and is indifferent to his personal needs. The epidemic crisis has forced a change in official policy and now Billy will be eligible for hospital surgery as well as a long-desired career in medicine. Billy happily anticipates the operation and the new options in his life.

Analysis. This science fiction tale is dynamic at the outset, but bogs down slightly in polemics when it deals with government interference in health care. Billy Gimp doesn't know his real name and accepts the derogatory appellation as his own. Although Billy is grumpy, suspicious, and hostile, he is also bright, brave, and tenacious. As he "saves" the populace, so now he is to be saved, at least in terms of a pain-free, serviceable foot and an opportunity for a respectable future. Although it is easy to relate to Billy and admire him, liking him is a different matter. Nevertheless, this portrayal is a strong, valid one. The plot is unusual for a junior novel and the gimmickry endemic to the genre is well managed.

O'Daniel, Janet. *A Part for Addie.* Boston: Houghton Mifflin, 1974. 230 pp. Reading Level: YA
Disability: Intellectual Impairment, General Health Problems

Addie, her father, and her younger sister are dancers who tour with a traveling theater troupe in the early years of the last century. After their father's death and a frightening and unsuitable proposal from the manager to Addie's sister, the two girls leave to find refuge in their grandfather's home. Once there, they find him desperately ill and a scheming cousin in charge of his affairs. The cousin, politically ambitious and badly in need of an inheritance to shore up his shaky financial business dealings, has confined the old man in his room and paid someone to poison him. Addie, agile and adept from her years on stage, manages to scale the outside of the house and enter her grandfather's locked room through a window. There she finds the supposed poisoner, an old friend who pretended to cooperate with the evil cousin so she might foil his plans. Her retarded son, Nathan, is with her. Addie, at first frightened of the boy because of his size and facial expression, realizes that he is kind, gentle, and reliable, and sends him with a plea for help. The grandfather is ultimately saved, and Addie, rejecting an offer of marriage, answers the call of the theater.

Analysis. This old-fashioned rousing drama of split-second timing and breathless escapes presents a retarded character in a cameo role. He is shown to be capable and valuable when given a chance, and although this is a message only peripheral to the main direction of the book, it is delivered convincingly.

O'Dell, Scott. *The Dark Canoe.* Illus. by Milton Johnson. Boston: Houghton Mifflin, 1968. 165 pp. Reading Level: YA
Disability: Orthopedic Impairment, Cosmetic Impairment, Emotional Dysfunction

Jeremy Clegg, the captain, and his brothers, Caleb and Nathan, sail in search of a sunken ship, the *Amy Foster.* Jeremy dies mysteriously, and Troll, the new captain, wishes to return to port. Caleb refuses since he feels the log of the lost vessel will prove his innocence of any responsibility for the ship's sinking. Caleb gives his younger brother a copy of *Moby Dick* for a birthday present and Nathan immediately notes the physical resemblance between his brother and Ahab. The words describing Ahab's scar "could have been written, every one of them to describe the scar that disfigured my brother's face." Although Caleb did not, like Ahab, have an ivory leg, "he did stand upon a leg that was stiff at the knee and short by a full two inches." What is even more disturbing to the boy is the similarity of their obsessive behaviors— Ahab's for the white whale, and Caleb's for the log of the *Amy Foster*. The sunken ship is at last located, and when Caleb raises a barrel of precious ambergris, the near-mutinous crew is pacified at the prospect of riches the recovered cargo can bring. The log is found and its entries exonerate Caleb of any wrongdoing in the loss of the ship. Nathan discovers a chest, which he hides on a small island, planning to return later to examine its contents. When Nathan goes with his brother to open the chest, in the daylight it uncannily resembles both a canoe and a coffin, but is most like "the dark canoe" Queequeg ordered built to contain his dead body. Troll presses to leave, and Nathan persuades his brother to sail for home.

Analysis. Caleb's impairments become the stigmata that propel him to submerge his own identify and assume that of the fictional captain. His scar and crippled leg have no meaning apart from those that attach to Ahab's—a meaning unlikely to be known to the audience to which this book is directed. Despite the absorbing style, the story line is confusing and leans upon the reader's presumed familiarity with *Moby Dick*.

O'Dell, Scott. *Sing Down the Moon.* Boston: Houghton Mifflin, 1970. 137 pp. Reading Level: MC/YA
Disability: Orthopedic Impairment

It is 1864 and times are difficult for the Navahos living in the Canyon de Chelly. Bright Morning, a fifteen-year-old member of the tribe, and her friend are kidnapped by Spanish soldiers and brought into a village to be household servants. Restless and angry over their loss of freedom, the two girls steal some horses and sneak away. However, they are seen and followed by the Spaniards. Tall Boy, a young Navaho, kills one of the Spanish soldiers, but is shot in the arm while fleeing. Although the Indians reach safety, the bullet that wounded the boy left his arm useless and he is no longer able to function in the esteemed roles of hunter and warrior. Soldiers from a nearby fort arbitrarily order all Navahos to leave their ancestral homes. The Indians' resistance is easily suppressed, their crops and orchards destroyed, and their people forcibly marched to Fort Sumner. Tall Boy, humiliated at the crushing of his dignity, becomes apathetic and despairing. Nonetheless, a marriage is arranged between him and Bright Morning. When his bride becomes pregnant, her obsession to return to her real home coalesces in a plan. She begins to hoard food from their meager supplies for their secret departure. Tall Boy is arrested for assaulting an Apache who tried to steal some wood he had harvested. He escapes and, with his wife, slips away from the encampment. Bright Morning insists that they return to their former home, claiming she knows where some sheep have been hidden. A son is born during the dangerous journey, but his birth only briefly interrupts their progress. At last they reach a hidden valley where some wild sheep remain. Using these animals as the basis for their livelihood and, with considerable ingenuity and fortitude, they begin to rebuild a life in keeping with their heritage.

Analysis. In a sense, Tall Boy's story is a metaphor for the experience of the American Indians. Tall Boy is injured by white soldiers while trying to protect his people. The injury is ruinous to his pride and to his status, diminishing his physical powers as well as his stature. Forced into an artificial and humiliating lifestyle designed by his oppressors, he suffers—conscious of the annihilation of so many of his people—but even more devastated by the impending collapse of his way of life. It is not until he takes control of his life again, with his wife as a strong model, and lives in a way compatible with his native traditions, that he has hope of regaining self-respect. The injury to his right arm symbolizes the impotence he now endures. The spare, lean prose precisely matches the content and tone of this powerful narrative.

Ogan, Margaret and George Ogan. *Water Rat.* New York: Funk & Wagnalls, 1970. 118 pp. Reading Level: MC/YA
Disability: Auditory Impairment, Speech Impairment

After being rescued by Race Arnold, an ex-Olympic swimmer, Bud Archer is invited to be his swimming student. He joins Lani, another pupil from Florida, who is deaf and mute. The thirteen-year-old girl was given lessons by her parents to help overcome her shyness and build up her confidence. Race grooms them aggressively, treating Lani like a potential champion, not a fragile, handicapped adolescent. The two teenagers communicate by finger spelling, although manual communication is forbidden by her parents. Both swimmers continue to improve. In the trial, Lani earns a new world's record. She has become popular at high school and is invited to give a swimming exhibition at the state institution for the deaf and blind. Lani beats her own record but magnanimously forgives the timer, who disqualifies the event by dropping his watch. Race is under pressure from other coaches who want Bud and Lani and from a newsman who once maligned him. Lani, despite continuing achievements, determines to give up her amateur status the following year and take a coaching job at the state school. Bud has problems but eventually qualifies at an important meet. Race meets the newsman to whom he explains the circumstances that led to his condemnation. It appears that Race will be exonerated and be able to restore his reputation; Lani will pursue a vocation that promises satisfaction and high achievement; and Bud will be able to focus his energies on qualifying for the Olympics.

Analysis. Lani is presented as a youngster with tremendous talent and drive who functions as a student, sportswoman, and friend. Although she is not developed in as much depth as the two major characters, one has a moderately good feeling about her naturalness, her determination, and her opposition to her parents who mistakenly try to limit her communication skills by confining her to oralism instead of total communication training. The heavy stress on swimming, information on racing competition, better-than-standard sports writing, and moderately well-paced story provide a vehicle that may be of interest to sports buffs as well as those who like an unusual story.

Oppenheimer, Joan. *On the Outside Looking In.* Chicago: Scholastic, 1973. 191 pp. Reading Level: YA
Disability: Orthopedic Impairment

Depressed and angry since the nightmarish motorcycle accident in which he lost his leg, Bruce seeks solitude at his grandparents' home on a secluded lake. Expecting to find privacy, he is outraged to discover Chris, a five-year-old boy, accompanied by Laurie, a teenage sitter, and vents his anger on the two surprised sunbathers. When Laurie discovers the reason for Bruce's outburst, she weaves this information into a story for Chris, hoping to help her young charge understand. Bruce overhears, is moved by her unexpectedly kind response, and invites the two to a picnic. When he finds that he is not rejected, he asks Laurie to go swimming with him—a major move toward recovering his self-confidence, since he will have to maneuver on one leg, unable to conceal the extent of his loss. They are just beginning to relax and enjoy each other's company when they are interrupted on the beach by Dooley, a local bully, who has been annoying Laurie and begins bothering her again. When Bruce comes out of the water, Dooley sees how vulnerable he is and proceeds to taunt and ridicule him, finally striking the helpless boy with his own prosthetic leg. Humiliated, Bruce becomes more withdrawn and morose than ever, refusing any further contact with Laurie. One night, when Laurie and Chris are home alone, Dooley forces his way in. Laurie signals the child to go for help. He returns with Bruce who manages to subdue the would-be attacker and hold him for the sheriff. With renewed confidence, Bruce is willing to go swimming again and to respond openly and without embarrassment to Chris' questions about his leg. Chris' parents plan to keep Laurie, who is orphaned, as a permanent member of the family.

Analysis. Despite some major flaws, this novel has many valuable qualities. Laurie is too good to be true, too free of scars over the loss of her parents and the experiences of a succession of foster homes. Sexist clichés abound, and the climax is too obviously contrived. Balancing this is the portrait of Bruce's emotional crisis caused by the loss of his leg. The full treatment of the young man is exceptionally well done. His fears, his tentative retreat, and his ultimate self-acceptance are realistically and convincingly developed. The scene of his humiliation is vivid and powerful. The final image is that of a person who has painfully and courageously dealt with both his disability and his handicap.

Ormsby, Virginia H. *Mountain Magic for Rosy.* Illus. by Paul E. Kennedy. New York: Crown, 1969. 137 pp. Reading Level: MC
Disability: General Health Problems

The Ray family barely ekes out a subsistence living on their Smoky Mountain farm. Their last two babies died and their most recent has a defective heart. The county nurse advises taking the infant to a clinic in Knoxville, but there is no money for medical expenses or even for the trip. Fearful that naming the infant would ensure his death, he is still just known as "the baby." The mother fears Granny Fite may have hexed him when she prophesied he would not live long. The old woman is suspected of being in league with the devil, and when visited by a stranger whose initials are known to be L. D., the local children decide he must be Lucifer Devil. In fact, the man is a folklorist who is collecting local chants, spells, and music. Through his work, Rosy, the unnamed baby's sister, and Granny Fite earn some modest fame and enough money to make a trip to the clinic possible.

Analysis. This gentle, folksy tale briefly explores some of the superstitions associated with disability and the oppressive restrictions on remediation created by poverty. Rosy, resentful of all the sacrifices necessitated by her sick sibling, briefly wishes the baby dead. This reaction and her consequent guilt are examined in simple comprehensible terms and are shown to be part of an inevitably ambivalent and complex response to the blue baby who demands so much of her parents' attention, love, and resources.

Ottley, Reginald. *The Bates Family.* New York: Harcourt, Brace and World, 1969. 175 pp. Reading Level: MC/YA
Disability: Orthopedic Impairment

The Bates family, drovers in the Australian outback, are suffering through one of the worst droughts in years. The oldest children, Linda and Albie, are seventeen-year-old twins and mainstays in the support of the family. Albie, injured as a child when his horse fell, has a damaged hip. The joint has stiffened, leaving him with a pronounced limp and considerable pain. Albie's work keeps him on horseback much of the time, jolting over rough country. The family lives a marginal existence, never far from real hunger. When at last the rains arrive, the parched land is unable to absorb the deluge and rivers swell, overflowing their banks and flooding the nearby land. A younger son is stranded on high ground when he tries to rescue a horse. The rising waters threaten him, and Linda fords the treacherous floods to save him while Albie remains on shore with a lifeline. His is punishing work, but he is ashamed that his hip prevents him from being the main actor in the rescue. Supplies are getting dangerously low and the father must cross the swollen river to replenish their stores. The twins devise a plan for rigging a line across the water to permit their father's safe return. Albie insists that he do the most dangerous chores this time. The first crossing is safely accomplished, but on the return trip his leg cramps and he is tossed helplessly about by the raging currents. Linda barely pulls him, half drowned, from the water. Soon the land is restored by the rains and the grazing grasses begin to grow again. The owner of the property they are camping on solicits their help in capturing some wild horses that are destroying the land. The father and older children participate in the work, which is dangerous and chancy. All seems to be going well when the pack suddenly turns and heads for a cliff. There is no way to stop the stampeding beasts from plunging over the edge to their deaths. One man is badly injured and the twins are stunned by the destruction of the great animals. Their father tells them that they need to be moving on; some sheep need to be herded to market and that will be their next work.

Analysis. The harsh, demanding conditions of the country provide a backdrop for this stark, well-wrought story of a drifting, marginal family. Albie, never free of pain, has the most difficult life. His leg, inadequately attended to, is further strained by the constant abuse of his work, his inadequate diet, and his frequent use of the hard ground for a bed. There is not much choice if his family is to exist; his labor is needed and there is no surplus income for comforts. Albie accepts this stoically and denies both to himself and to his family that there are any real limitations to what he can or will do. His twin is obviously sympathetic to his physical and psychological needs and makes numerous accommodations, while his parents, with only occasional exceptions, seem neglectful. This apparent lack of concern is in reality only an acceptance of their inability to affect an implacable fate. This taut, spare book presents a view of life and a value system probably at variance with those of most young readers, but is nonetheless fascinating.

　　Ottley, Reginald. *Giselle*. New York: Harcourt, Brace, 1968. 159 pp.
　　Reading Level: YA
　　Disability: Orthopedic Impairment

Giselle's unhurried bucolic life in New Caledonia is overshadowed by her parents' lack of communication, the possibility of her father's capture or punishment as a poacher, and especially by the weakening condition of her beloved uncle, Marcel. He had once been a strong and powerful man until "the big illness warped him until his limbs grew stiff. Now he is locked in hunchbacked shame." When she brings food to his cabin, they talk of his desperate desire to seek a cure at Lourdes. Giselle adds to his hoard of money by selling a stingray she speared in the act of saving the life of her friend, Edouard. The full cost of the trip is finally accumulated when Giselle's father and his friend obtain money from killing a bull while illegally hunting deer. Marcel is overwhelmed at the possibility of regaining his former physique, but the implication is that he will not be strong enough to make the trip. Edouard is accepted as a candidate for the priesthood and spends a last day fishing with his sister. A storm comes up and, despite desperate attempts at a rescue, he drowns.

　　Analysis. It is unclear what illness causes periodic fevers, "shrunken, twisted, stiffened limbs," and has deformed Marcel's spine. The key aspect of this story is the love, concern, and respect Marcel enjoys from the entire community. Although he disparages himself as "a gargoyle," others risk their lives for him, and helping him plan his pilgrimage gives them great pleasure. Unfortunately, this slow paced novel is burdened with patronizing attitudes about native life. Its lack of focus and abrupt conclusion detract markedly from the presentation.

　　Parker, Richard. *He Is Your Brother*. Nashville: Nelson, 1974. 98 pp.
　　Reading Level: MC
　　Disability: Emotional Dysfunction

The Lewis family has accommodated themselves somewhat to the autisticlike behavior of Orry, their youngest member. Mike and his sister, Jane, love their brother, and, depending on mood, tolerate, ignore, or are angered by his behavior. Mike's hobby of old trains is almost an addiction, and he judiciously locks his door to preserve the safety of his collection from the possible careless abuse by his family. Mike reluctantly takes his brother along when he and a friend search for railroad memorabilia in an old factory area. In the aftermath of getting lost, Mike and his sister hear Orry mimic regular speech, indicating the boy's unsuspected capacity to enunciate clearly when he is repeating the conversations of others. After Mike senses that Orry is also interested in trains, the youngster is allowed to enter his brother's room and even help prepare an old nameplate for display. When Mike goes to a play therapy session at his brother's clinic, he is puzzled to see Orry bury the father doll in the sand and to speak clearly to his therapist. Mr. Lewis has brought home a simple musical instrument for his young son. Fearing that Orry would reject a present, he decides to let the recorder simply lay around. Orry, who is only six, listens to his father's quartet rehearse and, despite never having had a lesson, readily duplicates a Dvorak piece. The two brothers become even closer after a tunnel accident in which Mike manages to save his injured brother. When they return home, Orry gives an uncannily accurate accounting of the episode. In precisely spoken words, the boy signals his improved level of functioning by the announcement that his name is Lawrence.

Analysis. Even though autism is frequently characterized by uneven development, the presentation of a child accurately playing a complex musical work at the age of six when he still fumbles with a fork and knife is not believable. Although some of Orry's actions are consistent with accepted constellations of behavior for autistic children, other scenes are neither compatible with that diagnosis nor with the developmental level of the child. Equally unbelievable is the pastiche of behaviors Orry displays, actually more manipulative than autistic. Jane's well-meaning explanation about her brother's acts is a brave attempt to place his behavior on a continuum, but the persistence and the extent of his disordered conduct preclude its being seen as "normal . . . only more so." The novel's best aspect is the depiction of each family member's individualized attempts to relate lovingly to Orry. Especially well done are the initial graphic vignettes of the troubled boy's behavior. It is only in the resolution that the story falters.

Parker, Richard. *Three by Mistake.* Nashville: Nelson, 1974. 128 pp.
Reading Level: MC/YA
Disability: General Health Problems

Arab terrorists have carefully noted the habits of Simon Farid, son of a senior official at the Jordanian Embassy in England. Their plans to kidnap Simon are altered when his sister and friend, Neil, stumble upon the bound and gagged boy. All three are now quickly abducted, roughly thrown into a truck, and driven to a remote hideout where they are to be kept until the terrorists' demands are met. Neil's serious asthma attacks are initially frightening to the two others, but the girl, especially, becomes sympathetic. Fearing for their lives, the children plan an escape and in a perilous adventure almost succeed. The captives are returned to their rooms but are able to overhear an argument among the plotters. One terrorist departs in a truck, another goes for assistance, and the third, who is the mastermind, enters the rooms where the frightened children are incarcerated. The door slams behind him and they all realize he has inadvertently locked himself in with them. The police arrive, but the kidnapper's attempt to escape, using Simon as a hostage, is foiled by the children's brave and ingenious actions.

Analysis. Neil's breathing difficulties are described in detail but, except for the actual period of the asthma attack, they do not restrict his behavior. This condition is peripheral to the plot development and his characterization. The story is fast-paced and moderately exciting. Although the children are scared, the experience seems more an adventure than a nightmare. While topical, the events have been reduced in seriousness consistent with the immaturity of the intended audience.

Paterson, Katherine. *Of Nightingales That Weep.* Illus. by Haru Wells. New York: Crowell, 1974. 170 pp. Reading Level: YA/MA
Disability: Orthopedic Impairment; also general health problems

Tako's life changes radically when her samurai father is killed in a battle and her mother is hurriedly married to a poor, dwarfed potter. Tako is repelled by Goro, her stepfather, her mother's pregnancy, and the poverty of their life, although Goro's sterling qualities emerge and the two grow closer. The young girl is made a lady-in-waiting at the emperor's court and becomes embroiled in the intrigue and turbulence of twelfth-century Japanese royal politics. Her increasingly precarious situation is complicated by a romance with a spy. Goro bribes his way to the royal island of exile and desperately begs his stepdaughter to return home since their house has burned and her mother is again pregnant. Refusing to give up her exciting life at court, she tells Goro that the tubercular emperor needs her, carefully concealing her relationship with her lover. Tako's fortunes decline and, after escaping from prison and returning home, she finds that her mother and brothers have died. The only one remaining is Goro who curses her and then himself for still being alive. Overcome with remorse, she joins Goro in working the fields, submerging her shame in gruelling labor. When her lover locates her, he is repelled by her coarse appearance. Deciding that vanity and selfishness have brought about her downfall, she plans to join a convent. She is dissuaded by the empress, who tells her to rebuild Japan with her little god. She returns home and bears the dwarf's child.

Analysis. In the text, Goro is sensitively portrayed—small in stature but strong and vibrant in love, anger, and grief. In the interplay between vanity and substance, between appearance and reality, Goro's physical condition is ironic: His short stature contrasts with his outsize virtues, and his reduced fortunes contrast with the empress' noble hopes for the future; it is in this context the designation of him as a god is made. Goro further symbolizes the fatuousness and hollowness of vanity. Tako's good looks are eclipsed by misfortune and drudgery, but Goro's strengths endure. It is only when Tako has paid for her weakness through the loss of her beauty, her family, her home, and her lover that she is eligible to assume the role of the dwarf-god's wife. The writing evokes a strong sense of time and culture and captures the attention of the reader in this action-filled exotic tale. Readers unaccustomed to Oriental names may have difficulty sorting out the warring factions and following the complex changes in nomenclature. The handsome pen and ink sketches unaccountably do not depict Goro despite his central importance.

Patton, Willoughby. *The Florentine Giraffe*. Illus. by William Hutchinson. New York: McKay, 1967. 149 pp. Reading Level: MC/YA
Disability: Orthopedic Impairment; also cosmetic impairment

It is Florence, Italy, near the close of the fifteenth century, and Guido, a fourteen-year-old boy, unenthusiastically works as an apprentice goldsmith, wishing all the while to be with animals instead. His beautiful, crippled sister, Tessa, contributes to the family's finances with her artistic embroidery. As she works, sitting in her crudely made wheeled chair, she dreams of becoming a queen and singing in Lorenzo the Magnificent's festival. When a strange animal called a giraffe is donated to Lorenzo's private zoo, Guido manages to see and become friends with the wonderful creature. He overhears a personal enemy of the prince converse with a man with a scarred face about stealing the giraffe. Guido conceals the animal in a church and, in trying to escape the wrongdoers, is shot with an arrow. Using a homing pigeon, Tessa warns the ruler about the plot. The conspirators are caught and, as a reward, Lorenzo grants Guido's request that Tessa perform in the festival. With Tessa invited to sing permanently in his court and Guido happily employed at the zoo, their economic future is at last assured.

Analysis. No information is presented about Tessa's condition, although presumably it was caused by polio. Tessa is beautiful, kind, generous, talented, ingenious, hard-working, and uncomplaining—in a word, perfect. As in all such tales, virtue is rewarded, but such romanticism detracts from the attempted realistic approach of this historically informative story. The treatment of the two criminals is harshly differentiated. The scarred man is hanged by being thrown naked off the castle with his neck in a rope. Guido requests that the other be spared because of his artistic talent and his kinder fate is to be banished. Tessa is a rare example of a disabled female in an historical novel.

> Perl, Lila. *No Tears for Rainey.* Philadelphia: Lippincott, 1969. 158 pp. Reading Level: MC/YA
> *Disability:* Emotional Dysfunction; also general health problems

After her father has been institutionalized for an emotional disorder, Rainey Brandt moves into a housing project with her mother. When she returns to her former neighborhood, one of the children taunts her, saying that her father is really in jail since no one could be hospitalized for so long. Rainey asks a friend to tell her former neighbors that her father has cancer, an explanation she finds less shameful than mental illness. Rainey makes friends with Anita, a Puerto Rican girl, who lives nearby. Anita's father has tuberculosis, a disease considered disgraceful by her grandmother. When Rainey's father is released for a visit home, he is detached and depressed. Mrs. Brandt, too obviously and extravagantly cheerful, insists that her husband is well and able to return to work. The only response he makes is to his daughter, who treats him in a straightforward manner, sharing her school problems with him. A sympathetic neighbor and Anita provide the emotional support Rainey needs at this difficult time. Problems worsen at home with bickering and bitter arguments until Rainey accuses her mother of responding inadequately to her family's needs. Mrs. Brandt rationalizes, saying: "Once a person finds a way of dealing with . . . things, well, one begins to tread a pretty well-worn path." When Rainey prepares some food for her father, the hot fat catches fire but he is able to quench the blaze and rescue his frightened child. He accompanies her to school and straightens out some difficulties she has been having, thereby further establishing his growing competence and providing his daughter with some sense of family support.

Analysis. The treatment of the family dynamics in responding to the father's problems is the best aspect of this story. Rainey's problem in remaining loyal to her father while simultaneously avoiding confronting the shame she feels is associated with emotional dysfunction is poignantly presented. The mother's inadequacy in responding to either her children's or her husband's needs because she is burdened by financial and social problems of her own is a facet of adult insufficiency not often found in juvenile books. Her denial of her husband's inability to resume full functioning appears, as it should, more pitiable than contemptible. Mr. Brandt responds best when needed, as revealed in his rapid physical response to the fire. Even more significant is his assistance in helping Rainey at school, which involves more demanding interpersonal functioning. The portrait of the sensitive and helpful black neighbor is too transparent a ploy, and the sexist message delivered is offensive: Rainey is told she should accept a cooking class with more grace, since cooking is a form of chemistry—a subject more to Rainey's liking. Unfortunately, the plot is contrived, the ending neat, the tone saccharine, and the message didactic—all of which deflect attention from the fine portrayal of an adult male coping with a paralyzing, incapacitating depression.

Peyton, K. M. (pseud.). Kathleen and Michael Peyton. *Flambards*. Illus. by Victor G. Ambrus. New York: World, 1967. 206 pp. Reading Level: YA/MA
Disability: Orthopedic Impairment; also visual impairment

Christina Parsons, an orphan, has been summoned by her uncle to live with him and his two sons at Flambards. The uncle plans for her to marry his oldest son so that when she is twenty-one and comes into her considerable inheritance, the money can be used to prop up the sagging economy of his estate. The day she arrives, William, the younger son, is brought home unconscious, having been badly hurt in a hunting accident. His father, whose legs had also been crushed in a riding mishap, is more angered at his son's lack of skill than distressed by his injuries. William heals slowly, disregarding his doctor's orders in an effort to damage his legs permanently. He sees this self-mutilating act as the only means by which he can be freed of his parent's cruel domination. His father arbitrarily decides to sell Christina's horse for dog meat. Horrified, she enlists the help of a groom to save her animal, but when the scheme is discovered, the man is fired. Christina visits his home and sees his invalided mother, who is in constant pain. The poverty they endure appalls her. When William interferes with his brother's chance to win a horse race, his father is furious and orders him to leave home. He does, but returns the next week to propose to Christina—an offer she happily accepts.

Analysis. This taut, literate story vividly evokes the times of pre-World War I England. William's attitude toward deliberately laming himself is shocking, but also somewhat romanticized. He is obsessed with flying, and the freedom symbolized by the primitive airplanes he pilots contrasts starkly with the imprisonment he endures in his own home. It is only after he is injured and cannot participate in his father's obsession for riding that his parent loses all interest in his son, and William is free to pursue his passion for flying. In a sense, he is willing to pay for his liberty by sacrificing the full use of his legs. His father, also crippled, is a malevolent figure; dreadful before his injury, he is even more bitter and vindictive afterward. The change is only a matter of degree rather than of kind. The groom's mother, also impaired, is pitiable, enduring terrible poverty and suffering. Linked by having the same kind of disability, the three orthopedically disabled characters are each completely different in situation and character. The illustrations nicely capture the uncle's various moods as well as William's pain and joy.

Phipson, Joan. *Birkin.* Illus. by Margaret Horder. New York: Harcourt, Brace and World, 1965. 224 pp. Reading Level: YA
Disability: Orthopedic Impairment

Two Australian high school boys take home a motherless calf to raise, but they soon lose interest. Tony, a boy with a hip deformity, brings milk for the calf, Birkin, when the other children's contributions drop off. Birkin has a few unpleasant adventures grazing and, frightened by the Mitchells' airplane, knocks down Frances, one of the girls. The calf is temporarily cared for at the Mitchell ranch. Birkin is in an accident, and while Frances goes for help, Tony stays with the calf, even though he is half-frozen in the process. Frances tries to persuade others that she and Tony should have exclusive ownership of Birkin. A violent storm occurs and the Mitchell's son is lost in a plane crash. When Tony and Frances go to the creek to check on the bull, they see Birkin on the other side of a swollen creek. As they watch, he is swept away by the current and carried helplessly downstream. Quickly, Tony commandeers an abandoned tub for a boat and follows the helpless animal, while Frances seeks assistance. Tony locates Birkin, wet but none the worse for wear, and subsequently finds the downed pilot. Sitting astride Birkin, Tony and the pilot return to the ranch and, in gratitude, Mr. Mitchell offers to pay for Birkin's food. The adolescents enter Birkin in a contest. They are horrified when Birkin wins and they realize he will be slaughtered. They plead with Mr. Mitchell to void the entry, which he does, and Birkin goes to live permanently on the ranch. Recognizing Tony's skill in caring for animals, Mr. Mitchell urges him to take up veterinary medicine or animal husbandry, programs that he will finance.

Analysis. This sensitive, old-fashioned story of considerable literary merit displays many themes common to this field: Outcasts together—Tony and Angus, the foreigner, are shunned by others and perforce become allies; the exceptional character as nature child—Tony has a special way with animals; and the Santa Claus theme—Mr. Mitchell provides direction and support for a career. Tony copes with pain, but it causes him to be testy and irritable. He is also courageous, intelligent, and tenacious. The illustrations give no indication of Tony's disability, but the characterization gives some insight into his pride and his ability to manage the vicissitudes of life.

Platt, Kin. *The Boy Who Could Make Himself Disappear*. Philadelphia: Chilton, 1968. 216 pp. Reading Level: YA/MA
Disability: Emotional Dysfunction, Speech Impairment; also orthopedic impairment

Roger is the son of two self-centered, ambitious, and rejecting parents. When they separate, he moves with his mother to New York where he enters an exclusive private school. There he encounters an instructor whose major disciplinary techniques are based on ridicule and sarcasm. Roger's lisping, babyish speech causes him considerable anguish. The rejection and hostility at home, combined with the anxiety generated by his school pressures, push him to retreat more and more into daydreams. As his situation progressively deteriorates, the world of fantasy appears safer and more reasonable than the real one and his withdrawal becomes complete. However, the presence of persons concerned about the boy's future suggests that Roger may have the support necessary to resume his interaction with the real world once again.

Analysis. Characterizations are excellent, particularly those of the rejecting mother, a supportive neighbor, a speech therapist, a young girl crippled in an automobile accident, and, most notably, Roger. This magnetic story gives some empathic understanding of how an individual's ability to cope with stress can be sabotaged by cruelty and indifference. Platt ends this sensitively written story on an optimistic note, perhaps overly optimistic in view of the extent of the boy's present functioning.

Platt, Kin. *Hey, Dummy*. Philadelphia: Chilton, 1971. 169 pp. Reading Level: YA
Disability: Intellectual Impairment, Emotional Dysfunction

Neil yells "Hey, Dummy" at a boy watching a neighborhood football game. The other boys think this is an apt description for Alan, and the label sticks. Neil uses Alan as the topic for his class report, which is perceived as hilarious by the students, but cruel by the teacher, Mr. Alvarado. Shocked and sobered by this reaction, Neil reluctantly becomes Alan's protector, a role that increasingly occupies a good deal of time, alienates him from his peers, and infuriates his father. Neil tries to disengage, but his sense of decency and a compassion for Alan he himself finds puzzling bind them together. Neil discovers that Alan's father is institutionalized, his sister hostile and withdrawn (erroneously labeled autistic), and his mother incapable of responding to her family's needs.

A little girl is hurt in the park and Alan, although innocent, is assumed to be the culprit. A mob flocks to his home and vents its violent anger on his sister, but Neil manages to rescue Alan, and desperate for assistance, reassurance, and a refuge, seeks out Mr. Alvarado in the barrio. The teacher, confronted with his earlier statements to Neil about humanitarianism and commitment, perceives any involvement as potentially damaging to his people, the Chicanos, whose social position is precarious at best, and hypocritically refuses the boys a haven. Exhausted and hungry, Neil rummages for food for himself and Alan outside a supermarket where he is fired upon by a watchman. The shot misses him but is fatal to Alan. Traumatized by the experience and unable to handle his feelings of guilt, Neil is institutionalized. Eerily, he soon begins to simulate the perceptions and behavior patterns of his dead friend.

Analysis. Platt has written an unusual and unsettling book. His depiction of Neil's dilemma and response is excellent, as is the presentation of the teacher's moral struggle. The representation of a severely retarded child's perceptions is effective and the reader is able to experience both insight into and compassion for Alan's plight, and even, to some extent, vicariously experience his limitations. The story's ineluctable increment of violence—name calling, teasing, rejection, stoning, arson, and finally murder—are carefully orchestrated and devastating in effect. Society is blamed for its criminal neglect of Alan's needs: The school placed him inappropriately and apparently assumed no responsibility for even his safety, much less his education; the community offered no support for this fragmented family; and society in its collective manifestation as the mob and in its individual personification in the character of the watchman (a social metaphor) grossly abuses the innocent. Although characters tend to be presented in extremes of virtue or villainy, the depiction of Alan is excellent and the plot is fast-paced and compelling.

Platt's intention to shock is obviously demonstrated in the offensive title. Many readers could be deflected from his humanitarian objective by looking only at plot and ignoring the themes. Although suffused with violence, the novel's message arouses the moral conscience. Persecution inevitably results in cowardice, violence, and wanton destruction, whether directed at the culturally different (the Chicano population) or the intellectually inadequate (Alan). Neil, Alan's mentor, is as much a victim of the mob as is Alan. Neil literally lives the commandment to be his brother's keeper, and when Alan dies, he assumes his persona. Alan's death is physical; Neil's psychological.

Platt's attempt to re-create the world as it appears to a severely retarded is moderately effective. His major focus, however, is not a comment on retardation but on the devastating effects of social abuse directed toward those who are different.

Pont, Clarice. *The Immediate Gift*. New York: McKay, 1961. 216 pp.
Reading Level: MA
Disability: Speech Impairment, Intellectual Impairment

Heather's stuttering has always aggravated her mother and exacerbates the strained relationship between them. After her mother's remarriage, Heather moves into the home of a warm and supportive teacher who simultaneously reduces the pressures on the girl and boosts her sense of self-worth—acts that noticeably improve her speech. Heather finds her college classes and fieldwork in speech correction demanding as well as exciting, and she is encouraged to pursue a career in this area despite her own disability. She immerses herself in the problems of a young retarded boy and is instrumental in arranging for free surgery to excise his brain tumor. The operation is a success, the child's prognosis is excellent, and Heather's professional and marital goals will soon be realized.

Analysis. Pont essentially has written an extended recruitment brochure for speech therapists. The significance and needs of the profession, ways in which society is unresponsive to children's real needs, and the techniques and implications of speech therapy are incorporated into a traditional teenage romance. The most interesting aspects of the book are the detailed descriptions of speech problems and their attempted remediation in clinical, institutional, and school settings. The influence of psychological and sociological factors in impeding or supporting corrective procedures is examined at length. The least satisfactory aspect, as might be expected from a work of this orientation, is the literary quality. The plot is a series of contrived events free of the restraints of probability. That Heather should select this field and have the potential for a successful career as a speech correctionist, despite her own stutter, is, however, neither unlikely nor impossible. The missionary tone of the book is oppressive but is balanced by the sheer quantity of relevant information.

Potter, Bronson. *Antonio*. Illus. by Ann Grifalconi. New York: Atheneum, 1968. 41 pp. Reading Level: MC
Disability: Orthopedic Impairment

In Antonio's Portuguese village where fishermen are highly esteemed, Antonio's "stiffened hand" excludes him from such arduous, demanding labor. Now he works as an ox-boy, who guides the huge animals as they pull returning boats onto the shore. The weather has been strange lately, but the fishing good. One day ominous storm clouds gather while the men are out and it is obvious that the fleet is in danger. Antonio persuades his teacher to help him load the oxen onto a truck and bring them to a beach closer to where the boats will land. A large signal fire is built and, despite the turbulent seas, most of the boats reach the shore safely. The boat owned by Antonio's father has been damaged and is foundering. The boy swims out to the boat and advises his exhausted father to head out to sea so that they can catch a big wave and ride it in. With Antonio at the throttle and his now proud father at the wheel, the boat is safely beached.

Analysis. Antonio is undervalued because of his disability. He gains status through his quick intelligence but also by a feat requiring strength and endurance. This simple, straightforward tale suggests that people should be valued for their actions, not on the basis of their presumed deficiencies. No hint of the boy's disability is present in the handsome illustrations. The text is written in the simple, choppy style commonly used to suggest a foreign locale.

Randall, Janet. *The Seeing Heart.* New York: McKay, 1965. 187 pp.
Reading Level: YA
Disability: Visual Impairment

Gay Sanders is expelled from college when the substitute she sent to take an examination for her is discovered. After a period of depression, she is persuaded to write for readmission and is reaccepted. No longer able to count on her wealthy aunt's support, she is obliged to accept a live-in, low-paying job with a woman disabled by cataracts. The woman gets her another job as a reader for Tony, a blind sophomore who is a major in Oriental languages, a ham radio operator, a chess player, a record collector, and a storyteller, and is physically attractive with "the walk of an athlete." She learns about talking book machines, becomes a volunteer at a recreation center for the blind, and considers working in this field as a career. She becomes reacquainted with Jim, a boy she once considered uninteresting, but whom she now views in a more attractive light, in large measure due to his volunteer activities with the disabled. Gay convinces a friend that she should not cheat on the same exam which was her own downfall, helps in revamping a college course, and ultimately gets a loan, awarded for her selection of such a worthwhile profession.

Analysis. Working with the blind is seen both as the impetus as well as the index of Gay's maturation. At the outset the heroine is indecisive, petty, and peevish. As she is exposed to the salutary influences of two strong individuals without sight, she begins to reconsider her values. When Gay begins to give of herself, her transformation is almost complete: She is now honest, courageous, and unselfish and has a raised consciousness and a "seeing heart." She prepares for an honorable career helping the blind and now knows the true value of a wonderful young man like Jim. Despite the noble disclaimer that "too many people who want to work with the handicapped are motivated by pity, which can do more harm than good . . . it takes a special mixture of compassion and the ability to face reality," the book tends to exploit blindness by using it as a device to educate the callous young woman. Although there are some positive portrayals of the blind, insensitivity is revealed through the decision to call the girls at the recreation center the "Three Blind Mice" and to bewail Tony's stubbornness in always wanting to do things for himself.

Raskin, Ellen. *Spectacles.* New York: Atheneum, 1969. Illus. by the author. unpaged. Reading Level: YC
Disability: Visual Impairment

Iris sees her world in a sort of murky fog. She mistakes her grand-aunt for a dragon and her babysitter for a horse. An eye examination confirms her visual problem, but she adamantly resists getting glasses. A clever optician wins Iris over by suggesting that the right frames will make her look like a movie star. Except when she removes her glasses, Iris has functional vision.

Analysis. This charming book has marvelously witty illustrations that simulate the heroine's visual deficit. The text is amusing and enter-taining. The lighthearted approach in the scenes with the medical men might help to minimize the anxiety a child can have about getting glasses.

Raskin, Ellen. *The Tattooed Potato and Other Clues.* New York: Dut-ton, 1975. 170 pp. Reading Level: MC/YA
Disability: Auditory Impairment, Speech Impairment, Intellectual Impairment, Cosmetic Impairment

Dickory Dock, a newly orphaned young art student whose parents were murdered during a robbery, finds a job as an assistant to a portrait artist named Garson. Living with him is Isaac, a deaf-mute, "a huge, disfigured monster of a man. A jagged scar cut across his smashed face, twisting his mouth into a horrible grin, blinding one eye white and unblinking." The two men were once young struggling artists together, but when Garson painted a picture of his friend as an untalented clown, the distraught youth rushed in front of a moving truck in an unsuccess-ful suicide attempt. He was so badly injured that "only a grunting vege-table survived." In an attempt at penance, Garson assumed a new identity and permanent responsibility for Isaac. Garson is an amateur detective who, in his guise as Inspector Noserag, solves various baf-fling crimes brought to him by the New York Police Department. His supposed ability as an artist to see through to the essential core of a person or problem and his adroit cerebral gymnastics are combined in a very broad spoof of Sherlock Holmes. Two unsavory tenants in their building, Manny Malomar and Shrimps Marinara, suspect Dickory of spying on their blackmailing activities. They grab her and tie her up, but she manages to escape through Isaac's intervention. The roomers are arrested and revealed to be the killers of Dickory's parents.

Analysis. This grotesque and highly offensive effort suffers from a strained and self-conscious attempt at cuteness. Impairments are used in egregious ways—obvious clues to a thief, disguises, establishing a character as pitiful or repulsive. The badly disfigured and irremediably injured Isaac is presented as a gentle Frankenstein, decent and kind, but barely human: "A loud howl erupted from the crippled mute like a clap of wondrous thunder. He rocked in his chair and threw back his head, uttering cries that echoed through the room. Dickory could hear his 'ung-ung-ung' through the thick glass. Isaac . . . was laughing." Obvious and childish name jokes—Dinkel, Finkel and Winkel, the detectives; Shrimps Marinara; Dickory and Donald Dock; Garson-Noserag—seem bizarrely out of place with such violent episodes as murders, kidnappings, and attempted suicide. The central concern of the book seems to be the relationship of illusion and reality. It seems a convoluted and hurtful way to say that things are seldom what they seem.

Rayson, Steven. *The Crows of War.* New York: Atheneum, 1974. 269 pp. Reading Level: MA
Disability: Visual Impairment; also emotional dysfunction

The Romans are invading Britain and the leaders of neighboring tribes have been called to join in a common defense. Beothainn answers the summons and brings not only a fighting force but also his daughter, Airmid, who, although shy and fearful, has prophetic powers. The place of defense is a seemingly impregnable fort known as Mai-dun. The Romans deploy a contingent to attack the fort and are met by a huge army of defenders. The invaders' assault was only a decoy, and the Britons are caught in a terrible trap in which Airmid's father and brother are killed and her intended future husband, Beon, appears mortally wounded. The Romans attack the fort again that night and the defenders are caught offguard. The battle plan is methodical, the Romans invincible, and the fort soon overrun. In the melee, Airmid is brutally slashed with a sword and blinded in one eye. The commander of the legion had prohibited wanton slaughter, and when evidence of the murder of women and children is found, a recruit is charged with insubordination. With Airmid testifying against him, he is found guilty and is crucified. Vertullus, the culprit's protector, is enraged and vows vengeance. He has Airmid kidnapped and puts out her remaining eye.

The Romans find amusement in a contest in which blind women, depending on their hearing to locate their opponents, are forced to fight each other armed with heavy staves. Airmid is trained by Vertullus in this barbaric sport and soon becomes subhuman, vicious, and bereft of reason. Discovered by a slave whose life she once saved, Airmid is returned to sanity through the grace of a Celtic goddess. The slave drugs Vertullus' drink and, when he is discovered apparently drunk while on watch, he is executed. Later Airmid discovers that Beon, the man she would have married, has survived his wounds. Now leader of their people, he asks her to be his wife. She refuses, reminding him of the prohibition against a chief marrying a physically imperfect woman. Beon reluctantly acknowledges her statement and Airmid leaves to live at the sacred grounds of the goddess who saved her. There she learns she has only been a pawn in the struggle between good and evil. But she is promised further knowledge of this and of other great cosmic mysteries.

Analysis. Several mythic themes are echoed in this complex, compelling work of historical fiction. Airmid is preordained to live out a destiny she is powerless to direct. Reminiscent of the Norse god Odin, her suffering is both payment and price: Blindness is simultaneously anathema to an association with leadership; nevertheless it is an incident that eventuates in her role as peacemaker. Endowed with a slight gift of foresight, by journey's end she is promised "A glimpse to the future, but of a time hence so distant that you could not conceive its form." The historical conceit of the blind seer is recapitulated in this story. The crucifixion, the act of blinding Airmid, and the terrible, sadistic contest, while not capitalized on for sensational effect, are described in sufficient detail to produce vivid repugnant images. The violence herein is pandemic, not simply directed at the disabled. The deliberate exploitation of the disabled for entertainment purposes is a devastating concept, which nonetheless has historical validity.

Renick, Marion. *Five Points for Hockey*. Illus. by Charles Robinson. New York: Scribners, 1973. 132 pp. Reading Level: MC
Disability: Visual Impairment

More than anything else, Stan Maxted wants to play on the local hockey team. All the regular players have been chosen, but Stan is excluded from even being an extra because of his notorious unreliability. The coach says that Stan will not be considered until he proves he is responsible. Stan hypothesizes that obtaining a strong recommendation from the local 4-H Club would suffice. One project, raising a puppy until it is old enough to be trained as a pilot dog, would give him many points toward that endorsement. Reluctantly and with misgivings, the program director gives the boy a puppy. Improving only moderately, Stan often forgets to feed or water the animal. One day Stan's hero, Bill Bell, shows up at the local coliseum where the team practices. Bell was blinded in an automobile accident and Stan envisions the possibility of his pup being the guide dog for the ex-hockey player. There is no refreshment stand in the coliseum and Bell is persuaded that he would be the ideal person to run one once he has a pilot dog. Stan finally demonstrates sufficient reliability to be allowed to practice with the team, although it is clear that no miraculous transformation has taken place.

Analysis. Extensive descriptions of hockey action should appeal to young sports fans. The presentation of the blind ex-hockey player is all positive, showing no vestige of deep bitterness or hostility over his sudden loss of sight. His vocational goal, although hackneyed, is appropriate and plausible. The formula plot is enlivened by the presence of the interesting, but obnoxious, central character who undergoes a slight, and hence believable, transformation by the book's end. There is substantive worthwhile information on pilot dogs. The dialogue is stilted and unlikely, especially when the boys express some of the prissier values of adults. The disabled character's role of inspiring the ne'er-do-well hero is somewhat of a literary cliché, but the pictorial treatment of the blind man and the relationships he has with other characters are presented in a straightforward and uncomplicated manner.

> Reynolds, Marjorie. *A Horse Called Mystery*. Illus. by Wesley Dennis. New York: Harper, 1964. 205 pp. Reading Level: MC
> *Disability:* Orthopedic Impairment, Cosmetic Impairment, Auditory Impairment, Speech Impairment

A lame boy, Owlie, so named because of his glasses, lives with his mother, who is deaf and mute, and his father, who is the caretaker on Dr. Delafield's estate. The physician has rented his island property to someone who seeks total privacy and instructs Owlie's father to supply provisions as requested but not to allow any breach of the desired seclusion. The boy has been saving money to purchase a bicycle, but when he discovers that the owner of a lame horse plans to sell the animal, Owlie impetuously buys it, naming his new pet Mystery. He foolishly takes a boat out in rough weather and, when it capsizes, he is knocked unconscious but is dragged to safety on the island by his dog. The boy awakens to discover not a tenant but Dr. Delafield himself ministering to his injuries. Disfiguring facial burns have led the physician to live as a recluse. Owlie promises to keep the doctor's secret, but when his mother is hurt, he successfully pleads for medical assistance and the physician and the boy ride Mystery back to the mainland. The horse trader now sees what a fine animal Mystery has become and insists it be returned, unscrupulously blaming Owlie for the horse's former injury. The boy who really was responsible for laming Mystery becomes ill from food poisoning. Once more the doctor responds to Owlie's entreaties for medical help, managing to get a confession from the sick boy, which exonerates Owlie. The townspeople, forewarned about Dr. Delafield's sensitivity to his scarring, appeal to him to return to his practice and he gratefully consents. Owlie's right of ownership of Mystery is confirmed, and for the first time the boy has some friends.

Analysis. The characterizations in this fast-moving but simple novel are all extreme. Every disabled character is shown in positive terms: The doctor is heroic and committed to his profession; the mother is considerate and kind; Owlie is brave, assertive, and tenacious. Owlie is more the victim of exploitation and exclusion than intended abuse. "From long experience he had learned that if you are short for your age, have a limp, and wear big round glasses that are always slipping," you have few social assets. Nevertheless by book's end, he has exemplified the author's theme expressed by the doctor: "Sometimes handicaps spur people on to greater efforts in the fields where they *can* succeed. In fact handicaps have made people great. It's what is inside people that counts. Not the outside."

The author uses certain formulas—the similarly handicapped animal, the disabled helping each other, the physically disabled needing to earn acceptance through physical accomplishments—but also shows Owlie's mother, a seriously impaired woman, functioning naturally and undramatically. The doctor's self-mockery—"Maybe now that I've got a face that would scare patients into a relapse, I'll be forced to become a sculptor or a steeplejack"—reveals the extent of his distress and seems to cancel the author's pious assertion about the maturational power of impairments. The conclusion is excessively neat, nevertheless it is a warm, engaging tale of adventure. The illustrations are attractive, but, except for Owlie's glasses, avoid picturing any of the impairments clearly.

Reynolds, Pamela. *A Different Kind of Sister.* New York: Lothrop, Lee, and Shepard, 1968. 192 pp. Reading Level: YA
Disability: Intellectual Impairment; also cosmetic impairment, orthopedic impairment

Sally Barnes, newly moved to rural Connecticut, wonders about her upcoming reunion with her eighteen-year-old sister, Debbie, who will be arriving home from a residential school for the retarded. Although Debbie is received warmly by her parents, Sally is ambivalent, afraid that Debbie might embarrass her. Sally is overawed by some of the snobbish girls she meets at the stable where her horse is boarded and is ashamed when the clique sees her there with Debbie. One of the girls calls Debbie "crazy," implying it is a family trait, and Sally angrily rebukes her. Later, when Sally becomes ill, she worries about not being able to exercise her horse. Frustrated by her enforced confinement and the unsettling fight she had at the stable, Sally displaces her anger onto Debbie, who, confused and perplexed, runs away. Debbie is finally found at the stable with Neely, who has a "bowed back" and a face that "had been smashed in by a horse." Sally regrets her unkind and intemperate remarks to her sister, and when Neely provides Debbie with a saddle and a safe and gentle horse, she is delighted. One of the girls has whipped Sally's horse in an attempt to unnerve the animal and eliminate it as a challenge in an upcoming competition. Neely tells her not to despair, that the horse may yet calm down enough to perform well. Sally realizes that Debbie is not the cause of the rejection she has experienced, but rather her riding talent has made her the object of the other girls' jealousy. As they line up for a special jumping competition, Sally sees the girl who injured her horse uneasily waiting her turn, fearful that Sally may win. At the conclusion of the story, the reader is uncertain whether Sally is going to gain the trophy, but feels that she has won back her self-respect and has discovered how to accommodate her own needs without sacrificing her sister's.

Analysis. Although the writing itself is not impressive, Reynolds has done an excellent job in exploring the dimensions of a real problem: The conflicts of loving a sibling but feeling trapped by social pressures about conformity and acceptability. The interpretation of the sisters' worlds—where they overlap and where they diverge—provides some useful insight. Debbie is portrayed as a girl who has serious intellectual deficits, but who is also capable of achievements, which, though modest, provide genuine pleasure. She has the same needs for acceptance and approval as anyone else, but when hurt or rejected, has fewer resources to assuage adequately the pain she feels. The varied reactions of different characters, from the overprotective mother to the understanding Neely, are convincing. However, one handicapped person helping another is an overworked plot contrivance, in this instance intensified by the suggestion that a victim of violence will inevitably be very sensitive toward another person's suffering.

Rich, Louise Dickinson. *Three of a Kind*. Illus. by William M. Hutchinson. New York: Watts, 1970. 151 pp. Reading Level: MC
Disability: Emotional Dysfunction

Eleven-year-old Sally, a ward of the state, has been placed with foster parents who live on an island off the Maine coast. Benjie, the grandson of these islanders, is excessively withdrawn, autisticlike in his lack of response to people or things. Distressed at plans to send him to a residential school, his grandparents take him into their home. Sally is at first jealous, but soon decides she and the boy are alike, both outcasts in a sense, and she feels she may be able to help relate to the boy. Initially, he displays no signs of contact at all, but soon Sally notices some slight nonverbal indications of awareness. Benjie is given an unwanted kitten named Reject by a man who considers the boy "backward." Benjie gets lost one day, and when found, begins to speak, explaining that he had been searching for his kitten. This event marks a breakthrough and Benjie at last seems headed toward other normal experiences.

Analysis. The "three of a kind" of the title are Sally, a homeless child; Benjie, a totally withdrawn little boy; and Reject, "the ugliest cat in Maine." The author's message, voiced by Sally, is that even though the trio is a "fine bunch of no-bargains," they can be mutually supportive. The positive benefits of being loved and having someone or something to love are endorsed in this gentle, compassionate book. Unfortunately, the characterizations lack credibility. Sally, a child who has never experienced security in her short life, adjusts marvelously to the intrusion of a child who has a stronger claim to the love of the first people ever to accept her unhesitatingly. Benjie is shown as a nature child who "looks like he's got a real way with critters." Another formula employed is the "cure" of one outcast by another. The rehabilitation of Benjie is so sudden and so complete as to seem miraculous. This astonishing change appears to proceed steadily uphill, with no backsliding and few plateaus. As an affirmation of the power of love and patience, it is a success; as an accurate portrait of a child recovering from severe maladaptive behavior, it misinterprets reality. The illustrations are a delight, nicely complementing the theme of the novel.

Richard, Adrienne. *Wings.* Boston: Little, Brown, 1974. 209 pp.
Reading Level: YA
Disability: Orthopedic Impairment

A school year in the life of young Pip provides her with encounters with a variety of unconventional characters, including Harold, a bright but friendless newcomer to Pip's class. Harold, pale and withdrawn, has two fingers missing to which the teacher responds with excessive protectiveness. The story revolves around Pip's Walter Mitty-like dreams of being an aviator, her Saturday matinee excursions to the local movies, her mother's flock of unorthodox friends, and the poultry-raising class project. Disgusted with her assignment of cleaning out the chicken coop, Pip boldly tempts Harold through a bribe of friendship to take over this odious chore. Excited by the possibilities of being rescued from his lonely condition, he eagerly agrees, motivated by the hope of social acceptance and the opportunity to perform physical labor from which the teacher unwisely has excluded him. From this first manipulative act, a real friendship grows. Harold contracts polio, and his all-too-real enforced passivity contrasts dramatically with Pip's dreams of thrills and freedom.

Analysis. Pip comes to understand how developing social concern and helping others are enlightening and liberating processes. Although Harold's characterization lacks the dimensionality of Pip's, nevertheless he plays a pivotal role in the movement in the story. This sensitive, gentle, and often funny evocation of the 1920s concentrates more on characterization than event. The author's skillful re-creation of the speech, attitudes, and perceptions in a time of relative innocence subtly relays the message: "We are more than we seem."

Rinaldo, C. L. *Dark Dreams.* New York: Harper, 1974. 154 pp. Reading Level: YA/MA
Disability: Intellectual Impairment; also general health problems

When twelve-year-old Carlo's father goes to war in 1943, Carlo moves in with his grandmother, a gloomy, fatalistic, protective Italian woman. His rheumatic fever, originally misdiagnosed as flu, has left him with an affected heart and a weak physical condition. Carlo is apprehensive about playing with a gang of toughs, who become contemptuous when he can't keep up with them, and, making him a butt of their game, they rope his ankles together and drag him. Carlo is rescued by a man and his dog but is nervous about accepting his invitation to visit a "castle." The boy recalls his grandmother's ominous warnings about strange men, but a local merchant tells Carlo that the man, Joey, is brain-damaged and likens him to a friendly child of six or seven. They play in Joey's castle, a deserted brewery, but their harmless games are interrupted by the gang who taunt Carlo, allegedly for being a homosexual, and inform his grandmother. Alarmed, she calls the police who take Joey to an institution. When Carlo visits Joey, he already seems changed, connecting less with what is said to him. Joey escapes and an appeal is made to the director of the hospital to let Joey remain at home with his mother. The man agrees but warns that Joey is capable of violence. The neighborhood boys continue to threaten Carlo and one actually pulls a knife on him. Joey angrily pulls the attacker off, breaking his arm in the process. Despite explanations, Joey is locked up again, since he has proven that he is dangerous. Joey becomes very lethargic and withdrawn and dies surrounded by his few friends.

Analysis. Dark Dreams is a superb book, heavily symbolic. The architecture of the book is particularly impressive. Parallels are developed between Carlo's persecution by a young mob and Joey's by an older society. Both retreat to darkness under stress—Carlo by fainting and Joey by hiding in his brewery haven. Both the impaired man and boy have the label of homosexuality, another pejorative that gives license for acts of aggression. The horror of calling the victim the aggressor is pointedly made as the underside of social protocol is revealed. Joey is loyal, gentle, and fierce but too innocent to cope with the casual misperceptions of the easily deceived, uninformed crowd. The effects of incarceration rapidly damage Joey's sense of freedom and integrity, and his death seems a welcome relief. Rinaldo's sense of setting and language is powerfully expressed and some images are exquisitely wrought. Although the tone of the book is often chilling, the humanity of Joey's portrayal contrasted with the victimization of those who are different is brilliantly presented.

Rinkoff, Barbara. *The Watchers.* New York: Knopf, 1972. 130 pp.
Reading Level: MC/YA
Disability: Neurological Impairment

Chris' home is torn by his parents' dissension over money matters. He often withdraws from the bickering and indeed from direct participation with his peers. Instead, he prefers watching people and hypothesizing about their lives. However, he is not a passive boy, and when Sanford, a new boy in his apartment building, is teased, Chris intervenes. Sandy is grateful, and as their friendship intensifies, Chris is increasingly astonished at the innocence and naivete of the younger boy. Sandy reveals he attended a special school before he moved, a rural center containing children with highly heterogeneous needs. Chris' mother warns him about associating with the newcomer, who is, she asserts: "queer, or retarded or something." Later, after Sandy gives him a telescope so they can watch people with it, Chris, surprised at the gift, finds pleasure and relaxation in being friendly with him. When Sandy attempts to use the instrument, "He was all thumbs, real clumsy, but is was more than that. He couldn't help being that way. That was part of what was wrong with him. Without saying a word he put the scope in his pocket." Chris tries to divert the embarrassed boy and they talk while Sandy envies his skill at repairing an ironing cord. He confesses that his parents never allow him to do such things, so Chris generously teaches him: "I put the knife in his hand and showed him what to do. His fingers twitched and his head jerked but he kept at it like it was a matter of life and death." Since this works well, Chris, warming up to his teaching role, helps him in reading and in physical activities. This resultant happiness is counterbalanced by his impulsive thievery, the increased tension in his own house, and the problems he has created for Sandy by purchasing a loud shirt that the boy admired, an explosive contrast to the neutral, nondescript clothes his parents provide for him. Sandy is angry at the punishment that is inflicted for accepting this gift, and assertively plays hookey with Chris. They have a pleasant day in the park but are faced with frantic parents when they get home late. When Chris explains that now Sandy can row, go on subways, and do common independent acts, his father is surprised and belatedly impressed with his son's potential. Subsequently, Chris' parents separate, but the boy derives some measure of comfort from his relationship with his new friend.

Analysis. It is not clear what the precise nature of Sandy's problem is, particularly because of the childlike perceptions of Chris, the narrator. One possibility is mild cerebral palsy. What is obvious is the quality of language, the sense of immediacy and honesty in the dialogue, and the vividness of the events. Sandy has been put into a double bind—he is incredibly overprotected at the same time that his parents are disappointed at his lack of achievement. There are flaws, for example, the incomplete characterization of the parents, especially Sandy's father, and the unsatisfying information about Sandy's former school. Moreover, the author leans on an old cliché about a loner helping a loner. Nevertheless, the main story line involving the maturation of a lonely disabled boy by exposure to new experiences with an affectionate, patient companion is beautifully executed.

Robertson, Keith. *Ice to India.* Illus. by Jack Weaver. New York: Viking, 1955. 224 pp. Reading Level: YA
Disability: Orthopedic Impairment, Cosmetic Impairment

A profitable voyage is vitally necessary so that Captain John Mason can recoup his lost fortune. Hooker Hance comes aboard, asking to be a member of the crew. His badly damaged face and hook in place of a left hand are no hindrance to the hard physical labor the job requires. Undecided about which cargo to carry, the owner's son agrees to Hance's surprising suggestion that taking ice packed in sawdust to India would be lucrative. Several agents who are in the pay of Mason's enemy, Traskill, also sign on and wreak havoc aboard. After the captain's leg is broken under suspicious circumstances, the sextant stolen, the log tampered with, the crew lied to, and the course of the ship changed, the new captain, Mason's father, is locked in his cabin and kept incommunicado. Hance hatches a scheme to foil this nefarious plot and uses his hook as an effective weapon in the subsequent melee. A confession is made implicating Traskill, but he is killed, presumably by one of his own men, before he can be brought to justice. The ice is delivered and the Masons avoid bankruptcy.

Analysis. Robertson has written a good, old-fashioned, rousing adventure story using a man with a prosthesis and disfigurement in a strong secondary role. Hance is the idea man and facilitator of the action. When the going gets rough, he is fierce but usually is shown as honest, hard-working, ingenious, and loyal. Hooker is portrayed on the book's cover with his upraised arm, signaling an exciting book of maritime derring-do.

Robinson, Veronica. *David in Silence.* Illus. by Victor Ambrus. Philadelphia: Lippincott, 1966. 126 pp. Reading Level: MC/YA
Disability: Auditory Impairment

Eric and his younger brother, David, who is deaf, move to a depressing industrial area near Birmingham, England. David is unable to make any friends except Michael, who tries to learn to communicate through finger spelling and mime. David's hobby is making constructions out of matchsticks and, although generally rejected, for this he is admired. Misunderstanding the shouts of some boys playing cricket, he unwittingly agitates them to team up against him. They chase him away, and in his haste and confusion he flees through a dark, perilous tunnel, takes a bus, gets lost, and finds that no one can understand his irregular speech when he asks for help. Luckily, Michael spots him and rescues his friend from the frightening situation. When David sees the raft the boys have constructed, his practiced eye tells him the craft is not balanced, but his explanation of the problem is discounted. However, when Eric interprets his analysis to the boys, they see that David is correct and plan to change the construction of the raft so it will be seaworthy. When Eric fights with a bully who abuses David, the roughneck falls onto the raft, which overturns, vindicating the deaf youth's judgment. When the deaf boy is taken onto the rebuilt raft, they all venture into the underground tunnel David had run through in terror. Afraid to continue, they look at him with new respect, since he was brave enough to dare the journey alone. His status with the group is marginally improved and the future looks socially promising.

Analysis. This is a gem of a story—gritty, realistic, and straightforward. Robinson clearly is knowledgeable about the ramifications of deafness. The family posture is admirable. They make sacrifices, but David is in no way made to feel guilty for this. Eric responds with patience to some reactions of his deaf brother, but realistically blows up in anger and frustration at others. The author, with rare skill, gives us many interior perspectives on David's own thoughts and feelings and the reader is treated to incident after incident that plumb the reality of children's puzzlement and curiosity about deafness.

Eileen was frankly curious. Though she had heard of deaf and dumb people, she could not believe that this boy was himself deaf and dumb, for he looked so completely normal. In spite of his curious behavior that morning, his smile was attractive, he looked as if he could be good fun, and she still hoped he was taking them in with a cunning practical joke. . . .

Michael and Eileen walked on either side of him while Paul and Tommy dropped behind to whisper. It had not yet occurred to them that whether they whispered or shouted made no difference, but it would have seemed wrong not to whisper. Michael and Eileen were feeling the same constraint. Eileen started to say something but stopped. If she leaned forward to speak across the boy, he would see and might wonder what she was saying; and if she dropped behind to talk to Michael, he might think they were being unfriendly. She thought of raising her voice so that Michael could hear her without having to get closer, but that too, felt wrong.

So they walked across the grass in silence, and only once did an odd grunt come from the strange boy. Paul nudged Tommy, but did not dare to giggle while Michael and Eileen were so close. Eileen was thankful that none of the other children of the estate were there to overhear. She felt her own cheeks flushing for the queer noise that the boy made.

Although outdated terms are used, for example, "affliction" and "dumb," these are minor flaws when viewed against the mountain of information on speech reading and communication problems. The author's ability to recapture the pain of an encounter blocked by disability and ignorance is excellent. Moreover, her skill in presenting the protagonist as a "normal" boy with problems but with interesting possibilities as a friend is admirable.

Rosevear, Marjorie. *The Secret Cowboy*. New York: Messner, 1955. 155 pp. Reading Level: MC
Disability: General Health Problems

Ten-year-old Cliff, recovering from rheumatic fever, spends the winter with his mother on a ranch in Arizona. He is infatuated with horses and wants to spend all his time at the stables, but his physician and mother insist he spend half of each day in bed. His mother is terribly afraid of horses, but she is finally persuaded by the ranch hands to check with a doctor to obtain permission for Cliff to learn to ride. The doctor deems this suggestion potentially useful in the rehabilitation process, and the boy eventually learns to ride well, even participating in a successful search in the desert for the ranch owner's lost son. When

Cliff's father joins them, he is excited about his son's vastly improved health and his physical growth and maturity and soon arranges for him to return the following winter.

Analysis. Cliff's rheumatic fever is treated as a serious condition requiring rest, and the story correctly suggests that environmental and psychological factors may be valuable in the rehabilitation process. The attitudes conveyed are realistic and straightforward, but no information is given at all about what rheumatic fever is or what treatment complications are. This easy-reading book contains only mildly exciting events, but nevertheless should be favored by horse fans.

Roy, Cal. *The Painter of Miracles.* New York: Farrar, Straus & Giroux, 1974. 132 pp. Reading Level: YA/MA
Disability: Emotional Dysfunction

Maclovio is a sixteen-year-old apprentice coffin maker and wheelwright in a small, impoverished Mexican village. His artistic talents are seen as a gift from God that must be shared with his neighbors. There are revolutionary stirrings among the villagers. During the government reprisals, many people are slaughtered and Maclovio is blinded. His uncle, the village healer, teaches him to use his other senses and takes him from his home to wander across the barren land. After the uncle is killed during a scuffle, a succession of strangers takes over his life, teaching him to beg for a living. Alone at night, he thinks about his short, painful life and imagines only he can see and everyone else is blind. One day a woman who has survived by selling his paintings takes him back to her home to live.

Analysis. This ponderous, brooding story exudes a feeling of compassion for people trapped by abject Mexican poverty. Maclovio is talented, kind, and well meaning, but directionless and unable to control his own destiny. As such, he may symbolize those whose gifts, and therefore whose future, are usurped by impoverishment, or his condition may embody a political statement. The fact that his blindness is hysteric rather than organic (he sees again momentarily) would tend to support such an interpretation. This slow-moving, bleak novel is most successul in conveying a sense of unrelieved poverty and exploitation.

Rydberg, Ernie. *The Dark of the Cave.* Illus. by Carl Kidwell. New York: McKay, 1965. 118 pp. Reading Level: MC
Disability: Visual Impairment

Ronnie hopes that his sight will be restored after his cataracts are removed, an operation scheduled before his tenth birthday. Garth, a black newcomer, and Ronnie become pals, and their many excursions offer opportunities for discussion about mobility training and educational adaptations. When Ronnie totes the injured Garth home on his back after a fall, the local paper prepares photojournalistic coverage until they see Garth. The community hears that the boys, a neighborhood bully, and a pal are missing and conclude they are lost in the cave. Getting together a rescue mission, searchers discover the boys, but are confused about the way out until Ronnie's sure touch of a unique rock establishes the correct direction. After his successful operation, Ronnie comments to his mother that he had been quite aware of Garth's color, but that the fact was irrelevant.

Analysis. This heavy-handed but positive treatment of the blind stirs memories of similar fictional efforts of the 1940s. The information on the Braille Code, adapted calendars, and talking books is extensive, and Ronnie is accurately presented making use of other senses as he functions. The brotherhood message is strongly but naively presented and the need for mutual cooperation overtly depicted. Certain assumptions are farfetched, including a scene where a nine-year-old boy is described as preferring to sit home listening to religious records rather than playing outside with a friend, or knowing the aeronautical design needed to cut wind resistance, yet unfamiliar with the word "fuselage." The neutral and simple illustrations aptly harmonize with the story.

Sachs, Marilyn. *Amy and Laura.* Illus. by Tracy Sugarman. Garden City, N.Y.: Doubleday, 1966. 188 pp. Reading Level: MC
Disability: Orthopedic Impairment

Amy and Laura await their mother's homecoming eagerly. Their aunt has been caring for them during the year that their mother was in the hospital recovering from her accident. They are shocked by their mother's appearance and her lack of responsiveness to their needs. The father compounds the problem by warning them not to upset their mother and by becoming furious when they disobey. A distinct barrier grows between the woman and her daughters and, as they behave artificially and react to her fears, their relationship erodes even further. The tension spreads and contaminates the relationship between the two sisters. One day they fight and the mother intervenes. It is the end of her role as passive bystander and she vows to stop being waited on like an invalid. The family unit starts the healing process and begins the return to its former status.

Analysis. Sachs deals with a relatively untouched problem: How does the family respond to the dislocations caused by an invalid whose image is diminished by such realities as the effect of pain, unpleasant medicine smells, passivity, and apparent uninterest? The author does a sensitive job in portraying the mother as a stranger in her own home.

The family dynamics involved in searching for homeostasis are well-described. Some scenes are not entirely plausible, such as a middle-class eighth-grader not knowing how to ride a bike. Much of the conversation between the girls is banal and the story seems childish. A slow-moving story, the book's major asset is its capacity to explore on an easy, comprehensible level the aftereffects of hospitalization.

Sachs, Marilyn. *The Bears' House.* Illus. by Louis Glanzman. Garden City, N.Y.: Doubleday, 1971. 81 pp. Reading Level: MC
Disability: Emotional Dysfunction

Fran Ellen and her four siblings try to cope with an absent father and an emotionally disturbed mother who has collapsed into a chronic crying, withdrawn state and is unable to care for the new baby. Afraid that their mother will be committed to a mental hospital and that they will be separated and sent to different foster homes, the children devise elaborate plans for concealment of her condition and for the allocation of her responsibilities. Fran Ellen is dirty, abused, friendless, and passive in school except when she immerses herself in fantasy play with a toy bears' house belonging to her teacher. In that tiny ordered setting, she finds the family she always wanted, where life is calm and manageable and everyone is bursting with admiration and love for her. The children have clearly undertaken more than they can cope with, and when the girl's teacher makes a home call, she is shocked by the consequences of the mother's behavior. The teacher now watches Fran Ellen carefully, and no longer allows students to victimize her. In an attempt to divert attention from her home, Fran Ellen does so well in school that she is awarded the bears' house as the student making the most progress. When the teacher brings the structure home, she sees that the situation is completely out of hand and determines to intervene. Fran Ellen seeks comfort and relief in her imaginary sanctuary where the father bear consoles her, telling her she did the right thing.

Analysis. In this beautifully written exploration of the manifestation and aftermath of stress, Sachs reveals the mother's relentless movement from trauma to withdrawal and the echo in her daughter's behavior. Fran Ellen's considerable strengths and the teacher's timely intervention will provide relief for the troubled child. It is clear that the mother is severely disturbed; however as a character she is not really known—her presentation is wraithlike and separate. The illustrations beautifully support this portrayal; she has literally turned her back on her family. Yet, they are a tough and loving brood who attempt to protect her and survive themselves. The devastation wrought when a single family head succumbs is feelingly developed and she is seen as victim, not ogre. Although Fran Ellen fantasizes excessively for a nine-year-old, she clearly has enough control and resources to manage stress and to choose a path different from her mother's.

>   Saint-Marcoux, Jany. *The Light*. Trans. by Frances Frenaye. New York: Vanguard, 1958. 158 pp. Reading Level: YA
>   *Disability:* Visual Impairment; also orthopedic impairment, auditory impairment

Miré, a young Basque orphan, is blinded when a smuggler, escaping the customs officials, pushes her roughly aside, injuring her. The lawbreaker, Luis Miguel, finds her wandering in the mountains a few days later. She tells him she plans to kill herself, and he learns for the first time the extent of the harm he caused. Conscience-stricken, he begs permission from her guardians, including her one-legged grandfather, to take her to his home where he and his mother will oversee her future. He gives up smuggling and begins a search for meaning in life. Everywhere he goes, Luis Miguel encounters a virtual blizzard of blind individuals. Visiting the local wise man, he discovers a blind lamb and realizes he is in the grip of immutable fate. The hermit advises the distraught young man to blindfold himself for three days during which time he shall surely be enlightened. When Luis goes walking with his dog, he is run over by a skier, who miraculously happens to be a famous eye surgeon. The doctor invites Luis to observe him performing a corneal transplant. The operation is a success and when the bandages are removed, the patient, trembling with excitement, points to Luis and exclaims, "Don't I see a doctor . . . a doctor there?" The die is cast and Luis embarks on studies that will lead to a great career in curing blindness. Meanwhile, Miré has grown into an attractive, cultured, socially responsible young lady. One day she encounters a deaf-blind child cruelly confined in a chicken coop and presumed "insane" by her mother. She takes the child home and enlists her dog's aid in instructing and civilizing the girl. Luis finds a school for deaf-blind children run by nuns, who take the child to their hearts. In the meantime, Luis is developing a revolutionary surgical technique and Miré generously insists that he test it on her. She claims restoration of her sight is immaterial to her, since "I often think how lucky I am that I cannot see." She expresses her gratitude for all he has done and begs: "Since you will have given me everything, please let me give you the one thing I can offer you—my eyes." The operation is a success and Miré recovers her sight in time to select a wedding dress.

Analysis. Coincidence is carried to unbelievable lengths in this heavy-handed effort. Some information is blatantly incorrect, for example, one does not use "exaggerated facial contortions" to teach deaf mutes. Pitiful, clumsy attitudes suffuse the story: "Has the sight of all those little mutes made you lose your tongue, too?" However, some few good models are presented, and there is some accurate information on eye banks, corneal transplants, and so on. But the maudlin treatment of the disabled characters, the ponderousness of the story line, and the awkwardness of the dialogue preclude much interest in this melodrama.

Savitz, Harriet May. *Fly, Wheels, Fly!* New York: Day, 1970. 90 pp.
Reading Level: MC/YA
Disability: Orthopedic Impairment

Joe Johnson coaches physically disabled youngsters for the Paralympics. He visits Chuck, a senior in high school, whose recent fall down a stairwell left him invalided and bitter. Joe tries to enlist Chuck's mother in encouraging her son to participate in athletics despite his injuries, but the woman has not adjusted to Chuck's new status and therefore is psychologically immobilized. At the request of the team doctor, Joe visits Jeff, an eleven-year-old boy with paraplegia, similarly depressed and resistant. Joe wins over both boys, and their increasing prowess in physical activities begins to alter dramatically their attitudes about themselves. Financial troubles plague the team, so the members must become involved in various schemes to raise money. A neighborhood block party is successful and the team is able to go to New York for the big competition. Jeff takes a first prize and Chuck a second, thereby making themselves eligible for the international games.

Analysis. Considerable information is presented in this novel about wheelchair sports, architectural barriers, and community indifference. Particularly effective are those scenes that convey the psychological pain that an unresponsive society causes the disabled. Unfortunately, the absence of subtlety makes the book and its messages, however commendable, more a sermon than a story. The plot is completely predictable, as are the characters.

Savitz, Harriet May. *The Lionhearted.* New York: Day, 1975. 149 pp.
Reading Level: YA
Disability: Orthopedic Impairment

Thrown from a motorcycle, Rennie Jackson's injuries permanently consign her to a wheelchair. At the rehabilitation center she learns how to be self-sufficient despite her impairment and makes friends with an otherwise friendless, talented, obese girl who "sang for herself, for all those watching her, who spent their lives on the outer fringe." Rennie is attracted to a young man at the high school she now attends. They meet as she is wheeling herself to school and Lee soon becomes her boyfriend. Rennie's mother has been urging her to walk and Lee adds his voice to this plea. Rennie does practice walking in her braces, but it is a painful ordeal for her. Her girl friend, admiring such determination and willpower, decides to stop overeating. At her New Year's party, Rennie shows Lee that she is able to walk in her braces. Sadly she realizes that he needs her out of the wheelchair because he is ashamed of her in it. She confronts him with this observation and he acknowledges its truth. They break up, but Lee soon realizes he cannot manage without her and they start a relationship anew on a more mature and honest basis.

Analysis. Although the plot, characterizations, and style are banal, *The Lionhearted* illuminates some aspects of disability that are significant but generally overlooked, that is, that behavior that most nearly simulates unimpaired functioning may not be the best for a particular disabled person. In other words, for some people like Rennie, a wheelchair is a better accommodation than walking with braces or crutches and the decision of which to use cannot be based on the needs or assumptions of others. The portrayal of the kinds of pressures to which Rennie is subjected is plausible. Problems of dating and of sexual relations are real, albeit clumsily presented. Additionally there is some realistic exploration of the problems and processes of rehabilitation and of surviving in a world in which architectural barriers are commonplace. The author has much insight to share, but deliberate inflation of the emotional tone, such as the trite description of the obese friend and the use of the disabled character as the noble model to change someone's life, reduces the credibility of the plot and thus the potency of the message.

Savitz, Harriet May. *On the Move.* New York: Day, 1973. 142 pp.
Reading Level: YA
Disability: Orthopedic Impairment

Since her recovery from polio, Carrie Dennis has been confined to a wheelchair. Her life is very circumscribed; she rarely leaves her house and her social contacts are restricted to her family. Her sister sees a wheelchair basketball game and notes that others, even more severely impaired than Carrie, seem to lead full, satisfying lives. The team coach is seeking support for his proposed comprehensive service center for the handicapped, which would include rehabilitative, athletic, social, and recreational facilities, and even temporary housing for athletes. When one of the team members receives notice that he must vacate his rooms, he encounters both racial bias and architectural barriers that interfere with locating affordable accommodations. Carrie becomes involved in this and similar crises in the lives of the team members and is inspired to reevaluate her own dependent patterns. She soon moves out of her sheltered environment into an apartment, learns to drive, and begins the difficult process of rebuilding her life. Despite the merit of the proposed center, the city council rejects it. But when a councilman's son, paralyzed in an accident, dies of his injuries, the coach's proposal is prepared for implementation and the center is designated as a memorial to the dead boy.

Analysis. The book is a compendium of information about the day-to-day functioning of orthopedically disabled young adults. The specifics of wheelchair maintenance and management, self-help skill development, environmental adaptations, and feasible social options are extensively explored. The restricting consequences of an overprotective family are illustrated through Carrie's struggle for independence. Community callousness—either deliberate, as in the lack of support of the proposed center, or inadvertent, as in the unavailability of usable housing—is effectively shown. Unfortunately, characterizations are weak, dialogue stilted, and incidents, rather than developing naturally, are marshalled to clear the way for neat solutions.

Sawyer, Ruth. *Old Con and Patrick.* Illus. by Cathal O'Toole. New York: Viking, 1946. 138 pp. Reading Level: MC
Disability: Orthopedic Impairment

Young Patrick Boyle is recovering from polio. His grandfather, known as Old Con, brings him a dog to cheer him up. Between Old Con's massages and the exercise required in scrambling after the dog, Patrick begins to regain some strength in his legs. Old Con finds a blue jay with an injured leg, which he brings to Patrick to nurse back to health. The blue jay, quite tame, becomes a village attraction. The local boys prevail upon Patrick to umpire their baseball games and his pets become team mascots. The improvement of the injured bird and its integration into community life precisely parallel and anticipate Patrick's own. This social involvement continues as summer comes, and when the boys go swimming, a raft is outfitted for Patrick so he won't be left out. Two younger boys take a canoe into the water and tip it over. Patrick rescues them, an incident he is too modest to mention at home. His inspiring friendship with a local ornithologist provides the impetus for him to submit an article to a magazine for bird fanciers. A letter arrives on the very day his mother has prepared a dinner party for his friends, and when Patrick opens the letter before his guests, the reader is not surprised to find that his article has been awarded first prize and a $50 check is enclosed in payment. He does not take that dramatic moment to throw his crutches away, but with his indomitable spirit, the reader can feel assured that he soon will.

Analysis. There is some brief communication of the isolation that disability imposes, but everyone rallies around so quickly that the fleeting moment of realism vanishes without a trace. Some few ideas are put forward to suggest the ease with which activities can be adapted. Patrick's improbable achievements and his patience, forbearance, and modesty suggest a literary genealogy tracing back to nineteenth-century tales. This is a cheery bit of sentimental fluff with a message: Charity, goodness, and effort inevitably ensure success.

Sherburne, Zoa. *Stranger in the House.* New York: Morrow, 1963. 192 pp. Reading Level: YA
Disability: Emotional Dysfunction

The news that her mother is coming home after years in a psychiatric hospital is upsetting to Kathleen Frazier. She, her younger brother Wimpy, her father, and their housekeeper have developed a comfortable living pattern that has excluded Mrs. Frazier. The housekeeper promises to stay if she is needed, but Kathleen remains uneasy, remembering the trauma of her mother's previous visits. Hoping to keep her free from stress, all but Wimpy treat her as an invalid. By excluding the mother from involvement in daily problems, they inadvertently but effectively exclude her from family membership. Having managed well without her before, they refrain from involving her now. One day, while Kathleen's mother is walking Wimpy's dog, the animal suddenly lunges after a cat and is run over. Soon after, her doctor visits and is distressed to see her regression. He berates the family for their lack of sensitivity and support. Mrs. Frazier disappears after the doctor leaves and the family fears that she may have tried to return to the hospital by herself. When she comes home hours later, she has a new puppy for Wimpy. She had interpreted the doctor's appearance as a prelude to her rehospitalization and she was determined to replace Wimpy's pet before she left. This incident vividly dramatizes to the family that overprotection is basically a rejecting behavior and manifestly deleterious to growth. Kathleen realizes that she had been selfish and punitive in the deliberate exclusion of her mother from participation in or knowledge of her school and social life. Kathleen begins to share confidences with her mother, who reciprocates. The improved relationship augurs well for Mrs. Frazier's ultimate adjustment.

Analysis. The hurtful aspect of local gossip is well presented, and difficulties attendant upon return to normal living after extended institutionalization are simply but effectively portrayed. Although both problems and solutions are unbelievably uncomplicated, the story is effective in introducing some ramifications of such situations and developing empathy for them.

Sherburne, Zoa. *Why Have the Birds Stopped Singing?* New York: Morrow, 1974. 189 pp. Reading Level: YA
Disability: Neurological Impairment

Katie's epileptic seizures have been controlled by medication, so her mother has only moderate concern about her planned bus trip to the northwest coast. Katie, excited about returning to where her ancestors once lived, promises to take her pills and not to overexert herself. Once there, one of her teenage friends points out an old portrait of a girl who looks exactly like Kathy. It contains an inscription that says: "Kathryn, May, 1873. A loving heart but a clouded mind." Compulsively, she searches for this girl's home, but, in her excitement, forgets to eat or take her medication. She falls, hits her head, and apparently has a seizure. When she awakens, she is discovered by a solicitous young man named Robbie who conducts her back to "her" house, believing she is another person. In this other life, she has "spells," which her uncle believes are cause for institutionalization, a move that will allow him to plunder her property with impunity. Robbie helps her escape and they make plans to be married the next day by a ship captain. She becomes agitated, runs after him, and falls. She awakens as Katie back in the hotel with her teacher and classmates. The girl goes to the local cemetery where she finds the headstones of the family she dreamed about, including those of Robbie and Kathryn. When home, Katie questions her mother about an ancestor with Robbie's last name. This jogs her mother's memory of a family heirloom which she gives to Katie who recognizes it as the very ring she wore while living the life of the girl in the portrait.

Analysis. This juvenile gothic presents an accurate if incomplete picture of the symptoms, ramifications, and means of control of epilepsy. The acceptance and accommodations made to the disorder by her contemporary family and friends provide a commendable model. The author's denial that the condition is inheritable while using it as a device to link different generations of family members is self-contradictory. Pacing is good, and the setting and characterizations are standard for this genre.

Shotwell, Louisa R. *Roosevelt Grady*. Illus. by Peter Burchard. Cleveland: World, 1963. 151 pp. Reading Level: MC
Disability: Orthopedic Impairment

Roosevelt Grady's most fervent hope is for his father to work permanently in one place, but this seems an impossible dream for a migrant worker's family. Roosevelt wishes he could go to school but their transient life precludes that aspiration. When he becomes sick, he is taken to a doctor, who notices his younger brother Matthew's foot. The physician abruptly inquires why the leg was not corrected earlier. Mrs. Grady, briefly and with simple dignity, gives a capsule view of what life is like for those who follow the crops. Humbled, he refuses money and explains that rehabilitation of the crippled foot would take at least three months. Roosevelt meets a boy in another picking crew and they have a stormy relationship. The two devise a scheme whereby Mr. Grady will have a fairly steady job and they manage this with the connivance of the mother. They are successful and the future looks promising for Matthew's rehabilitation and for some stability and continuity in Roosevelt's education.

Analysis. Although this migrant family is exceptionally poor, they are rich in their loving feelings for each other. Matthew is a special concern and his needs are a central focus for the family. The father hypothesizes the Promised Land as "a place where no little boy has to walk lame, not even if he's born with a bad foot." Matthew is portrayed as having both negative and positive qualities, and is a minor but balanced character. Much sensitivity is shown in this simple, well-illustrated story of a hardworking, caring, black family.

Shumsky, Lou and Zena Shumsky. *Shutterbug.* Illus. by Vic Donahue. New York: Funk & Wagnalls, 1963. 117 pp. Reading Level: YA
Disability: General Health Problems

Nine months ago Shep had been hospitalized but is now home, still recovering from the aftereffects of rheumatic fever. Sports are off-limits for him and he half-heartedly begins to use a camera, becoming increasingly skilled. With tutoring, he is able to enter high school but finds himself labeled a W. W. (Weak Willie) and is excluded from the company of his former friends, who are immersed almost exclusively in sports discussions. He encounters another isolate who has asthma and is further burdened by corrective lenses as well as his high ability in science, and they become supportive friends. Shep develops his photography talents, winning awards, earning money, and joining the yearbook staff. Having gained some insight into the practice of social segregation in the lunchroom and stung by the prejudice engendered by the letters W. W., Shep convinces some students that such practices should be discouraged.

Analysis. This well-intentioned story operates on a pleasant but superficial level and the reader becomes only casually involved in Shep's problems. Its major usefulness is in the suggestions for practicable hobbies for those with movement restrictions and the descriptions of rheumatic fever with its attendant long recuperation period.

Shura, Mary Francis. *The Nearsighted Knight.* Illus. by Adrienne Adams. New York: Knopf, 1964. 111 pp. Reading Level: MC
Disability: Visual Impairment

Prince Todd hopes someone will carry off Ethelrude, his unreasonable, unmannerly, unsightly, and unwed older sister. One day a likely candidate arrives, the Knight Before Glasses, a name derived from a witch's promise that such an object would be invented one day to cope with the man's serious myopia. Despite, or because of, his poor eyesight, he falls in love with Ethelrude, but the haughty princess decides she will not marry him unless he does some valorous deed. After rejecting such possibilities as ridding the woods of a dragon, a tournament is decided upon. In a preliminary contest, the hero's nearsighted horse is hurt and he is given a spirited steed, which he manages surprisingly well. As the competition nears its climax, an eclipse begins. The Knight Before Glasses, unaware of the darkening sky, keeps on going, but his opponent stops to look up at the event and is unseated. The myopic knight wins the contest and the prize, so to speak, of Ethelrude.

Analysis. In all other mythical, magical lands, it is a literary given that the princess is a beauty or, if not, she is transformed into one somehow during the trials undergone by the persevering hero. The handicapped knight wins more by chance and ignorance than by wit or muscle, and gets unquestionably the least desirable prize in the tradition of this genre. Certainly, this accidental hero does not merit a partner with such disagreeable attributes and to claim it makes no difference since he cannot see her anyway is to diminish him unconscionably. The disability is the uniting device for the story line and it permits the winning of the tournament by default. Thus the knight is seen more as a loser than a hero. Both the illustrations and the dialogue are witty and amusing, but much of the situational humor derives from the hero's impairment, a literary tactic of questionable taste. The author has sabotaged what appears to be the story's intent in her unusual postscript: "the charms of unique lives lie sometimes within the limitations of those lives . . . and therein may lie a special appeal." The suggestion that there is something enticing or desirable in those limitations is odious and is a position rarely taken by those who must sustain them.

Smith, Doris Buchanan. *Kelly's Creek.* Illus. by Alan Tiegreen. New York: Crowell, 1975. 71 pp. Reading Level: MC
Disability: Neurological Impairment

Kelly hasn't made any progress in the two months he has been in a special class. The nine-year-old's clumsiness cuts him off from his more athletic friends and, in truth, he has only one—Phillip, a biology student at a local college who is studying the marsh. To punish Kelly, his parents forbid him to visit the creek until he improves in school, a painful restriction, since in that environment he is competent, coordinated, and free of tension. The next day is no better and Kelly seeks the comfort of the marsh and Phillip's companionship. Kelly's parents are concerned about protecting him from the dangers of the marsh, but they are unaware of its meaning to him. His mother sees her son at the creek talking with Phillip, both proscribed acts, and Kelly is told he must never see his friend again. Sent to his room, Kelly finally draws a perfect square for the first time, and this skill is transferred to the school setting the next day. Phillip persuades Kelly's mother to encourage him to share his extensive knowledge about marsh life with his classmates, and after some initial skepticism, the students are greatly impressed. His former friend, Zach, now asks to accompany Kelly to the creek, but loses interest quickly and leaves. In frustration, Kelly dashes across a plank, an unexpected achievement in coordination. Saddened by losing Zach for a friend, Kelly is comforted by the security of the marsh and the belief that Phillip will be able to teach him to read and write.

Analysis. The hauntingly beautiful illustrations are the outstanding feature of this book. The marsh scenes and Kelly's feelings of frustration are well executed. The author projects a portrait of parents trying to cope with a child they don't understand, but the only time Kelly's parents treat him with love is when he achieves—not a very healthy message. In fact, one might get the impression that frustration and punishment are the best motivators, since this is when he achieves most. A further unfortunate impression is conveyed that Kelly's special class concentrates only on perceptual motor activities. Except for Phillip who is steady and constant, sudden reversals of mood and behavior occur frequently, thus providing a cast of shallow and unconvincing characters. However, *Kelly's Creek* does convey the frustrations and self-doubting often experienced by children with learning disabilities.

Smith, Doris Buchanan. *Tough Chauncey.* Illus. by Michael Engle. New York: Morrow, 1974. 222 pp. Reading Level: MC/YA
Disability: Orthopedic Impairment

Chauncey has been toughened by thirteen years of an infantile and self-absorbed mother, a succession of transient father figures, and grandparents who are uncommonly cruel and excessively punitive. He finds himself the presumed culprit at school and in the neighborhood whenever trouble erupts. Although lacking the basics of social savvy, he has one friend, Jack, a tough black boy. In attempting to escape his grandparents' house, Chauncey jumps from a freight train and rips the muscles from one leg. He is furious at having to return and is humiliated and hurt by his guardians. He is desperate to leave, but is unable to contact his mother for help. His sole consolation is a cat, and Chauncey is afraid that his grandfather will shoot it as he did another when Chauncey was younger. He begins his adjustment to the pain and to his crutches preliminary to his preparations for running away from this intolerable situation. Chauncey and Jack are tough, rough-housing competitors, but the black boy proves to be a responsive and knowledgeable companion. Ultimately Jack gives him the moral support he needs to initiate a search for a foster home where he might find love and could drop the "tough" charade. Chauncey cries out as he leaves, "You haven't seen the complete me yet!"

Analysis. Both the psychic and physical pain Chauncey sustains are powerfully communicated. The depth of his deprivation and his inability to make friends or to learn in school all contribute to the reader's understanding, if not approval, of his barely controllable rage. Chauncey's tenderness and humanity are revealed in his staunch, loving protection of the cat, and his insight is especially keen. The physical injury scenes and their aftermath are treated in an explicit manner. The resultant disability is yet another trauma this unflaggingly tenacious boy must fight to overcome. Smith writes movingly of a not always likeable, vulnerable boy who, nevertheless, is determined, feisty, and persevering—an indomitable survivor.

Smith, Gene. *The Hayburners.* Illus. by Ted Lewin. New York: Delacorte, 1974. 64 pp. Reading Level: YA
Disability: Intellectual Impairment

Will gets a poor steer to raise in a 4H drawing, but rapidly loses interest in the project. His responsibility is gladly assumed by Joey, a temporary farmhand who comes from an institution for the retarded. Joey cares for the scrawny animal devotedly and his ministrations revitalize the steer so that it becomes a serious contender in the competition. He embarrasses Will by his partisanship in the contest, and despite their growing closeness, the family is somewhat at a loss in dealing with Joey's directness, his honesty, and his open display of emotion. Everyone but Joey is astonished when the animal wins honorable mention and Joey's efforts are vindicated. This is a Pyrrhic victory since it presages the slaughter of the winner and the return to the lonely institution for Joey where he will ultimately die.

Analysis. The unusual title provides insight into the seemingly simple book; a hayburner is racetrack slang for a loser, and the ironic use of this metaphor provides the central concept. The plot is unconventional as is the portrayal of the main character, a decent, hardworking, generous retarded man. His qualities are contrasted with the character of Will, whose attributes are less admirable. The larger story is about how the weak are treated in society, particularly the abandonment of those who are presumably losers by conventional standards. As equine losers are sent to the glue factory, so those humans whom society has labeled "losers" are similarly disposed of. Below the surface melancholy, the story has an optimistic message: With care and love, even a hayburner can be a winner. Smith has written a most provocative and powerful book about a retarded character and Lewin has beautifully complemented his colleague's efforts. (See Figure 1.)

Smith, Vian. *Martin Rides the Moor*. Illus. by Ray Houlihan. Garden City, N.Y.: Doubleday, 1964. 181 pp. Reading Level: MC/YA
Disability: Auditory Impairment

An accident has deafened Martin Manningham, an eleven-year-old English boy. Fearing he appears foolish and different, he isolates himself from most social interaction, rejecting even Jane, his closest friend. His father brings him a pony but the boy refuses to accept it, disdaining its mongrel ancestry. During a gigantic snowstorm, Martin impulsively sneaks out to rescue the animal. He names it Tuppence, and invests much energy in constructing a stable for it. Martin is pleased with his efforts: "It's the kind of work the deaf can do well," and the pony appears contented with its new home. Because of the storm, trucks cannot reach the barn and the family income from milk is jeopardized. Martin builds a crude sled and Tuppence is able to drag some milk containers to the main road. Supplies are low and, despite the mother's protests, Mr. Manningham sends Martin and Tuppence for essentials. Martin's deafness contributes to a near tragedy on this trip. Adjusting to his new special education school is difficult for Martin, but the teacher cleverly elicits interest in academic performance by exploiting Martin's involvement with his horse.

Analysis. Laced throughout this fast-paced, literate animal story is much useful information about deafness. Martin's self-consciousness, his concern about his inability to monitor his voice, his special education teacher's skills, and his emotional volatility are illuminated with accuracy and sensitivity. The boy's frustration and exhaustion as he makes the effort to speech-read are validly presented, and the recounting of his family's efforts to assist him is especially poignant. Smith's theme is overtly stated as well as symbolically echoed through the destiny of the animal. In a hunting interlude, there is much violence toward animals, which the author staunchly opposes. He readily draws a parallel delineating similar insensitivity to human suffering. The unwanted pony, given care, affection, and opportunity, succeeds; the deaf boy, provided with love, education, and a chance, it is implied, will also be a winner.

Smith, Vian. *Tall and Proud*. Illus. by Don Stivers. Garden City, N.Y.: Doubleday, 1966. 181 pp. Reading Level: MC/YA
Disability: Orthopedic Impairment

Gail's physician insists that she exercise her left leg after polio has rendered it partially paralyzed. Unfortunately this advice is undercut by her mother's coddling. Despairing at his daughter's lack of progress, her father goes into debt to purchase a horse, which he hopes will motivate Gail to be more active. He has been able to buy the animal at a good price since it had pulled a leg and was no longer suited for racing. The horse proves to be a powerful magnet and Gail exerts herself more and more until she is able to ride and care for it. One day an escaped convict breaks into their remote cottage, but Gail is able to sneak out undetected and, with the help of a friend, inform the police. A plan to flush out the criminal is successful and he is recaptured.

Analysis. The exciting and unlikely ending seems appended as a device to demonstrate the heroine's restored ability. The author has used a similarly disabled animal to motivate and inspire the human character's recovery, an overworked and not particularly convincing ploy. The descriptions of Gail's rehabilitative problems are realistic and straightforward, although the overly dramatic illustrations somewhat negate this admirable, restrained approach. The strong, positive message about acceptance of human differences is contradicted by the mockery of the criminal because of his shortness. The book's strongest qualities are its honest treatment of the problems of postpolio rehabilitation and the effects that motivation, determination, and overprotection have on recovery.

Sommerfelt, Aimée. *The Road to Agra.* Illus. by Ulf Aas. New York: Criterion, 1961. 191 pp. Reading Level: MC
Disability: Visual Impairment

Only the lucky few can attend public school in India. Maya, a young Indian girl, has been chosen to be a student, but her failing eyesight jeopardizes this opportunity. Lalu, her thirteen-year-old brother, fervently had hoped she would in turn teach him to read, but this cannot occur if her admission to the school must be forfeited to someone else. Lalu hears of a hospital in the distant city of Agra where doctors are reputedly able to cure blindness. Determined not to lose his one chance to learn, Lalu leads his sister on the arduous walk to Agra. Despite many hardships and dangers, the two children arrive safely. The UNICEF doctors examine Maya and diagnose her condition as glaucoma, but she is denied admission to the overcrowded hospital. Impressed by the resoluteness of the children, some doctors agree to treat her anyway. They also find employment for Lalu while he waits for his sister to recover.

Analysis. Maya is a passive, placid character whose lack of dimensionality detracts from the likelihood of the reader identifying with her.

Little sense of the trauma associated with vision loss, especially when such loss would trap the family forever in poverty, is conveyed. The story is essentially a medium for illustrating and endorsing the work of those United Nations agencies that provide health care for impoverished peoples. As a result, literary concerns take a back seat to humanitarian goals.

Sorensen, Virginia. *Miracles on Maple Hill.* Illus. by Beth and Joe Krush. New York: Harcourt, 1956. 180 pp. Reading Level: MC
Disability: Emotional Dysfunction

Hoping that a return to the leisurely pace of the countryside will restore the emotional control of her husband, Marly's mother convinces her family to visit her childhood home in Maple Hill, Pennsylvania. Since "Daddy" had returned home from the war, he has been tense, irritable, and depressed. Mr. Chris, a neighbor, extends a dinner invitation, and Marly's father grows angry at the prospect of having his solitude interrupted. However, Maple Hill soon works its therapeutic wonders and the transformation of the ill veteran begins. One day Joe, Marly's brother, does not return home, delayed when he finds Harry, an old hermit, injured. A search party rescues them, and Harry spends his convalescence at Maple Hill where he can be taken care of. When Mr. Chris has a heart attack, Marly's whole family pitches in to harvest the maple syrup. The truant officer, instead of disciplining Marly and Joe, good-naturedly arranges for other schoolchildren to participate, giving them the opportunity to learn about the sugaring process too. The crop is saved, Marly's father is better, good deeds have been done, the syrup is excellent, and all's right with the world.

Analysis. The father's hostile withdrawn behavior has apparently been caused by his traumatic experiences in a prisoner-of-war camp in World War II. The proposition put forth in this book that direct daily contact with nature is restorative for such experientially caused emotional disorders is not without some validity. However, the superficial manifestations of emotional distress, the speed of recovery, and the unflinching, selfless support of everyone involved result in a shallow story of little insight.

Southall, Ivan. *Hill's End.* New York: St. Martin's, 1963. 174 pp. Reading Level: MC/YA
Disability: Intellectual Impairment

Adrian has boasted of his discovery of some aboriginal drawings in the mountain caves near the small lumbering community in Australia in which he lives. He is challenged about the truth of his claims, and six children and a teacher decide to climb to the caves in search of artifacts.

Since Adrian had lied about his findings, he is delighted and relieved when the little company actually discovers some drawings as well as some ancient animal bones. Butch, a retarded boy, had stopped along the way to rest. After a cyclone strikes, the teacher becomes terrified that he may have been killed or injured, and in the storm that follows retraces her steps to search for him. She collapses near him and, reversing roles, Butch finds her and protects her from the deluge. The other children discover them, but by now the teacher is seriously ill and all responsibility reverts to the youngsters. They make their way back to the now deserted town, experiencing various harrowing adventures. The children, forced to rely on their own resources, are often in conflict, yet see that they must work together for their common survival. Eventually, contact is made with some fathers who have been searching for them and the children, who once dreamed of a town without parents, are relieved to shift responsibility back to the adults.

Analysis. This excellent adventure story shows the impact of a crisis on the lives of several young people and their teacher. The events both reveal and change character, including that of Butch, whose behavior is complex—brave and frightened, competent and inept. He is shown as a boy who is slow to understand but who contributes as much as he is able. He is valued, plays his role, and makes a contribution to the survival of them all. Butch causes one problem when he remains behind, thereby necessitating a search, and another when he tries to make some sausage from spoiled meat. But he is also seen as courageous and dependable in his efforts to care for the sick teacher and in his attempt to kill an enraged and threatening bull. In all, *Hill's End* presents, through the medium of a tight, gripping, well-developed story, a balanced picture of a mildly retarded boy whose role in his little community is modest but important. Butch is not a central character, yet the picture presented of him is rounded and credible.

Southall, Ivan. *Let the Balloon Go.* Illus. by Ian Ribbons. New York: St. Martin's, 1969. 142 pp. Reading Level: MC
Disability: Neurological Impairment

John, a twelve-year-old cerebral-palsied boy, lives with his parents in Australia. His mother's overprotectiveness has stifled her son, frustrating him and restricting his maturation. He is astonished when one day, yielding to his protests, she permits him to remain home alone while she attends to business in the city. John's daydreams of physical prowess contrast sadly with his uncoordinated movements but, alone at last, he determines to achieve something truly admirable. Sloughing off his mother's nervous advice about limiting his activities, he decides to build a tree house. John trips and falls, but the feeling of weakness

passes and he is convinced he can succeed. In his yard is a gum tree—
perfect for climbing—and he drags a ladder from his father's shed to
launch him on the first stage of his enterprise. His start is shaky but he
persists in his climb to the lower branches of the tree, to higher ones,
and finally to the very top. Exhilarated, John hopes everyone will see
his triumph. Finally, he is spotted but all assume he is in trouble, unable to get down. The constable arrives but gets stuck when he attempts
a rescue. He forbids John to descend, cautioning him to wait for assistance, but John has had enough of suffocating advice. He descends,
freeing the constable's foot on his way down, but, now exhausted, falls
the last few meters. His mother is relieved that he is safe, but his father
understands that nothing can be the same with his son again:

> Ordinary boys and girls get knocks and bruises you've never
> dreamt of. Ordinary people have to live with ordinary treatment,
> and that's not what you're used to. You've been given special treat-
> ment; I doubt if you'll ever know how *special* it has been. But I
> gather you've had your fill of it. You'd prefer the knocks and
> bruises.

With this statement by his father, the goal of John's odyssey has
been achieved: He will at last be allowed to risk the "knocks and
bruises"—a price he is willing to pay for freedom.

Analysis. Although the plot may not appear very engrossing, the
author's expertise in dramatizing the boy's overpowering need to assert
himself and to prove the emptiness of the other children's derogatory
opinions of him is impressive. Equally skillfully, the reader is led to
empathize with John's reactions. Facts about cerebral palsy are insinuated into the story, providing an accurate and moving account of this
disorder:

> Ordinary boys had arms and legs that did the right thing; John's
> arms and legs only sometimes did the right things; and when his
> mum got upset about it, John usually got worse. He would start
> stumbling and dropping things and stammering, and sometimes
> had to beat his thigh with his fist over and over again very hard, to
> get out his words. His heart would pound like a hammer and some-
> times (to his own horror) he would cry.

Speare, Elizabeth George. *The Witch of Blackbird Pond.* Boston:
Houghton Mifflin, 1958. 249 pp. Reading Level: YA
Disability: Orthopedic Impairment

After Kit Tyler's grandfather dies, she leaves her home in Barbados
to live with relatives in Connecticut. Her new family is puritanical, and

the harsh, repressive atmosphere contrasts strongly with her former carefree life. Mercy, Kit's lame younger cousin, is a model of patience and humility who works without complaint, even when desparately sick, and readily accepts her situation. Kit befriends Hannah Tupper, an old Quaker woman widely regarded as a witch. After a devastating illness hits the community, the townspeople hysterically conclude that Hannah Tupper is to blame. Kit rescues the old woman, but is arrested herself on charges of witchcraft. The young sailor who originally delivered Kit to her new home brings a young child to Kit's trial who provides evidence of her innocence. As is typical of such books, all problems are resolved: The child, long abused, is reunited with a now more appreciative family; Hannah is safe from further persecution; all marriageable females, including even Mercy, are betrothed; and Kit and her uncle have accommodated their differences in a flood of mutual respect.

Analysis. Mercy's characterization is simultaneously highly idealized and taken for granted. She is not considered marriageable and her family makes no provision for a dowry for her. Being both female and crippled, her qualities of forbearance, self-effacement, and unassertiveness are thereby multiplied. Where others are shown having a spectrum of personality attributes, Mercy is shown in extremes—it is she who becomes the most ill from the epidemic; it is she who is "good enough" for the minister. The setting of colonial America adds some mild interest to this typical adolescent historical romance.

Spence, Eleanor. *The Nothing Place.* Illus. by Geraldine Spence. New York: Harper & Row, 1972. 228 pp. Reading Level: MC
Disability: Auditory Impairment

Glen has moved with his family to a suburb of Sydney, Australia. He recently has recovered from an illness that left him with a severe hearing loss and is very anxious to conceal this problem. Optimistically hoping that this difficulty will evaporate, his mother decides not to inform his new teachers. Since Glen does not mention it either, inevitably his school experiences are calamitous. Lyndall, a bright, assertive do-gooder, meets him as he is wandering about and immediately deduces that he is deaf. The community is planning a Captain Cook Bi-Centenary Exhibit that will contain numerous displays and activities. Lyndall bulldozes the reluctant neighborhood youngsters into joining her in creating a local display for the celebrations to which they will charge admission. She plans to use the profits to buy Glen a hearing aid, but is careful not to let him know of her benevolent mission since she intuits that he is very sensitive. She is beginning to have serious reservations about her high-handed plot and, although nagged by the possibility that he may be offended, is determined to proceed anyway. Assisted by some contributions from a kindly, generous derelict, the children raise $25 which Lyndall presents to the outraged boy, who sees himself as the object of neighborhood pity. One of Glen's teachers visits his home to speak with his mother about her son's school troubles and learns for the first time of the boy's hearing loss. After Glen overhears them talking about sending him to a special school, he decides to run away. With neither money nor plans, Glen finds himself at the shopping center where he is bitten by a watchdog. A guard and the derelict discover Glen, and after the boy cathartically speaks to them about his distress, he is able to return home. The next day there is a family council at which Glen agrees to consider the special school. Lyndall stops by to make amends and Glen agrees that wearing a hearing aid is probably not that much different from wearing glasses. He understands that her desire to help was an act of friendship, not pity.

Analysis. In this engaging, well-paced story, the problems of adjusting to hearing loss are dealt with in a matter-of-fact way. His impairment diminishes the hero's self-esteem and attempts to conceal it from teachers and friends seem in keeping with his character and immaturity. The obtuseness of his teachers and the insensitivity of his mother are less credible though. Characterizations of the children, particularly that of Lyndall, are good, and the pen and ink illustrations are a pleasant addition to this unusual novel.

Stein, Sara Bonnett. *About Handicaps: An Open Family Book for Parents and Children Together.* New York: Walker, 1974. Photog. by Dick Frank. 47 pp. Reading Level: YC (and adult)
Disability: Neurological Impairment; also orthopedic impairment

Joe has cerebral palsy, but *About Handicaps* is Matthew's story. Matthew is frightened and threatened by Joe's condition and reacts with mimicry, avoidance, and hostility. His mimicry is not mocking; it is an attempt to understand kinesthetically as well as intellectually how it would feel to walk as Joe does. Matthew has an insignificant defect in his little toe, but he worries about whether it could lead to a similar condition. Matthew dresses in the toughest clothes he owns, a futile, pitiful attempt to cloak his vulnerability in the garb of power. His father, understanding the root of Matthew's behavior, sets up an encounter with Mr. Bello, a veteran with an artificial arm. Mr. Bello shares with Matthew not only the information about how his arm prosthesis works but tells him of his initial fears that people would no longer like him after he lost his arm. Weeks of discussion with his father allow Matthew to resolve his anxieties and free him to relate naturally to Joe.

Analysis. About Handicaps is a flawless example of a fictionalized problem book. Two parallel and complementary books are found within one cover: a story for children and an accompanying interpretive text for adults. The message of the adult text is that neither hiding from issues nor resorting to magic is an effective way to deal with problems. Confrontation, buttressed with information and awareness of child development, yields the most promising means for coping with fears. Stein's insight into children's thinking and parents' needs is impressive. The exquisitely sensitive photographs perfectly support the direct, unsentimental text. Concept, content, implementation, and graphic design are all splendid.

Stewart, Agnes Charlotte. *Elizabeth's Tower.* New York: Phillips, 1972. 222 pp. Reading Level: MC/YA
Disability: Orthopedic Impairment

Elizabeth is living with her aunt while her father is away in the army. One day, in the adjacent woods, she encounters a lame stranger, Lawrence Willoughby, who is lost, exhausted, in pain, and desperately in need of a place to rest and spend the night. Impulsively she invites him to stay in her tower, the remains of a former castle that she has remade as her own sanctuary. The stranger insists that Elizabeth inform her guardian of his presence. Still in great agony from his injured leg, Lawrence is astonished by the child's extraordinary competence and sensitivity and the two become fast friends. When she questions him about how he was hurt, he reports that he was a hit-and-run victim and will never have full functioning restored. The pair enjoy a few hours at a fair where Elizabeth observes two men who seem to be watching them. On her next trip to the tower she finds Lawrence missing and is alarmed by signs of a struggle. She follows the traces of two sets of footprints into a forest and eventually to a cabin where Lawrence is imprisoned. In a hairbreadth escape, they elude the kidnappers and return home exhausted, Lawrence having suffered further bodily damage. He has learned that his captors have been working with traitors and are after details of his work in armaments design. He and Elizabeth's uncle reluctantly theorize that it is her father who has cooperated with the spies, although he judiciously avoided disclosing critical information. When the child realizes that her adored father is being blamed, she panics and determines to prove their unspoken accusations false. When her absence is discovered, Lawrence appreciates the danger to the child and rushes in pursuit. Not finding her in the tower, he concludes she may have returned to the cabin. In great distress, he follows her, finds evidence of a struggle, and discovers her in the topmost branches of a tree where she sought refuge from her angry pursuers. She has sprained her arm, is exhausted, and clearly unable to help herself. With super-human effort, he climbs the tree and retrieves the injured child. Eliza-beth, while recovering, is further devastated by an army telegram an-nouncing her father's death. Lawrence has only a few more days before he must leave the tower and complete plans for joining his brother in Australia. Elizabeth, disconsolate, has avoided him, but finally comes to say goodby. Lawrence knows that he has been the instrument of her suf-fering and realizes that this encounter will be crucial to his hopes. Her aunt's family while accepting responsibility for Elizabeth, nonetheless finds her a burden. In a well-crafted scene, Lawrence, who wishes to take over as her guardian, suggests that he could use her assistance and com-panionship on the journey and in Australia and proposes that she ac-company him as his ward. Responding to his sensitivity and to her own need to be helpful and appreciated, she accepts.

Analysis. This gripping story of mystery and intrigue contrasts idyl-lic, pastoral scenes with interludes of tension-filled confrontations. Stewart's literary skill is most apparent in her sensitive development of the admirable, many-faceted heroine. Lawrence's herculean rescue of Elizabeth strains belief, but it is the only flaw in this otherwise master-fully written story.

Stinetorf, Louise A. *A Charm for Paco's Mother.* Illus. by Joseph Es-courido. New York: Day, 1965. 127 pp. Reading Level: MC
Disability: Visual Impairment

Paco's mother sells cacti to tourists passing through Oaxaca, Mexi-co, and, since she has become blind, people are embarrassed to haggle with her. A curious American tourist discusses the curative possi-bilities of an operation, and Paco, in his innocence, asks if operations are like charms. Receiving a partially affirmative answer, Paco decides to pray at a huge stone cross. He departs and is delayed innumerable times by stopping to help solve the problems of a series of people he encounters. He is heartbroken when he discovers that it is after mid-night and too late to pray with the other pilgrims. Disheartened, he returns home where he is startled to discover that his mother's eyes are bandaged. She reports that the inquisitive tourist was an ophthalmolo-gist who requested that she be a volunteer patient. When Paco confesses he did not have time to pray for her recovery, she replies that there is no charm like good and charitable deeds.

Analysis. The story is a simple parable with the message of virtue rewarded. The premise behind the coincidental selection of Paco's mother to be "chosen" is farfetched, but reality is not a prerequisite for such stories. Many will also be offended at the cliché of the Mexican in the opening line description: "Paco curled his back into a little round hump and rested it. . . ." Although there is some valid description of the onset of the loss of eyesight, the passive acceptance of pity in the sales transactions contributes subtly to certain stereotypes of blindness. The loving and concerned relationship between son and mother is probably the story's strongest asset, but the concept of a reward or "cure" for evidence of piety its most unfortunate feature.

Stinetorf, Louise A. *Musa the Shoemaker*. Illus. by Harper Johnson. Philadelphia: Lippincott, 1959. 183 pp. Reading Level: MC
Disability: Orthopedic Impairment

Unable to contribute to the town's coffers as do other males—his lameness precludes being a traveling acrobat—fourteen-year-old Musa is apprenticed to a cobbler. He demonstrates great skill, particularly in designing footwear for the orthopedically disabled. During a family wedding in his North African town, Musa's leg is hurt and a caravan is formed to accompany him to a city hospital for treatment, which they reach after many adventures. The boy tries to enter the hospital to request treatment but, since he has no money, is refused. He has several occasions to display his quick mind, such as protecting a family and himself from a vicious bear, but his most opportune moment arrives when he trips up a thief who has stolen the purse of a princess. His next recollection is waking up in the hospital to discover that the expenses for his operation are being paid in gratitude. Coincidentally, the royal child also has a foot problem and the two patients go to rehabilitation therapy together. Musa's operation is successful in that he can walk again but not to the extent that he can be an acrobat. Musa is critical of the remedial shoe the girl is wearing but the medical staff is unimpressed with his comments. Happily, one physician listens while Musa precisely explains to him the nature of the girl's medical problem and how a corrective shoe should be made. The doctor tells Musa he will help him, should he decide to become a "foot doctor." The shoe designed for the young princess is extraordinarily effective. Musa is invited to live at court and, when ready, is promised his choice of any college in North Africa to fulfill his ambition.

Analysis. The obvious absurdities hardly require belaboring. Musa's understanding of physiology and rehabilitation, his role as a consultant to doctors and therapists, and his outrageous good fortune ask too much from even the most credulous reader.

Stucley, Elizabeth. *The Contrary Orphans*. Illus. by Charles Mozley. New York: Watts, 1961. 192 pp. Reading Level: MC/YA
Disability: Visual Impairment, Speech Impairment, Orthopedic Impairment, Intellectual Impairment

Carlotta lives with her grandmother, known locally as Mrs. Dirty for painfully obvious reasons. When the old woman must be hospitalized, Lotta, whose crossed eyes make her the object of ridicule, is taken to a small institution for homeless children. Independent, quick, and defiant, Lotta is deterred from running away by the retarded cook, Maggie, who "had never even learnt to give change for a shilling, but she was the nicest, kindest person imaginable." Frankie, another newcomer to the home, is shy, withdrawn, and often subject to embarrassment because of his stammer. One of the members of the institutional committee benevolently decides to treat the children to a party at her home. Her own son, Walter, who is invalided in a wheelchair, takes an immediate liking to Frankie and the young orphan stays on as a companion. Walter's tutor informs Frankie that he stammers because: "It's the chip on your shoulder that gets between your lips." With a few lessons in breath control and some exercises, Frankie improves wonderfully. Frankie is packed back to the home when Walter's father returns, since the pain of watching an ablebodied child run about while his own son is immobile is unbearable. Frankie, not unsurprisingly, views this as another instance of rejection, although the boy's social worker insists that he is strong enough to survive this incident. Frankie and Lotta share a surrogate "Auntie," a plain dumpling of a woman who is precisely the kind of accepting, undemanding person Frankie needs. The local handyman, whom Frankie admires, marries the woman. The couple then adopt the no longer hostile boy whose speech impediment has disappeared. Lotta has an operation that vastly improves her appearance. Now pretty enough to be a maid at the local festival, her picture appears in the paper, leading to a reunion with her missing father. Surgery has also restored Walter's ability to walk, leaving only Maggie, the retarded cook, uncured.

Analysis. All problems are solved by love and good fortune in this story. The best characterization is of Maggie, who is a simple, but sensitive and accepting person—yet even she is overdrawn. Lotta's Italian and gypsy ancestry is considered wondrously exotic and a key to her colorful but untamed and impulsive behavior. Frankie was first discovered, it is reported—apparently without intentional humor—abandoned in a phone booth, and his fortunes have proceeded steadily downhill. He stutters when it is literarily convenient that he do so, and recovers almost miraculously from a life of near total emotional deprivation. Walter is a true descendant of Tiny Tim, indomitably cheerful despite his father's rejection. The most prevalent message the characters deliver is that no matter how forlorn one is, there is always someone with worse troubles. The plot is contrived and the tone unflaggingly optimistic.

Sutcliff, Rosemary. *Warrior Scarlet*. New York: Walck, 1958. 207 pp.
Reading Level: YA
Disability: Orthopedic Impairment; also visual impairment

Drem, an adolescent boy with a withered arm who lives in England during the Bronze Age, aspires to wear the scarlet cloak awarded only to warriors. Discouraged by his grandfather's contemptuous dismissal of him as inadequate, Drem runs away to the forest where he meets Talore, who lost an arm in battle, but is a respected member of the tribe. Talore becomes his mentor, teaching him to use a spear and assuming the role of sponsor for the wolf test, which marks the rites of passage. Each boy must single-handedly kill a wolf. During his test, Drem slips. Only a friend's quick action saves him from certain death. Shamed, Drem is banished to the low-status shepherds' community where he learns their ways but remains an outsider. In the winter following his failure, a shepherd is lost in a snowstorm but when Drem finds him, the man is dead. The boy cannot leave the lamb the man had sought to rescue, nor can he carry it to safety with one useless arm. He sends his dog for help, but just before assistance arrives, some wolves attack. He kills two and his rescuers kill the third, but Drem has been badly mauled. The elders revise their earlier verdict and accept this encounter as evidence of Drem's worthiness to wear the scarlet cloak.

Analysis. Sutcliff writes of an age when courage and physical strength could mean the difference between survival and death. The hero is not discriminated against because he is disabled. In fact, his impairment does not disqualify him from the trial, a unique presentation in this genre. In the historic context, Sutcliff appears to set up the following dramatic dilemma: The leaders have two interlocked responsibilities—to ensure the perpetuation of the tribe by preserving intact their cultural mores and to guarantee the competency of all those on whom the safety of the tribe depends. Thus Drem's rejection is based on his inability to meet standards rather than on the physical condition, per se. His other virtues are extolled—loyalty, integrity, commitment to duty—but these qualities cannot substitute and ultimately he is confronted with proving himself in the very context in which his disability is most handicapping. Although the author eschews stereotyping in access to manhood rites, the bracketing of an orphan outcast with Drem, the use of the blind person as seer, and the description of Drem as "a bird with a broken wing" are certainly humdrum devices. Talore provides the theme: "If the thing is worth a fight, fight for it and do not hear the Grandfather [the critics] too clearly. There are ways—ways round, and ways through, and ways over." Sutcliff has created two noble heroes who are both wise and disabled.

Sutcliff, Rosemary. *The Witch's Brat.* Illus. by Richard Lebenson. New York: Walck, 1970. 143 pp. Reading Level: MC
Disability: Orthopedic Impairment

This is an historical tale, set in Norman England, of Lovel, a young lad with a spinal deformity. He is stoned by the villagers after the death of his grandmother, a herbalist. The superstitious community both sought and feared her and found it easy to accuse her grandson when livestock languished. Lovel flees to a monastery where he learns how to tend a medicinal garden and gradually takes over more specialized healing responsibilities. He meets the king's juggler, Rahere, who later invites him to be the healer in a new hospital. Although racked with self-doubt about his capability in this role, when Lovel meets a youth crippled in a fall, he is able to massage and brace the boy's leg, restoring the boy's ability to function.

Analysis. The development of Lovel is well executed and the reader comes to share his worries and aspirations. Despite the jarring speech, Sutcliff is at her usual masterful level in recreating a vivid historic setting peopled by memorable characters. The illustrations beautifully abet the goal, giving sensitive, artistic expression to this admirable novel.

Swarthout, Glendon and Kathryn Swarthout. *Whales to See The.* Illus. by Paul Bacon. Garden City, N.Y.: Doubleday, 1975. 121 pp. Reading Level: MC
Disability: Neurological Impairment

Miss Fish plans to take her class of ten learning-disabled children to see a pod of migrating whales. On the chartered boat, a class of non-impaired children, perhaps prompted by Miss Fish's grotesque medication administration routine, teases the ten. The weather deteriorates but, spurning safety considerations for the glory of the anticipated spectacle, Miss Fish urges the captain not to turn back. The whales are sighted and the children are thrilled. One of the disabled children balances on the railing and falls into the ocean but is miraculously rescued by a child from the other class. The regular grade teacher reverses her original negative opinion of the learning-disabled children and then prevails upon two of her children to call on the others with an offer of friendship. They do so, but cynically, assuring each other that friendship with such undesirables is an absurdity:

> "And I'm not being mean," Gloria added. "I will be nice to John, but nice and nothing else. I'm not tying myself down next year to any boy who wears hearing aids and tries to commit suicide."

[Todd responded:] "Sure, I'll be polite and say hello and stuff, but any girl who stumbles and bumbles around is off my list."

"I don't blame you," Gloria agreed. "You're too normal—we both are. Anyway, I think people should solve their own problems, and not be so dependent on others."

Analysis. This final incident is so astonishingly cruel and inhumane that the shocked reader fumbles for additional pages, convinced the story cannot end on such a heartless note. The intended ironic contrast in the final paragraph between the supportive whale society and this selfish, uncaring human one scarcely mitigates the misanthropic observations of the children. The characterizations and plot elements are specious and the progression of events unlikely. Miss Fish is one of the most incompetent teachers ever to stagger through a novel. Although her presentation suggests a loving, nurturing personality, her behavior is so monumentally stupid as to ensure catastrophe. The children are all pictured as uncontrollable, heavily medicated losers. Their behavior is presented in its most extreme manifestations with an excessive emphasis on symptomology, labeling, and chemical control, and no development of positive admirable characteristics. In sum, the book presents an almost perfect model of pernicious, exploitive, distorting treatment of handicapped characters in juvenile literature.

Tate, Joan. *Ben and Annie.* Illus. by Judith Gwyn Brown. Garden City, N.Y.: Doubleday, 1974. 79 pp. Reading Level: MC/YA
Disability: General Health Problems

The isolation and loneliness caused by Annie's increasing invalidism is relieved by her warm friendship with Ben. They communicate regularly on an improvised intercom and, with much trepidation, Annie's mother occasionally permits them to go browsing in a local store. Deciding that Annie needs more excitement in her restricted life, Ben persuades his skeptical eleven-year-old friends to let her watch them play soccer. Surprised and elated by the pleasure this gives everyone, the boys devise a safe but makeshift arrangement in which they hoist her wheelchair onto a swing and all very gently push her. Rewarded by her utter joy, they, almost knightlike, plan new pleasures for her on their excursions. They push her wheelchair down a gentle slope and hear her cries of delight. Suddenly a stranger intervenes and, without provocation, furiously shoves and batters the boys. All are so terror-stricken that they are unable to defend themselves. The man herds them all to Annie's home where he explains to her mother that he has rescued her daughter from these boys who have been tormenting and abusing her. Annie's mother becomes hysterical and her father rips out the communication device the children used and then yells: "And don't let me hear you speaking to our Annie again . . . ever, ever again." Ben's mother asks him what happened. "But Ben can't say a single thing. Not a word comes out of his mouth and his stomach has curled up and his whole brain has stopped working with the shock of what Annie's dad has done and what they all think, all of them." Ben realizes that their marvelous fun, Annie's brightest moments, and their very precious friendship are over.

Analysis. Annie's mother is trapped by her legitimate concern for her weakened daughter, her terrible fear of the hopeless future, and her desire to allow Annie some joy while keeping her safe from harm. The stranger is so overwhelmed by what appears to him to be danger to the fragile child that he is unwilling and unable to conceive of any benign explanation. Ben is so outraged at the irony and injustice of the accusations that he is unable to speak out in his own defense. Annie is so devastated by the intrusion, the violent scene, and the destruction of their innocent pleasures that she cannot protest either.

Annie, weakened and clearly dying, is shielded by her parents from danger but, in doing so, they also keep her from participating in life. Only the children seem to understand that a life without friendship, pleasure, and joy is meaningless. The joy is not hers alone, but also the boys'. Ben's eager involvement in Annie's life brings him direct as well as reflected gratification. This powerful story is unique and masterfully crafted, moving from its happy serene mood to a violent, jolting climax. Although the conclusion is disconcerting and destroys the reader's profound hopes that all will be happily resolved, the memory of the characters, particularly the humane, honest, and admirable Ben, alleviates the distress. Superb soft pencil drawings beautifully project the overwhelming sense of both happiness and pain in the story. (See Figure 6.)

Tate, Joan. *Tina and David.* New York: Nelson, 1966. 95 pp. Reading Level: YA
Disability: Emotional Dysfunction

Tina and David first meet when he is the new boy in class. Desperately shy, he blushes and grows visibly distraught when called upon to speak. He has no friends and speaks to no one. Once when Tina writes him a note, he answers back in writing, thus establishing his sole means of communicating with anyone in school. When Tina leaves for an all-girls' school, she loses track of David and it is not until after she graduates and begins work in a manufacturing plant that she comes across him again. He is employed as an accountant in the same place, has noticed her, and leaves her a message stuck in a tree near where she catches a bus. The note says only: "Tina Carter?" She responds in writing and this strange nonverbal relationship resumes. Finally, knowing he has a car, she asks for a ride home. He drives her in silence, now using the glove compartment instead of the tree as an exchange center for their communications. David lives only a few blocks from her home, but has never offered to pick her up in the mornings on his way to work. She walks over to see him one day and finds he lives in a dismal flat in the back of a house. Tina speaks to him but he is terribly distressed and does not answer. Seeing a notepad, she writes him a message. Calmed, he is able to respond. She asks him out loud to come to tea, but he becomes very agitated and writes: "Don't ask me." His next note, delivered via the glove compartment, says: "I'm no good. But don't leave me." After Tina returns from a vacation, David suddenly begins to speak to her. He explains that he had always been able to talk to people who mean nothing to him, but is totally incapable of speaking to girls or to anyone about things of a personal nature. He finds his work nonthreatening because it concerns figures and balance sheets, not people. Tina's parents are anxious to meet David, suspecting from their daughter's odd behavior that something is wrong. They are amazingly understanding and supportive, and David finally works up the courage to visit them. They carefully avoid conversations concerning anything of a personal nature and do not pressure him in any way. Greatly relieved, he is able to kiss Tina on her cheek for the first time. The following day, Tina is alarmed to see the tree that had been used as their message center has been chopped down. She rushes to tell David, but he dismisses it: "Oh, well. . . . It's a pity. I liked that old tree. But we don't need it any longer."

Analysis. The desperate loneliness of someone for whom any human contact represents a threat is effectively conveyed. However, that such extreme dysfunction should not find expression in other aspects of his personality and that it should be so amenable to remediation is hard to swallow and results in a story that is disappointing and ultimately unconvincing from the point of view of logic or plausibility. It is almost impossible to relate to a character as remote and uncommunicative as David or to comprehend his appeal to Tina. Despite these major faults, *Tina and David* is a strangely compelling story.

Tavo, Gus (pseud.). Ivan, Gustave, and Martha Ivan. *Ride the Pale Stallion*. New York: Knopf, 1968. 180 pp. Reading Level: MC/YA
Disability: Orthopedic Impairment

Unable to pursue his career on a riverboat because of a leg lost in the Civil War, embittered, taciturn Simon and his son, Abe, try to homestead in New Mexico. They have had difficult times, including the critical loss of a bull, but work hard in the fields to make the ranch function. After a silent arduous day, Simon retires to look at his dead wife's cuckoo clock and, in his reminiscences, isolates himself further from Abe. Chief Pomosino drops in, accepts hospitality, and becomes entranced with the cuckoo, baldly requesting ownership. Abe trades his horse, Star, to get money for a bull, and Simon, feeling guilty that he was unwilling to swap his clock for the bull, becomes even more distant. Pomosino cannily allows Abe to ride one of his horses, Yucca, and predicts that Simon will soon trade the clock to him for the horse. After the two see a bear maul an eagle in a fight, Abe defies his father's orders to shoot the injured bird in a "scene of insight"—the only heavy-handed symbolic segment in the story. Later, Simon, seeing the one-legged bird feed, is inspired and begins to deal more constructively with his pain and self-pity. Pomosino's men rescue him from a near fatal encounter with a wounded bear and he rethinks his relationship with Abe, agreeing with the chief that the most valuable memento his wife gave him was Abe. There is a round of giving—Pomosino at last gets the cuckoo clock, Abe gets Yucca, but, most importantly, Simon gets to be able to accept his son's deep feelings of love and to feel free to abandon the burdens of the past.

Analysis. This is a simple, clean, well-crafted story. It deals with various manifestations of love, but is a story of action, agony, and humor, as well as one that stresses characterization and emotional relationships. The handicapped character is seen struggling with his problem, not complaining about the pain and fiercely resistant to being pitied. His stoicism blocks his ability to move toward his son and his early self-evaluation as an incapacitated person with feelings of worthlessness is paralleled in his violent reaction with the similarly injured bird. The ending is neat and expected, but not a cliché. This story of growth through struggle is developed with economy, color, and affection.

Taylor, Theodore. *The Cay.* Garden City, N.Y.: Doubleday, 1969. 137 pp. Reading Level: MC/YA
Disability: Visual Impairment

Curaçao seems a likely target for attack at the beginning of World War II. Mrs. Enright always regretted leaving Virginia and seizes on the anticipated danger as an excuse to return with her son, Philip, to the United States. The tanker they leave on is torpedoed and Philip, separated from his mother and injured by a blow on the head, finds himself adrift on a raft with an old West Indian man. Philip had absorbed his mother's virulent racial prejudices and is contemptuous of Timothy, whom he perceives as ugly and stupid. The pain from his injury is terrible and, when it at last subsides, Philip is blind. Filled with terror, he rages at Timothy and the old man comforts him as much as he is able. At last they reach an island, and Philip, his arrogance exacerbated by his ordeal, is uncooperative and complaining. He insists that he is helpless, but Timothy compels him to learn to weave mats, to fish, to find his way around the island, and ultimately to be self-sufficient. When a hurricane hits the island, Timothy dies protecting Philip. Ably prepared by the West Indian, the boy survives until he is rescued by an American ship. He is reunited with his parents and after several operations his vision is restored.

Analysis. Blindness provides the central metaphor of this story. Philip, programmed by his mother's bigotry, is unable to see Blacks clearly. It is not until his actual sight is lost that he becomes "color-blind" or, ironically, "sees" clearly for the first time. Told in the first person by Philip, the descriptions of events are revealed through his gradually changing perceptions and his slowly developing maturity. Timothy is unschooled but intelligent, compassionate to the point of self-sacrifice, and patient with the frightened and abusive youngster. The character of Philip is more fully developed as it is revealed directly through descriptions of behavior and more subtly as his response to his blindness and to Timothy transforms him. His initial fears and his instinctive desire for dependence are convincingly pictured as are his growing competence under Timothy's tutelage and self-assurance despite his loss of sight. Timothy personifies the prototype teacher, even sacrificing self to give love and insight, and as such is an heroic figure. A skillfully written, controversial book, *The Cay* speaks primarily of human relations and secondarily of blindness.

Taylor, Theodore. *Teetoncey.* Illus. by Richard Cuffari. Garden City, N.Y.: Doubleday, 1974. 153 pp. Reading Level: MC/YA
Disability: Emotional Dysfunction

In 1898, on the remote outer shoreline of North Carolina, 11-year-old Ben lives with his mother who broods about the death of her husband and other son at sea. During a storm, Ben finds a girl who has survived a shipwreck. She is aphasic from shock and no one knows her identity, but under his mother's care she gradually begins to improve physically. Ben and his mother also have a problem in communication complicated by different perceptions of his father's death. In desperation at her lack of responsiveness, the boy takes the newly named girl, Teetoncey, to the site of the wreck where her parents drowned, and she begins to scream and yell. This shock treatment reestablishes her communication, both on a verbal and conscious level, with the world.

Analysis. This is an excellent book enlivened with a superb feeling of local color. Teetoncey has her own persona, but the local inhabitants have contempt for her and describe her variously as a burden, an unpleasant bother, a "loony," and a "vegetable." She also has a symbolic function for Ben, proof that he could be manly and rescue victims like other adults, especially his father. Moreover, this silent girl is the means by which Ben's mother accepts her husband's death in a healthier context and by which the boy and his mother come to terms with each other's needs. The novel's theme of death and rebirth, of ebb and flow of feelings, is echoed in the ocean which dominates the background, and in Teetoncey's behavior which occupies the surface story.

The reader learns only a minimum amount about this impairment, but a model of persistent, loving care toward a mute, amnesiac child is carefully described. Cuffari's moving illustrations target it on Teetoncey's vulnerability and emotional fetters.

Terris, Susan. *The Drowning Boy.* Garden City, N.Y.: Doubleday, 1972. 189 pp. Reading Level: YA
Disability: Emotional Dysfunction

Mr. Hurd wishes his reflective and unaggressive son, Jason, were more "manly." Mrs. Hurd, who reluctantly gave up a career as a chemist to manage the family's newly purchased farm and to care for her own senile mother, has become increasingly withdrawn and despondent since the move. Mr. Hurd's plans for Jason's summer involve informally apprenticing his son to Sam Slavin, a teacher at the school for "problem" boys that Jason attends, who will teach Jason carpentry. The Slavins' six-year-old nephew, Buddy, is spending the summer with them. The child is still not toilet-trained, will not look at or talk to anyone, and becomes hysterical at any change in routine. Jason is more interested in the child than in woodworking and takes the boy on walks in the woods, reads to him, and shows him his pet mouse. Buddy seems slightly more responsive as a result of Jason's attentions and the older boy desperately hopes that the Slavins will agree to keep their nephew with them. The Hurd family is invited for dinner one evening, and Jason's father, contemptuous of Buddy, insists on labeling the boy "autistic," whereupon he confidently predicts a gloomy future for the child. Jason, naively hoping to force Buddy to alter his behavior, takes him to see his silent, senile grandmother, threatening the now terrified child with a similar fate if he does not show immediate improvement. Mr. Hurd berates his son for his foolish efforts at amateur psychiatry and for wasting his time with a "hopeless case." Forbidden to see the child again, Jason returns to the Slavins to say good-by. After exchanging angry words with his teacher, he rushes to the quarry, planning to drown himself. Once in the water, however, he changes his mind and swims for shore. Buddy is sent to a residential school, but will stay with the Slavins on weekends. Jason is assigned the job of teaching the boy the days of the week so he can comprehend that he is not being abandoned, but can anticipate regularly returning to his adoptive home.

Analysis. This sensitive, well-written, complex story explores three varieties of emotional dysfunction: The grandmother suffers from the physiological ravages of age that have reduced her intellectual functioning; the mother has been removed from a satisfying profession to live out her husband's ambitions without regard for her own needs or desires, and, devoid of support or affirmation of her worth, she withdraws from all but the most minimal contact with life; Buddy, responding to parental neglect, retreats into a private world. The picture of Buddy is vividly etched and easy solutions or signs of unwarranted optimism are soundly suppressed. The diagnosis of autism is neither clearly affirmed nor denied. Jason is presented as a sensitive boy whose coarse and unfeeling father is totally unsympathetic to his son's needs. When Jason eschews suicide as a solution to his problems and calls upon previously unacknowledged reserves to save himself, this is clearly a model for his future course of action if he is to survive. The dark and depressing tone of the book is the weakest feature of this unusual novel.

Terris, Susan. *Plague of Frogs.* Garden City, N.Y.: Doubleday, 1973. 180 pp. Reading Level: YA/MA
Disability: Cosmetic Impairment; also intellectual impairment, orthopedic impairment

Jo is a self-centered girl, cool and manipulative, who is interested in frogs and tennis, but mainly in herself. She encounters Marcella, a pregnant, unwed teenager, whose behavior gives the impression of mild intellectual impairment. Jo's mother compassionately offers Marcella a job as a domestic until her baby comes. Jo and her tennis partner, Roger, listen to Marcella's claims about a plague of frogs in her Ozark mountain home and exploit her fears for their own amusement by teasing her with a frog. This scares the expectant mother, who angrily tells them that her own facial strawberry mark was the result of her pregnant mother being frightened by such a creature. She threatens to kill them if the same thing happens to her unborn child. Jo and Roger become absorbed in the pregnant girl's life and in her tales of frogs and convince her to take them with her for protection when she attends her sister's hometown wedding. Jo is shocked at how repellent people find Marcella's face and how cruelly she is treated by her family. After wild accusations and an ax attack by her enraged father, Marcella retreats to a cabin where she starts her delivery. The midwife, after admitting she inflated and spread stories about frogs to encourage Marcella to leave her inhospitable environment, helps in the birth. Examining the newborn, she tells Marcella that the child is fortunate to have a lucky caul over her face; however, the baby also has a mark on her back that looks like a jumping frog. When Marcella's father arrives to harass her further, she bravely confronts him, revealing that she knows he has exploited her facial blemish to divert attention from his own vanity and ineptitude. As they leave, Jo reviews her early condescending attitude toward Marcella, which has now been replaced by a considerable measure of respect.

Analysis. Superstitious perceptions of disability are explored in this unique and disquieting story. The first intimation of this connection occurs on the day when Jo first sees a legless vendor and later listens to Marcella who talks of the evil eye, a lucky charm, and a plague. Marcella is seen as a victim of superstition, circumstances, and deliberate ill will and as a person who is easily gulled, but whose efforts to deceive others are transparent and consequently unsuccessful. Although the convoluted plot is interesting and unusual, characterizations are incomplete and unconvincing. Jo's mother seems not the type to allow her young daughter and a younger friend to travel unsupervised to an obscure mountain village. The midwife is presented as one who quotes Shakespeare and is also a gossipy promoter of superstitious ideas. It is insinuated that the father of Marcella's baby may be either her brother-in-law or even her own father, but the accusations remain unsubstantiated. Some of the behaviors of characters seem incompatible and there are hints of connections that are left dangling, all of which contribute to the sense of tension and unease generated by the plot itself. The story obliquely suggests that response to disability is capricious—some impairments are assigned favorable meanings and others negative. In sum, this demanding book, although flawed, develops a chilling feeling of foreboding, and vividly re-creates an isolated rural community that is accepting of casual violence and virtually untouched by modern thinking.

Thomas, Dawn C. *Pablito's New Feet.* Illus. by Paul Frame. Philadelphia: Lippincott, 1973. 63 pp. Reading Level: MC
Disability: Orthopedic Impairment

Unable to walk since he had polio, Pablito, a young Puerto Rican boy, is brought into a New York hospital for analysis. Tests indicate that surgery may help, and the boy undergoes an operation. This medical intervention appears successful, but, despite therapy and braces, the patient still does not walk. Months go by during which Pablito languishes in the hospital without any noticeable improvement. Finally, another operation is performed and corrective shoes prescribed. Still no recovery of function occurs until one day a famous baseball player visits the children's ward. Pablito, an avid fan, wishes desperately to see his hero: " 'Goodness me,' he whispered, 'those autographed balls are almost gone. Maybe, just maybe. . .' He got up and put on his shoes. He reached for his crutches. And then slowly, very, very slowly he walked."

Analysis. This story is misleading, absurd, and deplorable. The premise that rehabilitation from polio is simply a matter of desire is emphasized and repeated. When the boy first enters the hospital, a family member predicts: "Pablito will walk, I know he will, if he wants to and is not afraid." When the boy asks if his new shoes are "walking shoes," the doctor replies: "Only if you want them to be." As Pablito finally walks for the first time after months in the hospital, he does not just barely manage but he "felt very strong on his feet." There is an implied promise that not only will the boy walk again but he will soon be playing baseball. The hospital, staffed by a benevolent and unhurried crew, oddly enough has such few demands on its facilities that it can house a lad for half a year, and is unprofessional enough not to require the recalcitrant lad to attend physical therapy. The attitude toward the Puerto Rican family is patronizing, the writing is stiff, and the concept of willing away immobility is a serious disservice to individuals with real problems.

Thompson, Mary Wolfe. *Snow Slopes.* Illus. by Frank Kramer. New York: Longmans, Green, 1957. 179 pp. Reading Level: YA
Disability: Orthopedic Impairment

Hoping to supplement her loving but inept widowed mother's attempt at earning a living by managing a guest house, Arleigh gets a job working weekends at a nearby ski lodge. The young woman has made a few friends but resents the fact that polio has affected her mobility. The muscles in her thigh and the condition of her bones preclude dancing, skiing, and other such physical and social experiences. She meets a young man, Garry, at the lodge and he and his parents become regular weekend guests at her home. This casual relationship is cemented when Arleigh's uncle and Garry's father share their conviction that the guest house was part of the Civil War underground escape network. A budding romance is impeded by Sonia, who sees Arleigh as a serious rival for Garry's attention, and Arleigh is both astonished and pleased to be considered a femme fatale. When Sonia receives a spinal injury in a skiing competition, Arleigh discovers how hard-hearted the injured girl's parents are and now understands Sonia's contemptible behavior. The incipient marriage of her uncle and widowed mother, combined with the proof that the house does have historic value, promise relief for Arleigh's financial woes, and she and Garry discuss their future college plans.

Analysis. Snow Slopes is a standard teenage romance, enlivened mildly by its discussions of the Underground Railroad and its exploration of feelings of low self-worth associated with disability. Arleigh is presented as a bright, hardworking girl, naturally upset at her loneliness but who blossoms through the affection of a sensitive and caring boyfriend. The book is a modest example of a positive portrayal of a heroine adjusting constructively to the aftereffects of polio, but is marred by pale characterizations and a shallow plot.

Thrasher, Crystal. *The Dark Didn't Catch Me*. New York: Atheneum, 1975. 182 pp. Reading Level: MC/YA
Disability: Cosmetic Impairment, General Health Problems; also intellectual impairment

During the Depression, the Robinson family moves to the Indiana hills, lured by rumors that jobs are available there. Seely, the daughter, meets Freida, a girl with a badly repaired cleft lip and palate who becomes her friend, and Teddy, a slow-learning boy who later dies of a fever. Belatedly, Seely's father learns that there will be no jobs locally until a government factory is started. He takes work in a distant town, living away from his family during the week and returning home on weekends. Jamie, Seely's brother, is late coming home one day. Their frantic search recovers his drowned body in the rising flood waters where he presumably died during an epileptic seizure. Freida becomes engaged, Seely graduates, and her family moves closer to her father's work.

Analysis. This beautiful portrait of a poor family struggling to survive economic and personal hardships is essentially a story of the maturing of the young heroine. The handicapped characters have minor roles, but their depiction is so natural, so unencumbered by symbolic or didactic intent, as to be a model for this genre. The heroine's response to each is open, accepting, and free of judgmental components.

Travers, Pamela L. *Friend Monkey*. New York: Harcourt Brace Jovanovich, 1971. 184 pp. Reading Level: MC
Disability: Auditory Impairment, Speech Impairment

A monkey boards a ship and causes near havoc with his overly helpful ways. When the boat docks at London, Mr. Linnet, a mild-mannered clerk, impulsively takes the creature home. As the monkey rapidly dismantles the way of life of his staid family, Linnet becomes more and more fond of him. Soon they are obliged to accept the hospitality of their neighbor, Miss Brown-Potter, an intrepid explorer, since Monkey has been responsible for his protector's loss of job and the burning down of the family residence. Included in the woman's household is

Stanley Livingston Fan, a deaf-mute boy whom she rescued in Africa when he was abandoned to the crocodiles, presumably because of his impairments. The combined households soon set sail for Africa and, when the ship sinks under strange circumstances, they row to a paradisiacal island. They learn that they have unknowingly participated in the plan of a surreptitious network of people devoted to the welfare of animals and a return to a more naturalistic lifestyle.

Analysis. This tiresome story is unenlivened even by the wild antics of the irrepressible, larger-than-life monkey. The brittle, clever dialogue is very self-conscious and the final message seems self-righteous. The child's deafness is a gratuitous inclusion, useful only in establishing the generosity of the explorer and in artificially complicating the plot.

Treece, Henry. *The Dream Time.* Illus. by Charles Keeping. New York: Meredith, 1967. 107 pp. Reading Level: YA
Disability: Orthopedic Impairment

Crookleg, who lived when human societies were just forming, was given that name by the community after he fell and his bones mended badly. Crookleg is able to draw pictures, but his tribe considers them bad magic. The men agree to take him on a raiding party with the proviso that he sacrifice the right forefinger which guides his drawing sticks. The raid is unsuccessful and he runs away, wisely concerned about the consequences. He wanders from tribe to tribe, during which time he is renamed Twilight, and finds that his gifts are honored and valued among peace-loving communities. A young girl named Blackbird becomes his friend and he is distressed when she is taken prisoner. He encounters members of another tribe who value his pictures and ultimately rescue Blackbird for him. In a foray, the others are killed except for a baby, who is entrusted to Blackbird and Twilight to care for. When bad times come, he decides he must live by his dreams. After this decision, his leg appears cured and he walks seemingly without a limp. The three head toward a new and peaceful village where there is no need for fortifications and "the people came out to meet them laughing."

Analysis. This story, unsatisfactory in many ways, is burdened with too many incompletely developed symbols and messages. Crookleg is the artist, prophet, peacemaker. Asked to accept maiming as the price for remaining with the tribe, he refuses. But he seeks to protect others as well as himself and pleads unsuccessfully for mercy for those who are vulnerable. He is in tune with nature and can converse with the animals as well as duplicate their forms in his art. His more gentle name replaces the cruel descriptive one and his impairment magically disappears almost without notice. The story is episodic, replete with violence, weighted with images, and heavy-handed in its statement of hope that peace will replace war. Rigid, dark strokes dominate the somber illustrations of a primitive time.

Treece, Henry. *Viking's Sunset*. Illus. by Christine Price. New York: Criterion, 1960. 182 pp. Reading Level: YA
Disability: Orthopedic Impairment

Harald Segurdson, a Viking chieftain, returns to find his village desolated and his sons grievously wounded by raiders. He and the other men of the village set out to seek revenge. They trail the invaders to Greenland where they are detained through the winter. When spring comes, they sail west, finally landing in North America. Although claiming to come in peace, they are nonetheless challenged by Wawasha, one of the two sons of the Indian tribe's chief, who is deafeated in the confrontation. Instead of killing him, the Indian's courage is proclaimed and the Viking champion calls him brother, whereupon the strangers are welcomed by the tribe. Their storytelling skills are greatly admired and Harald mesmerizes them with the legend of Baldur, the beautiful and beloved god whose blind brother was tricked by the evil Loki into being the instrument of his death. The Indians are deeply moved by this tale, but the Viking, Grummock, misinterpreting their response, assures them that Wawasha is as brave and handsome as Baldur. The Indian chief tells the Vikings that he has two sons, and although the other one, Heome, is not blind, his hands are useless: They were mauled by a bear during initiation rites and since then have been a badge of his inadequacy. When Harald kills a wolf, he allows Heome to take credit, hoping to improve the Indian's status among his people. Instead, Heome becomes boastful, arrogant, and more contemptible than ever. The Vikings accompany the Indians on their annual migration. During an attack by another tribe, Heome disgraces himself through his cowardly behavior. Seeking the power and respect that have always eluded him, Heome plans an ambush in which Wawasha and all but five of the men are killed. The survivors return to camp bearing the chief's murdered son. Shamed before his Viking brothers when he discovers Heome's duplicity, the chief offers the boy's life in forfeit. The Vikings reject the suggestion, but the enraged plotter, hearing this discussion, lunges for their leader; in the ensuing struggle the two topple from a cliff to their deaths. Harald, Wawasha, and Heome are all placed in the Viking boat, which becomes their funeral pyre. The chief sadly and cynically observes that "at last Heome shall be with warriors."

Analysis. The deliberate recapitulation of the Baldur legend presages its inevitable reenactment within the course of the story. Heome, the object of well-deserved contempt, is the agent for the killing of his handsome and admired brother. The mythic Hoder was duped by the evil god Loki, but Heome, his counterpart, is the victim of his own failings. It was his inadequacies that resulted in the maiming, thus rendering him incapable of assuming his proper tribal role and setting in motion those events that could only end in tragedy. The depiction of this disabled character reveals only contemptible qualities and suggests that his impaired body reflects an equally impaired soul. Although this presentation of a handicapped character is wholly negative, *Viking's Sunset* is written with great skill. The nature of the tragedy can be predicted early in the tale, yet reader interest is unflagging. The illustrations suggest the harsh and difficult times in which the story is set and ably convey the force and vigor of these early people.

Trevor, Meriol. *The Rose Round.* New York: Dutton, 1964. 176 pp.
Reading Level: YA/MA
Disability: Orthopedic Impairment

The imperious Mme. Ayre has employed Matt's half-sister, Caro, as a cook on her estate and he joins her there. The 13-year-old boy meets the owner's granddaughter, Alix, and her uncle Theo, whose birth defect Mme. Ayer, his mother, loathes. The old woman is bitter that of all her children, only Theo remains alive. No matter how self-effacing his efforts in accepting her insults or concealing his malformed arm in a sling, he remains the object of her scorn. She calls him "a throwback" and considers him useless, an opinion he comes to share. This is patently untrue, since he is a sensitive man, enjoys poetry, does translations, and volunteers his time in a school for multiply-disabled children. That institution is in dire financial condition, and although Theo is afraid of his mother, he summons up the courage to announce he is bringing the orphaned, crippled children home for Christmas. His mother is violently opposed to this plan, but Caro, with whom Theo is secretly in love, agrees to help. Matt pitches in and even Alix assists when she sees how much work needs doing. Since she has never before had responsibilities, being completely pampered by her grandmother, Alix carelessly leaves one of the children alone. When a fire starts, Theo courageously puts it out and saves the untended, helpless child. Alix, much chastened and humanized by the experience, becomes friendlier with Matt. Her grandmother, outraged at the unsuitability of such a relationship, forbids further contact, but Alix disobeys the old woman and, in an attempt to get to Matt's room, loses her footing crossing a roof. Theo is able to save her but falls from the building, sustaining multiple fractures. His mother becomes ill and, when confronted with her own mortality, asks Theo's forgiveness for her reprehensible behavior, and dies. Alix and Matt conspire to get Theo and Caro to admit their hidden feelings for each other and the story concludes as they decide to marry.

Analysis. Rose Round is a tightly structured story, steeped in religious and metaphysical symbolism. The characters undergo metamorphoses as they encounter difficulties and defiance. Most complex is Theo, who accepted abuse from peers as a child and from his mother as an adult, having internalized other people's appraisals of his total unworthiness. Inspired by children whose problems surpass his, he is able to slough off the infantile, passive role he had once tolerated. As he begins to act like an adult and becomes less preoccupied with his own inadequacies, his impairment loses its stigmatic character. The handicapped children function as catalysts for the maturity and redemption of Theo. Even the old woman, who had been unflinchingly cruel to her own son throughout his life, is reconciled to her church after encounters with a disabled child, and is able to die in a state of grace.

Turnbull, Agnes Sligh. *The White Lark.* Illus. by Nathan Goldstein. Boston: Houghton Mifflin, 1968. 57 pp. Reading Level: YC
Disability: Orthopedic Impairment

Suzy has had to wear a leg brace since her accident, but the doctor has told her it may come off some day. She has come from America to visit her English aunt and there she meets a greengrocer, Mr. Prettyford, who has "short legs." After a brief, blunt conversation about leg problems, they become good friends. She accompanies him out to the country to purchase produce from farmers and helps prepare food for sale. A customer comes to purchase foodstuffs and reveals that once when her cat had gotten stuck in a pipe, the grocer's short stature was critical in rescuing the animal. The man tells Suzy about the white lark, which represents hope, but he despairs of seeing it because it is so rare. Their pleasant visit is marred by bullies who tease the grocer. On the last day of their visit, they see the white lark which has the effect of making the man feel tall. Suzy reports: "When I saw it and listened to its song, I forgot all about my brace. I won't ever feel sad again that I can't run. I'll just be patient and happy."

Analysis. The symbolic white lark is incongruous with the mundane, prosaic nature of the rest of the story, which begins as a straightforward naturalistic account of a child and an adult finding support and consolation in their shared problems. The grocer is presented in a positive light—hardworking, kindly, and brave. The intrusion of the lark, a symbol of hope, seems to negate the validity of the accommodations Mr. Prettyford has made which, up to that point, had seemed both admirable and adequate. What he could hope for, certainly not remediation of a congenital condition, is not clear, and, since her doctor had predicted improvement for Suzy, her need for a mystical white bird seems equally pointless. Suzy's pious words offer an unfortunate contrast with the handsome, honest illustrations and the otherwise satisfactory presentation of a young girl and an old man making the best of their situations.

Underhill, Ruth M. *Antelope Singer*. Illus. by Ursula Loering. New York: Coward-McCann, 1961. 280 pp. Reading Level: MC
Disability: Orthopedic Impairment

The Hunt family is part of the great American westward migration. Tad and Mitty, the children, discover a young Paiute Indian boy with a malformed arm desperately ill with measles at one of their stops. They bring him water and food from their meager supplies, but he barely responds. Their father, searching for a stray ox, is bitten by a rattlesnake and the family is forced to remain until he recovers. One day, Nummer, the Indian boy, disappears but returns with several adults from his tribe. Nummer's grandfather brings an antidote for snakebite and the boy teaches Tad trapping to replenish the family's dwindling food supplies. Pa still is not well enough to travel and each day it becomes more dangerous not to do so. Although eager to reach California, the Hunts have tarried too long for safety and so accept the invitation to stay with the Paiute Indians at their winter camp. The Indian boys shun Nummer, considering him bad luck. He was the second twin to be born and, according to custom, should have been left to die. His grandfather, Dago, would not allow it, and when the firstborn twin died, Nummer was blamed. Dago is the tribal Antelope Singer. He dreams of where the antelopes graze and sings the ancient songs that lure them. Then, adult men of the tribe prepare a trap for the animals. If the singer dreams well, the tribe prospers. Nummer prepares to take over this role, but the first time he sings, the antelopes break through the barrier and Nummer is more an outcast than ever. Nummer then finds more of the animals. This time when he sings, it results in the best antelope hunt in memory. Nummer is at last accepted and it is clear that he will hold a position of great honor in the tribe.

Analysis. In this charmingly old-fashioned story, all problems are relatively simple and amenable to solution. It is a comfortable tale of kindly people unhampered by larger social or historic problems, although mention of trading exploitation is included. The ostracism of Nummer is more related to his twin birth status than to his disability, but the withered arm is a visible symbol of his luck. He is shown as a bright, adaptable child, compensating for his near useless arm in intelligent ways. He is finally fully accepted when his aura of bad luck disappears. The illustrations do not hide his disability and support his positive depiction. This gentle, upbeat story emphasizes the need to concentrate on strengths rather than impairments and delivers its low-key, straightforward message without sermonizing.

Valenti, Angelo. *Hill of Little Miracles.* Illus. by author. New York: Viking, 1942. 200 pp. Reading Level: MC
Disability: Orthopedic Impairment, Emotional Dysfunction

Hoping to stretch his short leg to the same length as his other one, young Ricco Santo nightly ties a brick to it. While awaiting this unlikely event, he is fitted with a new pair of shoes, one of which has a built-up sole, an improvement sufficient to allow him to abandon his crutches. Since the death of her husband, Ricco's neighbor seems obsessed with the need to pick all the flowers in the world. Escaping from her yard, she wanders into the path of a car and the resultant injury restores her mental balance. Old Jonah, another neighbor, is a mender of nets, a superstitious and crusty old character who tells Ricco that he must wear a wooden leg to replace the one a whale swallowed. The community events that comprise Ricco's adventures include attending a family wedding, getting lost at sea during a fog, building a clubhouse, and painting a picture of Jonah, which the latter destroys, fearing it has "stolen his soul." By tale's end, Ricco's leg has lengthened, an event he is uncertain whether to attribute to the brick or the religious medal he wears around his neck.

Analysis. Less a continuous story than a series of incidents loosely woven around the character of Ricco, this book is a romanticized, sentimental look at a pasteboard world. The presentation of disabilities is unreal: Ricco is marvelously free of pain or discomfort as he changes from crutches to corrective shoe and the resumption of leg growth is completely implausible. He is oblivious to pity and casual about accepting charity. The old woman's spontaneous restoration of mental health is only the most extreme in a sequence of unlikely events.

Vance, Marguerite. *A Rainbow for Robin.* Illus. by Kenneth Longtemps. New York: Dutton, 1966. 88 pp. Reading Level: MC
Disability: Visual Impairment; also speech impairment

Now fourteen, Robin has been keeping a diary for the past two years in which she has recorded her experiences, fears, and hopes. Blind since birth, she has learned to be self-sufficient and participate in family and school events, but her absorbing interest is in her music. Her family is totally supportive, including a brother whose stuttering she occasionally mimics. Rosemary's first recital is a success, her original musical composition wins the top prize, and, to her great joy, it is performed by the local symphony.

Analysis. Robin emerges as a plastic child in this tale where everything is beautiful, wonderful, and marvelous. When Robin is a bridesmaid and must hold the bride's bouquet during the ceremony, she worries: "I must be careful to take it from her nicely, not grab it or—my goodness—drop it." The heroine expresses her thoughts that blind people may have a special sensitivity to music: "Of course, all musicians are very, very interested in perfect technique, but sometimes I think no sighted person can feel the pictures in tones that a blind person can." Teasing her brother is mistakenly considered playful and this provides the only sour note in an otherwise sugar-coated world. The writing is stilted and unconvincing and the pictures are particularly inept, displaying a poor sense of proportion and a faulty knowledge of anatomy.

Vance, Marguerite. *Windows for Rosemary.* Illus. by Robert Doares. New York: Dutton, 1956. 62 pp. Reading Level: YC
Disability: Visual Impairment

Nine-year-old Rosemary explains what adjustments have been made at home to accommodate her blindness. The permanence of all furnishings, the orientation she requires in new settings, the modes she uses to learn about the world, and the misperceptions of some of her friends about blindness are described. Her parents' gift of a typewriter leads to the observation: "I had the happiest birthday any girl ever had and that I was the luckiest girl in the whole world."

Analysis. This syrupy tale superficially explores some of the problems associated with blindness, concluding that a loving family and an optimistic attitude profoundly reduce their seriousness. The book's strongest features are the depiction of Rosemary functioning in all family activities, the attractiveness of the heroine, and the clarity of the illustrations of her instructional tools.

Vinson, Kathryn. *Run with the Ring.* New York: Harcourt, 1965. 225 pp. Reading Level: YA
Disability: Visual Impairment; also auditory impairment

During a track meet, Mark Mansfield, a junior in high school, falls, injures his head, and is blinded. Convinced that Curt, a competitor, deliberately caused him to fall, bitterness overwhelms Mark. Listening to his ham radio, he learns that one of his old contacts is also blind. He is surprised at the man's obvious enjoyment of life and begins to hope his own life can yet be worth living. After Mark admits to himself that his blindness is permanent, he enrolls in a residential state school for blind and deaf students. He sets up his ham gear, meets some other students, and begins classes. Mark learns braille, mobility techniques, and how to compete in track events despite his blindness. When he loses his first competition, he becomes despondent, convinced he could easily have won had he been sighted. He passes up the dance afterward and retreats to his room. There is a storm that night and lightning causes a fire in one of the dormitories. The phone lines are down, but Mark is able to call for help on his ham radio. He then rushes to another dormitory where he helps save the disabled children inside and later collapses. He is honored for his bravery at graduation ceremonies where a medal is awarded to him by the president. He returns home to find that the boy he suspected of fouling him is being considered for a scholarship. The coach questions Mark about rumors concerning the accusations but, no longer bitter, Mark says Curt should be given the scholarship.

Analysis. Despite the extravagant unlikelihood of many of the events in the story and a dialogue replete with outdated, overly cheery slang terms, the plot is fast-paced and interesting. The factual information about blindness and rehabilitation is sound. Techniques for circumventing learning problems, the freedom engendered by mobility training, and the many things blind people can do successfully are stressed—and this information is organic rather than intrusive to the story. The humiliation of being pitied is effectively conveyed, as is the trauma of adapting to a totally new lifestyle. Despite the superhero climax and the characterization of Mark as compassionate, brave, forgiving, and socially admired, earlier scenes show him to be resentful, stubborn, and willing to play pranks. In sum, he is shown in balance as a plausible character—one of the strongest aspects of this novel.

Walker, Pamela. *Twyla.* Englewood Cliffs, N.J.: Prentice-Hall, 1973. 125 pp. Reading Level: YA/MA
Disability: Intellectual Impairment

The death in an auto accident of Twyla Krotz, a fifteen-year-old retarded girl, is reported in the local newspaper. Through her letters to Wally, a former student at the high school with whom she is infatuated, the events of her life are revealed. Twyla wants a boyfriend, girl friends, some moderate success in school, and security and support at home. Her pitiful letters unfold the hopelessness of these modest aspirations. Wally, away in college, has no real interest in her and is embarrassed and bewildered by her attentions. Basically a decent person, he neither wants to encourage nor hurt her, but soon finds himself entangled in a unilateral romantic relationship. Naive and easily hoodwinked, Twyla is readily deceived by other adolescents she thinks of as her friends. They cruelly induce her to compete in a school beauty contest, aware that she will be humiliated, and cynically cheat her in a bogus car-buying scheme. Her best friends are unable to control their own lives and can scarcely provide Twyla with the support she needs. Her teachers accurately assess her modest academic skills and suggest a trade school, but are insensitive to the uncontrollable panic this prospect causes. Her mother, although loving, is manifestly inadequate to the task of providing her daughter with either the skills or the psychological strength to cope with an overwhelmingly callous environment. No help is available from her father whose whereabouts are unknown. Twyla's last pathetic letter to Wally tells him she hopes she will be missed when she is gone and suggests that the auto crash was deliberate—the circumstances of her grinding, totally unrewarding existence inexorably force her to this terrible act.

Analysis. Twyla is the devastating portrait of the consequences of intellectual insufficiency in a hostile, unsupportive environment. The story focuses on the often painful social and societal ramifications of retardation. Twyla's simplistic thinking, her unrealistic assessment of either her abilities or prospects, lack of savvy, poor predictive and interpretive skills, and extreme gullibility are almost classically typical. Letting Twyla speak for herself intensifies the portrait and reveals the thought processes and expressive limitations of such an adolescent in a moving and poignant manner. The misspellings, typing errors, and poor grammatical constructions make difficult reading at first, but ultimately add to the overall impact. Walker's daring revelation of Twyla's death at the outset, followed by a recapitulation of the antecedent events, in no way detracts from the book's tension or the reader's involvement in this skillfully crafted, compassionate novel.

Walsh, Jill Paton. *Goldengrove.* New York: Farrar, Straus & Giroux, 1972. 130 pp. Reading Level: YA
Disability: Visual Impairment

Each summer Madge and Paul return to Goldengrove, their grandmother's Cornwall home near the sea. They play happily as always until they meet Ralph, a blind professor, who has rented a cottage nearby, ostensibly to finish a manuscript. Madge is strangely drawn to the man, to Paul's dismay and, in a heavy emotional scene, the professor tells Madge about the life of the poet, Milton, and about his own wife who left him, concluding that one must adjust to life's vicissitudes. Overwhelmed, Madge, in a gush of self-sacrifice, proposes that she stay with him. However, she perceives that she has been rejected by the professor, echoing her father's abandonment of her at the time of her parents' divorce. Madge becomes ill and when Paul comes to cheer her up, their closeness is reestablished. Madge learns that Paul, whom she thought was her cousin, is really her brother. Recalling Ralph's philosophy, she is able to accept this traumatic revelation. But the blind man, totally self-absorbed, is trapped by inertia; unable to profit from his own advice, he is estranged from life, withdraws and waits.

Analysis: Although Goldengrove is initially conceived of as a child's paradise, the setting soon projects a brooding sense of peril and near tragedy. Patterns of abandonment are pervasive. The story is essentially a mood piece examining the barriers, real or contrived, that interfere with personal relationships. The slow-paced, reflective novel recounts approaches and retreats from relationships and how these are perceived differently from various perspectives.

Warwick, Dolores. *Learn to Say Goodbye.* New York: Farrar, Straus & Giroux, 1971. 179 pp. Reading Level: YA
Disability: Emotional Dysfunction

For eight years, Lucy Brannan and her younger sister, Marcella, have lived in orphanages run by nuns. Their mother, an alcoholic, has not seen her younger daughter since she was removed from her custody, but sees Lucy intermittently. The older girl is bitter, filled with doubts and hostility, but has managed to adjust. Marcella is emotionally disturbed; her behavior is inappropriate, bizarre, and morbid. She combines poetic innocence with an icy astuteness. When Marcella gets off a bus labeled "Annual Orphans' Picnic," she says to the waiting television cameramen, "I've gone around the world on a drop of water. . . . Your sign there is only a reminder of where we've all been, what we've all lost. It's strange, though, to see you trying to hide your loss by advertising ours. Don't you see how it's all the same thing?" The people watching are aghast at the seemingly irrational words of the child, which contain a crystalline truth. Lucy, able to reach her sister at last, vents her anger at the cameras and drags Marcella away. Soon after, would-be foster parents who had seen Lucy on television request permission to have her live with them. The nuns, who have been preparing her for independence, permit her to go. She visits Marcella one last time to promise she will always come whenever she is needed.

Analysis: Lucy is portrayed as a strong, albeit bristly and insecure adolescent. Despite the psychological abuse she receives from her mother, the woman's weak, inadequate, and punitive love still does provide her daughter with some periodic relief from the abandonment and lovelessness she has experienced. Marcella, by contrast, and despite the care she receives from the nuns, is too devastated to keep her ego intact. In this literate novel the author explores how the pressures of lovelessness and insecurity eventually force the development of coping skills that are inimical to normal functioning. Internal development is more critical than external action in this study of children under stress.

Watson, Sally. *Other Sandals*. New York: Holt, Rinehart and Winston, 1966. 223 pp. Reading Level: YA
Disability: Orthopedic Impairment, Speech Impairment; also intellectual impairment

Two Israeli families each decide that their children would benefit from a different environment. Eytan, self-pitying since the car accident that damaged his leg, is sent to a kibbutz, changing places with Devra, a hyperactive girl whose stuttering speech reflects her body tension. In addition, Devra is an anti-Arabist, but her personal involvement with a young Arab woman ultimately moderates her antipathy. Eytan, anticipating rejection, takes offense at the friendly overtures from the kibbutzniks, and his prickly behavior ensures that his prediction will come true. Turning to an African student in the community, he learns judo and is gradually made to exercise his leg, which he had unwisely avoided using. He also meets Zorik, one of the youth group who is acknowledged as retarded, but who nonetheless is included in all the action. Returning from an orchard where he has been humiliated, Eytan discovers a girl bitten by a viper. Despite his fear and aversion, he kills the snake, drains the wound, and attempts to carry her to the compound on his back. Just before his weakened leg gives way, he gets assistance and the injured girl is saved. Eytan now has his own self-respect as well as the reluctant esteem of his peers.

Analysis. Watson's theme is broadcast in her title: changing perspectives will change perceptions. Both Devra and Eytan undergo some modulation of their views but no excessive metamorphosis takes place. No one demeans or spends time in extensive corrective therapy with Devra; her stutter is perceived of as simply another example of her impulsiveness, speed, and energy in dealing with the world. Responses to Zorik vary and are based on his real limitations rather than unreasoning rejection. The others interpret, reexplain, but sometimes ignore him or act exasperated—all possible, if not admirable, reactions. Zorik's inner thoughts are simply stated but not in a deprecating manner. A man with an amputated leg is shown in a cameo part, ostensibly as a model of a well-adjusted, outgoing adult. Eytan's growth comes from addressing his physical problem indirectly through the judo training and by insight painfully gained through interaction with his peers. Watson's analogue of disability and prejudice as inhibitors of understanding is the central theme of the novel.

Watson, Simon. *The Partisan*. New York: Macmillan, 1975. 143 pp.
Reading Level: YA
Disability: General Health Problems

Two adolescent boys encounter Dom, the young heir to Lammercot, a walled estate near their homes. They enjoy an idyllic interlude at
the estate with Dom, who is severely asthmatic and often must use a
wheelchair because of his weakened condition. Some brutish louts in-
vade their domain and when one of them seizes leadership the group
changes to a destructive, aggressive gang whose climactic act is an invasion of Dom's house. They steal some ancient weapons, including the
partisan, an enormous ceremonial pike that is a family symbol of prestige and honor. Energized by the threat to his family's symbolic survival, Dom, as if impelled by an implacable destiny, challenges the usurper
for the leadership of the group. In his weakened and fragile condition,
it is inevitable that he lose, and he almost dies in the confrontation.
Dom is hospitalized, the partisan is broken, and the peaceful, happy
days at Lammercot are over.

Analysis. Dom's strength of character is contrasted with his extreme
physical weakness. The debilitation caused by his condition makes his
willingness to take on the bully seem exceptionally courageous. The
asthma is only a device to heighten the conflict and set up the inevitable
tragedy. Dom, who personifies gentility and reverence for traditional
virtues, is savaged by the coarse, cruel, but more powerful opponent.
The plot is slow-moving and the ending abrupt, but the mood of impending disaster is successfully sustained.

Weber, Lenora Mattingly. *Beany Has a Secret Life*. New York: Crowell, 1955. 262 pp. Reading Level: YA
Disability: Orthopedic Impairment

Beany Malone resents her new stepmother, a woman more interested in pursuing her artistic talents than in being a homemaker. Recently asked to join a secret club by the glamorous Maurine, Beany is
happy to be distracted from what she perceives as a disastrous development in her home life. One of the boys in the club has a sister who is
confined to a wheelchair because of polio. Rosellen is kind, gentle,
patient, sensitive, and wise. Having "suffered so much herself" she can
even hear the pain in other people's voices. One night Beany uses her
stepmother's car for an errand and unintentionally leaves the keys in
the ignition. The next morning the car is missing, but is later located.
Beany is angry because she thinks her stepmother suspects she took the
car, damaged it, and is clumsily trying to conceal her negligence. All
problems come to a climax when it is revealed that Maurine and her
boyfriend took the missing vehicle. As in all such books, issues are

resolved neatly: The guilty young woman is reconciled with her family, her boyfriend does not lose his job, Beany appreciates the virtues of her father's new wife, and every female not previously spoken for begins a new romance.

Analysis. Rosellen is not a central character in this bubblegum romance; however, she embodies, in excess, all those passive virtues apparently presumed suitable for one in her condition. The effervescent, impulsive, action-oriented heroine is counterbalanced by the less mobile, quiet, sagacious girl in the wheelchair who functions as the resident saint. To endorse Rosellen's role as an object of charity when this is totally unwarranted is patronizing, exaggerated, and condescending. It is typified by Mr. Malone's benevolence reported to Beany by Rosellen: "And once—I'll never forget it—your father passed me in my wheel chair in the aisle, and he leaned down and squeezed my hand and said, 'Here's an orchid for you, sweetheart,' and left a five-dollar bill in my hand."

Weber, Lenora Mattingly. *A Bright Star Falls.* New York: Crowell, 1959. 260 pp. Reading Level: YA
Disability: Orthopedic Impairment

The school principal's restrained praise is disappointing to Beany Malone, newly appointed editor of the high school paper. The administrator criticizes the paper as too flippant and too engrossed with trivial affairs at the expense of serious student concerns. In an odd response to this criticism, the staff institutes an advice column. When a letter appears bemoaning the fate of the poorly dressed coed, Rosellen, a friend of Beany's who has been crippled by polio, suggests a used-clothing sale at rock bottom prices. Beany's brother is infatuated with a vicious, exploitive, dishonest girl, and the central concern of this story is the evolution of this unpleasant relationship and his eventual enlightenment. Rosellen lets fall various broad clues that her health is failing, but her parents and friends are oblivious to her declining physical state. Weakened, she falls, breaking several ribs, but nobly refuses hospitalization. Her accommodating doctor does not insist, nor does he advise her parents of the seriousness of her condition, and, without benefit of x-rays or other diagnostic basics, treats her at home. Rosellen fades quickly and dies just before Christmas. Beany's brother finally awakens to the moral shabbiness of his paramour, while Rosellen's brother, distraught over her death, is finally reconciled to its inevitability and resumes his status as Beany's boyfriend. The clothing sale is a great success, the newspaper staff is developing a new closeness, and the poorly dressed coeds are now modishly garbed and consequently much happier.

Analysis. This soap opera is steeped in demeaning attitudes toward the disabled. Rosellen is portrayed as one whose thoughts are all of others and there seems no limit to her self-effacing, long-suffering nature. Reflecting on her life while she is very sick, she avers: "I'd rather die than be a burden. Hospitals—and being helpless—and having to be waited on—and upsetting lives." This proposition that the disabled are a burden to others and themselves is never countered. Even the doctor who attends her does not bother her parents with specifics about the extent of her illness and the priest who delivers her eulogy says: "Perhaps the kindest angel . . . was the angel of death that touched her arm." The implication that family life should not be interrupted or "burdened" with the need to care for the legitimate health needs of disabled family members is odious.

Weber, Lenora Mattingly. *Come Back, Wherever You Are*. New York: Crowell, 1969. 240 pp. Reading Level: YA
Disability: Emotional Dysfunction

Beany's friend, Kay, is hospitalized with leukemia. Beany agrees to take over the care of Kay's "out of kilter" son, Jody, since the father, Joe, cannot afford a housekeeper because of the tremendous medical expenses. Jody is sullen, negativistic, boastful, and panicky whenever his father leaves. Beany is advised that the child's misbehavior probably has deeper roots. She subsequently learns that he has alternately been indulged, then beaten or otherwise abused. Beany manages to sneak the boy into the hospital to see his mother one last time before she dies. Kay's bracelet, a gift from Joe, is stolen by Yvonne, his former girl friend, who hopes to be Joe's next wife. Jody blanches at the sight of Yvonne and it is soon revealed that she was working at the hospital when he was sick and it was she who pushed Jody's bed into a dark storage room where he remained alone and unattended all night. This trauma precipitated his subsequent emotional instability. Joe severs all contact with Yvonne, moves into the roominghouse of a friend of Beany's, and makes arrangements for appropriate schooling for his son. Jody responds positively, and, for the first time since Beany has known him, he laughs.

Analysis. This melodrama is replete with simplistic explorations and quickie resolutions of complex problems. Years of abuse and unintentional neglect are cancelled by gestures of good intent. The writing is pure treacle: "The world was right again. A time for words, a time for keeping still. So she didn't say, 'Husbands need TLC—meaning tender, loving care—too, and I've certainly shortchanged you.' But she moved closer to him. He pulled the clasped hands up and held hers against his cheek. It was almost as though he said, 'Together we can work it out—somehow.' " The only redeeming feature of this banal book is the por-

trayal of Jody's behavior, not as simply obnoxious but as the manifestation of a deeply traumatic event. Moreover, Jody functions as a device
to propel others to action, exemplified in the decision of a character to
become a psychiatrist as a result of dealing with Jody's problems.

Weik, Mary Hays. *The Jazz Man*. Illus. by Ann Grifalconi. New
York: Atheneum, 1966. 42 pp. Reading Level: MC
Disability: Orthopedic Impairment; also intellectual impairment

Reality and illusion merge, intermingle and disperse in Zeke's life.
Although nine years old, he cannot read. Whether this is a result of
deprivation or retardation is unclear. He is home alone much of the
time when other children are in school. His parents appear at odd times
and respond sporadically and inadequately to his needs. Although he is
loved, the pressures of their own unmet wants render the parents incapable of providing either sustenance or structure. The most important
person in his life is the jazz man who lives in a brightly painted room
across the courtyard. The man's music is wild and vibrant and fills Zeke
with hope, curiosity, and excitement. Zeke's parents, ground down and
disheartened by their poverty, abandon him. The boy searches for them
in an agonizing dream in which he finds the jazz man. His parents
return home to love and care for him, but whether this later event really
happens or is only a dream is not known.

Analysis. The many unexplained elements and lack of precision,
oddly enough, do not diminish the impact of the story: Rather they
underscore the impression that the "jazz man" should not be perceived
literally, but responded to as a metaphor for a rich, though unfulfilled
and elusive, promise. Zeke is a child hobbled by limitations, untended
by either his family or society, and locked into a barren, isolated environment. Nevertheless he hungers after a fuller life as represented by
the jazz man's music. The important but ambivalent roles of the family,
school, and environment find surrealistic expression in this memorable
work. Weik requires that the adult reader work hard to deal with the
imagery in the story; child readers, while able to relate to surface elements, may be confused about deeper meanings. Youngsters may be
further troubled by the behavior of adults in the story. Zeke's mother
pulls him onto her lap for a reading lesson, reads him the same story
twice, and inexplicably begins to cry. She seems unable to protect or
nurture him and eventually deserts him. His father, although previously loving, also abandons him. Grifalconi's stark and powerful
woodcuts underscore the conflicting verbal images.

Wersba, Barbara. *Let Me Fall before I Fly*. Illus. by Mercer Mayer.
New York: Atheneum, 1971. 31 pp. Reading Level: MC
Disability: Emotional Dysfunction

A boy sees a miniature circus in his yard. He becomes enchanted with these tiny people and watches them every day as they set up and perform their acts and then relax at the end of the day. Soon the boy's whole life is absorbed with this fantasy. When his mother tells him it is vacation time, he becomes panicky and pleads to stay home, but this odd request is rejected. He spends a week at the beach collecting shells he hopes his special friend from the circus will like. The night before his return there is a wild storm and the boy finds that nothing remains of his miniature world. His parents, worried about his morose and disconsolate behavior, persuade their son to explain his deep unhappiness. He does and, at first, his parents don't believe him but "when they saw his seriousness and his suffering, when they realized that he wanted to die because his friends had died," they arrange for him to see a psychiatrist. The child begins to doubt whether his tiny world ever existed. After a time he returns to school. "He had become more selfish and frequently argued with other children," pretending to be like everyone else. Later, in the boy's dream about his circus, he becomes as small as the performers and joins his favorite on the trapeze. "Without understanding what it meant, he whispered to himself, 'Let me fall before I fly.' " He does fall, but is unhurt and resumes his acrobatics. When he awakens, he sees that his circus people are still with him.

Analysis. It is never really clear whether the boy's imaginary world should be considered fantasy or hallucination, but as a fantasy, the story is unsatisfactory because of the presence of the psychiatrist and the child's death wish. The author contrasts the boy's generosity and selflessness while hallucinating with his selfish, belligerent, and dishonest behavior needed to accommodate reality, leaving the reader to wonder if the author is suggesting that a world of irrationality is preferable to the real one. The format suggests a child's book, but the confusing and quasi-surrealistic style renders it an unlikely choice for that audience.

Whitney, Leon F. *That Useless Hound.* Illus. by Ernest Hart. New York: Dodd, Mead, 1950. 211 pp. Reading Level: MC
Disability: Orthopedic Impairment

Dave Ward is the only child of the warden of a southern prison. His bout with polio left him with one weakened leg, which severely impedes his free movement. His two best friends are Abe and Shorty, black trustees at the prison. Shorty ties Dave's weak leg to his own so that the boy is forced to move it in a vigorous and near normal manner. Despite his father's disdain, Dave, with the help of his friends, trains his bloodhound to be a skilled tracker. Useless, the hound, proves his value when he successfully trails an escaped prisoner, rescues Dave from his kidnappers, and locates a lost little girl and a 90-year-old woman. When the child's parents offer to buy Useless, Dave, although heart-broken, agrees, knowing that his parents urgently need money to pay his hospital bills. Useless will not trail for anyone but his original masters and when his talents are needed to trace the kidnappers of another youth, Dave and the trustees are called upon. The boy is rescued and his kidnappers caught. Useless remains with Dave and Abe and Shorty are granted pardons but they vow their friendship with Dave will continue.

Analysis. This well-intentioned work excoriates the southern prison system, particularly in regard to its brutal treatment of black prisoners. Unfortunately, the tone is condescending and paternalistic. Dave, although a child, appears as the leader of his adult black friends and their proper role, apparently, is subservient to his. The warden refers to these men as "the boys" and this accurately, though inadvertently, defines their status. This novel concentrates less on illness and more on aftereffects and attitudes of the person undergoing rehabilitation. Dave begins to recover from the effects of polio when his interest and energies are directed away from his limitations and he becomes absorbed in a new project—the training of his hound. The unlikely therapy provided by Shorty yields too complete and uncomplicated a recovery to be believable. Although the plot is brisk, many improbable events strain the credulity of the reader.

Whitney, Phyllis A. *Mystery of the Haunted Pool.* Illus. by H. Tom Hall. Philadelphia: Westminster, 1960. 223 pp. Reading Level: MC/YA
Disability: Orthopedic Impairment

Since Gene was hit by a car two years ago, he has had to wear braces. The cost of rehabilitation has been tremendous, and his grandfather may have to rent his home to meet the mounting expenses. Susan, a young newcomer, observes Gene futilely trying to play basketball, and when she is seen, she brazenly asks to be taught to shoot baskets. He happily demonstrates, eager to emphasize his skills rather than his disabilities. In addition to hearing that one of Gene's ancestors was murdered by pirates who boarded his ship, taking the valuables he was transporting, she also hears a rumor that Gene's house is haunted. An eccentric woman claims that she sees a face in a pool but this turns out to be a figurehead from the old captured ship. The children investigate and discover the whereabouts of the long-missing jewels. The grandfather's financial problems are consequently ameliorated, and Gene's self-pity and withdrawal are replaced by self-confidence.

Analysis. Through the agency of a good juvenile mystery, the author has examined a youngster's feelings of guilt and frustration over the consequences of carelessness, the acknowledged cause of the accident that resulted in Gene's disablement and his family's financial crisis. His loving and insightful grandfather understands Gene's abrasive acts and self-denigrating feelings and the old man participates in several discussions devoted to the obligation of coming to terms with one's problems. Gene's involvement with solving the mystery diverts his neurotic self-absorption. His new young friend's sympathy and support are shown as instrumental in promoting his improved attitude.

Whitney, Phyllis A. *Nobody Likes Trina*. Philadelphia: Westminster, 1972. 187 pp. Reading Level: YA
Disability: Orthopedic Impairment

Sandy is unimpressed with the first two girls she meets when her family moves to a rural area: Melissa, the daughter of her father's partner, is snobbish, rude, and the arbiter of the social scene, and Trina is an unpleasant, crippled girl Melissa has warned her against. Sandy's classmates treat Trina as a leper, exclude her, make wild accusations, pretend she's invisible, and engage in other hateful acts. The girls pressure Sandy to join them in their persecution, which she does, but is then sickened by her own cowardice. When Cliff, another neighbor, invites Sandy to visit Trina, she sees something of the lonely girl's barren life. Trina's fabrications and obnoxious behavior become understandable as the fantasies she requires to withstand her sterile, isolated existence. The harassment becomes so intense that Sandy shoves Melissa and the two girls begin to fight. After Trina rescues Sandy, the teacher drives her home, explaining more about Trina's background. Sandy approaches the crippled girl and, as they start to talk, understanding and the beginnings of closeness are felt. Their teacher subtly tries to manipulate the situation, assigning Trina, Sandy, and Melissa and her buddies to one group to study the environment, a topic on which Trina is exceptionally knowledgeable. When this group is sent on a field trip, Melissa ignores Trina's warning about a bear. As the huge animal approaches, Melissa becomes paralyzed and Trina runs out, throwing logs to divert the bear, which then turns on her. Trina's twisted leg impairs her sprint back to the cabin. Her dog attacks the animal and Trina is saved. Melissa tries to explain to the adults that Trina was at fault. However, when Melissa's cohorts are confronted with this outright lie, they look at her in shock, presaging the collapse of their unified support for her cruel behavior.

Analysis. Trina wears a mask of stupidity to fend off intimacy. Although she is sullen and unattractive, her virtues are also presented. She has high intelligence, expertise in several subjects, especially ecology, and feelings of tenderness about her dead mother. Further, she is able to set the leg of an injured dog whose limp thereafter echoes her own. The author does some preaching in showing parallels in human and animal ecology and in suggesting the rejection of a philosophy that is based on feelings of superiority for a more egalitarian, sharing point of view. Trina's behavior is well explained and her anger perfectly justified. A thought-provoking theme Whitney proposes in this slow-moving, convoluted novel is that the victim and persecutor are essentially operating from the same motivations.

Whitney, Phyllis A. *Secret of the Emerald Star*. Illus. by Alex Stein. Philadelphia: Westminster, 1964, 233 pp. Reading Level: MC/YA. *Disability:* Visual Impairment

Robin, thirteen, a new resident of Staten Island, is curious about the puzzling behavior of the Devery family, her neighbors, and particularly that of the volatile Stella, a blind girl about her age. The two youngsters become friendly, despite the stony opposition of Stella's imperious grandmother, who suffocates the sightless girl with foolish and inhibiting restrictions. Stella seeks comfort and solace from a star-shaped emerald pin given to her by her Cuban grandmother and defiantly wears it against Mrs. Devery's instructions. Stella is reluctantly allowed to pose for Robin, who envisions using the model of her new friend's sculptured head as an entry in an art competition. Robin not only learns braille from Stella but, as their friendship deepens, learns about blindness and empathizes with Stella's frustrations. Feeling secure in their closeness, she chastises Stella about her tantrums and criticizes her callous manipulation of other people. An unsavory stranger, claiming to be a relative of Stella's dead father, attempts to coerce Mrs. Devery by demanding money to buy guns for Cuban insurgents, a cause her son supported. The two girls suspect his motives before the old woman takes action against him, but he makes his escape with Mrs. Devery's jewels after locking the girls in a dark basement. Fortunately, Stella had retrieved her pin earlier and hidden it in the moist clay of Robin's sculpture. Stella has matured enough not to feel compelled to reveal the pin's whereabouts, which would ruin her friend's excellent work. Robin's sensitivity is also demonstrated when she realizes the depth of her friend's sacrifice and unselfishly destroys her completed model, returning the cherished jeweled star.

Analysis. Woven into this mystery is a series of highly palatable and knowledgeable lectures about blindness and attitudes toward the blind. Whitney, despite her evident admiration for the blind heroine, nevertheless shows Stella's considerable faults as well as her numerous strengths. The writing is crisp and the major characters are developed well; however, the criminal and his scheme are presented less convincingly. This lack of emphasis seems appropriate, since in this instance, the author seems less concerned with the trappings of the evildoer than with an exploration of how blindness affects individuals, what stress does to relationships, and how stereotyped thinking in labeling people who are different can become an emotional straightjacket.

Wibberley, Leonard. *Flint's Island*. New York: Farrar, Straus & Giroux, 1972. 166 pp. Reading Level: MC/YA
Disability: Orthopedic Impairment

It is August 1760, and Captain Samuels is searching for some land containing a tree suitable for replacing his broken mast. An island, once the property of a notorious pirate, is sighted and the ship puts in for repairs. Whelan, a young lad, and Arrow, a seaman, go ashore. After the two become separated, Whelan hears a shot and finds his companion murdered. A peg-legged man approaches the boy, identifies himself as Long John Silver, and, upon meeting the captain, asks to be allowed to leave the island with the ship. The captain is suspicious, but agrees. Using a subterfuge, the cunning pirate, with the aid of his hidden gang, entraps the captain and takes control of the ship. Whelan and another seaman free the crew and recapture the ship in a bloody battle. Shorthanded, the captain must use the services of Silver, who gains favor with the crew and leads a successful mutiny. The captain, Whelan, and two others are set adrift in a small boat that safely reaches the Georgia shoreline. The government dispatches a crew to capture the pirate. The ship is destroyed, but once again the villain manages to elude justice. Whelan is offered a plot of land once belonging to Silver. He recalls a story his father often recounted of a mock funeral on the property and discovers the fraudulent gravesite from which he unearths the pirate's buried treasure. He generously distributes the fortune among the families of the crew members who perished and to his remaining loyal shipmates.

Analysis. The author's infatuation with *Treasure Island* is clearly discernible in this stirring blood-and-thunder sequel. The lame pirate is an eighteenth-century villain with a heart of iron but a tongue of gold. His peg leg is clearly a prop, a mark signifying an evil nature that he cannily employs to elicit sympathy. Although he is the embodiment of wickedness, Silver is really a character in a celluloid swashbuckler, and as such, his crutch and peg leg are but part of his costume.

Wilder, Laura Ingalls. *Little Town on the Prairie*. Illus. by Garth Williams. New York: Harper & Row, 1941. 307 pp. Reading Level: MC
Disability: Visual Impairment

The Ingalls family's strength, resiliency, and ingenuity are effective bulwarks against the frigid winters of the unsettled Dakota Territory.

Their love and cohesiveness are important contributions to the functioning and optimistic attitude of Mary, their oldest daughter, who is blind. She is expected to make her contribution to the family's economy and only partial lessening of responsibilities is made for her in accordance with her impairment. The family willingly scrimps so that Mary can go to college. Laura, the narrator and middle child, does her share by first hiring herself out to a seamstress and later, at fifteen, teaching school. Her salary of forty dollars is to be reserved for her sister's tuition and such related costs as braille slates. Although Mary's presence is only peripheral in these episodes, concern for her permeates the story.

Analysis. This classic story and marvelous illustrations provide a delightful, warm model of a family and their concern for a young adult with an impairment. The entire series reveals how a family responds without overprotection, and Mary's adult functioning vindicates the validity of their approach. The novel is a fictionalized autobiography but, while historically accurate, the unfortunate minstrel sequence that is included flaws this otherwise satisfying and absorbing book.

Wilder, Laura Ingalls. *These Happy Golden Years.* Illus. by Garth Williams. New York: Harper & Row, 1943. 289 pp. Reading Level: MC
Disability: Visual Impairment

This continuation of the Ingalls' adventures chronicles the period after the family settled in the sparsely populated Dakota Territory. Mary Ingalls, the blind older sister, now away at college, plays only a peripheral role in the book but maintains her cherished position in the family's thoughts and conversations. When she returns to visit, her actions reveal her as competent, mature, and playful. As she gives her father his present, she recounts how she and her college roommate chose it. "We went downtown to find something for you. She can see colors if they are bright, but the clerk didn't know it. We thought it would be fun to mystify him, so Blanche signaled the colors to me, and he thought we could tell them by touch. I knew by the feeling that it was good silk. My, we did fool that clerk!" There are some few descriptive passages in which Mary shows her family how she has learned to write in braille, but for more substantial information, the earlier volumes in this series should be consulted.

Analysis. The presentation of Mary's saintliness is tempered by a realistic approach to her activities of daily living. She is pictured in idealized illustrations but no more so than others. This series is unique in looking at an impaired character during the growing-up process. How different age levels place varying demands upon both the family and the character with a disability are revealed in this warm family portrait.

Windsor, Patricia. *Home Is Where Your Feet Are Standing.* New York: Harper & Row, 1975. 247 pp. Reading Level: YA/MA
Disability: Neurological Impairment

Colin, a difficult, clumsy child, lives with his mother and two sisters in a tiny village in England. He is a very poor student in a totally unsympathetic school. Moreover, his vacillating, manipulative behavior is exasperating to his family and teachers. Some apparently inexplicable events have occurred at home, which his mother suspects are the work of ghosts. Actually, Colin's two disagreeable sisters (who hope their mother will move back to America) as well as the housekeeper have been responsible for objects sailing through the air, noises that seem to emerge from the walls, and the extensive breakage of fragile objects. Colin overhears a discussion his mother has about these events in which he is also mentioned, as are poltergeists. He deduces he has a dread disease known as "poltergice" and decides to run away from home, managing to travel as far as London. He is pleased to find that he can read a map, take trains and subways, purchase food, and behave in ways exceptionally competent for one with ostensible learning problems. In the city he encounters Chris, a would-be poet, who returns Colin to his home. Chris finds Colin's mother attractive and a kindred spirit. The school continues in its criticism of Colin, thereby further antagonizing the boy and exacerbating his conduct. Surprisingly, he enjoys reading and does well in math; the unidentified specific learning disability clearly does not affect those activities.

Analysis. Colin's mother is overindulgent, as random and spontaneous in her responses to him as she is to other aspects of her life. When the boy throws a tantrum while with Chris, he is removed from the car, so he abandons that tactic. It is implied that equivalent firmness at home could greatly improve his character. The frustrations of a boy unable to meet the demands of the world he lives in are extensively developed despite the flippant, impertinent style and mildly humorous, offbeat tone. His learning enigma remains unexplained.

Windsor, Patricia. *The Summer Before.* New York: Harper & Row, 1973. 241 pp. Reading Level: YA
Disability: Emotional Dysfunction

After the death of her best friend, Bradley, and the traumatic events compounding it, Alex was committed to a psychiatric hospital. Even though she has recovered sufficiently to be released, terrible nightmares and uncontrollable fears continue to torment the girl. Her mother hovers over her, afraid for her daughter, but also worried about what the neighbors might think. Alex reflects upon her relationship with Bradley and their experiences. Bradley was a gifted, spirited nonconformist whose harmless but unconventional behavior led to several encounters with the police. One afternoon he and Alex were seen swimming nude in a secluded area. The interlude became the topic of neighborhood gossip and Alex was consequently forbidden to see him again. Her parents planned to send her away to camp but when she learned that Bradley was leaving home, she joined him. They found their way to a puritanical, dirty, and ineptly run commune. The two friends hardly ever saw each other, and Alex became depressed with the drudgery and boredom and was frightened at the untended serious illness of one of the members. She and Bradley finally left with a man Alex disliked intensely. Drunk, he demolished the car; Bradley was killed and Alex hospitalized.

After many months her fears abate and her nightmares become less frequent. Sessions with a psychiatrist help her to work through her guilt and anguish over her friend's death. At last she is able to return to school where she finds that the teachers and students casually accept her and she is even warmly welcomed by some. She writes in the journal that has been a source of relief during her long ordeal, addressing herself by the various names that signal different aspects of her life: "Apple Alex Sandy Alexandra. Welcome to the earth."

Analysis. Alex is seen as a conventional adolescent experiencing many of the doubts, insecurities, and conflicts of her generation and who, through a series of tragic and enervating experiences, has been catapulted into a dysfunctional state. Her naive and simplistic expectations that life in a commune would be freer and less stultifying are cruelly shattered. Alex has strong feelings about what she is leaving behind, but no sense of where she is going. The mindless irresponsibility that resulted in her boyfriend's death is a shocking, incomprehensible intrusion into what had been a rather cloistered life. The reader sees all events and characters through Alex's eyes, and the painful recovery from her emotional disorder is vividly conveyed, but each event and feeling is explored in such ponderous detail that the story proceeds sluggishly. The first-person narrative flashback technique is an appropriate one for this content. The depiction is realistic—neither exaggerating nor minimizing the effects of such an experience—and the tempered, optimistic ending seems plausible.

Winthrop, Elizabeth. *A Little Demonstration of Affection.* New York: Harper & Row, 1975. 152 pp. Reading Level: YA
Disability: General Health Problems

John, the oldest of three children, initiates a family project of digging a hole large enough to be used as a hideaway. Soon after the enterprise begins, he takes off with a friend, leaving the two younger siblings to finish. Charley, the middle child, has had asthma, and the restrictions it imposes have resulted in exclusion from most of his siblings' activities. The family rents a farm for a two-week summer vacation during which a vicious neighbor shoots Charley's dog, claiming the animal was chasing his chickens. It was a deliberate act of cruelty, but their father has no legal recourse, and Charley, heartbroken at his pet's death, sees his father's inaction as near betrayal. Jenny, the youngest child, begins work on the hole when they return home, encouraging her brother to help in an effort to distract him from his grief-induced depression. Charley discharges some of his pain through the writing of a story about his dog. After he and his sister become closer, he rewrites the tale involving her in a key role. When he reads her the new version, Jenny is very moved and begins to cry. Charley holds her until she is able to stop. To the girl, this affectionate gesture assumes sensual overtones. Charley becomes healthier during the summer as his asthmatic troubles fade and the physical activity builds his strength. Jenny's best friend returns from her vacation and comments on Charley as a potential boyfriend, a suggestion that unreasonably angers and anatagonizes his sister. When the hole is finished, Jenny persuades Charley they should camp out in it one night. She tries to recapture the moment of tenderness she felt when he comforted her after reading the story of his dog, but he pushes her roughly away. Jenny angrily withdraws from the whole family, including John, who has just returned home. Her behavior becomes increasingly distressing to her family as she reacts to her unspoken guilt and fears. She finally talks with her father, pouring out her feelings of attraction to Charley and alarm at the possibility that, had he not discouraged her, she might have neither stopped him nor wanted to stop him. The act of unburdening herself to her father and his reassurances comfort the distraught adolescent after which she is able to place the incident in its proper perspective and to resume her former role in the family structure.

Analysis. Scenes dealing with Charley coping with his asthmatic attacks are realistic. Although the condition had once been severe enough to require hospitalization, his increased age and vigor have apparently reduced its impact by the story's end. The boy is angered by his parents' concern and, although it is certainly within reasonable limits, his resentment is a plausible response. The author handles the incestuous attraction with great delicacy and implies it stems in part at least from the parents' near total lack of demonstrativeness. The characterizations are excellent and the use of language skillful, but the book's outstanding quality is its beautiful and sensitive exploration of the feelings of the central character.

Wise, William. *The Cowboy Surprise.* Illus. by Paul Galdone. New York: Putnam, 1961. 47 pp. Reading Level: YC
Disability: Visual Impairment

Mike and Sally are the butt of teasing at their school since they are the only children who wear glasses. Mike persuades Wild Bill, a cowboy who also wears glasses, to come to school. When Wild Bill arrives astride his horse, he informs the students that lots of people, even Indians, sometimes need glasses. The children are so astonished at this intelligence that they cease tormenting Sally and Mike and even wish for glasses of their own.

Analysis. Using an heroic model to sell or oversell an idea is not new. Although the story is preposterous, the book has value as an example of using simple stories for sensitization purposes.

Witheridge, Elizabeth. *Dead End Bluff.* Illus. by Charles Geer. New York: Atheneum, 1966. 186 pp. Reading Level: MC/YA
Disability: Visual Impairment

Although he is blind, Quig Smith is his town's best hope of winning the free-style event at the next swim meet. His speed is good, but every time he approaches the raft that is used as a marker, he goes off his time, afraid he will slam his head against the hard surface. Quig is offered a job by George Munson helping with the new litter at his kennels. While he is on the job, a couple drive up, examine the litter, and express an interest in Quig's favorite pup. Both boy and animal take an immediate dislike to them. They return one day when Quig is alone with the dogs, steal the pups, and conceal them on a nearby island. Although Quig can identify the thieves, having recognized the woman's perfume and the sound of the car, the sheriff is unable to find them. Convinced that the dogs are hidden along the river, Quig persuades his friends to search there. The dogs are found, but the culprits escape. Quig swims well enough to tie for first at the meet, allowing the other members to clinch first place for the team. Tommy, Quig's younger brother, climbs down Dead End Bluff where Quig has been forbidden to go. The youngster becomes frightened and Quig climbs down after him, retrieving him from the rapids into which he had fallen and keeping him safe until both are rescued by the fire department. Through this courageous act he signals his independence from parental restrictions.

Analysis. Dead End Bluff neither exaggerates nor diminishes the effects of blindness on an otherwise average youth. Quig is presented as a normal boy with a moderately overprotective father and friends who accommodate their responses to his disability but are in no way condescending. He is moody, excitable, happy, worried, discouraged, or hopeful—in short, subject to the same vagaries of feeling as everyone else and struggling for the same goals as other adolescents. His achievements, while outstanding, are only moderately so and in no sense heroic. The illustrations fully support this image of an average, nice, decent kid—who happens to be blind.

Wojciechowska, Maia. *A Single Light.* New York: Harper & Row, 1968. 149 pp. Reading Level: YA/MA
Disability: Auditory Impairment, Speech Impairment, Orthopedic Impairment

Anna is born to a Spanish peasant who dies in childbirth. The superstitious villagers conclude that her mother "must have died of the shame of having given birth to such an unnatural child" and interpret the infant's deaf-mute condition as "God's punishment." Her father ignores her and only her armless grandfather, who intends for Anna to assume his chores, accepts her. Some years later, when an infant entrusted to her care dies soon after she takes him to church, she becomes a pariah, finding refuge in this same sanctuary. Desperate for affection, she lavishes her unspent love on a statue of the Christ Child. An art historian discovers the girl with the religious object and tells the priest and townspeople that it is very valuable. He suggests that they advertise its presence, turn the church into a shrine, and reap some financial advantage from the icon. The statue is taken from Anna and encased in glass, but she steals it back and runs away. The townspeople, seeing their dream of riches evaporate, search for her. Led by a crippled man, the now frenzied mob comes across a shepherd who they assume is concealing Anna's whereabouts. "The sight of the sleeping boy enraged them and they were further angered by the hunchback's gesture that told them to stop and wait. He had presumed too much. They had followed him mindlessly and listened to him for too long. His crooked back was an ugly reminder of the ugliness in their lives, and the Garcia boy reminded them of the deaf-and-dumb girl who had run away with their future." Completely out of control, the hysterical villagers turn on the crippled peasant and stone him to death. Shocked at the results of their fury, the mob is chastened and repents. The historian asks to take Anna back with him to the United States where he can devote his life to her, but the priest resists. " 'Don't you see,' he whispered, 'the girl has changed both of us. She can do the same for the people of Almas.' " Anna herself is, of course, not consulted, since she has no importance as a person.

Analysis. This harrowing tale is one of unharnessed violence and abuse, most of it directed against disabled characters. Anna and the crippled man are sacrificed for the selfish ambitions of the priest, who seeks affirmation of his ministerial skills, and the art historian, who seeks recognition of his genius. However, their suffering serves an important symbolic purpose also; the crippled man becomes the mob's scapegoat: "The rage was against their very lives, against the trap of never-changing days, as much as it was against the hunchback and his treachery. When they raised their hands against him, it was as if they had taken up arms against him, it was as if they had taken up arms against evil, sin, and death." His death provides a catharsis for the villagers. After their savage act they are able to repent, seek expiation for their sins, and aspire to a state of grace. To dramatize the relief that killing an innocent man has on a mindless mob or to suggest that hounding and persecuting an innocent child can be an act so easily and readily atoned for is offensive. The style of writing is impressive, exhibiting considerable skill in the creation of vivid imagery and in the re-creation of a stark and barbaric society. But the uncritical use of the disabled as natural victims perpetuates a pernicious model.

Wolff, Angelika. *Mom! I Need Glasses.* Illus. by Dorothy Hill. New York: Lion, 1970. 40 pp. Reading Level: YC
Disability: Visual Impairment

When Susan plays with other friends her age, she has trouble with such games as catch and jumprope. She also has trouble seeing the blackboard and must frequently take her work home to do it over. Her teacher suggests that she should have an eye checkup and her mother tells her that wearing glasses is common in their family. Although Susan is somewhat fearful, she sees Dr. Sugarman for her examination who confirms that she is myopic. He uses this opportunity to deliver a long lecture on how the eye functions. Susan visits the optometrist, is happy with the glasses she orders, and no longer has to sit in the front of the class, isolated from her friends.

Analysis. The easy-reader format is in startling contrast to the content, which deals with technical information and explains visual functioning using schematic drawings of cross sections of the eye complete with terminology well beyond the comprehension of first- or second-graders. The explicit illustrations, particularly those that detail the massive equipment often used for eye examinations, may be more intimidating than enlightening.

Wolff, Ruth. *A Crack in the Sidewalk.* New York: Day, 1965. 288 pp. Reading Level: YA
Disability: Intellectual Impairment

Linsey Templeton is one of six children. Her younger brother, seven-year-old Pleas, is severely retarded. The Templetons are a poor, close-knit family who are devoted to each other and resentful of the implication made by well-meaning strangers that they and Pleas would be better off if he were institutionalized. The father, a religious fundamentalist, sees Pleas as a "beautiful soul in a sorry body." The painter upstairs says Pleas is working out his karma until he learns enough to go on to the next level. Linsey rejects their perceptions and is sad that her brother is excluded from participating in so much of their life, but muses that he may be luckier and have secret happiness the rest don't have. Later events leave the problem of supporting the family largely to Linsey. She joins a group of young folksingers who have some modest success, finds a boyfriend, and sings on television.

Analysis. This cozy, homey story is narrated by Linsey and suggests the rhythms, pace, and beliefs of poor hill folk. Pleas never speaks and is unable to walk or care for himself but he is obviously an important and loved member of the family. A message specifically repeated throughout the story is that all kinds of people are important and necessary. The theme of Pleas as a child of nature is reiterated and dominates other characters' perceptions of him. People frequently talk about the retarded character but no real understanding of the child's internal perception emerges. He is both a central focus and provides the test by which others' values and character are judged. The treatment is at once ordinary and mystical and the title evokes the image of a place where life pushes through, despite the unlikely environment.

Woods, Hubert C. *Child of the Arctic.* Illus. by Doris Reynolds. Chicago: Follett, 1962. 173 pp. Reading Level: MC
Disability: Auditory Impairment

Despite the congenital deafness and consequent lack of language development of his twin brother, Kumalik, Tooruk can understand him by interpreting his facial and gestural language. Their Eskimo community considers the deaf boy a retarded, dangerous, and unstable person. Only Tooruk shares his brother's frustrations at their neighbors' exclusionary behavior. He acts as guardian, companion, and buffer between his hostile neighbors and the simmering anger of his brother.

Influenza spreads throughout the isolated colony and the only physician does not have enough sulfa for the emergency. However, the twins find a supposedly abandoned ship, locate the needed medication on it, and hastily return with the lifesaving drug. Tooruk generously gives deserved credit to his brother who forced open the crates until he finally located the medicine. The doctor asks Tooruk: "How *did* he know about the medicine?" The boy replied: "He knows because he is smart! He sees things, and then he thinks and thinks and then he understands!"

Analysis. The theme of high achievement in an area of presumed incompetence is replayed using a deaf central character. Unfortunately, none of the boy's feelings is directly shared with the reader. His inner being is known only indirectly through the sensibilities and perceptions of his loving and strongly protective brother. The parents are shown as caring, but confused about how to treat their impaired son and how to counter community belligerence. The author and illustrator provide a strong sense of place. The importance of the Caucasian in the life of the Eskimos is seen as crucial, and although the necessity of mutual respect is implied, it is clear whose way the author considers superior. The story ends on a strong note of hope, heralding new and improved status for the former pariah.

Woody, Regina J. *Almena's Dogs.* New York: Grosset & Dunlap, 1954. 240 pp. Reading Level: MC
Disability: Orthopedic Impairment

Almena, a young black child, loves dogs but cannot have one because she and her family live in a rented house where their lease prohibits it. Her father works as the head stableman for a very wealthy man. When he takes Almena to his employer's kennels, she discovers a runt who is not nursing properly. She persuades the manager to see that the pup gets special attention and so embarks on a career filled with successful canine rescue missions. When school starts, Almena learns that the class for handicapped children has been transferred to her school. The children need help at recess and Almena's class is asked to assist. Almena suggests that the disabled students be their class project for the year. Almena saves a puppy from drowning in a rain barrel and participates in a demonstration with Knee-Hi, the safety dog who teaches children proper traffic safety and bicycle habits. Miss Seligman, the teacher of the handicapped children, has a deaf dog she is training by hand signals. She explains: "If I really were a good teacher I could teach a handicapped dog as successfully as I could teach the handicapped children in my class." Miss Seligman prepares an auditorium program on "scent detection by dogs." Crystal, one of the special class children, is a participant. During the performance, the fire bell is accidently rung and Crystal's disappearance is overlooked. When the staff realizes she is missing, everyone joins in the search. The deaf dog finally locates her on a fire escape. On the way home, Almena is hit by a car and her arm and leg are broken. Soon after she recovers, her father brings the news that the family will be moving near his employer's kennels and she will have an entire kennel of dogs to love.

Analysis. Although apparently well intentioned, this book is patronizing in its treatment of Blacks, teachers, children, and especially those who have disabilities. Almena, described as "colored," although having no formal dance training, has "an excellent feeling for rhythm." The handicapped children project functions as a vehicle for the display of benevolence on the part of others: That such children should be treated as "a project" demonstrates a lack of sensitivity. The comparison between teaching the deaf dog and the children is unfortunate. The depiction of Almena as Lady Bountiful, distributing her largess in the form of attention to "saving" animals and later "saving" children with special needs, is offensive. The plot is contrived and the characterization and dialogue unimaginative. This formula book is irretrievably marred by a narrow conceptualization of how people speak and behave, and of what comprises a wholesome interaction between a disabled and nondisabled person.

Woody, Regina J. *Second Sight for Tommy*. Philadelphia: Westminster, 1972. 159 pp. Reading Level: MC
Disability: Visual Impairment

While playing with a chemistry set, nine-year-old Tommy Weatherley is blinded. A young orphan girl is hired to teach him orientation, mobility, and self-help skills. Tommy is bitter and resistant, but his tutor's patience and concern and the example of an older blind boy are inspiring. The boy's blindness is a terrible burden to his father; it interferes with the man's business, running a country inn, and makes an unfortunate impression on potential customers. He angrily berates the boy: "You're just taking advantage of the fact that you can't see. Already some guests have moved on because seeing a blind child spoiled their enjoyment of their vacations and said as much." Ironically, the boy accepts this vicious assessment, which the author does not dispute. The mother, distressed at her son's handicap, is inspired by the example of Ben "who is blind, but you'd never guess it except for the glasses and the guide dog." Tommy learns to ride a bike, skate, play a bugle, and swim, yet his inadvertent clumsiness angers his parents. When Tommy manages to fall into 24 pies, a feat of such magnitude that one would seem to need sight to accomplish it, this is seen as the last straw and his father banishes him to a summer camp since "a blind boy doesn't belong at a country inn." The father's plans for expanding his business seem doomed since he was counting on his son's contribution. But Ben saves the day when he demonstrates his typing proficiency, a talent being developed by Tommy and apparently predictive of success in the "hospitality" business.

Analysis. Although there are a few morsels of information about adjustment to blindness, the misperceptions, false premises, unwarranted deductions, and outright errors totally eclipse whatever usefulness the book might possess. The text exaggerates the implications of having a blind family member and underestimates the difficulties, especially the psychological adjustments, a blind person must make. A fraudulent sense of difference is promoted and, although intended to be commendatory, is actually patronizing: "Though Ben was a year younger, he looked more mature than Andy. There was an inner glow about him, a sense of peace and security that puzzled Kim, since Ben was blind and Andy wasn't." The rampant verbal cruelty and condescension leveled at just about everyone negate whatever commendable objective may have motivated this work.

Woody, Regina J. *A Time to Dance.* New York: Chilton, 1963. 156 pp.
Reading Level: YA/MA
Disability: Emotional Dysfunction

Janet Sherwood, only a college junior, is invited to choreograph a national television show. This golden opportunity is withdrawn and she goes to California to complete her education but remains preoccupied with dance problems and performances. She does manage to notice that her roommate, Hilaire, is behaving in an erratic manner. Hilaire threatens to jump to her death from a roof, but instead climbs down of her own accord when the crowd below disperses. At spring break, she announces that she is going to Hawaii with some friends, but is subsequently found, suffering from amnesia, and is committed to a mental hospital. When Hilaire sees a dance performed to some music she wrote, her self-made cocoon is penetrated and she is propelled along the road to recovery. A rosy future is also projected for Janet, who marries her fiancé the day after graduation.

Analysis. This book promulgates some lamentable attitudes toward disability. Just as emotional dysfunction is exploited as a device to illustrate the uses of dance, so Hilaire is constructed as an object on whom the therapeutic effects of the arts can be demonstrated. Indeed, Hilaire's function is to provide the excuse for some extensive ruminations on dance therapy and inferentially to yoke talent to mental instability. A particularly depersonalizing comment is made after the heroine berates herself for being insensitive to her roommate's problems. " 'Don't blame yourself,' Suzy said, 'You're not particularly concerned about people's mental health, and there's no good reason you should be, but I am, and Hilaire's behavior fascinates me.' " The instant panacea artifice is foreshadowed in Janet's formulation: "If we could get Hilaire interested enough through hearing her music to realize that there *is* more for her to do, she just might snap back to normalcy and decide it would be *fun* to do." And, unsurprisingly, upon hearing her song, Hilaire tosses off her apathy, withdrawal, and amnesia, dashes to the piano, and finishes a major composition. The writing is shallow, sexist, and cliché-ridden. The idea that one can at will "snap back" from psychosis is appealing, but unfortunately untrue. The trivialization of illness as well as the effort needed for recovery is highly irresponsible.

Woody, Regina J. *Wisdom to Know.* New York: Funk & Wagnalls, 1964. 179 pp. Reading Level: YA
Disability: Emotional Dysfunction

Karen, a junior Red Cross aide, is assigned a job handing out passes to visitors at the state mental hospital. She is so absorbed in her work that she fails to notice her own father until he asks for a pass to visit his sister-in-law, her aunt, a long-term patient in the hospital. Karen is surprised to learn that he is not only a frequent visitor but also works as a volunteer. She tours the facilities and finds they are "beautifully clean," staffed by aides who are "good-looking Negro women in well-fitting nylon uniforms. Trained, acting with authority, proud of their wards and their patients. . . ." The director of nursing, "a handsome woman . . . was evidently someone deeply admired and loved." It is reported that this remarkable woman "says something new and wonderful" every time she speaks. In a new building "there were fine sunny wards opening off a small lobby. Karen was impressed by the color, the cleanliness, and the vases of fresh flowers."

Karen visits her aunt on a locked ward. The woman is uncommunicative, responding only momentarily at the mention of her prodigious brownie-making skills. When the girl plays the piano for her aunt, the woman becomes very agitated, and it is clear that her niece has penetrated her protective shell and precipitated a Turning Point. Karen's friend, Joannie, has exhibited increasingly erratic behavior, including memory lapses. Her brother is in the marines, her mother is an alcoholic, and her father has deserted the family. Having no adult to turn to, Joannie desperately requests admission to the state hospital. Karen visits Joannie where she has the opportunity to see the wonders of poetry therapy. Her friend explains how a therapist used "poetry with strong rhythms, poetry like 'Casey at the Bat' and 'Hiawatha.' She did this on very bad wards and she proved she was right. Patients listened, answered questions, and began talking just as they used to before they had come to the hospital. And believe it or not, some of those patients hadn't spoken a word in five, ten or even fifteen years." Karen's aunt requests some music, thereby indicating a desire to rebuild her life. She is moved to a rehabilitation cottage where her "cure" is acknowledged and she is joyfully reunited with Karen's mother, who had refused to see her for the past ten years. The state hospital hosts some students from Joannie's high school who are invited to attend a psychodrama session. The principal proposes that the director conduct a similar session at the school to explore techniques for helping released patients to readjust. The school, which formerly had been a hostile environment, is now supportive; Joannie's parents have joined Alcoholics Anonymous and she is in Alateen. Joannie is invited to participate in a major dance exhibition and Karen has decided on a career in dance therapy.

Analysis. As if maudlin sentimentality and patronizing attitudes about Blacks were not enough, this effort presents some groundless claims and misleading information about emotional dysfunction and public institutions. The hospitals described herein resemble expensive spas more than typical state institutions and the personnel appear to be candidates for beatification. Claims for "cures," a term more popular with novelists than psychotherapists, are patently absurd and minimize the problems. Assertions that poetry, drama, and music therapy have powers to induce almost instantaneous remission of symptoms would embarrass even their most ardent supporters. While apparently intending to promote acceptance for residents of mental hospitals, such falsification of reality provides a distinct disservice.

Woolsey, Maryhale. *The Keys and the Candle.* Illus. by Don Bolognese. New York: Abingdon, 1963. 215 pp. Reading Level: MC/YA
Disability: Orthopedic Impairment

Rowan, an English boy living in the eleventh century, has an underdeveloped left side. He is sent to a monastery to be instructed in the creation of manuscripts. Injured by one of the boys, he loses consciousness and is discovered by a brother who questions him about the etiology of the illness that resulted in his physical anomalies. Rowan tells the monk that his infirmities were God's punishment for the sins of his parents, but this explanation is rejected by the brother. A program of massage and physical therapy is initiated in an effort to restore better functioning. Some slight improvement ensues and this is abetted by a specially cushioned shoe. The disabled boy prays for a sign that he is worthy of the honor of copying bibles. One day, he sees a falcon swooping down on a beautiful white bird, which miraculously manages to injure its assailant, dropping a feather into Rowan's hands. This event is interpreted as divine approval of his petition and the improvement in his gait is a further sign of special favor. The lord of the manor for whom his father worked proposes that Rowan become his adopted son and also marry his daughter. Rowan demurs, wishing to pursue his rewarding religious vocation, but agrees to postpone his final decision for a year.

Analysis. The miracle of Rowan's recovery is both claimed and denied. The brothers' ministrations, in tandem with the adapted shoe, provide improvement, but further unexplained recovery appears to take place as the boy uses his previously functionless hand to catch the feather and as his walk appears suddenly stronger. Some discussion of physical therapy is presented as well as descriptions of specifically designed prostheses, including an unusual sling for his arm to ease the discomforts of travel. The story line is a fictional pageant. Its setting in the Middle Ages presents considerable information about social classes, work roles, and the functions of monasteries. The pen and ink drawings are attractive, but do not show the extent of Rowan's impairments.

Wright, Anna Rose. *Land of Silence*. Illus. by Pru Herric. New York: Friendship, 1962. 143 pp. Reading Level: MC
Disability: Auditory Impairment; also neurological impairment, orthopedic impairment

Toby Truxton, a seventh-grader, is a troublemaker, a poor student, and a frustrated and unhappy boy. He sneaks away from the playground one day and discovers a nursery school room for deaf children. He is invited in by a friendly special education teacher and instantly becomes immersed in the instruction of these children and the problems of deafness. His own school work has been badly neglected, but he agrees to improve and so is allowed to continue his visits to the room for the deaf. Buzz, a brain-injured, crippled, deaf child, becomes his special interest. The little boy is very hostile and Toby relates readily to this attitude, which Buzz apparently senses. The transformed Toby writes a composition on deafness that appears in the school newspaper and takes over the disciplining of another child who had been teasing the deaf students. Toby attends a lecture on deafness with his father and dreams of a career in which he can invent some devices for assisting deaf people. The reformed boy directs the year-end play performed by the deaf children, becomes closer to his own father, is cited as the boy who made the most progress that year in school, and is given a book about auditory impairment as a token of that achievement.

Analysis. Land of Silence is a combination instructional bulletin on the implications of deafness and a tract praising good deeds done for deaf persons. In the former capacity it presents considerable valid descriptions of language development, auditory training, orientation to hearing aid usage, lipreading, signing, and a host of other behavioral or instructional ramifications of hearing loss. In the latter role it presents a thoroughly unbelievable character in improbable situations. The quality of the writing is poor, particularly the dialogue, and postulates about human behavior and motivation are naive. The general treatment of deafness is as a purely physical and communicative problem and most social, emotional, and developmental implications are ignored.

Wrightson, Patricia. *A Racecourse for Andy*. Illus. by Margaret Horder. New York: Harcourt, Brace, 1968. 156 pp. Reading Level: MC/YA
Disability: Intellectual Impairment

Andy and his friends live in Sydney, Australia. Andy is retarded and the boys make allowances for his slowness in understanding and his inability to participate fully in some activities. He has a bright and amiable disposition, and since he is "always warm and admiring, always glad to see them and careful not to be a nuisance, the others were still his friends." One of their favorite games involves claiming ownership of some highly desirable public property. Andy cannot seem to understand the rule that private property does not count and, although he wants to play, he always seems to miss the point. Andy decides that owning the racetrack would be fun, and a tramp, realizing how easy it will be to cheat the boy, agrees to "sell" the racecourse to him for three dollars. Andy turns the money over to the man and is now convinced he owns the property. The boys are at first merely amused and frustrated at Andy's insistence that the track is his and then become concerned at what they correctly see is a situation that is rapidly getting out of hand. The workers of the track are diverted by the boy's fantasy and go along with the game, but he is becoming more and more of a nuisance to the real owners. His friends begin to worry in earnest: "He's getting in deeper all the time. He's got to come out of it." When Andy begins to "fix" the racecourse, decorating the stands, painting the benches, and "repairing" the mechanical rabbit used in the dog races, events come to a head and the owners are out of patience. Andy discusses with a friendly groundskeeper some strangers' offer to pay him to give some special food to the horses. The food is drugged and the groundskeeper provides information that leads to the apprehension of the men, but it is clear that Andy must not be allowed to continue his delusion. The owners decide to "buy back" the track from Andy. They offer him ten dollars, which he accepts, using his profits to buy a model airplane. His friends help him assemble it, but one complains that Andy is too clumsy and may break it. "What does it matter? . . . He's got to have things sometimes, even if he does bust them." And this summarizes Andy's situation: Even if he is unable to understand or make or use things as well as others, he must still be a participant.

Analysis. Wrightson uses the image of a window to convey the impression of Andy being a part of, yet separated from, the other boys:

Andy lived behind a closed window. When he smiled his warm smile and spoke a little too loudly, it was as if he was speaking through the glass. When he listened carefully to what people said and paused for a second before he answered, it was as though their words came to him through the glass. . . . He had moments of noisy laughter or fierce anger when it seemed that he was knocking against the window. Even his face looked a little distorted, as things sometimes look through glass.

Andy is seen as gullible and readily deceived by appearances: He is sure that the man collecting money from the parking meters must be rich and he is adamant in his belief that he owns the racecourse. His friends, although sometimes annoyed or exasperated, acknowledge their responsibility not to abandon him despite the difficulties his stubbornness causes. The story is beautifully written, with marvelous characterizations, vivid imagery, a unique story line, and a compelling style.

Yolen, Jane. *The Transfigured Hart*. Illus. by Donna Diamond. New York: Crowell, 1975. 86 pp. Reading Level: MC/YA
Disability: General Health Problems

Since his recovery from rheumatic fever, Richard feels suffocated by the overbearing solicitude of his aunt and uncle. He seeks escape, order, and comfort through an immersion in folklore, bestiaries, and classical literature. One day he sees a solitary albino deer, which he becomes convinced is a unicorn. Heather, a young friend, spies it also and the two make plans to capture and tame it. The impulsive and voluble girl blurts out their secret to her brothers, who are hunters. The two children are reconciled after her accidental perfidy and they search for the animal, impelled by the need to protect it. When the creature arrives, Heather captures it with a ribbon, thereby magically transforming the forest. After an idyllic interlude, the unicorn escapes, leaving the two children bound together by this transcendent experience that they know must remain their secret.

Analysis: Except for the heavy-handed use of names, places and the parallel between the hart and "bruised heart" of the hero, the book is a delicate and exceptionally well-crafted story. The tale winds a tricky path between fantasy and reality and it is the interplay between love and destruction, between withdrawal and approach, between faith and skepticism, that gives tension to this tender story. Since this book is highly allegorical, only a miniscule amount of information about rheumatic fever is presented. Richard's recovery is marked by some pain and a need for restricted activity. This situation not only justifies aspects of his characterization but also allows for a contrast between the dreamy, thoughtful youth and the dynamic, effervescent heroine. As the deer is transformed through an exhibition of faith, this act presages for Richard a metamorphosis in his life from passivity to self-assertion and a feeling that he can capture and control his destiny. The illustrations are perfectly attuned to the rhythm of the narrative—sensitive and representational, yet imprecise enough to blur perceptions and certainties.

Title Index

This index provides access by title to the Chapter 5 annotations. The page references to any of these titles discussed earlier in Chapters 1–4 may be found by consulting the Subject Index.

Subject Index

References by title to the Chapter 5 annotations are separately listed in the Title Index. Page references to any of these titles discussed earlier in Chapters 1–4 are included here.